RUSSIA'S MISSING MIDDLE CLASS

RUSSIA'S MISSING MIDDLE CLASS

The Professions in Russian History

Edited by Harley D. Balzer

Routledge
Taylor & Francis Group

LONDON AND NEW YORK

First published 1996 by M.E. Sharpe

Published 2015 by Routledge
2 Park Square, Milton Park, Abingdon, Oxon OX14 4RN
711 Third Avenue, New York, NY 10017, USA

Routledge is an imprint of the Taylor & Francis Group, an informa business

Library of Congress Cataloging-in-Publication Data

Russia's missing middle class : the professions in
Russian History / edited by Harley Balzer.
p.   cm.
Includes bibliographical references and index.
ISBN 1-56324-707-0 (cloth : alk. paper)
ISBN 1-56324-748-8 (pbk. : alk. paper)
1. Middle classes—Russia—History.
2. Professional employees—Russia—History.
3. Professions—Russia—History.
4. Russia—Social conditions—1801–1917.
I. Balzer, Harley D.
HT690.R9R866   1995
305.5'5'0947—dc20   95-42117
CIP

ISBN 13: 9781563247484 (pbk)
ISBN 13: 9781563247071 (hbk)

To Kendall Bailes,
colleague and friend.

Contents

About the Editor and Contributors

HARLEY D. BALZER is Associate Professor of Government and Director of the Center for Eurasian, Russian, and East European Studies at Georgetown University. He received his Ph.D. in History at the University of Pennsylvania. He is author of *Soviet Science on the Edge of Reform* (Westview Press, 1989) and editor of *Five Years That Shook the World: Gorbachev's Unfinished Revolution* (Westview Press, 1991), which was selected as a *Choice* outstanding academic book in 1992. He is currently completing a book on the social history of engineers in Russian and Soviet society and a volume on science and education in Russia since 1960.

KENDALL E. BAILES was Professor of History at the University of California, Irvine. He received his Ph.D. from Columbia University. His many publications included *Technology and Society Under Lenin and Stalin: Origins of the Soviet Technical Intelligentsia, 1917-1941* (Princeton University Press, 1978), which received the American Historical Association's Herbert Baxter Adams Prize, and *Science and Russian Culture in an Age of Revolution: V.I. Vernadsky and His Scientific School, 1865-1945* (Indiana University Press, 1990).

JULIE V. BROWN is Associate Professor of Sociology at the University of North Carolina, Greensboro. She received her Ph.D. in Sociology from the University of Pennsylvania. She is currently completing a monograph on the history of the Russian psychiatric profession.

JOHN F. HUTCHINSON is Professor of History at Simon Fraser University. He received his Ph.D. from the University of London. He is author of *The Cleansing Hurricane: Politics and Public Health in Revolutionary Russia, 1890-1918* (Johns Hopkins University Press, 1990), and coeditor (with Susan Gross Solomon) of *Health and Society in Revolutionary Russia* (Indiana University Press, 1990). His *Champions of Charity: War and the Rise of the Red Cross* will be published in March 1996 by Westview/Harper Collins.

SAMUEL KASSOW is Professor of History at Trinity College. He received his Ph.D. in History from Princeton University. He is author of *Students, Professors, and the State in Tsarist Russia* (University of California Press, 1989).

BRIAN L. LEVIN-STANKEVICH is Vice Provost at Eastern Washington University. He received his Ph.D. from the State University of New York at Buffalo, writing a dissertation on Russian legal development. He has written on the Russian educational system and the academic profession in Russia.

DANIEL T. ORLOVSKY is Professor of History and Chairman of the Department of History at Southern Methodist University. He received his Ph.D. in History from Harvard University. His publications include *The Limits of Reform: The Ministry of Internal Affairs in Imperial Russia, 1802-1881* (Harvard University Press, 1981) and a forthcoming monograph on the Russian provisional government.

SAMUEL C. RAMER is Associate Professor of History at Tulane University. He received his Ph.D. in History from Columbia University. In addition to several articles on Russian feldshers, his research focuses on Russian social and cultural history in the period 1861-1941.

RICHARD G. ROBBINS, JR. is Professor of History and Chairman of the Department of History at the University of New Mexico. He received his Ph.D. in History from Columbia University. His publications include *Famine in Russia, 1891-92: The Imperial Government Responds to a Crisis* (Columbia University Press, 1975) and *The Tsar's Viceroys: Russian Provincial Governors in the Last Years of the Empire* (Cornell University Press, 1987).

SCOTT J. SEREGNY is Associate Professor of History at Indiana University at Indianapolis. He received his Ph.D. in History from the University of Michigan. He is author of *Russian Teachers and Peasant Revolution: The Politics of Education in 1905* (Indiana University Press, 1989) and coeditor (with Rex Wade) of *Politics and Society in Provincial Russia: Saratov, 1590-1917* (Ohio State University Press, 1989).

Preface

We daily entrust our personal and collective well-being to professional specialists: the engineers who build our roads and bridges, the architects who design our buildings, the physicians who not only diagnose illness but decide what medical procedures will be used and for whom, the lawyers and judges who determine who walks the streets, not to mention the military and scientific experts who control (we hope) weapons of inconceivable destructive power. Who are these arbiters of expertise in a society? How do they come to wield the enormous power that our scientific-technical civilization bestows upon specialists? And why do we defer to their expertise? These questions are being asked with heightened urgency as it becomes apparent that neither the model of self-sacrificing servant of humanity nor the image of self-seeking monopolist adequately characterizes professionals.[1]

Professional communities are a quite remarkable phenomenon. Their earliest origins were in religious leadership and the priesthood, yet they claim special status based on scientific knowledge. Their knowledge base is developed and transmitted in educational institutions that are constantly in the process of reform. Status and leadership within a professional community generally accrue not to the most community-oriented or politically capable, but to the specialists with greatest command of the most esoteric knowledge. Practitioners frequently expend enormous energy and resources striving to meet standards that only a small group of professional peers will ever notice. Aberrations are tolerated in the name of autonomy and self-regulation.

If in a more credulous time it was possible to suggest that some issues were too important to be left to nonspecialists, many of the questions society now confronts appear to be too important to be left to specialists. Developments in science and technology pose increasingly complex ethical dilemmas. What are the risks and benefits of nuclear power, and how much risk is acceptable? In a nation of more than a billion people (China), who decides where to place the first six dialysis machines? Who determines the criteria for their use? And who decides who makes the determination?[2] We are increasingly aware that professional expertise is a two-edged implement that can be used as a sanction to enforce conformist behavior within a profession even as a group uses it to assert its autonomy.[3]

Russia is rejoining the global community in confronting issues of expert and professional power at a time when there is little consensus on these questions. Prior to 1917 there were active professional communities in Russia. In the Soviet era, these communities were subjected to harsh deprofessionalization, and issues of specialist influence took other forms.[4] Since 1991 professional activity has revived, giving examination of the earlier history an additional dimension of comparison.

This volume was begun when comparative study of the professions was at a relatively early stage. It has now become a cottage industry, with a significant literature focusing on the Anglo-American and Continental experiences. One of the questions underlying our efforts involves whether the history of Russian professions might contribute anything to the comparative history and theory of professions.

The volume had an unusually long gestation period for an edited collection, in part because at two key junctures I made career choices that diverted my attention from academic writing. In 1983 I accepted a Congressional Fellowship, and spent much of the year working on a piece of legislation called the "Soviet and East European Research and Training Act of 1983." More commonly known as "Title VIII" of the State Department appropriation, this legislation has provided substantial sums to support scholarly research and advanced education. Even after I returned to full-time academic work at Georgetown, the annual appropriation steeplechase called for much attention. I am enormously grateful to Robert Huber and others who have assumed much of this burden. A second diversion from academic life came in 1992-93, when George Soros asked me to take on the task of helping to establish the International Science Foundation, his $100 million initiative to support basic research in the Baltic nations and NIS. While I would probably make the same choices if I had it to do again, I do regret the limitations these activities imposed on my ability to push academic writing projects to completion.

Given the long delays, I am particularly grateful to the contributors to the volume, almost all of whom were willing to persist. Some took advantage of the hiatus to add material to their essays; others felt that they had said what they have to say on the subject, and their own research interests are now in other areas.

Kendall Bailes provided a valuable commentary at the conference where the essays published here were discussed. It was our intention for that commentary to serve as the basis for a concluding chapter to the volume. Unfortunately, Ken's death meant that he was not able to see the final versions of the essays or to incorporate material that has been published since he first drafted his comments. Bailes's contribution is included as an introductory essay discussing a number of important thematic issues appearing in the individual contributions. My "Introduction" grounds the material on Russian professions in the context of recent theoretical discussions and the growing comparative literature on professions, and provides a brief historical summary of early Russian professional development. My concluding chapter summarizes some of the themes in light of the profound changes that have taken place in Russia since this project was begun. It represents an initial effort to project the story of Russian professions through the Soviet period, and to consider the issue of the reemergence of professional life in post-Soviet Russia in the context of democracy and the middle class.

The specific professions included in the volume, while covering the "core" groups of medical, legal, technical, and pedagogical personnel, hardly exhaust the range of Russian professions. Many other groups might have been included. Recent research has provided valuable data on journalists, pharmacists, architects, and some of the cultural occupations.[5] Our conference discussions included groups that formed professions in other countries, such as charity workers, who had only begun to constitute a profession in Russia.[6] Here the barriers to professional development and the degree of professionalization achieved by particular groups can tell us something about the social processes at work in Russian society.

An entire volume could be devoted to Russia's "professional *intelligenty.*" The Russian system of higher education also fostered a substratum of professional students. At one stage in developing this project, we considered a chapter on "professional revolutionaries."[7] But if the cursed questions of the Russian intelligentsia have not been resolved by a century of scholarship, we do not expect to settle the issue in this forum. Our goal is more modest: to begin to portray a large and until recently largely neglected portion of the Russian intelligentsia who in their education, career patterns, and collective action aspired to professional status.

Despite the publication of a growing number of monographs dealing with individual professions, students and scholars interested in the phenomenon of professionalization in Russia still must consult a range of individual studies to extract material on the topic. By collecting these essays in a single volume, we hope to make the material more accessible and to encourage further research.

*   *   *

A project with this long a history accrues more than the usual number of debts. The initial impetus came from a session at the convention of the American Association for the Advancement of Slavic Studies (AAASS) at Asilomar in 1980. Reginald Zelnik provided valuable advice and encouragement, which helped induce us to seek support for additional collaborative activity. The Research and Development Committee of the AAASS, which at that time was in a position to make modest grants supporting group projects, provided funds to support a working conference. We are grateful to the committee and in particular its chairman, Brian Silver, for expeditious handling of the application and wise advice about the organization of the conference. The committee also provided support to prepare the manuscript for publication.

The conference was held in conjunction with the University of Illinois Summer Research Laboratory, which provided support in the form of housing and meeting space and offered a wonderful atmosphere for our discussions.

Several of the papers presented at the conference could not be included in this volume for various reasons. Nancy Frieden's pioneering work on the medical profession was already in print at the time of the conference. William Fuller's book on army officers appeared shortly thereafter. Ben Eklof's paper on teachers became part of a larger work, and Adele Lindenmeyr's paper on charity workers is included in her forthcoming monograph. We are grateful to each of them for contributing to the collective effort and for enriching the discussions.

Other scholars who added their wisdom to the conference deliberations included Kendall Bailes, David Ransel, William Wagner, Bruce Adams, Paul Josephson, and Ronald Charbonneau. All of them helped sharpen our understanding of comparative and broader social historical issues.

The Science, Technology, and Society Program at the Massachusetts Institute of Technology and Georgetown University provided much needed administrative and logistical support. My own research has been supported by the International Research and Exchanges Board, Fulbright-Hays, the National Academy of Sciences, the National Science Foundation, the Carnegie Corporation of New York, and the National Council for Soviet and East European Research.

I was fortunate to have help in preparing the manuscript from my research assistants Susan Trapp, Jennifer Long, and Christine Zapotocky. Vicki Mills edited and formatted the manuscript under stringent time pressures and consistently provided wise suggestions about both form and content. At M.E. Sharpe, Patricia Kolb was willing to take on the project and to believe our opinion that colleagues will want to use this volume in the classroom. We hope her faith will be justified. Ana Erlic and Elizabeth Granda were especially helpful in seeing the manuscript through to completion.

The volume has benefited from comments by a number of colleagues and anonymous reviewers. If I have mercifully forgotten many of the details, I sincerely hope that I have not forgotten any of the individuals who generously provided encouragement and assistance at various stages. I am grateful for suggestions made by Joseph Bradley, Loren Graham, Norman Naimark, Dave Ransel, Alfred Rieber, Blair Ruble, Susan Solomon, Richard Stites, William Wagner, Reginald Zelnik, and by several groups of Georgetown students.

Marjorie Mandelstam Balzer knows that if it were not for her, not only would the book have been less coherent, it might never have existed.

Harley D. Balzer

Notes

1. Thomas L. Haskell, ed., *The Authority of Experts: Studies in History and Theory* (Bloomington: Indiana University Press, 1984); and Steven Brint, *In an Age of Experts: The Changing Role of Professionals in Politics and Public Life* (Princeton, NJ: Princeton University Press, 1994).

2. For examples in medical ethics, see Edmund D. Pellegrino, Robert M. Veatch, and John P. Langan, eds., *Ethics, Trust and the Professions: Philosophical and Cultural Aspects* (Washington, DC: Georgetown University Press, 1991); Stephen Hilgartner, *Nukespeak: Nuclear Language, Visions and Mindset* (San Francisco, CA: Sierra Club Books, 1982).

3. *The New York Times,* 4 August 1995, A15. The Dean of Harvard's Medical School warned John E. Mack "not to let his enthusiasm for UFO research steer him from the path of professionalism." This is an example of using the concept of professionalization to circumscribe scientific inquiry, keeping it within a paradigm recognized as legitimate by mainstream practitioners. Once someone is certified as a member in one of the knowledge-based professions, who has the authority or the right to sanction their professional activity (scientific research) on grounds other than ethical violations?

4. For an excellent treatment of the differences in specialist response to issues of ethics and political interference, see Loren R. Graham, *Science, Philosophy and Human Behavior in the Soviet Union* (New York: Columbia University Press, 1987), chapter 6.

5. When I spoke about this project at the Institute of History in Leningrad, Russian (then Soviet) colleagues expressed shock that the "artistic intelligentsia" was not included. Some sense of how our Soviet colleagues might have cast such a volume can be derived from the works of V.R. Leikina-Svirskaia, *Intelligentsiia v Rossii vo vtoroi polovine XIX veka* (Moscow: Mysl', 1971) and *Russkaia intelligentsiia v 1900-1917 godakh* (Moscow: Mysl', 1981).

6. Adele Lindenmeyr's paper on charity workers has been incorporated in her forthcoming Princeton University Press monograph on charity in tsarist Russia. The value of examining social work for both professional and gender studies is demonstrated by Young Sun Hong, "Femininity as a Vocation: Gender and Class Conflict in the Professionalization of German Social Work," in *German Professions, 1800-1950,* eds. Geoffrey Cocks and Konrad H. Jarausch (New York: Oxford University Press, 1990), 232-51.

7. For a good sense of what this might have been like, see Norman M. Naimark, *Terrorists and Social Democrats: The Russian Revolutionary Movement under Alexander III* (Cambridge: Harvard University Press, 1983). We also declined the offer from Richard Stites to contribute a chapter on "the oldest profession." Recent work by Laurie Bernstein points in this direction, *Sonia's Daughters: Prostitutes and Their Regulation in Tsarist Russia* (Berkeley: University of California Press, 1995).

A Note on Dates, Archive References, and Transliteration

In 1918 the Bolshevik regime abandoned the Julian calendar in favor of the Gregorian calendar used in the West. Scholars who work with pre-1918 materials are used to adjusting dates thirteen days for the twentieth century and twelve days for the nineteenth century. All dates given in this volume are those that were in use in Russia at the time.

After the demise of the Soviet Union, names of most Russian state archives were changed. Those referenced in this volume include:

RGIA. Rossiiskii gosudarstvennyi istoricheskii arkhiv. The Russian State Historical Archive is the former TsGIA (Central State Historical Archive).

GARF. Gosudarstvennyi arkhiv rossiiskoi federatsii. The State Archive of the Russian Federation is the former TsGAOR (Central State Archive of the October Revolution).

RGAE. Rossiiskii gosudarstvennyi arkhiv ekonomiki. The Russian State Archive of the Economy is the former TsGANKh (Central State Archive of the National Economy).

Russian archive citations include the following abbreviations:

- f. *fond* (an archival collection)
- o. *opis* (a list of the materials in a collection, usually handwritten by the archivists)
- d. *delo* (a packet of material that may contain anything from a single page to hundreds of pages)
- l. *list* (a page)
- ob. *obratnaia storona* (the reverse side of a page of material; many archival documents are numbered 1, 1 ob, 2, 2 ob, and so on.)

The Library of Congress transliteration system has been used, except for those proper names that have become widely accepted in English in other forms.

Glossary

Antisepsis. Destruction of microorganisms that cause disease or putrefaction in wounds. Antisepsis and the use of antiseptics became a major factor in improving the efficacy of medical treatment beginning with Lister's techniques in the 1860s. By the 1880s a better understanding of bacteriology led to use of asepsis—maintaining a surgically clean environment. The scientific understanding of bacteriology produced a revolution in the efficacy of medical care which enhanced the professional status of medical practitioners.

Artel'. A cooperative association of workers or craftspersons, usually working under the direction of an elected elder (*starosta*).

Bloody Sunday. On Sunday, 9 January 1905, troops in St. Petersburg attacked marchers seeking to present a petition to the tsar. This event became a cause célèbre and is generally considered the starting point of the Revolution of 1905.

Bulygin. Aleksandr Grigorevich Bulygin (1851-1919) replaced Prince Sviatopolk-Mirskii as minister of the interior in January 1905 (after Bloody Sunday) and served until October 1905. In February, the tsar issued a rescript instructing him to prepare a proposal for a consultative assembly. Following protracted wrangling over the provisions, a proposal for a consultative assembly to be chosen by indirect suffrage was published on 6 August 1905. While such a proposal might have been accepted a year earlier, it was generally considered inadequate and did little to stem popular unrest.

Chinovnik. Bureaucrat, civil servant. The term derives from holding *chin* (rank) in the Table of Ranks established by Peter the Great. As is the case for bureaucrats almost everywhere, the term generally has a pejorative connotation.

Deprofessionalization. Process of declining autonomy and social status of professional groups. The phenomenon was seen in the Soviet Union after the Bolshevik Revolution and in a somewhat different form in Nazi Germany. A different variant of deprofessionalization has taken place in advanced industrial societies where many professionals have found themselves working in large organizations.

Desiatina. A measure of land equal to approximately 2.7 acres.

Duma. Literal translation: "thought." The name has been given to a variety of bodies playing either a consultative or legislative role in Russian politics at both local and national levels. After the municipal reform of 1870, elected city dumas were established in many urban areas. At the national level, in addition to the boyar duma that functioned in medieval Russia, there were a number of proposals (the last being Bulygin's) for a consultative duma. After the October Manifesto, four state dumas were elected between 1906 and 1917. The term was revived as the name for the lower house of the legislature in Russia in the 1993 constitution.

Feldsher. A physician's assistant.

Great Reforms. During the reign of Alexander II (1855-1881), reforms were promulgated affecting many areas of Russian life. They included emancipation of the serfs (1861), a reform of local government that established *zemstva* in European Russia (1864), a legal reform establishing jury trials and providing more judicial independence (1864), education reforms reducing the class bias in education and permitting greater university autonomy (1864), a municipal reform providing for elected local dumas in urban areas (1870), and a military reform ending twenty-five-year service in favor of a reserve-based system (1874).

Guberniia. Province. This territorial division was introduced by Peter the Great and reorganized multiple times thereafter. In 1900 there were fifty *gubernii* in European Russia, each headed by a governor and divided in to an average of ten districts (*uezdy*).

Gymnasium/progymnasium. The gymnasium was a secondary school at which the curriculum emphasized classical languages and mathematics, encouraging a student body drawn mainly from the nobility. Graduation from a gymnasium was the route to university entrance. The progymnasium offered the fist four or five years of the gymnasium curriculum. Progymnasia usually existed in more remote areas, and it was assumed students would complete their secondary education at a gymnasium in a larger town.

Holy Synod. Lay council set up by Peter the Great to supervise the affairs of the Russian Orthodox Church. In effect, it established state control of church affairs.

Kadet Party. Common name for the Constitutional Democratic Party (from the Russian initials KD). The Kadet Party, led by Paul Miliukov, was the major liberal political party in Russia after 1905.

Khoziain. Can be translated as "master," "owner," "proprietor," or "landlord." In the 1897 census Nicholas II gave his occupation as "*Khoziain* of the Russian Lands."

Land Captains (*Zemskie nachal'niki*). Rural officials created in 1889 in an effort to undercut the *zemstvo* reform and increase the authority of the central government and the nobility. This was one of several "counterreforms" introduced in the reign of Alexander III.

Meshchanstvo. The lower middle class of individuals engaged in petty trade and crafts. Used colloquially, the term connotes philistinism and vulgarity.

Narod. The people. Generally used by members of the intelligentsia to refer to the "masses."

October Manifesto. Decree by Nicholas II on 17 October 1905 promising the creation of an elected legislative body (the State Duma). The manifesto satisfied many of the political demands of the professional middle class and liberal gentry and *zemstvo* activists, splitting them from the social and economic demands of workers and *meshchane* and helping to quell the Revolution of 1905.

Octobrists. Common name for members of the Union of October 17, a political party organized by moderates including Dmitri Shipov and Alexander Guchkov after the October Manifesto to support the new political system. The party won a sizable portion of the vote in elections to the Third Duma (1907) and initially provided a parliamentary majority supporting Stolypin's reform program. The party soon became fragmented, was unable to push through the proposed reforms, and split into several factions in the Fourth Duma.

Okrug. An administrative district in pre-1917 Russia. An *okrug* occupied the same position in an *oblast'* that an *uezd* occupied in a *guberniia*. There were also educational districts (*uchebnye okruga*), military districts (*voennye okruga*), and judicial districts (*mirovye okruga*), each with their own boundaries.

Pirogov Society (Society of Russian Physicians in Memory of N.I. Pirogov). Association of Russian physicians founded in 1883. Physicians employed in public institutions, and particularly by *zemstva*, played a major role in the Pirogov Society. It became a model for other professional groups wishing to establish organizations.

Privat-dotsent. A university teacher's rank corresponding to assistant professor.

Progressists. The Progressists were members of a liberal political party that attracted some support in elections after 1905. In elections to the Third Duma P.P. Riabushinskii sought to make the party a focal point for entrepreneurial interests. The party should not be confused with the Progressive Bloc, a union of centrist parties in the duma during World War I.

Provisional Government. Self-proclaimed official government of Russia following the February Revolution of 1917. Recognized by Russia's allies in the war against Germany, the Provisional Government considered itself a caretaker administration until elections could be held for a Constituent Assembly. It was forced to share power with elected councils (*sovety*) and was overthrown by the Bolsheviks in October 1917.

Raznochintsy. Individuals who did not belong to any of the legally defined social estates in tsarist Russia. The Code of Laws recognized nobles, merchants, clergy, peasants, and a few special groups. The *raznochintsy* were often sons of priests or other individuals who attained some education which enabled them to rise above their hereditary social status but did not confer new status. In the mid nineteenth century, many became part of the radical student movement and the left-wing intelligentsia.

Second Element. The elected deputies to the *zemstvo* from various *soslovie* at district and provincial levels. The "First Element" refers to appointed administrative personnel. See also "Third Element," listed below.

Senate. Created by Peter the Great in 1722 as a temporary administration during his campaign against Turkey, the Senate evolved into a supreme court of cassation by the nineteenth century.

Soslovie. Estate, a legally defined social class. Around 1900 Russian law and census categories recognized nobles and officials, merchants, clergy, *meshchane*, peasants, *inorodtsy* (native peoples of Siberia and Central Asia), and Cossacks.

State Council (*Gosudarstvennyi sovet*). Established in 1810 as an appointed body to advise the tsar on legislation, the State Council frequently served as a place to park retired ministers and other high officials. On some occasions it played a significant role in developing or modifying legislation. After 1906 the State Council became the upper chamber of the Russian legislature, with half its members appointed by the tsar and half elected by social organizations: thirty-four from provincial *zemstvo* assemblies, twenty-two from assemblies of landowners in the non-*zemstvo* provinces, eighteen from provincial societies of the nobility, twelve from trade and industry associations, and six each from the Russian Orthodox Church and the Academy of Sciences. It had the power to veto measures adopted by the elected lower house (State Duma).

Studenchestvo. Russian term for the student body in higher education. Up to and during 1905, the term had a connotation of radical or left-wing political sympathies. After 1905 this remained true, but the student movement became more diverse.

Third Element. The growing group of professional employees who worked for the *zemstvo*. It included medical, educational, technical, veterinary, statistical, and other specialists who as *zemstvo* employees had a significant influence on policies and the political attitudes of the *zemstva*. The term was used in an address by Samara Vice-Governor Kondoidi in January 1900 to warn of the dangers of trained specialists from the intelligentsia influencing the elected *zemstvo* members.

"To the People" Movement. In the mid 1870s, thousands of young, educated Russians opted to "go to the people" to help spread education and bring about social and political change. In most instances these well-meaning student radicals were met with incomprehension or outright hostility in the villages. The lack of results led to a split in the radical movement between those who advocated more education and those who decided to kill the tsar in an effort to shock the people out of their lethargy.

Uezd. District. An administrative subdivision of a province. In 1900 there were 504 *uezdy* in Russia, 350 of which had *zemstvo* organizations.

Union of Unions (*Soiuz soiuzov*). Established during 1905 in an effort to coordinate the activity of the various professional and other unions that were active in the revolutionary movement. It ceased to exist in January 1906.

Vekhi. Landmarks. Title of a collection of essays first published in 1909 at the initiative of M. Gershchenzon. The contributors produced a diverse but scathing critique of the Russian intelligentsia and set off a major debate.

Zemstvo (plural: *zemstva*). Organs of local self-government established in 1864 in thirty-four of the fifty *gubernii* of European Russia as part of the Great Reforms. Nobles, urban residents, and peasants each chose representatives to *uezd* assemblies, which elected governing boards and chose representatives to *guberniia* assemblies. The *zemstvo* organizations in many regions gradually assumed an important role in local administration, especially education and public health. In 1911 and 1912, *zemstvo* institutions were extended to nine additional provinces.

RUSSIA'S MISSING MIDDLE CLASS

1

Introduction

Harley D. Balzer

In postemancipation Russia and the Soviet Union professional specialists constituted the largest component of the nascent middle class. Before 1917 specialists were growing rapidly in numbers and played an important role in the political process, but an estate-based social structure and cleavages cutting across their occupational and social identities inhibited concerted political action. The primary goal of this volume is to provide a preliminary portrait of the development and expansion of Russian professions in the years before 1917.

Questions about the character of Russian professions have acquired an additional dimension with the demise of the Soviet political system. Policies adopted by the Soviet regime resulted in a massive increase in the number of specialists in the knowledge-based professions within a system where political controls and stringent deprofessionalization precluded collective action. Since 1991 the attempt to create a democratic polity in Russia has invited, if not demanded, the participation of the professional middle class.[1] Yet, as in the period before 1917, it has proved difficult for these groups to act in concert or to firmly establish a professional or middle-class identity. Exploring the history of Russian professions helps us to learn more about the professional specialists and the role they might play in the future. Russia's professional intelligentsia provided many of the ideas and much of the support for perestroika. These communities of specialists might be expected to join Russia's new commercial and industrial groups in supporting economic reforms and political change. But in the face of social change and economic crisis a danger exists that rapid downward social mobility could lead professional specialists to support more extreme political movements.

Approaches to the Study of Professions

Early studies of professions focused mainly on Britain and America and generally adopted an uncritical approach. The existence of professions was accepted as part of the natural order of things, and professional communities

3

were portrayed as having the good of society among their highest values. The British literature has been described as "Whiggish."[2] In America, despite a healthy skepticism in the work of some social critics, the dominant paradigm was provided by Talcott Parsons's functionalist approach. Professions were seen to be ethically motivated and service-oriented.[3] After World War II, the image of professionals as selfless public servants was called into question by scholars, many writing from a neo-Marxist perspective, who emphasized issues of conflict and power. In these analyses, professions seek to dominate the market for their services, relying on the state to regulate entry. While presented as actions to protect the public and guarantee proper standards of training and behavior, these professional programs also (or, for some analysts, primarily) are manifestations of self-interest and concern for status.[4]

Despite significant differences in their views about the motivation for and implications of professional programs, the functionalists and the radical critics developed a rough consensus in defining professions. The models derived from study of the Anglo-American experience emphasize cognitive, normative, and evaluative attributes: members of a profession share a knowledge base acquired through formal training; they adhere to standards of conduct reinforced by a socialization process emphasizing service; and the professions are self-governing, asserting that the professionals themselves are the most competent gatekeepers and arbiters of appropriate behavior. Training, socialization, and regulation are carried out through institutional structures including universities, specialized journals, and professional organizations. Scientific societies, study circles, and various informal groups also play a role in developing and maintaining professional identity.

Some scholars have amplified these criteria with longer lists of specific attributes.[5] The elements of the definition they emphasize fluctuate in response to social, economic, and political conditions that manifest different forms in different national contexts. In an effort to transcend list making, Eliot Freidson has offered a more parsimonious definition: "I use the word 'profession' to refer to an occupation that controls its own work, organized by a special set of institutions sustained in part by a particular ideology of expertise and service. I use the word 'professionalism' to refer to that ideology and special set of institutions." Freidson recognizes that in the way he uses the concept, it is probably limited to Anglo-American experience in a particular time period. Yet his call for a rebirth of professional theory invites broader comparisons.[6]

Scholars studying the professions may tend to overestimate their role. Harold Perkin elevated the professions to the central place in English social history.[7] Burton Bledstein makes less grandiose but quite strong claims for their role in America.[8] Geoffrey Cocks and Konrad Jarausch slip into formulations where a disembodied "professionalization impetus" becomes an actor on the historical stage.[9] Harold Wilensky suggested the ultimate extreme in "The Professionalization of Everyone?"[10]

Placing on professions and professionalization a load the concepts cannot support impairs our understanding of history. Professionalization is not the single thread running through the fabric of modern society that will enable scholars to unravel and explain their material. It is an important phenomenon, indeed one of the dominant social processes of the nineteenth and twentieth centuries, but it must be viewed in the broader context of social history or it distorts more than it reveals. Professionalization cannot be accorded an existence separate from social-political environments and human actors.

But to reject excessive claims about the role of professions is not to reject the utility of the concept. Recent work emphasizes the situation of specialists functioning in the complex organizations characteristic of postindustrial society.[11] In this context, the crucial distinctions become those between manager and subordinate, salaried and nonsalaried labor, and the relationships inside and outside of the organization. Increasingly, the identity of being part of a large bureaucracy transcends professional identity.

Or does it? Are we not dealing with a situation of multiple identities in increasingly complex societies? Even professionals employed in large universities or corporations may derive a significant part of their identity from their professional role, and their professional community may provide an important forum for political expression. I tend to agree with Eliot Freidson regarding the significance of professions: they are not merely knowledge-based occupations embedded in large organizations. To comprehend diverse social and political contexts, the elements of perceived status and autonomy are crucial. No matter how completely the specialist's activity is subsumed in a large organization, the professional specialist maintains a reference group and an identity (increasingly one of multiple identities) as a member of a profession. Professional identity may be a delusion that results in acquiescence to the condition of a "one-dimensional man"; it may be a status payoff that substitutes for material benefits; but it may also be a source of strength in confronting the organizational structures. Not enough attention has been paid to the enduring power of the professional specialist, even in seemingly rigid organizational settings.

Professions take on their greatest significance in the context of the intermediating structures crucial to democratic political development. Professional autonomy, rarely complete but also rarely completely obliterated, is one of the components of most democratic political systems.[12]

Professionalization is not a developmental model, and there is no ultimate resolution. Conflicts and the need for renegotiation of the arrangements are perpetual. At the same time that professions, the occupational environment, and the types of questions asked by scholars of the professions are all changing, the state, too, is changing. This gives the search for a "unified theory of professions" the quality of four-dimensional chess. Scholars coming to the problem from diverse perspectives based on different discourses are studying changing social and occupational structures in relation to state and administrative contexts that are themselves in flux.[13]

Professions and the State in Europe

Models based on British and American experience do not always lead us to the most important questions about professions in the Continental nations. In France, Central Europe, and especially in Russia, the relationship of professions to the state had a different character, stemming from their origins in systems of formal academic training administered by the government. Rather than independent professional groups seeking to invoke state authority to enforce their control over training and membership, the Continental pattern consisted of states fostering the professions through specialized educational institutions, with practitioners organized in state-sanctioned corps. While different in each national context and each profession, the professional programs inevitably involved a tension between establishing some degree of autonomy and enjoying the status, protection, and control over credentialing that the state provided. The model of the civil servant as bureaucratic modernizer was a powerful alternative to the model of the free professional.

Realization of professional agendas always implies some reliance on state power. At a minimum, the state guarantees professionals a monopoly vis-à-vis practitioners lacking proper credentials (in the name of protecting the public). In conditions where professionals perceive their role to be encouraging social transformation as well as performing professional services, the state may be viewed as both a serious obstacle and an opportunity; professionals may see in state power an important means to achieve their program, provided that state power can be harnessed to advance the professionals' goals without unduly infringing their autonomy.[14] When the state in the guise of bureaucratic modernizers advances its own program of development, there is a strong temptation to ignore autonomy in favor of (perceived) efficacy.[15]

Recent scholarship on professions in continental Europe clearly shows the important role played by the state and the complexity of professionals' relationships with state power. In France, old elites first resisted the growth of professionalizing educational institutions and then sought (rather successfully) to restrict access to those institutions in ways favoring individuals from the traditional privileged classes. Introducing a volume on French professions, Gerald Geison decries the neglect of the state in studies of professions, attributing the lacuna to the "political cultures and traditions in which scholars are embedded." He notes that "even powerful professional groups depend ultimately on the borrowed authority of the state."[16]

Both Geison and Matthew Ramsey emphasize the role of the French state while underlining the importance of political culture and the history of individual professions. "In France, professional 'autonomy,' 'power,' and success virtually required dependence on the state."[17] Yet they also note that the character of the relationship and degree of dependence vary; physicians in France managed to retain considerably more independence than many other professions, for example engineers and scientists.[18] These differences suggest a range of relationships between professions and the state in any national context that are subject to change over time.[19]

Similar judgments about the diversity of professional programs and the importance of longitudinal changes emerge from an examination of German professions. The German case is closer to the Russian experience geographically, culturally, and also in terms of political discontinuities. German professionals in the mid-nineteenth century strove to gain independence from the state while simultaneously seeking control over such mechanisms of government authority as the system of state examinations. By the end of the century, faced with competition for a limited employment market, many German professionals sought state protection to support their incomes and status. In the Nazi era, German specialists experienced severe deprofessionalization. Since World War II they have provided an example of relatively successful reprofessionalization in a context of increasing specialization and organizational bureaucratization.[20]

Several scholars of the German professions suggest that the civil service bureaucracy developed an ethos and orientation essentially similar to Anglo-American professionalism.[21] Gispen provides an extensive analysis of the basis for the similarities:

> From a comparative historical perspective, the professions are not so much *sui generis* as just one version of a larger phenomenon that encompasses Weber's bureaucracy as well: The rise of expertise and certification as specifically middle-class techniques for advancement and for legitimizing privilege, rank, and power (vis-à-vis aristocratic resistance and democratic pretensions alike), intertwined with ideologies of 'culture,' science and public service that function in a context of all-pervading instrumental rationality, specialization, and secularization."[22]

The approach leads to a focus on specialist employment in large organizations and suggests Hans Rosenberg's Prussian bureaucrat as the original "organization man."[23]

A somewhat different analysis is given in Mária Kovács's study of Hungarian professions, which helps us to understand just how different things appear from a Central European perspective. For Kovács, "real" liberalism is represented by the Hungarian government's setting state education standards that determined access to the professions, thereby breaking the self-interested monopolistic control exercised by guildlike corporate groups. Where American, British, and French physicians succeeded in restricting entry to the medical profession, Hungarian doctors accepted the state's "rational liberal policies" that maintained open access via state-regulated education.[24]

In Kovács's analysis, as in the work of many students of German professions, the professional structure resulting from government policy is more important and more "rational" than self-regulating professional organizations. She sees this as fully liberal, with antiliberal elements introduced only after World War I, when ethnonationalism colored the response to a situation where overproduction of specialists resulted in unemployment and underemployment.[25]

Kovács's work presents an important challenge to equating self-regulating professions with liberalism. But she does not address some of the broader historical questions posed by the fate of Hungarian professions after World War I. Had these groups been able to counterbalance bureaucratic domination by developing self-regulating communities or corporations, might they have been better able to resist the demise of liberal politics? Is the "liberal state" the best guarantor of liberalism and professional goals? What happens if the state becomes less liberal, or even fascist? It is here that broader issues of the relationship among professional organizations, the public sphere, and democracy become central.

Historical and cultural approaches to comparative study of the professions hold much promise.[26] Konrad Jarausch outlines an ambitious and important agenda for comparative research on Continental professions. One of the most significant points in his account is the reversibility of professional development, particularly in the face of economic crisis.[27] In the case of German (and also Hungarian) professionals, rapid expansion in numbers resulted in pressure to restrict entry or even remove some practitioners.[28] Cocks and Jarausch note the vulnerability of downwardly mobile professionals to right-wing extremism, and pose the question in terms of a dilemma between "narrow selfishness and broader public interest" that "will determine whether professions are a scourge or a benefit to humanity." The Soviet case (and that of Poland, Hungary, and other East European countries) suggests that professionals may also be vulnerable to left-wing extremism, leading us to pose the question somewhat differently. Rather than making a choice between altruism and self-interest, might professionals have reacted in a typical human way by shunning difficult choices, taking refuge in the shelter of disinterested expertise?[29]

Professions in Cultural Context

Not only was the professional game on the Continent distinct, but so was the discourse. The English vocabulary used to discuss professions, professionals, and professionalization is not easily translated into French, German, or Russian. It requires extensive explanations and notations to convey the meaning of "liberal professions." The prevailing Marxist terminology in French social science can make it problematic to even address the issues.[30]

There is some irony in the linguistic difficulties, given the origin of the term "liberal profession" in the liberal education English gentlemen received, as opposed to learning a trade or skill.[31] The usage suggests a commonality with the classical education and culture that are central to Continental professional self-definition. In Central and Eastern Europe, the academic aspects of professionalism became tinged with a strong element of sociocultural elitism. An educated person was also a cultured person (and in Russia an intellectual). The Central European profession is more than an occupation, or even a calling: it is a way of life, and the state monopoly on certifying graduates for employment reinforced cultural patterns. For example, in nineteenth-century Germany shop-educated engineers were not able to displace academic elites and attain the legitimacy or leadership in professional organizations enjoyed by their American counterparts.[32]

The differences in language and social structure are reflected in the European convention of using "estate" to refer to professional groups. In Germany, physicians and other professionals belonged to the *Stand*. Russian doctors and lawyers referred to themselves as members of the "medical estate" (*meditsinskoe soslovie*) or "legal estate" (*iuridicheskoe soslovie*), and other groups sought this label as a symbol of status.[33]

Emphasis on estates reflects the importance of the cultural element in Central European professional identity. In German the key concepts are *Bildung* and *Wissenschaft*. *Bildung* may be loosely translated as "cultivation," but in educational terms almost always implies a classical gymnasium education. *Wissenschaft* in this context is best rendered as "scholarship" in the broad sense.[34]

Russian professionals were influenced not only by education and social structure, but also by Russia's intelligentsia culture. The Russian intelligentsia differed from other Continental cultural elites in its almost narcissistic self-awareness. It is tempting to deflect the "cursed question" of defining the intelligentsia by suggesting that it was made up of those people who were themselves concerned with defining the intelligentsia. A good working definition might be individuals concerned with making general statements about humanity and about society in a context of criticism, if not outright opposition, vis-à-vis the state.[35] Where *Bildungsburgertum* was a retrospective label applied in the 1920s, Russian *intelligenty* constantly referred to the term and debated the changing boundaries of membership.[36] The intelligentsia ethos included a strong element of social service and responsibility for the enlightenment of the people (*narod*), tinged with opposition to the tsarist government.[37] Family tradition plays an important role—any *intelligent* can describe a process of *vospitanie* (literally "upbringing," but implying moral education and inculcation of values). Members of the intelligentsia most often refer to a specific family member or surrogate relative who was their *vospitatel'*, and will distinguish between where they received their formal education and where they received their *vospitanie*.[38]

The family or personal element is a striking feature of the Russian intelligentsia. *Bildung* could be acquired in state institutions of higher learning, as could *Wissenschaft*, but the Russian intelligentsia never trusted the state to act as the arbiter of its cultural norms. *Vospitanie* was inculcated by one's family or by an individual with the moral and cultural authority to serve as a role model; the state could never play this role for the critical intelligentsia in either tsarist Russia or the Soviet Union.[39] Intelligentsia skepticism toward the state helps explain the negative public assessment of most bureaucratic modernizers.

Affinities based on education and knowledge combined with a sense of cultural isolation make Russian professionals closely resemble the intelligentsia, and there is significant overlap between the two groups. But they are not identical. One could be an *intelligent* without being a professional, much less a member of a profession, and not all professionals meet everyone's definition of an *intelligent*. The real importance of the intelligentsia culture for Russian professions was in leadership and ideology. At least until 1905, leadership of virtually all Russian professions was in the hands of radical activists inculcated with intelligentsia values.[40] In addition to political radicalism, professional programs were imbued with a strong ethos of service to the people that had deep roots in intelligentsia traditions.[41] Brint's discussion of profession as a "calling" resonates with the concept of the intelligentsia.[42] It is a highly cultural definition. But the nineteenth-century Russian professional was more a culture-bearer than a rational actor. *Intelligenty* were far more likely to organize a study circle for workers, foster an *artel'*, or propose a labor union than to organize themselves into a group capable of coherent collective action.[43]

The Development of Russian Professions

The character of their relations with the state set Russian professionals apart from their British and American counterparts, and also from colleagues in Western Europe. Russian professionals perceived the state to be simultaneously a greater obstacle to organizing independent professional groups and a more important partner in fulfilling their aspirations for social and economic development. Russian rulers generally rejected even the most nonthreatening proposals for independent collective action, and this was far more the case under the Soviet regime.[44]

Conditions for the development of professions in Russia were created by the Great Reforms following Russia's defeat in the Crimean War (1853-55). In this period, higher education, group communication, specialized publications, and professional associations became important elements of specialists' occupational self-definition. The efforts began among lawyers, physicians, and engineers, and were rapidly imitated by other groups. By the last decade of the nineteenth century, professional aspirations were articulated by a broad range of Russian specialists.

Prior to the reform era, most individuals in specialized occupations were members of militarized corps fostered by the tsarist government. A majority of the physicians in the empire were trained in military medical academies, and three-fourths were public employees.[45] Engineers were educated and spent their careers in militarized corps run by the mining and transportation departments. More than three-fourths of the transport engineers and 94 percent of the mining engineers were graduates of the two specialized corps.[46] Perhaps a half-dozen graduates of civilian technical schools managed to become private entrepreneurs.[47] Most lawyers graduated from elite government schools and served in state administrative positions.[48]

The reforms of the 1860s replaced the militarized corps with higher education at universities and specialized institutes.[49] The corps of mining and transport engineers became open higher educational institutions, and the precedent of engineers trained in new types of institutes was established at the Petersburg Technological Institute and Moscow Higher Technical School.[50] Military academies ceased to be the major supplier of physicians, and the role of university juridical faculties in educating legal specialists was greatly enhanced.[51]

The number of specialists involved in the shift to open education was less important than the qualitative change. A significant increase in numbers of students, institutes, and professionals came only at the end of the nineteenth century, when Sergei Witte expanded the Finance Ministry role in education and forced other departments to follow suit.[52] However, the norm of public higher education for professional specialists was clearly established in the 1860s.

Russian higher schools were overwhelmingly engaged in professional training. Rather than studying the "liberal arts" or natural sciences, the great majority of Russian university students were in the medical and law faculties.[53] By the end of the century the nine universities were dwarfed by a large network of institutes training specialists in a broad variety of professional skills.[54] Once again, new institutions did not replace those that already existed, but rather added another "sedimentary layer," so that alongside the older ministerial institutes there now existed schools emphasizing new specialties and polytechnical institutes oriented to the needs of developing industry.[55] Rapid expansion accentuated the increasing diversity of the student body.[56]

Professional journals became an important part of most specialists' lives by the 1860s. Almost all the specialized periodicals that existed before the Great Reforms were published by government departments or educational institutions. In the 1860s regular publications by social organizations became common fare.[57] The Russian Technical Society inaugurated its *Vestnik* in 1866. The law societies in St. Petersburg and Moscow introduced specialized journals.[58] Twenty-three new medical periodicals appeared in the decade after 1856, compared to a total of fourteen in the previous half century. The St. Petersburg architecture society journal *Zodchii* was initiated in 1872. By the 1890s even feldshers (physicians' assistants) had multiple publications.[59]

In addition to the "official" professional journals, private (and privately financed) periodicals appeared. An independent medical journal, Manassein's influential *Vrach,* began publication in 1880. Russia's first completely independent engineering journal, *Inzhener*, was inaugurated in 1882. Lawyers were less quick to establish an independent organ, and one did not appear until the early twentieth century.[60]

Expanded communication and travel, particularly railroads, provided an impetus for professionals to congregate, and foreign models spurred efforts to organize professional congresses. Convening a national congress was regarded as a crucial manifestation of professional development. In part this reflected the isolation felt by members of some professions—physicians and teachers in particular—who worked in remote rural areas. But the desire to hold congresses was no less strong among groups like lawyers, who were overwhelmingly concentrated in urban centers. Along with providing opportunities to exchange information, the congresses were a substitute for permanent associations. The government recognized this and demonstrated its fear of independent public activity by resisting efforts to make these gatherings regular events or to extend the right to hold congresses to new groups.

Physicians sought to use their Pirogov Congresses as a basis for professional organization, and these gatherings became the model other Russian groups strove to emulate. Meetings of medical specialists were convened to deal with specific problems at the provincial level, but physicians wanted a national gathering. The first Pirogov Congress met in 1885, followed by nine more before 1914. Physicians were relatively successful at maintaining this form of organizational activity, in part out of sheer necessity: if embarrassing and costly epidemics were to be controlled, it was imperative that the medical specialists gather to share information about existing conditions and to elaborate measures to protect public health.[61] Other groups were less successful. The government permitted lawyers to meet once, in 1872, but prohibited further national congresses. Engineers did not overcome the government's strictures against an all-Russian congress until after the February Revolution in 1917.[62]

Private journals and congresses of independent specialists reflected growing levels of private employment in an economically and socially more complex society. Changes in the character of economic activity meant that following their education, professionals entered an increasingly diverse occupational world, where the state, while still attractive to many, was no longer the sole major player. As in education, a greater numerical expansion came at the end of the century, but the reforms created the conditions for substantial private employment.

Private legal activity had existed before the reforms, but it could hardly be called professional. The prereform solicitors (*striapchie*) had no requirements for education or socialization, and their ethical conduct was universally condemned. A few engineers worked outside government ministries before the 1860s, but thereafter occupational diversity increased enormously and engineers began to formulate arrangements for that ultimate hallmark of the independent professional—consulting. Before the reforms, the number of independent physicians was small, and most were foreigners. While private medical practice expanded in the second half of the century, physicians illustrate an important characteristic of Russian professions: despite the development of the economy and diverse career patterns, many specialists—lawyers and engineers as well as physicians—continued to prefer the security of government positions guaranteeing fixed salaries and pensions, and continued to emphasize the intelligentsia's mission to serve the Russian people.[63]

Even if many specialists remained in government service, the prevailing model was no longer the bureaucratic official (*chinovnik*). With the expansion of local self-government (*zemstvo*) activity in the final decades of the nineteenth century, additional roles and opportunities were created for physicians, engineers, statisticians, agronomists, and a growing number of other specialists.[64]

It is difficult to overemphasize the importance for professionals of ending the state's monopoly position as employer. Career alternatives reduced (though hardly removed) the threat of economic retribution for professional and political activity. Even within the government there could be multiple opportunities for employment, as in the case of professors dismissed from the universities who were hired to teach at institutes administered by the Finance Ministry.[65]

Changes in education, communication, and employment created the conditions for professional development, and professionals sought to express their new identities in formal organizations. Physicians, lawyers, engineers, and teachers regarded their congresses as the first step to establishing permanent professional societies modeled on those of their European colleagues.

Lawyers were provided with a professional organization, the Councils of the Bar, as part of the judicial reform. Although limited to only a few cities, these institutions encompassed the major portion of Russia's lawyers, who were concentrated in urban centers. The councils were the strongest organs of professional self-government created by the tsarist state, yet even they did not satisfy lawyers' aspirations for professional association.[66]

Engineering societies were for the most part school alumni associations. Initially, this meant they were organized by specialty. But among engineers a desire persisted for two types of professional organization: alongside groups based on increasingly narrow specializations and subspecialties, they sought a single association uniting all engineers.[67] Physicians, too, sought multiple forms of organization. Attention has focused most often on the Pirogov Society, but there were other medical associations as well.[68] Like engineers, they sought both specialty-based societies and also a broad organization that could speak for all medical personnel on important political and social issues.

Administrative resistance to convening congresses or establishing professional associations encouraged Russian specialists to exploit whatever organizational opportunities were available. Mutual assistance societies established to aid needy practitioners became one focal point for group activity.[69] Scientific societies and circles (*kruzhki*) were also a way to circumvent restrictions on professional contact. Not only did the scientific societies provide opportunities to meet and to assist colleagues, they also served as "fronts" for prohibited meetings.[70]

In addition to creating new opportunities, the growing private economic sector posed new ethical dilemmas for professionals. Where the state might be in a position to credential and monitor its employees, the open market was a different matter. Each profession expected its members to adhere to an ethical code embodying norms of disinterestedness and proper moral conduct. Physicians stated this directly when they took their oath.[71] For Russian lawyers, achievement of a less corrupt court system and self-policing legal profession were among the most dramatic changes wrought by the Great Reforms. Subsequent accounts were effusive in praising the transformation in legal ethics resulting from the new system.[72]

Compared to lawyers and physicians, engineers took longer to voice their commitment to ethical norms. Moral precepts played a less important role in technical education, while the opportunities for profit were far greater. Memoirs and fictional accounts provide ample evidence that bribery remained a common feature of technical work in government departments.[73]

While law, medicine, and engineering provide the most vivid examples, these were hardly the only professions to develop in postreform Russia. Teachers, auxiliary medical personnel, technicians, statisticians, and many other groups formulated professional agendas.[74] By the end of the nineteenth century, the list was greatly expanded, growing even more rapidly as a result of the liberation movement's union-fostering activities and the role of the Union of Unions in 1905.[75] What transpired was a general phenomenon of "professionalization," where activists within an expanding number of occupational groups aspired to the corporate identity, social status, and frequently the autonomy of the free professions. Efforts to establish professional norms were visible among Russian government officials, army officers, and the clergy.[76]

The tsarist government's ambivalent attitude toward professional development reflected both its internal divisions and its aspiration to achieve the economic and political power of societies in which professional life was more developed. To compete with England, France, and Germany, there appeared to be no choice but to grant specialists more influence—not as much as they enjoyed in other nations, but just enough for Russia to match western achievements. The concessions were never granted willingly. Each shred of professional autonomy had to be wrested from a resistant administration that was likely to seek to reimpose restrictions at the first sign of adverse consequences or "irresponsible" behavior. The professions increasingly found support from specialists within the government, but they were never dominant. In the end, the issue always reverted to the power of the autocrat.[77]

The autocracy's unwillingness to compromise meant that in the decade before 1905, professional programs became increasingly political. This is clear in the essays that follow. The events of 1905 feature prominently in the history of every Russian profession. This history has been recounted elsewhere.[78] While activism and professional organization grew markedly after 1891, the period of significant politicization among professionals was quite compressed. Professions were not part of the strike movement in 1903, and they played little role in 1912 and after.[79] It was only in the revolutionary year of 1905 that most professions joined the assault on autocracy. For a few months they believed that radical professionals might displace professional radicals as the agents of change in Russian politics.

Russian professionals failed to consolidate either strong professional organizations or a participatory political system. In the essays that follow, we can see both the aspirations and the failures. Examining the history of the individual professions provides a basis for us to return in the Conclusion to the broader questions of Russia's social and political history. Was the professional middle class truly missing, or was it too small, too fragmented, and too inept politically, or was the Russian autocracy too strong an obstacle?

Professionals themselves emphasized their uniqueness, and this tendency has been echoed by the scholars who study them. It is an important cognitive element of professional self-definition: the professions derive their identity not only from a program of collective action, but also from exclusion and differentiation. Every profession contained a faction arguing that their "professional program" was essential to Russia's salvation. Professors claimed a special responsibility for the higher education system, physicians for public health, lawyers for the legal basis of the state, and engineers for economic and technical progress. In most cases, at least before 1905, professional messianism was linked to a belief that the necessary actions could be taken only in conjunction with a political transformation limiting autocracy and liberating society (and the professions) to improve Russian life.

*   *   *

The editor's essay on Russian engineers focuses on their aspirations to play a role in economic and political life, and the tension between increasing specialization and yearning for a united national organization. Leading Russian engineers advocated a major expansion in the number of technical specialists trained in the country, along with introduction of new types of education. They got their wish at the end of the nineteenth century, when Sergei Witte fostered a major increase in the number of schools and students in Russian specialized higher education. The larger number of specialists alone eventually would have stimulated initiatives for stronger professional associations. But in Russia such developments were frequently compressed: A downturn in the economy created an employment crisis encouraging engineers to turn to professional societies for assistance, and these larger and more aggressive organizations became mobilized politically during the Revolution of 1905. The last section of the chapter emphasizes the increasing diversity within the engineering profession, relating it to Russia's more complex economy.

The next three essays deal with medical professionals. John Hutchinson's contribution demonstrates the diverse varieties of Russian professional programs. The pioneering work on Russian physicians by Nancy Frieden focused on *zemstvo* medicine, a theme continued by other researchers.[80] Hutchinson reminds us that *zemstvo* doctors did not constitute the entire medical profession—about one-third of Russian doctors were in private practice. More important, he shows that even if opposition to autocracy was the most popular stance among physicians, it was not the sole option. G.V. Rein sought not to confront the state but to harness its power. He represents the emergence of a coherent conservative model for Russia's medical profession, and similar phenomena can be seen in other groups. In particular, Rein's efforts within the government should be compared with the careers of the several conservative university professors who became ministers of education in the years after 1905.[81]

After 1905-6 leadership in many professional groups began to pass from the hands of the activists who dominated the liberation movement and Union of Unions. The activists did not always abandon the field, but they were increasingly compelled to share it with leaders advocating less politically oppositionist programs. Hutchinson suggests the community medical tradition was "potentially subversive." In the eyes of some, this was certainly the case. Others might view as subversive the efforts to establish an organization on the model of Germany's Chambers of Physicians, with compulsory membership.

Rein's prescriptions sound similar to structures that developed in the Soviet period: a two-tiered system of medical education with physicians working as state-supervised practitioners, not autonomous professionals. Thus, a model of state-dominated professions was available for the Bolsheviks to apply. Both the messianic professional impulse and the sources of Soviet technocracy were apparent in Rein's proposals, which Hutchinson points out were guided by the belief that "intervention by the state, employing the latest technology, could achieve dramatic success."

But could it? Rein's effort to create a super-ministry ran aground due to bureaucratic opposition, but also due to the bureaucracy's inability to carry out the tasks it sought to perform. In a vast empire, it was simply impossible for the government to do everything, much less do it in a way that could cope with local diversity. Only by mobilizing society could "modern" levels of development be achieved.[82] The story of the medical profession underscores that professions depend on a relationship to the state, rather than simply escaping its tutelage. Now that Russians are reconstituting the professions, many of the difficulties that inhibited professional development in the period after 1905 are again apparent.

Julie Brown's essay on psychiatrists suggests that the conservative reaction described by Hutchinson was neither broadly popular nor irreversible. But even psychiatrists were more supportive of universal suffrage in the political realm than of inclusiveness in administering the asylums. Having fought for decades to establish their professional identity and status as specialists, they were loath to share responsibility with other groups. Here we see the roots of the divisions that became apparent in 1905. In most professions, the October Manifesto satisfied the political goals of the elite, while promising a forum for advancing their professional programs. But it did little to assuage the demands for inclusiveness by auxiliary personnel. Rather, these demands drove many professionals to the right in an effort to preserve their hard-won but fragile gains.

Psychiatrists were confronted by well-organized and highly politicized second-echelon personnel and also by ordinary workers who demanded a share in decisions about the mental hospitals.[83] This may well have helped to sharpen the sense of professional uniqueness; it was not an issue of democracy, but rather one of training, competence, and ethical codes. When psychiatrists sought accommodation by involving other groups in administration on a consultative basis, government and *zemstva* rejected this, and in the wave of reaction, it was reversed.[84] Psychiatrists were frustrated by having to deal with nonspecialists in the guise of both nonpsychiatrist medical administrators and less educated public administrators.

The small number of psychiatrists meant that many, often most, day-to-day decisions were made by paraprofessionals, a situation similar to that of feldshers. The Russian feldsher was in theory a physician's assistant. Samuel Ramer shows that the shortage of doctors in many areas of the Empire frequently meant that feldshers worked alone, often combining their rudimentary training with traditional practices derived from folk medicine. Such "unmodern" techniques and the feldshers' efforts to legalize and institutionalize their activity brought them into conflict with the physicians who were their superiors. This conflict was overshadowed in 1905 by a unified struggle against autocracy, but in the following years more narrow group interests reasserted themselves. Like the primary school teachers, feldshers were extremely concerned to overcome their isolation.

Ramer demonstrates that feldshers shared much with rural teachers. They had taken a first step up the ladders of education and social mobility and were cut off from their illiterate village past. But they were not highly educated specialists and were not accepted as peers by the self-defined intelligentsia elite. They might be patronized, with talk about the need for enlightenment, but they were never equals. It is hardly surprising that feldshers sought to become colleagues of physicians and enter the Pirogov Society at the same time that they denied status and recognition to the military (*rotnye*) feldshers. Virtually every professional group defined itself by who it excluded as well as who it admitted.

Feldshers' fate in the period after 1917 is also instructive. As "paraprofessionals," they lacked the cachet of being real proletarians and therefore did not benefit from policies favoring workers and peasants. Bolshevik policies in 1918 lumped all medical workers—physicians, feldshers, midwives, and others—into "mass" unions. This egalitarianism satisfied the demands of paraprofessionals for more equal treatment, but simultaneously debased the professional standards of all specialists. Lenin rejected the approach in 1919, but it was revived by Stalin with suffocating results. Feldshers were an important component of the Soviet health care system, and difficulties recruiting medical personnel in the USSR encouraged increasing reliance on their contribution.

Ramer's essay touches on the key issue of identities. At a time when both political and vocational identity were in their formative stages, self-identification was highly malleable. It was not unusual, and probably typical, for individuals to belong to a number of organizations related to their work. And given the newness of public political life, it would be surprising if individuals did not experience an evolution in their views over time.

Moving from medicine to education, the reader may be struck by similarities between feldshers and village teachers. Scott Seregny notes that teachers in virtually every society find themselves extolled as critically important molders of future citizens while being rewarded at a level suggesting their skills are neither unique nor esteemed. In Russia these difficulties were compounded by the nation's low cultural level and government suspicion of any collective activity to overcome backwardness and isolation. Seregny shows the ways government opposition and conflicts with *zemstvo* officials led to radicalization of Russian village teachers.

Russian teachers' organizations resembled engineering associations in the important role mutual-aid societies played in organizational development. Yet for village teachers, cultural issues came to have more salience than economic concerns. This may be attributable to the demographic composition of the teaching profession (specifically the enormous increase in the number of young, single teachers in the decade before 1905), but also reflects the genuine idealism characterizing elementary education in these years. Teachers' major demands at the turn of century were cultural replenishment and the right to association, rather than economic benefits. They were culture-bearers, but they simultaneously felt tremendous cultural insecurity—a situation that explains the important role of congresses and summer courses among their demands.[85]

Unlike the authors of the other essays in the collection who focus mainly on 1905 and after, Seregny devotes his attention to the period before 1905. This emphasis points up the history of professional development beginning with the reforms of the 1860s. That development, hardly unilinear, was plagued by false starts, twists and turns, and administrative opposition. The reform era generated a spurt of professional initiative that was thwarted by government resistance in the 1870s and 1880s. The efforts were revived after the famine of 1891-92, which convinced many Russians that increased public activity was crucial for the nation's development. The leap in corporate consciousness in the decade before 1905 had a long preparation.

The condition of village teachers also reminds us that Russia was an underdeveloped country. While teachers aspired to professional models from European societies, they were also aware of developmental needs.[86] These tensions were acute in all the professions. Some specialists in the knowledge-based professions reacted by seeking to join the broader international community, either through emigration or employment with foreign firms. Others, including most of the service professionals, sublimated their tensions and emotions, often through a service ethos.[87]

Samuel Kassow's discussion of university professors provides an even more vivid illustration of the multiple identities specialists juggled. A professor was a member of a specialized scientific society, was likely to join the Academic Union, and was a member of a faculty council. In the last role, he was essentially a state official.[88]

The Kadets have been described frequently (and accurately) as a "party of professors," and this helps to explain their character and behavior. The professors were the most conservative of the groups making up the liberation movement in 1905, and this moderation is attributable in large part to their multiple identities. Impulses to radical political activity were generally curbed by their responsibility for educating the next generation of Russia's leaders and protecting the universities. Participation in running the universities caused professors to perceive themselves as different from other professional groups and other state employees. The self-image of being "above" class and party came to characterize university professors and the entire Kadet Party. But the illusion of being above politics did not make professors immune from punitive administrative measures. The purge of professors in 1908 echoes the dismissal of radical teachers after 1906. In the case of the professors, the numbers were far smaller, and they were more likely to have someplace else to go.

The moderate character of academics' political stance was clearly apparent in 1905. Where most professions broke from the united front against autocracy after the October Manifesto, professors reached their turning point in August with the Bulygin Rescript and Temporary Rules for university governance. These modest concessions, which to most unions represented at best a first step, appear to have satisfied the Academic Union's political agenda. Even in 1911-14, a period Kassow calls the "nadir of relations between the academic profession and the government," professors' dissatisfaction did not translate into political activism. Some professors were able to compromise. Others saw their pedagogical responsibility as paramount. The cleavages within the academic profession were numerous: between conservative and liberal professors, between junior and senior faculty, between faculty and students, and among the professors' diverse roles. Theirs was one of the few professions to have a right-wing movement in the years before 1914.

Many of those who seek a basis for "civic society" in postcommunist Russia look to the legal system created in the second half of the nineteenth century. But as Brian Levin-Stankevich reminds us, the reformed, western-looking part of the system was precisely that—a part. As in so many aspects of Russian life, "modern" institutions coexisted with more traditional forms. Alongside the new courts and the legal professionals organized into Councils of the Bar, a large number of state legal experts and a parallel system of administrative law remained in place for matters "too important" to be left to the vagaries of a jury system.[89]

By stressing an attitudinal rather than an occupation-based definition of the legal profession, Levin-Stankevich provides a framework permitting inclusion of the state law occupations as well as lawyers and jurists. The relationship between "private" and "state" legal professionals is one of the most informative examples of Russian professional development and has important parallels to the development of specialist input in subsequent periods. The state legal officials and private lawyers shared a common educational background, read the same journals, and often belonged to the same law societies; in Levin-Stankevich's term, they shared the same "legal culture." The categories were fluid, with many of the state officials subsequently entering private practice. They also shared a frustration at the lack of full acceptance of that culture. Many state legal officials did not agree with the government's views on policy issues. Individuals had to make their personal choices between resisting from within and resigning from government service. There were numerous examples of both responses. The complex web of possible legal careers in tsarist Russia clearly illustrates the ambiguity and contradictions rife in a profession encompassing highly educated, self-governing professionals on a western model, state employees who formed a distinct but closely related community of potential colleagues, and a variety of nonspecialists who nevertheless were permitted to function parallel to the professional community.

Levin-Stankevich identifies the core issue for the autocracy. From the time of Peter the Great, Russian rulers wanted formal and technical modernization without the accompanying social consequences. Reform might be on the table, but not autocratic prerogatives.[90] He shows the regime's need for a legal system, the consequent development of a corps of experts trained in the specialized knowledge required for such a system to function, and the inevitable corollary of an independent outlook among the emerging corps of professionals.

Without the professionals, who frequently did not share the autocratic world view, the government could not function. Even "safe" administrative judicial processes could disappoint the government when its specialists were not as well-versed in the law as defense attorneys.[91] This cuts to the heart of issues that remain central to Russian development. The contradiction between a Europeanized world of "modern" culture and the persistence of traditional behavior patterns is a recurring theme in Russian history. Anyone who suggests that post-Soviet Russian development must be in a West European direction should look carefully at similar assumptions in the years before 1917. The inchoate legal system suggests disturbing parallels, and Russia probably had a more developed legal profession in 1914 than in 1994.

Russian professionals constantly interacted with government officials who themselves were becoming more professionalized, as can be seen in the final two essays dealing with government administrators. Including governors and state officials in a volume on professions is surprising only to those who see professions solely in an American (and perhaps nineteenth-century American) context. Anyone attending meetings of American Federation of State, County, and Municipal Employees (AFSCME) in the 1990s would not find it unusual. Jane Caplan made a strong case for including civil servants in a volume on German professions.[92] Charles McClelland goes even further, suggesting that the German civil service was the first modern profession.[93]

Richard Robbins notes that the Russian governor was a classic administrative generalist, and in this guise might seem out of place in a collection on professions. But if our focus is extended from specific professional groups to the phenomenon of professionalization, the changes taking place in the tsarist administration are both relevant and important. The essays by Robbins and Daniel Orlovsky help us to focus on the context of increasing education, specialization, and professional expectations in Russian society.

Russian governors were subject to a job market monopolized by the state.[94] Their basis for association was weak, since they had no standard education or career pattern. Yet Robbins presents evidence that governors' careers became increasingly standardized, that education levels were rising and more likely to involve legal training, that their knowledge base included expertise acquired through on-the-job training, and that by the turn of the century a pattern had developed consisting of service in the provinces and in the post of vice-governor. The process remained incomplete, a result of the government being caught among conflicting goals, needs, and imperatives, but even within the MVD, generally the most conservative and gentry-oriented of tsarist ministries, a pattern of professional service was developing.

The autocracy could base appointments on loyalty rather than professional expertise, and often did. But ignoring the specialists involved costs, and these costs were increasingly high. In the case of the governors, not enough "professionalized" candidates were available. This has been one of the enduring problems of Russian administration. Frederick Starr noted that Russia's provinces were undergoverned. Merle Fainsod's portrait of Smolensk indicates that things did not improve significantly after the Bolshevik Revolution. Jerry Hough suggests that similar ambiguity persisted after World War II.[95] A cursory look at Yeltsin's governors in the post-Soviet era indicates that the loyalty-versus-professionalism issue remains quite salient.

Robbins's account of the scandalous situation in Riazan during Vice-Governor V.A. Kolobov's tenure also provides some perspective on the proliferation of advertisements for secretaries "without inhibitions" (*bez kompleksov*) in postcoup Russia. Rather than emerging into a world of post-materialist values, as some might have hoped, Russian society retains many of the gender and other stereotypes characteristic of preindustrial society.[96]

Despite the conflicts between the state and professional groups in the last years of the tsarist era, there was no real alternative to increasing reliance on professionalized officials. The simultaneous development of bureaucratic professionals and independent professional organizations offered two competing models for professional development. Rather than battling the state to secure professional independence, some professionals were tempted to try to utilize state power to further their "professional program." The example of Rein in the medical profession was duplicated in a number of areas where bureaucratic specialists proliferated. Orlovsky describes the emergence of professional specialists in many departments of the tsarist government.

Orlovsky's definition of professionalism among ministerial staff corresponds to the description of professional experts, rather than autonomous professionals. It was characteristic of both tsarist and Soviet experience and of Central Europe more broadly. He portrays the growing specialization and the role of the tsarist bureaucracy as an intermediary institution. Conflicts developed between the bureaucracy and would-be professionals, and also within the bureaucracy among proponents of rival concepts of professionalism and service.

The essays by Robbins and Orlovsky and material on German and other European officials bring us back to the issue of competing models of professions. Early theorists emphasized autonomy as the sine qua non of professionalism. At the opposite extreme, Charles McClelland seems to dismiss it entirely. Scholars examining processes of bureaucratization in large organizations have suggested that autonomy was a transient phase for most professionals; increasingly, work is performed in hierarchical structures where autonomy exists only as a stabilizing myth. But a narrow focus on autonomy within occupational structures ignores larger issues of professionals and politics.

A theme that runs through these pages is the inhibited development in Russia of "civic society." There were many elements of "civil society": voluntary and societal organizations, a critical public, and after 1905, political parties. But there was not a cohesive middle class. Most important, Russian society was not able to develop the network of intermediating institutions that allow social groups to play a role in the political system.

It was not just that Russian society was becoming more diverse. The diverse elements of the society were themselves becoming less homogeneous. Not only were the social groups more complex, but the range of acceptable discourse was expanding markedly. The *Vekhi* group is probably the most oft-noted symptom of heightened heterogeneity. Aileen Kelly has stressed the diminishing of radical self-censorship in the period after 1890 and especially after 1905. Laura Engelstein has documented reduced inhibitions in literature, discourse, and lifestyle. Don Rawson has provided a more nuanced portrait of the radical right. Joan Neuberger's account of societal responses to hooliganism shows the divisions and tensions over social issues that were developing in Russian society. Other recent studies explore similar phenomena. Russian society was in the throes of diversification similar to changes taking place throughout Europe in the first decades of the twentieth century.[97] Diversity can be a source of either weakness or strength, depending on the social context and particularly the intermediating institutions that make democracy work.[98]

As elaborated in the Conclusion of this volume, the failure of democracy in Russia resulted from a complex interaction involving divisions within the nascent middle class and resistance of the Russian government to collective action by its subjects. In the essays that follow, we repeatedly encounter instances where the Russian government refused to sanction national organizations of professionals or to permit congresses and other meetings. The excuse most commonly given was that the individual gatherings were "inappropriate at this time" (*prezhdevremenno*). But the reasons run deeper, to the very character of the autocratic political system. Russia's rulers never committed themselves to legal limitations on their power. Autocracy injected a personal element into decisions inhibiting institutionalization. Up to the end of the Russian Empire, the tsar continued to personally approve the formation of every commercial corporation. Similar tutelage extended to every effort to foster public activity, making professional congresses and national societies hostage to the whims and fears of the sovereign and his favored bureaucratic servitors.

Notes

1. In a recently completed doctoral dissertation, Marc Garcelon suggests that the Soviet specialists should more properly be termed a "state-engineered bureaucratic status group." Marc Garcelon, "Democrats and Apparatchiks: The Democratic Russia Movement and the Specialist Rebellion in Moscow, 1989-1991" (Ph.D. diss., University of California at Berkeley, 1995).

2. A.M. Carr-Sanders and P.A. Wilson, *The Professions* (Oxford: Clarendon Press, 1933); W.J. Reader, *Professional Men: The Rise of the Professional Classes in Nineteenth Century England* (New York: Basic Books, 1967).

3. Talcott Parsons, "Professions," *International Encyclopedia of the Social Sciences*, vol. 12, 536-47; and his *Essays in Sociological Theory* (New York: The Free Press, 1964). For an uncharacteristically intelligible account, see Parsons, "The Intellectual: A Social Role Category," in *On Intellectuals*, ed. Philip Rieff (New York: Doubleday & Co., 1970), 3-26. Eliot Freidson and Konrad Jarausch give summaries of the study of professions in America suggesting progression (and implying progress) from uncritical (at best neutral) acceptance to a more probing approach relying on comparative and social-historical perspectives. See Eliot Freidson, *Professionalism Reborn: Theory, Prophecy and Policy* (Chicago, IL: University of Chicago Press, 1994); Konrad Jarausch, "The German Professions in History and Theory," in *German Professions, 1800-1950*, eds. Geoffrey Cocks and Konrad H. Jarausch (New York: Oxford University Press, 1990); and Jarausch, *The Unfree Professions: German*

Lawyers, Teachers, and Engineers, 1900-1950 (New York: Oxford University Press, 1990).

4. One of the earliest critiques was J.A.C. Grant, "The Guild Returns to America, I," *Journal of Politics* 4, no. 3 (1942): 304-36. For a good example of a well-documented but one-sided assessment, see Randall Collins, *The Credential Society: An Historical Sociology of Education and Stratification* (New York: Academic Press, 1979). The most influential and most strident is probably Magali Sarfatti Larson, *The Rise of Professionalism: A Sociological Analysis* (Berkeley: University of California Press, 1977). Also see Larson's "The Production of Expertise and the Constitution of Expert Power," in *The Authority of Experts: Studies in History and Theory*, ed. Thomas L. Haskell (Bloomington: Indiana University Press, 1984), 28-80. A more nuanced critique is found in the work of Eliot Freidson; see *Professionalism Reborn*, and also his *Professional Power: A Study of the Institutionalization of Formal Knowledge* (Chicago, IL: University of Chicago Press, 1986).

In his introduction to *The Authority of Experts* (xxii), Haskell described the difference between Freidson and Larson in the following terms: "Freidson's essay is like a sunlit room full of familiar furniture; the one that follows, by Magali Sarfatti Larson, is like a shadowy corridor, with doors opening off in all directions. From Larson's Marxian perspective, everyday concepts, such as 'profession,' 'knowledge,' and 'university training' appear in an unfamiliar light and tend to blur at the edges, merging imperceptibly with larger systems of control and authority."

5. Larson provides a good summary of this literature in chapter 1 of *The Rise of Professionalism*.

6. Freidson, *Professionalism Reborn*, 10, footnote 1. Freidson's treatment of profession as a "folk concept" to be derived from "how people in a society determine who is a professional and who is not" (20) opens the door to introducing cultural elements in the definition, but it would produce quite intriguing and also confusing ramifications in the Soviet and post-Soviet context.

7. Harold Perkin, *The Origins of Modern English Society, 1780-1880* (London: Routledge & Kegan Paul, 1969). Perkin has extended the argument in *The Rise of Professional Society in England Since 1880* (London: Routledge, 1989).

8. Burton J. Bledstein, *The Culture of Professionalism: The Middle Class and the Development of Higher Education in America* (New York: W.W. Norton, 1976).

9. Cocks and Jarausch, eds., *German Professions*, "In spite of increasing difficulties, the professionalization impetus continued to involve new occupations during the first third of the twentieth century" (5); and "Though the professionalization impulse made further headway during the Third Reich . . ." (6). In fairness, it should be noted that they do better at putting professionalism and other "isms" in context on pages 6-7.

10. Harold L. Wilensky, "The Professionalization of Everyone?" *The American Journal of Sociology* 70, no. 2 (September 1964): 137-58.

11. In addition to efforts by scholars of Germany to find a link between civil service officials and Anglo-American professionals, much of this discussion is being driven by changes in systems of medical care and insurance. See Edmund D. Pellegrino, Robert M. Veatch, and John P. Langan, eds., *Ethics, Trust and the Professions: Philosophical and Cultural Aspects* (Washington, DC: Georgetown

University Press, 1991); Freidson, *Professionalism Reborn*; and Steven Brint, *In an Age of Experts: The Changing Role of Professionals in Politics and Public Life* (Princeton, NJ: Princeton University Press, 1994).

12. Freidson, "Are Professions Necessary?" in *The Authority of Experts*, ed. Haskell, 3-27; reprinted in Freidson, *Professionalism Reborn*, 149-68; and Freidson's "Nourishing Professionalism," in *Ethics, Trust and the Professions*, ed. Pellegrino et al., 193-220; reprinted in *Professionalism Reborn*, 199-216.

13. H.M. Vollmer and D.L. Mills, *Professionalization* (Englewood Cliffs, NJ: Prentice-Hall, 1966). Vollmer and Mills note that definitions and models must be continuously reinvented. Any profession is "inextricably linked to the kind of society in which [professionalization] takes place—to its political form, its cultural norms, and its social structure, as well as its stage of technological development" (62). Brint, *In an Age of Experts*, 13, notes that professional communities are always conflict-ridden, and they change over time. We might add that in Russia we have seen repeated instances of compressed development.

14. Bureaucratic modernizers are an important theme in the history of most European nations. George Yaney in *The Urge to Mobilize: Agrarian Reform in Russia 1861-1930* (Urbana: University of Illinois Press, 1982) has elevated it to a major theme in Russian and Soviet history. The literature on increasing specialization tends to merge with that on professions. See Brint, *In an Age of Experts*; Freidson, *Professionalism Reborn*; John A. Armstrong, *The European Administrative Elite* (Princeton, NJ: Princeton University Press, 1973); and Forrest Miller, *Dmitri Miliutin and the Reform Era in Russia* (Nashville, TN: Vanderbilt University Press, 1968).

15. Again the German material provides some of the most suggestive examples. One of the first scholars to pose these questions was Hans Rosenberg, *Bureaucracy, Aristocracy and Autocracy: The Prussian Experience 1660-1815* (Boston, MA: Beacon Press, 1966, 1958). His work has been expanded by Kees Gispen, "German Engineers and American Social Theory," *Comparative Studies in Society and History* 30 (1988): 548-72; Jarausch, *The Unfree Professions*; and Fritz K. Ringer, *The Decline of the German Mandarins: The German Academic Community, 1890-1933* (Cambridge: Harvard University Press, 1969). For a rich analysis of the early Russian experience that also sheds valuable light on France, see Alfred J. Rieber, "The Rise of Engineers in Russia," *Cahiers du Monde Russe et Soviétique* 31, no. 4 (Octobre-Décembre 1990): 39-68.

16. Gerald L. Geison, ed., *Professions and the French State* (Philadelphia: University of Pennsylvania Press, 1984), 2. Geison finds even Larson's analysis inadequate in its appreciation of the role of the state in France. On the relationships between elites and professions, see the chapter in *Professions and the French State* by John Weiss, "Bridges and Barriers: Narrowing Access and Changing Structure in the French Engineering Profession, 1800-1850," 15-65. Also Ezra N. Suleiman, *Elites in French Society: The Politics of Survival* (Princeton, NJ: Princeton University Press, 1978).

17. Geison, ed., *Professions and the French State*, 9.

18. Matthew Ramsey, "The Politics of Professional Monopoly in Nineteenth-Century Medicine: The French Model and Its Rivals," in *Professions and the French State*, ed. Geison, 225-305; also Ramsey, "Review Essay: History of a Profession,

Annales Style: The Work of Jacques Leonard," *Journal of Social History* 17 (1983): 319-38.

19. The most studied French profession has been medicine. The extensive work of Jacques Leonard demonstrates the persistence of regional differences, a phenomenon that also remained critically important in Germany and Russia. Leonard's massive thesis is not easily available. Matthew Ramsey has performed an enormous service by summarizing this work and the rest of Leonard's opus in "Review Essay." On regional differences in France, see Eugen Weber, *Peasants into Frenchmen: The Modernization of Rural France, 1870-1914* (Stanford, CA: Stanford University Press, 1976). For a summary treatment of French education and professions, see Theodore Zeldin, *France, 1848-1945* (Oxford: Oxford University Press, 1977).

20. On German professions, see Charles E. McClelland, *The German Experience of Professionalization: Modern Learned Professions and Their Organizations from the Early Nineteenth Century to the Hitler Era* (Cambridge: Cambridge University Press, 1991); Jarausch, *The Unfree Professions*; Cocks and Jarausch, eds., *German Professions*; and Gispen, "German Engineers and American Social Theory."

21. Jarausch, Gispen, Rueschemeyer, McClelland, and others who focus on Germany have stressed the civil-service ethos in German professions.

22. Gispen, "German Engineers and American Social Theory," 563.

23. Rosenberg, *Bureaucracy, Aristocracy and Autocracy*, 89. Gispen stresses the ethos, service, and public welfare aspects of the equation, but may downplay the autocratic element. Rosenberg adds, "In order to make the personal will of the ruler supreme, his agents, therefore, were to be regimented with an iron hand, driven to their work, compelled to acquire a new frame of mind and attitude of service, watched all the time and spurred to greater exertions by the hope of material reward and social honors and the fear of stern punishment."

24. Mária M. Kovács, *Liberal Professions and Illiberal Politics: Hungary from the Habsburgs to the Holocaust* (New York: Oxford University Press, 1994). Compare McClelland, *The German Experience of Professionalization*, 6-7.

25. Kovács, *Liberal Professions and Illiberal Politics*, 31-36, 49-54.

26. One important area of comparison between Russia and Germany is the evolving role of nationalism in professional programs. In Germany, where professional development preceded national unity, nationalism competed with or merged with liberalism in the various professional programs. Nationalism was frequently viewed as subversive. It is particularly instructive to compare the events of 1848 in Germany with the Revolution of 1905 in Russia. In Russia, national unity preceded professional development, and ethnonationalism rarely played a role in professional programs before 1917. There were strong right-wing and nationalist groups in 1905, but they did not find much support in the professions. The radical intelligentsia culture and self-censorship played a role here. After 1905 the situation began to change, but the numbers were not large. One notable instance was professors' supporting right-wing organizations. See Samuel Kassow's essay in this volume, 213. Also see his discussion of the right-wing student movement in Odessa and Kiev in *Students, Professors, and the State in Tsarist Russia* (Berkeley: University of California Press, 1989), 362. Since 1991, there has been a major development of nationalist professional organizations, inviting comparison with both Germany and Hungary.

27. Jarausch, "The German Professions in History and Theory," 20.

28. This is a situation where comparative analysis is particularly interesting. In ˚Russia at the turn of the century, unemployment spurred development of professional organizations and mutual assistance initiatives. We have good evidence from eighteenth-century America that market pressures can result in efforts to restrict professional membership even in a situation where the efficacy of professional services is not established. See Peter Dobkin Hall, "Inquiry and Uplift," in *The Authority of Experts*, ed. Thomas L. Haskell, 107-41.

29. When Cocks and Jarausch discuss the "maturation" of studies of professions, they flirt with the fallacy committed by virtually every generation of scholars who perceive the weaknesses of their predecessors and think they have achieved the ultimate synthesis of objective analysis. Cocks and Jarausch, "Introduction," *German Professions,* 3-4. Those who argue for viewing phenomena in their specific cultural context may find that they are ignoring broader issues.

30. Geison writes that "in private correspondence with me, Ramsey has pointed out the need to add qualifiers or modifiers to the French terms *profession* (any occupation) and *un professionnel* (one who does something for a living) to capture their current Anglo-Saxon connotations. Weiss reports that at a recent conference in Paris on 'Social Taxonomies as Ideology,' the French participants repeatedly insisted that the American occupational category 'professionals' was 'completely meaningless' to them." Geison, ed., *Professions and the French State*, 10-11, footnote 7. Also see Ramsey, "History of a Profession," and William H. Sewell, Jr., "*Etat, corps* and *ordre*: Some Notes on the Social Vocabulary of the Old Regime," in *Sozialgeschichte Heute: Fetschrift für Hans Rosenberg*, ed. Hans-Ulrich Wehler (Gottingen, 1974), 49-68. I had a similar experience with specialists at the Institute of History in Leningrad, who assumed that references to professions meant the official (and broadly inclusive) *profsoiuzy*. For the difficulties with terminology in German, see Jarausch, "The German Professions in History and Theory," 10-11.

31. Reader, *Professional Men,* 10.

32. As always, these differences are matters of degree. The tie between education and professionalism in America is the focus of Bledstein's *Culture of Professionalism*. But in America it was a distinctly middle-class culture, whereas in Europe the aristocratic tinge of high culture, enlightenment, and "being cultured" played (and plays) a much greater role.

33. McClelland, *The German Experience of Professionalization*, 23. Nancy Mandelker Frieden, *Russian Physicians in an Era of Reform and Revolution, 1856-1905* (Princeton, NJ: Princeton University Press, 1981); John Hutchinson, "Society, Corporation or Union? Russian Physicians and the Struggle for Professional Unity (1890-1913)," *Jahrbucher für Geschichte Osteuropas*, Band 30 (1982), Heft 1, 37-53; and Brian Levin-Stankevich's contribution to this volume. For Russian pharmacists' claim to be an estate, see Jonathan Sanders, "Drugs and Revolution: Moscow Pharmacists in the First Russian Revolution," *The Russian Review* 44 (1985): 351-77, here 362. For a critique of the traditional use of *soslovie,* see Gregory Freeze, "The *Soslovie* (Estate) Paradigm and Russian Social History," *American Historical Review* 91, no. 1 (February 1986): 11-36. Freeze notes the important role of professions as social entities outside the official estate structure.

34. *Wissenschaft*, like the Russian *nauka*, is a more general term than the English "science." In both Russian and German, the words are used to refer to all spheres of knowledge and do not imply a distinction between "natural" and "social" sciences.

35. This definition stems from discussions with Alfred Rieber, but he should not be blamed for any faults in the version given here. For discussions of the Russian intelligentsia, see Richard Pipes, ed., *The Russian Intelligentsia* (New York: Columbia University Press, 1961); Philip Pomper, *The Russian Revolutionary Intelligentsia* (New York: Crowell, 1970); Boris Kagarlitsky, *The Thinking Reed: Intellectuals and the Soviet State from 1917 to the Present*, trans. Brian Pearce (London and New York: Verso, 1988); Michael Confino, "On Intellectuals and Intellectual Traditions in Eighteenth- and Nineteenth-Century Russia," *Daedalus* 101, no. 2 (Spring 1972): 117-49; and Christopher Read, *Religion, Revolution and the Russian Intelligentsia 1900-1912: The Vekhi Debate and Its Intellectual Background* (London: Macmillan Press, 1979):

Soviet scholarship offered a definition of the intelligentsia that is convenient but analytically not of much value—those with higher education. Soviet scholars also identified subgroups like the "*raznochinskaia intelligentsia*" and the professional intelligentsia. For example G.N. Vul'fson, *Raznochinno-demokraticheskoe dvizhenie v povolzh'e i na urale v gody pervoi revoliutsionnoi situatsii* (Kazan': Izdatel'stvo Kazan'skogo universiteta, 1974). Soviet scholars were primarily interested in the intelligentsia and professions only to the extent they contributed to "democratic" or revolutionary activity. When they focused on the professions, Soviet scholars characteristically devoted their attention to counting the professional intelligentsia and mapping the education system that fostered it. For the prereform intelligentsia, see L.A. Bulgakova, "Intelligentsiia v Rossii vo vtoroi chetverti XIX veka" (Kandidat diss., Leningrad, 1983). For the period after 1861, a good introduction is the two volumes by V.R. Leikina-Svirskaia, *Intelligentsiia v Rossii vo vtoroi polovine XIX veka* (Moscow: Mysl', 1971), and *Russkaia intelligentsiia v 1900- 1917 godakh* (Moscow: Mysl', 1981). Also see L.K. Erman, "Sostav intelligentsii v Rossii v kontse XIX i nachale XX v.," *Istoriia SSSR*, no. 1 (1963): 161-77, and his *Intelligentsiia v pervoi russkoi revoliutsii* (Moscow: Nauka, 1966). Erman's statistical data appear reliable; his biographical material is not. Also see A.V. Ushkov, *Revoliutsionnoe dvizhenie demokraticheskoi intelligentsii v Rossii, 1895-1904*. On the geography of the education system, see A.E. Ivanov, "Geografiia vysshei shkoly Rossii v kontse XIX-nachale XX vv.," in *Istochnikovedcheskie i istoriograficheskie aspekty Russkoi kultury* (Moscow: AN Institut istorii, 1984); Ivanov, "Upravlenie vysshei shkoloi Rossii v kontse XIX-nachale XX vv.," in *Istoriograficheskie i istoricheskie problemy russkoi kul'tury* (Moscow: AN Institut istorii, 1983); and Ivanov's monograph, *Vysshaia shkola Rossii v kontse XIX-nachale XX veka* (Moscow: Akademiia nauk SSSR. Institut istorii SSSR, 1991).

Particular mention should be made of the studies by N.M. Pirumova, *Zemskoe liberal'noe dvizhenie: Sotsial'nie korni i evoliutsiia do nachala XX veka* (Moscow: Nauka, 1977); and especially her more recent *Zemskaia intelligentsiia i ee rol' v obshchestvennoi bor'be* (Moscow: Nauka, 1986). The second volume presents a survey of "third-element" *zemstvo* employees, including an effort not only to count them but also to describe working conditions and relations between occupational and professional groups. Despite omitting some groups, such as the *zemstvo* technicians, the book was a promising departure in Soviet scholarship, and a sequel going beyond 1902 would be particularly welcome.

36. *Bildungsburgertum* implies a middle class based on education. Jarausch, "The German Professions in History and Theory," 17. A recent work on the Soviet intellectuals and the intelligentsia by Vladimir Shlapentokh is a good example of the categories of definition and thought produced by Soviet scholarship. Shlapentokh puts the number of intellectuals at perhaps 700,000, mostly in Moscow and St. Petersburg, but suggests that only some 10 percent of them were the "real" creative intellectuals. While he notes in passing the scientific and technical intelligentsia, they do not represent a major concern, and most are not among his "real" intellectuals. Vladimir Shlapentokh, *Soviet Intellectuals and Political Power: The Post-Stalin Era* (Princeton, NJ: Princeton University Press, 1990), x.

37. Was Konstantin Pobedonostsev, that seemingly omnipresent bearer of pessimistic tidings, a member of the intelligentsia? What about Mikhail Katkov and other conservative publicists? When I ask Russian colleagues and acquaintances these questions, they respond in the negative. But when asked whether these men were *intelligenty* when they worked on the Great Reforms in the 1860s, but not when they supported counterreform in the 1880s, the response is usually silence. The issue continued to be divisive in Soviet society, with some analysts finding the need to codify the popular reference to *nastoiashii* [real] *intelligent.* "Podvizhniki: O traditsiiakh otechestvennoi intelligentsii," *Pravda,* 10 March 1987, 3.

38. Based on observation of the contemporary Soviet intelligentsia. For historical instances, see the archive of intelligentsia autobiographies collected by S.A. Vengerov, housed in Pushkinskii Dom, f. 377. I am grateful to Alan Kimball for bringing this material to my attention.

39. The closest that persons in "official" positions might come to playing this role was in cases where a teacher in a secondary school or an institute might become the *vospitatel'* for a selected student or group of students. One small group of prominent historians at the St. Petersburg branch of the Institute of History trace their *vospitanie* back to a mentor who played this role. There was, of course, an "official" Soviet intelligentsia, and in the early years after the revolution, many *intelligenty* devoted their talents to building socialism. But under Stalin and after, the intelligentsia returned to its critical stance. See John Bushnell, "The 'New Soviet Man' Turns Pessimist," in *The Soviet Union Since Stalin,* eds. Stephen F. Cohen, Alexander Rabinowitch, and Robert Sharlet (Bloomington: Indiana University Press, 1981), 179-99; Kagarlitsky, *The Thinking Reed*; and Shlapentokh, *Soviet Intellectuals and Political Power.* The debasement of the language in the Soviet period is visible in the hideous coinage, "mass intelligentsia."

40. For a good discussion of the radical political element in intelligentsia and especially student culture, see Daniel Brower, *Training the Nihilists: Education and Radicalism in Tsarist Russia* (Ithaca, NY: Cornell University Press, 1975). Leadership of professional groups by radical activists is noted for physicians by Frieden, *Russian Physicians*; for lawyers by Levin-Stankevich in his contribution to this volume; for statisticians by Robert E. Johnson, "Liberal Professionals and Professional Liberals: The Zemstvo Statisticians and Their Work," in *The Zemstvo in*

Russia: An Experiment in Local Self-Government, eds. Terence Emmons and Wayne S. Vucinich (Cambridge: Cambridge University Press, 1982), 343-64; and for engineers by Harley D. Balzer "Educating Engineers: Economic Politics and Technical Training in Tsarist Russia" (Ph.D. diss., University of Pennsylvania, 1980). Roberta Manning notes the general phenomenon in *The Crisis of the Old Order in Russia: Gentry and Government* (Princeton, NJ: Princeton University Press, 1982), and in "Zemstvo and Revolution: The Onset of Gentry Reaction," in *The Politics of Rural Russia, 1905-1914,* ed. Leopold H. Haimson (Bloomington: Indiana University Press, 1979), 30-66.

41. The intelligentsia is a cultural category, with characteristics similar to the German *Bildung*; professionals are defined by education, socialization, and adherence to norms. While both imply moral evaluation, the moral and ethical standards for professionals apply to a limited sphere; those of the intelligentsia are absolutes.

42. Brint, *In an Age of Experts,* 7.

43. In her study of urban teachers, Christine Ruane suggests that what existed in Russia was a professional intelligentsia rather than a professional middle class. Christine Ruane, *Gender, Class and the Professionalization of Russian City Teachers, 1860-1914* (Pittsburgh, PA: University of Pittsburgh Press, 1994). But Samuel Kassow's discussion in this volume of the professors' making a distinction between themselves and the intelligentsia suggests a problem with Ruane's description of Russian professionals as a professional intelligentsia. The intelligentsia identity was one more of the cleavages that cut across professional and middle-class identities in tsarist Russia. On the issue of the professional intelligentsia, see Karl Mannheim, *Ideology and Utopia: An Introduction to the Sociology of Knowledge,* trans. Louis Wirth and Edward Shils (New York: Harcourt, Brace & World, 1936), 10-12, 156-61.

44. The tone is brilliantly captured by Vladimir Voinovich in *The Life and Extraordinary Adventures of Private Ivan Chonkin,* trans. Richard Lourie (New York: Farrar, Straus & Giroux, 1977), 138, where he has the District Committee tell a village party organizer to disperse and then reassemble the villagers for an announcement of the outbreak of war because "[s]pontaneity, comrades, must be organized."

45. Frieden, *Russian Physicians,* 16; and L.A. Bulgakova, "Intelligentsiia v Rossii vo vtoroi chetverti XIX veka" (Kandidat diss., Leningrad, 1983), *Avtoreferat,* 15.

46. Bulgakova, *Avtoreferat,* 19.

47. Vul'fson, *Raznochinno-demokraticheskoe dvizhenie,* 134.

48. Samuel Kucherov, *Courts, Lawyers and Trials Under the Last Three Tsars* (New York: Frederick A. Praeger, 1953); Richard Wortman, "Judicial Personnel and the Court Reform of 1864," *Canadian Slavic Studies* 111, no. 2 (Summer 1969): 224-34; Wortman, *The Development of a Russian Legal Consciousness* (Chicago, IL: University of Chicago Press, 1976); and Levin-Stankevich's contribution to this volume.

49. On the Prussian mining corps as the model in Germany, see Eric Dorn Brose, *The Politics of Technological Change in Prussia: Out of the Shadow of Antiquity, 1809-1848* (Princeton, NJ: Princeton University Press, 1993), chapter 4. For France, see Weiss, "Bridges and Barriers," and Thomas R. Osborne, *A Grande École for the Grands Corps: The Recruitment and Training of the French Administrative Elite in the Nineteenth Century* (Boulder, CO: Social Science Monographs, Inc., 1983).

50. More important for the long term, a private Polytechnical Institute established in Riga introduced both the model of community-funded higher education and the European polytechnical pattern of training. See Balzer, "Educating Engineers," 47-50.

51. See Frieden, *Russian Physicians*, 38-41; Levin-Stankevich's contribution to this volume; Kucherov, *Courts, Lawyers and Trials Under the Last Three Tsars*; and Charles Timberlake, "Higher Learning, the State and the Professions in Russia," in *The Transformation of Higher Learning 1860-1930*, ed. Konrad H. Jarausch (Chicago, IL: University of Chicago Press, 1983), 321-44.

52. Balzer, "Educating Engineers"; A.E. Ivanov, "Geografiia vysshei shkoly"; and Timberlake, "Higher Learning."

53. Timberlake, "Higher Learning," 327-30.

54. Ivanov, "Geografiia vysshei shkoly."

55. Alfred J. Rieber, "The Sedimentary Society," in *Between Tsar and People: Educated Society and the Quest for Public Identity in Late Imperial Russia*, eds. Edith W. Clowes, Samuel D. Kassow, and James L. West (Princeton, NJ: Princeton University Press, 1991), 343-71.

56. Balzer "Educating Engineers," 405-6; James C. McClelland, *Autocrats and Academics: Education, Culture and Society in Tsarist Russia* (Chicago, IL: University of Chicago Press, 1979), 50-54; Frieden, *Russian Physicians*, 41-42. Rapid expansion in specialized education was common throughout Europe and the U.S. in this period. See McClelland, *The German Experience of Professionalization;* Kovács, *Liberal Professions and Illiberal Politics*; Ringer, *The Decline of the German Mandarins*; Jarausch, ed., *The Transformation of Higher Learning;* and George Weisz, *The Emergence of Modern Universities in France, 1863-1914* (Princeton, NJ: Princeton University Press, 1983).

57. This is not meant to imply that diversity, discussion, and debate did not exist before the 1860s. Bruce Lincoln has demonstrated that in even the official ministerial periodicals it was possible to present a range of opinions and lobby for change. W. Bruce Lincoln, *The Great Reforms: Autocracy, Bureaucracy and the Politics of Change in Imperial Russia* (DeKalb: Northern Illinois University Press, 1990), 46-48.

58. The Moscow Society published *Iuridicheskii vestnik.* The journal of the Petersburg Society was inaugurated as *Zhurnal grazhdanskogo i ugolovnogo prava.* It subsequently appeared as *Zhurnal iuridicheskogo obshchestva pri St. Peterburgskom universitete,* and then as *Vestnik prava.*

59. William C. Brumfield, "Building for the Bourgeoisie: The Quest for a Modern Style in Russian Architecture," in *Between Tsar and People,* eds. Clowes et al., 310. For feldshers, see Ramer's contribution to this volume. Lenin was in the mainstream of the professional intelligentsia when he insisted on a journal as one of the crucial aspects of Bolshevik activity. V.I. Lenin, *What Is to Be Done?* trans. Joe Fineberg and George Hanna (Harmondsworth: Penguin, 1988).

60. Once they initiated private periodicals, lawyers did not limit themselves to a single publication. The list of private law journals included *Voprosy prava, Vestnik grazhdanskogo prava,* and *Iurist,* among others.

61. Characteristically for the development of Russian professional groups, the first gathering of *zemstvo* physicians took place under the auspices of another group,

the Seventh Congress of Natural Scientists and Physicians, in Odessa in 1883. Frieden, *Russian Physicians*, 118. Russian professionals were persistent and imaginative in their struggle with recalcitrant officialdom. They constantly sought alternative venues for meetings that were prohibited. Among the many examples were the jurists, who held their first congress in 1875. When subsequent gatherings were put off by the government, they managed to host an international conference on prisons in 1890 and conduct their meeting within its framework. Statisticians were not allowed to convene their own congresses after their first session in 1887, but managed to meet in subsections of the Ninth Congress of Naturalists and Physicians (1894), the Moscow Juridical Society (1898), and the Free Economic Society (1900). The Eleventh Congress of Naturalists and Physicians in 1901 was "essentially a congress of statisticians." Pirumova, *Zemskaia intelligentsiia*, 138-39. Also see Leikina-Svirskaia, *Intelligentsiia v Rossii*, 199. Statisticians formed a statistical section within the Moscow Juridical Society, and after 1905 gathered under the auspices of the Twelfth Congress of Russian Naturalists and Physicians, the Chuprov Society, and other groups. See Johnson, "The Zemstvo Statisticians," 347, 350. Perhaps the ultimate example of "camouflage" was in 1904, when the meeting of the Union of Liberation in St. Petersburg got "lost" due to the simultaneous gathering of two much larger professional meetings.

62. See Levin-Stankevich's contribution to this volume and Kendall E. Bailes, *Technology and Society Under Lenin and Stalin* (Princeton, NJ: Princeton University Press, 1978), 42-43. Teachers were one of the first groups to use congresses (*s"ezdy*) as a mechanism of professional association. For teachers scattered in the countryside, these gatherings helped to overcome isolation as well as served professional purposes. F.G. Panachin, *Uchitel'stvo i revoliutsionnoe dvizhenie v Rossii (XIX-nachalo XX v.)* (Moscow: Pedagogika, 1986), 85-89; Seregny's contribution to this volume; and Ben Eklof, *Russian Peasant Schools: Officialdom, Village Culture, and Popular Pedagogy, 1861-1914* (Berkeley: University of California Press, 1986). As in the case of physicians, functional utility appears to have resulted in a wavering government policy. An all-Russian teachers' congress in Moscow attracted 700 delegates in 1872, but subsequent meetings were subject to very strict regulation. A congress on technical education in 1902 was closed by the MVD before its official end.

63. In addition to security and state pensions, government employment frequently included housing or a housing allowance, and might provide other benefits as well. The tradition persisted in the Soviet era and is one of the factors causing some individuals to resist leaving work in the state sector.

64. George Fischer noted that *zemstvo* organizations provided a large share of positions for "lower" intelligentsia. See *Russian Liberalism, From Gentry to Intelligentsia* (Cambridge: Harvard University Press, 1958), 60. On the *zemstvo* specialists see Pirumova, *Zemskaia intelligentsiia*, chapter 3; Frieden, *Russian Physicians*, 53-65, 105; and Bulgakova, "Intelligentsiia v Rossii." Lawyers were not usually *zemstvo* employees, which may explain why they are ignored by Pirumova and Leikina-Svirskaia (the latter provides statistical material but does not include a chapter on the lawyers).

65. The Petersburg Polytechnical Institute became a refuge for radical economists and others. See Balzer, "Educating Engineers," 399. A similar phenomenon can be

seen in scientific research institutes in the Soviet period. See Mark Adams, "The Founding of Population Genetics: Contributions of the Chetverikov School, 1924-1934," *Journal of the History of Biology* 1, no. 1 (1968): 23-39; and Adams, "Science, Ideology and Structure: The Kol'tsov Institute, 1900-1970," in *The Social Context of Soviet Science*, eds. Linda L. Lubrano and Susan Gross Solomon (Boulder, CO: Westview Press, 1980), 173-204; Kendall Bailes, *Science and Russian Culture in an Age of Revolution: Vernadsky and His Scientific School, 1863-1945* (Bloomington: Indiana University Press, 1989); and Werner G. Hahn, *Postwar Soviet Politics: The Fall of Zhdanov and the Defeat of Moderation, 1946-53* (Ithaca, NY: Cornell University Press, 1982), 166-81.

66. The first law society was created in Moscow in 1863, and similar organizations followed in St. Petersburg and Khar'kov in the 1870s. The law societies began largely as organizations of state legal officials rather than private lawyers, though the latter usually assumed leadership positions. See Levin-Stankevich's contribution to this volume.

67. The phenomenon of engineers' simultaneously endeavoring to create both a national organization and more specialized associations was seen in other countries as well. Kees Gispen, *New Profession, Old Order: Engineers and German Society, 1815-1914* (Cambridge: Cambridge University Press, 1989): 137-39; on American engineers, see Edwin Layton, *The Revolt of the Engineers* (Cleveland, OH: The Press of Case Western Reserve University, 1971), 40-42.

68. See Hutchinson's contribution to this volume, 93-94, 108.

69. F.G. Panachin, *Uchitel'stvo i revoliutsionnoe dvizhenie v Rossii (XIX-nachalo XX v.)* (Moscow: Pedagogika, 1986); and Balzer, "Educating Engineers," 412-15.

70. Statisticians were not allowed to convene their own congress after a first session in 1887, but managed to meet in subsections of the Ninth Congress of Naturalists and Physicians (1894), the Moscow Juridical Society (1898), and the Free Economic Society (1900). The Eleventh Congress of Naturalists and Physicians in 1901 was "essentially a congress of statisticians." Pirumova, *Zemskaia intelligentsiia*, 138-39. Also see Leikina-Svirskaia, *Intelligentsiia v Rossii*, 199.

A.D. Stepanskii provides important detail on the role of scientific societies in "Nauchnye obshchestva i s"ezdy Rossii na rubezhe XIX-XX v. i literatura voprosa," in *Istochnikovedcheskie i istoriograficheskie aspekty russkoi kultury* (Moscow, 1984); and "Nauchnoe obshchestva pri vysshikh uchebnykh zavedeniiakh dorevoliutsionnoi Rossii," in *Gosudarstvennoe rukovodstvo vysshei shkoloi v dorevoliutsionnoi Rossii i v SSSR* (Moscow, 1979).

71. Russian physicians swore an oath upon graduation from medical school. See Frieden, *Russian Physicians*, 27, 267. For the text of the oath, see 326-27.

72. Kucherov, *Courts, Lawyers and Trials Under the Last Three Tsars,* 92. Kucherov's assertion that bribery and venality vanished probably overstates the "success" of the reforms of the Russian judicial system. There is little doubt that some abuses continued. However, there is no question that a new concern for legality and ethics influenced not only the legal profession but other groups as well.

73. E.O. Paton, *Vospominaniia* (Moscow, 1956), 31; L.N. Liubimov, "Iz zhizni inzhenera putei soobshcheniia," *Russkaia starina* 157 (March 1914): 596-602; and

N.G. Garin-Mikhailovskii's novels, *Studenty* and *Inzhenery* (Moscow: Khudo-zhestvennaia literatura, 1964).

74. Priumova, *Zemskaia intelligentsiia*, chapter 3; Scott J. Seregny, *Russian Teachers and Peasant Revolution: The Politics of Education in 1905* (Bloomington: Indiana University Press, 1989); Ronald H. Hayashida, "The Unionization of Russian Teachers, 1905-1908: An Interest Group Under the Autocracy," *Slavic and European Education Review*, no. 2 (1981): 1-16; Ruane, *Gender, Class and the Professionalization of Russian City Teachers*; Ramer's essay in this volume; Johnson, "Liberal Professionals and Professional Liberals"; Henry Reichman, *Railwaymen and Revolution: Russia, 1905* (Berkeley: University of California Press, 1987); Louise McReynolds, *The News Under Russia's Old Regime: The Development of a Mass-Circulation Press* (Princeton, NJ: Princeton University Press, 1991), 153-61.

75. Jonathan Sanders, "The Union of Unions: Economic, Political and Human Rights Organizations in the 1905 Russian Revolution" (Ph.D. diss., Columbia University, 1985); Abraham Ascher, *The Revolution of 1905: Russia in Disarray* (Stanford, CA: Stanford University Press, 1988); Shmuel Galai, *The Liberation Movement in Russia, 1900-1905* (Cambridge: Cambridge University Press, 1973); and Terence Emmons, *The Formation of Political Parties and the First National Elections in Russia* (Cambridge: Harvard University Press, 1983).

76. See essays in this volume by Orlovsky and Robbins. On army officers, see William C. Fuller, Jr., *Civil-Military Conflict in Imperial Russia, 1881-1914* (Princeton, NJ: Princeton University Press, 1985), chapter 1; on the clergy see Gregory L. Freeze, *Parish Clergy in Nineteenth-Century Russia: Crisis, Reform, Counter-Reform* (Princeton, NJ: Princeton University Press, 1983). What might be termed the "mainstreaming" or "maturing" of study of the professions in Russian history is evident in two outstanding recent monographs that integrate analysis of the professions with broader themes of social history. See Laura Engelstein, *The Keys to Happiness: Sex and the Search for Modernity in Fin-de-Siècle Russia* (Ithaca, NY: Cornell University Press, 1992); and William G. Wagner, *Marriage, Property and Law in Late Imperial Russia* (Oxford: Oxford University Press, 1994).

77. The phenomenon of bureaucratic interest groups that included professional specialists is discussed by Rieber in "The Sedimentary Society," 358-59.

78. Harley Balzer, "The Problem of Professions in Imperial Russia," in *Between Tsar and People*, eds. Clowes et al., 183-98; Sanders, "The Union of Unions"; and Ascher, *The Revolution of 1905*.

79. Diane P. Koenker and William G. Rosenberg, *Strikes and Revolution in Russia, 1917* (Princeton, NJ: Princeton University Press, 1989); Victoria E. Bonnell, *Roost of Rebellion: Workers' Politics and Organizations in St. Petersburg and Moscow, 1900-1914* (Berkeley: University of California Press, 1983). The difference between 1905 and 1917 can be seen quite clearly by comparing the books written about Moscow in the two revolutionary years. Laura Engelstein notes the role of coalitions and professional and administrative personnel during 1905. In Diane Koenker's book on 1917, the workers are virtually the sole topic. Laura Engelstein, *Moscow, 1905: Working-Class Organization and Political Conflict* (Stanford, CA: Stanford University Press, 1982). Diane Koenker, *Moscow Workers and the 1917 Revolution* (Princeton, NJ: Princeton University Press, 1981).

80. In particular see Peter Krug, "Russian Public Physicians and Revolution: The Pirogov Society, 1917-1920" (Ph.D. diss., University of Wisconsin, 1980); Susan Gross Solomon and John F. Hutchinson, eds., *Health and Society in Revolutionary Russia* (Bloomington: Indiana University Press, 1990).

81. They were the ministers most hated by their colleagues. See Kassow's contribution to this volume.

82. This was the lesson learned, in different ways, by both Sergei Witte and Mikhail Gorbachev.

83. In reading about Russian psychiatrists, it is important to remember that mental health care in this period was asylum care. Virtually all Russian psychiatrists carried out their work in the setting of a mental hospital. This institutional factor had an important influence on the developing psychiatric profession.

84. The *zemstva* were active in reversing the policies of inclusion. The tension between "second-element" *zemstvo* nobles and "third-element" *zemstvo* employees played a major role here. See Priumova, *Zemskaia intelligentsiia*.

85. Seregny's account of village teachers may be usefully compared with Christine Ruane's study of urban teachers. Ruane notes varied strategies in formulating professional programs and the different uses to which these programs could be put. Peasant men teachers sought to define urban women as "outsiders" who could not function effectively in the villages. When women teachers in St. Petersburg were faced with a ban on marriage they endeavored to portray themselves as educated specialists whose private lives were being disrupted by unwarranted interference. Ruane also does a good job portraying the lines of cleavage within the teaching profession—urban-rural, primary-secondary, and male-female—though she does not suggest which identities tended to dominate in different contexts. Christine Ruane, *Gender, Class and the Professionalization of Russian Teachers*. Other recent work on teachers includes Eklof, *Russian Peasant Schools*; Panachin, *Uchitel'stvo i revoliutsionnoe dvizhenie*; Hayashida, "The Unionization of Russian Teachers"; Seregny's contribution to this volume; and Ruane and Eklof, "Cultural Pioneers and Professionals: The Teacher in Society," in *Between Tsar and People*, eds. Clowes et al., 199-211.

86. See Theodore H. von Laue, *The World Revolution of Westernization: The Twentieth Century in Global Perspective* (New York: Oxford University Press, 1987). It is not necessary to embrace von Laue's entire argument to appreciate his sensitivity to the profound psychological impact on educated Russians of feeling they were equal to western colleagues, and also understanding that Russia had a vast distance to go to achieve comparable levels of social and economic development.

87. The service ethos is visible in all Russian professions. It is particularly evident among teachers and physicians. See Ruane, *Gender, Class and the Professionalization of Russian Teachers*; and Frieden, *Russian Physicians*. Compare McClelland's comments on the "service professions" in *The German Experience of Professionalization*, 98-105.

88. The tensions among their roles as scholars, teachers, and officials mirror those in Germany. McClelland, *The German Experience of Professionalization*; also Ringer, *The Decline of the German Mandarins*.

89. Also see William Pomeranz, "The Emergence and Development of the Russian Advokatura: 1864-1905" (Ph.D. diss., University of London, 1990).

90. Andrew M. Verner demonstrates the anguish over this issue in the reign of Nicholas II in *The Crisis of Russian Autocracy: Nicholas II and the 1905 Revolution* (Princeton, NJ: Princeton University Press, 1990).

91. In some instances this was frankly admitted, for example when the government stated that it could not dismiss politically unreliable faculty from polytechnical institutes because there were no adequate cadres to replace them. Rossiiskii gosudarstvennyi istoricheskii arkhiv, f. 25, op. 5, d. 3, l. 67. The polytechnical institutes were administered by the Ministry of Finance. The Ministry of Education seems to have been less concerned about retaining skilled instructors. Koni's description of the difficulty finding someone to prosecute Vera Zasulich demonstrates the extent of internal resistance among the staff of the Ministry of Justice. It is in some ways similar to accounts from 1988 to 1989 of Soviet Central Committee staffers being turned away from meetings of the Moscow Popular Front by militia following the orders of local Party officials. (Based on personal conversations with individuals involved.)

92. Jane Caplan, "Profession as Vocation: The German Civil Service," in *German Professions*, eds. Cocks and Jarausch, 163-82. Caplan states: "My proposal here is that the professional civil service, the *Berufsbeamtentum*, occupied the same ideological space for nineteenth-century Germany as the free professions did for England or the United States, that is, the space of an institution defined by an ethical identity that—as an element in its 'cognitive basis'—places it outside capitalist relations, and permits the 'protection of the social fabric' against the subversive effects of the market" (166).

93. McClelland writes in *The German Experience of Professionalization*, "The discourse of professionalization has only been a relatively recent import into Germany, whereas that of the civil service has been a flourishing concern since the early nineteenth century. The difference is to be explained not simply as the result of an uneven process of research, but also as the effect of a more profound cultural displacement. For there has indeed been a copious literature celebrating the significance of the professional civil service for the national history and character of Germany" (32-33). This is certainly also true of Russia/the Soviet Union.

94. In this they were similar to army officers. See Fuller, *Civil-Military Conflict in Imperial Russia,* 3. Fuller develops a definition of military professionalism based on consciousness, 5-6.

95. S. Frederick Starr, *Decentralization and Self-Government in Russia, 1830-1870* (Princeton, NJ: Princeton University Press, 1972); Merle Fainsod, *Smolensk Under Soviet Rule* (New York: Vintage Books, 1963); and Jerry Hough, *The Soviet Prefects* (Cambridge: Harvard University Press, 1969).

96. But those who suggest that precommunist society and values were "frozen" and will emerge intact are not correct. Adam Przeworski, *Democracy and the Market: Political and Economic Reforms in Eastern Europe and Latin America* (Cambridge: Cambridge University Press, 1991), 93. A similar approach is found in the work of Ken Jowitt, "The Leninist Legacy," in his *New World Disorder: The Leninist Extinction* (Berkeley: University of California Press, 1992), 284-305. On ecological issues, for example, Russians evince views that might be described as "post-dialectical-materialist."

97. William Wagner, "Ideology, Identity and the Emergence of a Middle Class," in *Between Tsar and People,* eds. Clowes et al., 149-63; Aileen Kelly, "Self-Censorship and the Russian Intelligentsia, 1905-1914," *Slavic Review* 46, no 2 (Summer 1987): 193-213; Joan Neuberger, *Hooliganism: Crime, Culture and Power in St. Petersburg, 1900-1914* (Berkeley: University of California Press, 1993), 7-8; Engelstein, *Keys to Happiness;* Don C. Rawson, *Russian Rightists and the Revolution of 1905* (Cambridge: Cambridge University Press, 1995); and Koenker and Rosenberg, *Strikes and Revolution,* 35-38.

98. Robert D. Putnam, *Making Democracy Work: Civic Traditions in Modern Italy* (Princeton, NJ: Princeton University Press, 1993); and Charles S. Maier, ed., *Changing Boundaries of the Political: Essays on the Evolving Balance Between the State and Society, Public and Private in Europe* (Cambridge: Cambridge University Press, 1987).

2

Reflections on Russian Professions

Kendall E. Bailes

A comparative perspective helps bring into focus some of the issues raised by a study of the professions in late imperial Russia. William Bouwsma, in an article on the emergence of lawyers as a profession in early modern Europe, suggests studying the professions is "an opportunity unique in its concreteness to study the sources and nature of social change."[1] The modern British historian Harold Perkin would concur. In his controversial book, *The Origins of Modern English Society, 1780-1880*, he makes the rise of the professions a major theme of late nineteenth-century British history. Perkin agrees with the traditional emphasis on the importance of the middle class in the historiography of the nineteenth century, but he thinks that the middle class has been an amorphous concept which needs more empirical investigation and analytical sharpness to make it useful. He makes a distinction between the capitalist or entrepreneurial middle class, with its emphasis on economic growth, individual competition, profit making, and laissez-faire in nineteenth-century Britain, and what he calls a noncapitalist or professional middle class, which he sees emerging after the 1840s and 1850s.

He considers the professionals to be "a class curiously neglected in the social theories of the age but one which played a part out of all proportion to its numbers."[2] For example, he sees the great social reforms of the middle decades of the nineteenth century in Britain as mainly the result of the initiatives of professionals such as physicians, statisticians, lawyers, and civil servants. This he believes was true of reforms in the legal system, factory inspection, police and prisons, public health, education, control of emigration traffic, and so on. The great social and administrative reforms were part of the professionalization of government which he calls "the greatest political achievement of nineteenth century Britain."[3]

But perhaps even more important than that achievement, in terms of its lasting consequences, is what Perkin perceives as the divergence of "the professional ideal from the entrepreneurial in social policy, which was ultimately to help to undermine entrepreneurial society."[4] The mid-Victorian age was, for him, a key period for the emergence and consolidation of the leading professions and the crystallization of the professional ideal as a separate entity, increasingly critical of the entrepreneurial. The professional's ideal society was a functional one based on expertise and selection by merit. For professionals, trained and qualified expertise—rather than property, capital, or labor per se—should be the chief determinant and justification of status and power in society. For them, merit meant ability and diligence in one's chosen field, and this could be judged only by other professional experts in the same field. Perkin sees the epitome of the professional ideal in nineteenth-century Britain in Benthamite utilitarianism. Not all professionals, of course, were conscious Benthamites, but Bentham was very popular among them because he spoke to their professional condition. Benthamite utilitarians stood for expert, efficient administration in the interests of the greatest happiness of the greatest number. Bentham expressed articulately the professional's preferred way of dealing with problems of government or society: first, organizing an inquiry; then, issuing a report; third, enacting legislation; and finally, guaranteeing enforcement and proper execution of the laws through state inspection.

Perkin does not claim that professionals became anticapitalists, but he sees a drift toward statism with advocacy by professionals for greater state intervention and a state that acts in the public welfare. Prominent Benthamites like J.S. Mill came to distrust the competitive ideal of entrepreneurial society and put more emphasis on the alternative of producer cooperation, while the Fabians at the end of the century eventually severed all connection with capitalism and aimed, he says, at a purely professional socialist society as the best way to achieve the ideal of the Benthamites: the greatest happiness of the greatest number.

Perkin, in other words, tries to identify the origins of the modern British welfare state and the trend away from entrepreneurial society.[5] Not all historians accept his interpretation or see professionals as either so influential or so distinct from the dominant capitalist values of nineteenth-century Britain. Perkin himself admits that professionals constituted only about 3.8 percent of all employed males in 1867, but he argues that their numbers grew rapidly and their influence on culture and public policy outstripped their numbers. Between 1841 and 1881, the professional occupations trebled in number, compared with only a two-thirds increase in the general population; already by 1867, professionals constituted about one-sixth of all the nonmanual occupations.

I have spent so much time on Perkin's book because it helps provide a context for considering the professions and professionalization in late imperial Russia. Perkin points to some answers to the question, why study the professions in Russia during this period? For one thing, his approach suggests that the problem is important because professionals are part of the middle class, and we need to know more empirically about the composition, attitudes, and activity of the middle class in modern history. In contrast to Britain, of course, most historians have stressed the weakness of the middle class in late imperial Russia. What they have overlooked, or not stressed sufficiently, is that the Russian middle class that did exist was not homogenous. It was as much a professional middle class, perhaps more so, than an entrepreneurial class. One of the problems that requires further exploration is the relative growth within the nineteenth-century Russian middle class of entrepreneurial groups like merchants, industrialists, and bankers versus the growth of professionals. I would guess, but at present this is speculative, that the professional occupations grew even more rapidly between 1850 and 1914 than did the entrepreneurial middle class. If so, this would be in contrast to the pattern in Britain, where the entrepreneurial group became well established in its dominance before the rapid growth of modern professions. The latter accelerated with the formation of the British Medical Association in 1857 and passage of the Medical Registration Act of 1858, which set precedents for state regulation of a labor market to ensure professional standards.

For imperial Russia, it would seem that the entrepreneurial ideal was undermined within the Russian middle class even before it had a chance to establish itself. The evidence in Alfred J. Rieber's book, which documents considerable conflict among entrepreneurial, merchant, and professional groups, strongly suggests such a conclusion.[6] This requires further research, of course, on the growth and composition of the Russian middle class, but certainly tensions between the ideals of the Russian professionals and those of Russian entrepreneurs are evident in this period and received quite different political expression after the legalization of parties following the Revolution of 1905 (compare, for example, the Kadets, Octobrists, and Progressives).

The Russian middle class was weak not simply because it was small in numbers, but also because it lacked homogeneity and cohesion in its values and outlook. Professor Rieber's book documents particularly well this lack of cohesion and even calls into question the use of the term "middle class" when applied to late imperial Russia, at least in the sense that there was no self-conscious "bourgeoisie" that could unite effectively to achieve its aims on a national level. There certainly were growing intermediate occupational groups that were increasingly conscious of their common interests, as well as conflicts among them, whether one chooses to call them a middle class, the middle classes, or use some other label, like entrepreneurial and professional groups.

The history of the professions in tsarist Russia was neglected for so long, I think, because they were perceived as small, scattered, and having little influence on the course of events. Historians directed most of their attention toward the social groups they viewed as major actors in the historical process: the tsarist state (or at least its upper reaches), the revolutionaries, the peasantry, the working classes, and various nationalities. The essays in this volume suggest that an understanding of late imperial Russia and the background to the Russian Revolution is incomplete without including the professions or incipient professions. The authors remind us that, despite formidable obstacles, professionalism was a growing ideology among important occupational groups that contributed both to the state bureaucracy and the revolutionary and reform movements. The present volume does for many of the professions in late imperial Russia what Alfred Rieber's and Thomas Owen's books do for the entrepreneurial and merchant groups: illuminate much of their activity and significance in a rapidly changing society.[7]

Though small by comparison to the overall Russian population and often weak, professional groups nonetheless are important for several reasons. First, professionals were key sources both for criticism of the status quo in tsarist Russia and for alternative visions of the future. Professionals disseminated their views widely through their own journals, congresses, and professional associations, as well as through the educational system and the wider media. As Nancy Frieden, Harley D. Balzer, and others have made clear, Russian professionals frequently made comparisons with similar occupational groups in Western Europe and America as a way of criticizing the Russian situation. Second, professionals formed groups that tried to influence government policies and attempted to direct social change in areas such as education, public health, defense policy, and economic development. As Perkin's book suggests, then, a study of professionals is important as a way of understanding social change.

The record of Russian professions in effecting successful social changes during the late imperial period is, of course, much more mixed than in the case of Victorian Britain. But this forms part of the value of the Russian case, a sobering reminder that professionalization is far from being a smooth process, and that the kinds of change favored by professionals are not always readily accepted and institutionalized. The Russian experience may, in fact, be more typical and instructive for many modernizing societies than the British experience. The experience of professionals in Western Europe and America has provided most of the empirical base for the sociological and historical literature on professionalism. A comparison of Russia with Britain in this respect highlights significant differences which theorists of the middle class and of professionalization need to take into account. The essays included here expand our understanding and supply a needed corrective to generalizations formed from too narrow and restrictive a base.

A third reason for studying Russian professions involves the question of the breakdown of the tsarist regime. The frustration of professionals at the slowness of change and their anger at the bureaucratic obstacles to effective practice of their professions contributed considerably to the disillusionment of educated Russian society with the tsarist system. As Julie V. Brown notes in her essay on Russian psychiatrists, these professionals were adamant that "the authority of knowledge should never be subservient to the authority of office." Out of their professional frustrations, they were promoting a new form of legitimating authority in tsarist institutions, one profoundly subversive to the autocratic principle and the privileged position of the hereditary nobility.

Although Russian psychiatrists may have been among the more radical professionals in their welcoming the regime's overthrow and its successors in 1917, they were only part of a continuum of opposition that made some form of political change seem necessary to many, if not all, Russian professionals. Samuel Kassow, in his essay on university professors, reminds us of the limits of professional opposition and serious splits within the professions on the nature of opposition to the regime. Nonetheless, the gap between professional ideals and Russian realities is a frequent theme in the memoirs and literature that deal with late imperial Russia. As John F. Hutchinson notes, "all the wrong people are in charge" was one of the most common laments among Russian professionals in the last decades of the tsarist regime.

What links groups as seemingly dissimilar as engineers, psychiatrists, primary school teachers, legal professionals, university professors, army officers, and others is the fact that frequently many of them were key sources for criticism and for views and programs that affected the policies of the tsarist—and later on, the Soviet—government. One could argue that much of early Soviet history in economic, military, social, and cultural areas is illuminated by studying the professionals and their debates in late imperial Russia. Whether or not professionals form a noncapitalist class, as Perkin contends, these groups eventually made the transition to Soviet state socialism more smoothly, although not without considerable tension and opposition, than did the entrepreneurial middle class, which emigrated in large numbers after the revolution or was eventually abolished or driven underground in Stalin's Russia after 1929. What many Russian professionals shared, therefore, is of some historical significance. The differences among these groups may also be useful to students of both professionalism and Russian history. The studies included here are a rich mine for understanding the differing composition and views of the various groups examined, and their differing levels of professionalization.

Some critical distinctions among professional groups alluded to in this volume merit further consideration. One is the significance of differences among the knowledge bases of various groups, particularly those groups that had an effective knowledge base and those whose knowledge was less demonstrable or convincing (for example, physicians treating epidemics of infectious diseases versus psychiatrists). Another critical distinction in this area can be made between groups that had achieved a consensus on what constituted a body of professional knowledge and those groups within which there was still considerable disagreement and dissension. The former tended to be more cohesive and capable of presenting a unified front to outside groups, whereas various factions among other professional groups might appeal to outsiders, like the state, for support against their professional rivals.

These essays also suggest that there may be important differences between professional groups that are primarily creators of new knowledge and those that are practitioners. For example, the former may put more emphasis on civil liberties, such as freedom of speech and association, may advocate more vigorously the end of censorship, and may have more desire for contacts with an international professional community, while the latter may at times be less concerned with such issues and seek the support of a strong state, even an autocracy, in effectively applying their body of professional knowledge in a particular national or regional setting. While all such generalizations need qualification and testing, they are worth further consideration. Another distinction which merits emphasis is between those professions whose work environment is limited primarily to one institution (such as Russian psychiatrists) and those groups that can choose between a variety of institutional settings (such as physicians, engineers, and legal professionals). Finally, in assessing differences among professional groups we need to look at the role played by the existence of an international community for a particular profession. Some professionals, seeking a sense of moral support as well as sources of ideas and criticism of Russian conditions, seem to have been far more oriented than others toward such a community.

I would like to mention a few of the most frequent and important themes running through these essays and indicate briefly some of the conclusions suggested by comparing them. I will also indicate some of the areas where problems exist and further research seems merited. The themes to be examined here include: the sources and levels of professionalization; obstacles to professionalization, including the role of the state, Russian cultural values, and internal divisions and conflicts within an occupational group; relations between professionals and paraprofessionals; and finally, relations between the radical intelligentsia and professionals.

One of the strongest attributes of professionalism is the claim professionals make for autonomy and self-regulation: their desire independently to determine the knowledge base of their occupation, who should belong to a profession and who should be excluded, how education should be structured to ensure competence, what professional standards and ethics should prevail, and how the profession should be policed to maintain these standards. An occupational group's effectiveness in achieving professional autonomy may depend on a variety of factors, but the role of the state is obviously a crucial variable. This points up one of the major differences between professionalization

in Russia and in countries like Britain and America. As Nancy Frieden notes
in her book, Russian physicians, unlike their medical colleagues abroad,
perceived the need to reduce official interference in their professional activity.[8]
If one of the major spurs to professionalization in the West was to raise the
status and economic position of an occupation by having the state intervene
to enforce a monopoly and control a labor market (i.e., to license practitioners with accepted knowledge and standards of behavior and exclude those
considered charlatans and incompetents), in Russia the relationship of professionals to the state was different, and the stimulus for professionalization also
differed. Political obstacles to doing one's work effectively, rather than economic issues or social status, seem to have been the strongest spur to
professionalization, although these other issues at times played a role. One of
the major battles of professionalization in the West was against the
laissez-faire ideology of free markets and nonstate intervention. In Russia,
professionals did not have to battle a strongly entrenched entrepreneurial ideal
in the culture that limited the role of the state. The state already was interven-
tionist and, in fact, helped to bring into being most of the modern professional occupations.

In Russia, the dilemma of the professionals was to free themselves from
the tutelage of the state, while still using the state for their own ends. This
Janus-faced relationship, as Frieden dubs it, more often than not led to frustration, as long as the tsarist state was led by an elite unsympathetic to professional goals and frequently themselves untrained in modern knowledge.
Samuel Kassow indicates how few of the tsarist upper bureaucratic elite came
from the universities and higher technical schools, which were important
sources of professional ideology. Most were from schools reserved for the
nobility, or from the military. Daniel T. Orlovsky sees a struggle in late
imperial Russia not only between the professions and the elite of the tsarist
state, but within the state bureaucracy over rival notions of professionalism.
"The tension between the ideology of 'free professions' and the very real
demands, powers, and magnetism of the ministerial bureaucracy was one of
the hallmarks of political and social conflict in the last years of the tsarist
regime. Even more important," he writes, "this conflict took place not only
between the bureaucracy and those who had begun to break away and form
professional associations and markets apart from the state, but it took place
in slightly different terms within the ministerial bureaucracy itself . . ." (270-
71).

When we speak of professionals in the ministerial bureaucracy, then, we
are really speaking of several groups across a spectrum. On one end, we
have specialists (teachers, statisticians, doctors, etc.) at the lower and
middle levels of ministerial hierarchies who come closest to the western
type and who identify with the ideals of free professions despite the reality

of their existence in government hierarchies. Moving to the center of the spectrum, we have higher ranking specialists in provincial and central ministerial hierarchies (engineers, lawyers, financial specialists, agronomists, or those with legal training, and the like), who maintain much closer degrees of identification with the state bureaucracy and who coexist, sometimes uneasily, with their professional counterparts in the private sector. Finally, at the other end of the spectrum, we have the traditional generalist, who, whatever his degree of education or specialization within the bureaucracy, regards himself morally also as a professional, but in this case as a nonamateur representative of a set of ethical and political norms tied to the autocracy and deeply rooted traditions of Russian administration. (290-91)

By the end of the tsarist period, Orlovsky concludes, rival notions of professionalism and service contended for political power in the autocracy, and later for the right to shape the new revolutionary society. For professional occupations outside the higher ranks of the bureaucracy, it was the uninformed meddling of the state that spurred professional organization in most of the cases examined, although economic issues of low status, low pay, and unemployment were at times important sources of professionalization (judging from Balzer's essay, particularly so in the case of engineers).

Despite the extremely low economic position of primary school teachers, for example, Scott J. Seregny concludes that it was mainly values picked up in their university education and reinforced by what educated society expected of them, later combined with a sense of isolation and cultural deprivation, that spurred many of them to professional activity in the 1890s and later.

If professional attitudes and ideology grew among many occupations in Russia after the reforms of the 1860s, as most of these essays attest, the actual level of professional organization and activity varied widely, and no professional occupation examined here became truly autonomous or self-regulating in the decades between 1860 and 1914. It was easier to unite an occupation against a common enemy like the state, or a symbol like the Hospital Statute of 1895 or the University Charter of 1884, than it was to create a high level of cohesion supporting a positive program of professional activity. The occupations that became most professionalized appear to have been physicians and lawyers, but even here the record seems quite uneven.

Public health physicians were one of the few groups that was able to create and sustain a nationwide professional organization before 1905. They effectively countered some of the state's measures with which they disagreed, such as the Hospital Statute of 1895, and they achieved considerable, if incomplete, influence on the local level. Primary teachers and university professors, although participating in short-lived national organizations during the Revolution of 1905, never achieved permanent national professional associations comparable to the Pirogov Society. Even the Pirogov Society did not represent all physicians before 1905, but only those who were engaged in public health, working primarily for the *zemstva*. Local faculty councils were foci of professional activity for university teachers, but Kassow sees them as generally ineffectual and riven by divisions within the professoriate. In fact, he believes, "in many respects the professional situation of the professoriate was much worse after 1908 than it had been before 1905," as the Stolypin government tightened its noose around the universities, and professors themselves were increasingly polarized between liberals and conservative factions that supported the government, more frightened of violent revolution than of state control.

As far as legal professionals are concerned, only one national Congress of Russian Jurists was held in this period (in 1875). Brian L. Levin-Stankevich notes that attempts to hold a second congress were put off repeatedly. Law societies sponsored by the law faculties of various universities and national journals did provide centers of activity for legal professionals, but in his own conclusions Levin-Stankevich indicates that professionalization was essentially frustrated by the policies of the government. State legal professionals after the 1870s were increasingly dominated by careerists who identified with the goals of the state rather than with independent professional activity per se, as the result of government persecution of lawyers for performing their lawful functions. He sees the legal occupations as increasingly polarized between "missionaries" and "careerists," with less ground in between for the growth of professional-service types oriented toward the ideals and knowledge of their profession and toward a colleague group outside the immediate work environment.

The Councils of the Bar, set up by the government beginning in 1865, which some have viewed as a model of professional self-regulation, he sees as having a more limited role. For one thing, they were brought into existence by the state, not generated by pressure from legal occupations. They were limited to European Russia, and new ones were prohibited from 1875 to 1904, being only gradually extended thereafter. They did set and enforce standards and ethical behavior for lawyers, but their autonomy was limited through external supervision by the courts. Their authority was also limited because not all lawyers were subject to their authority; membership was not mandatory.

A comparison of these occupational groups, therefore, leads to a conclusion that public health physicians, although far from fully professionalized, were the most successful in their struggle for self-identity and against measures by the state with which the majority of practitioners disagreed. Why was this so? Frieden explains it by the growing effectiveness of the knowledge base of the medical profession, that is, changes in medical knowledge in the late nineteenth century and the growing practical value of physicians to the community. She also credits the growth of medical associations which acted for the interests of public health physicians and their uneasy alliance with the *zemstvo* opposition, an alliance which strengthened their position vis-à-vis the central state bureaucracy before 1905, but was fraught with tension because the interests of physicians often conflicted with the *zemstva*, which were dominated by the landed nobility.

With the increased danger from epidemics as Russia modernized and internal migration speeded up, the need for effective public health strengthened the leverage of public health physicians with the state. Especially from the 1880s on, "with increased understanding of the etiology of diseases and discovery of techniques to reduce their impact, physicians would become impatient with their subordinate position," that is, subordinate to nonmedical bureaucrats.[9] In other words, the change in the knowledge base of medicine gave substance to the physicians' claims to authority and gave them political leverage that other occupations did not have.

As Seregny points out, primary teachers looked to the physicians as a model of professional influence and particularly sought to emulate national medical congresses and local medical councils, which had won the right to make their opinions known to the *zemstvo* assemblies and exerted some influence over appointments and other decisions affecting medical work. In 1899, the minister of education did permit local teachers' congresses, but school inspectors were given near dictatorial powers over them. Only a few local congresses of teachers were actually held and only a handful of *zemstva*—the more liberal ones—established school councils similar to the local medical councils. Teaching was viewed as a less expert field, that is, the knowledge base of primary school teaching was seen as less esoteric or specialized. The field was increasingly dominated by women, a fact which Seregny believes lowered its influence among the male-dominated *zemstva*. But perhaps most crucially from the standpoint of the central government, teachers were considered more dangerous than physicians. Educating the people was viewed as much more sensitive politically and subject to closer external regulation and control than raising the level of public health.

While Frieden, dealing with the period prior to 1905, sees the achievement of some autonomy by public health physicians as impressive—indeed, by comparison with other occupations examined here it was—Hutchinson strikes a more somber note for the period after 1905. After 1907, the membership of the Pirogov Society declined, and the profession was riven by internal dissension and estrangement over differing models of professionalism. Hutchinson sees the search for unity in national organizations abandoned by 1913 in favor of a concentration on local medical societies. He finds the conflict among physicians over differing conceptions of professionalism crucial to the history of this occupational group. He considers the inability to achieve a viable national professional body a major failure of medical professionalization which "had serious consequences during the war and revolution." After 1905, he states, the autocracy was never faced with a unified profession, and he places the onus for this more on the profession itself than the autocracy.

However, he does find a fresh attempt at an accommodation between physicians and the tsarist regime in the work of the Rein Commission during the period just prior to 1914. The commission favored a limited and controlled professionalism unacceptable to public health (community) physicians, but one with which both the regime and the majority of physicians could live. Rein's idea of the physician as a medical servant of the state enjoyed a marked revival after 1907, resulting in plans to bind physicians more closely to the state than to each other. World War I spoiled these plans and played into the hands of the supporters of professional autonomy. Nonetheless, by the time of the fall of the dynasty in early 1917, the tsarist regime was poised for a major assault against the drive to professionalize Russian physicians according to the ideas of the public health tradition. Already in 1916, the chief mechanism for such an assault was created within the government (the nucleus of a Ministry of Public Health), and Rein was named chief administrator for State Health Protection. The fall of the monarchy temporarily foiled these plans, but the establishment of the Soviet regime gave new life to the type of professional organization that Rein had hoped to create. Hutchinson concludes that the quest for corporate autonomy favored by public health physicians was only one type of professional model and formed no more than a transitory episode in the history of relations between physicians and the state.

This raises an interesting historical problem, which we can see in the cases of university professors, legal professionals, public health physicians, and other occupations. Did the drive for professionalization, which seems to have been increasing in the decade before 1905, actually wane between 1906 and 1914? If so, why? Is the explanation to be found in a more hard-line policy by the state, or was it the result of growth, diversification, and dissension within these occupations themselves? I am not sure that we yet have an adequate explanation. It is an important problem, particularly in terms of the debate over social stability in Russia on the eve of World War I. If these occupations were less united in their opposition to the tsarist state in 1914 than in 1905, then what implication does this have for the outcome of any revolutionary situation that may have been developing in the final years before the outbreak of World War I? This seems particularly important if peasants were also more quiescent than in 1905, leaving Professor Haimson with only his urban workers and the revolutionary intelligentsia to carry out a revolution in 1914, a much less formidable brew than in the failed Revolution of 1905.[10]

The essays in this book not only raise new questions about the Haimson school of historiography concerning social stability in late imperial Russia;

they present a rather different picture of Russian professionals than one finds in a book by the most notable Soviet historian of these groups, Vera Romanova Leikina-Svirskaia. [11] She sees the professionals as far more cohesive and united in their "revolutionary democratic" opposition to the autocracy throughout the period from 1900 to 1917 than they appear in a number of the essays included in this volume. While probably none of the authors represented here would disagree with the central role played by professional groups (particularly the Union of Unions) in the Revolution of 1905, some would quarrel rather strongly with the impression one gains from Leikina-Svirskaia's work that this political cohesiveness among the professions continued in the years between 1905 and 1917. Her data on the period after 1905 is admittedly sketchy. One of the present volume's services to scholarship is to paint a far richer, more complex, and heterogeneous picture of the professional intelligentsia in the decade prior to 1917 than can be found in other works, Soviet or western. One of the major conclusions suggested by these essays is to call into question the cohesiveness of the professional intelligentsia as a revolutionary force in Russian life after 1905.

Another unsolved problem, which several of these essays explore but only Samuel C. Ramer probes in detail, is the question of stratification within the occupations considered here, and the relations between professionals and paraprofessionals, particularly their relations in the workplace. Ramer states that feldshers felt great ambivalence toward physicians, who had always been both role models and objects of feldsher envy and hostility, since these paraprofessionals viewed physicians as their major barrier to recognition and professional mobility. Kassow mentions the importance of the junior faculty and its conflicts with the senior faculty over democratization of the university, conflicts which helped undermine the cohesion of the faculty. Julie V. Brown sees as an important issue among psychiatrists the question of collegial administration of mental hospitals and whether psychiatrists should share power with paraprofessionals and other hospital employees. Finally, Balzer mentions the importance of the *praktiki* who assumed engineering duties without higher technical education. Conflicts between graduate engineers and *praktiki* were important before 1917 and continued to be an issue well into the Soviet era.

I would like to suggest that this is a general issue worth further exploration, in part because no occupation is fully understood without looking at the overall work environment, and at the attitudes and activity of all those involved in it. Power relationships in the workplace—the role of professionals as supervisors—need more attention by historians. In part this area deserves more attention because, as the Soviet historian S.A. Fediukin suggests in his books on the intelligentsia after 1917, the Bolsheviks took a major stand against professional autonomy and sought to exploit conflicts between professionals and paraprofessionals as a way of further weakening the cohesion of professional groups that initially opposed the October Revolution.[12]

Fediukin's work and western studies of the medical and engineering professions after 1917 further suggest that a major source of recruitment into professional occupations during the early Soviet period was from the ranks of paraprofessionals. Do we know how much mobility of this kind occurred in the late tsarist period? Ramer indicates that for feldshers, at least, membership in that paraprofessional group was an occupational dead end before 1917, whereas under the Bolsheviks after 1917 medical faculties were opened up to the more competent feldshers who wished to better their positions, and the job ceased to be a professional cul-de-sac. However, the early Soviet regime failed to improve the situation of feldshers in most other areas where they had articulated grievances prior to the establishment of Soviet power. In fact, in some respects their situation grew even less favorable, for example, by the loss of freedom to organize an autonomous association to represent the interests of feldshers when the Soviet government forcibly merged all feldsher societies into the larger *Vsemediksantrud*, an industrial union that represented all medical workers from cooks to surgeons and that was integrated closely into the power structure of the Communist Party.

Did most paraprofessional groups experience something similar before and after 1917? We do not yet have comprehensive studies that would answer this question. Was lack of upward mobility a source of tension or conflict in the workplace which helped shape the mentality of both paraprofessionals and professionals before 1914? What can we learn of the psychology of paraprofessionals and their attitudes toward their professional supervisors among the occupations we have examined? Did paraprofessionals tend to be more radical politically? Ramer suggests that those feldshers who chose to participate in politics definitely were more radical by 1917 than most physicians; most such feldshers, he states, were Socialist Revolutionaries, Mensheviks, or Bolsheviks in 1917, considerably to the left of most politically involved public health physicians. But the proportion of feldshers and other paraprofessionals who were politically active in 1917 or before is still an unanswered question, as is the more precise nature of their political activity.

This leads to another general question which is important to the Russian case and may help further distinguish the history of Russian professional occupations from those in English-speaking countries. That question relates to the relative influence of radical political culture on Russian professionals. Barbara Engel wrote in an article concerning women medical students in the late nineteenth century that there was an inherent tension between radical political roles and the process of professionalization among Russian students in higher education.[13] The process of professionalization, her study suggested, tended to undercut radical activity. But one wonders whether professionalization necessarily undercuts radicalism or can, in certain contexts, actually stimulate dissent and radical activity.

The evidence in several of the studies here (for example, those of teachers, lawyers, psychiatrists, and to some extent public health physicians) indicates that Russian professionals' frustrations with the conditions of their work sometimes brought them closer to accepting radical political roles or at least tended to make them at times sympathetic toward radical political activity and attitudes. However, liberal professors, Kassow notes, drew a sharp line between themselves and the radical intelligentsia. Russia, they felt, needed people who were disciplined, competent, and efficient—people who knew their jobs and who did them well. They viewed the radical intelligentsia as too lazy and intolerant to undertake steady and often unglamorous work at a chosen profession.

I have no quarrel with this characterization of the liberal professoriate. But at the same time, I wonder if this typifies many other professions. Certainly the high level of arrests of primary school teachers and physicians during the Revolution of 1905, as well as the radicalization of many lawyers after the 1870s, is testimony that in a time of upheaval members of many professional occupations would be drawn to radical political programs. Certainly the radical intelligentsia and professionals shared at least one major ideological point: their ethos defining their role in terms of service to society rather than service to the state per se. Where they may have differed was in the nature of that service and the degree to which one could work for the state or with the state while "serving society." Yet I think it would be correct to view the intelligentsia and professional occupations as partially overlapping groups in late imperial Russia. One of the curious things is that in the Soviet period the terms "intelligentsia" and "professional expert" became almost interchangeable. The meaning of the word intelligentsia changed in official Soviet jargon to stand for all nonmanual occupations for which specialized secondary and higher education was generally required. I would like to suggest that the change in the meaning of the term intelligentsia from that most common among the nineteenth-century Russian intelligentsia to the official Soviet usage after the October Revolution may not have been a historical accident. The great prestige enjoyed by the Russian radical intelligentsia after 1917, thanks to its oppositionist role versus the discredited tsarist regime, was used to legitimate a change in the function of the intelligentsia from a revolutionary and reform-minded group to a group of persons increasingly involved in professional specialist and bureaucratic roles within the official structure of Soviet society.

After the Bolshevik revolution, it became increasingly difficult to follow the traditional role of the revolutionary or reformer, whereas major opportunities opened up for those who wished to pursue professional roles in the bureaucracy. Revolutionaries and reformers who persisted in the traditional oppositionist role usually found themselves silenced, particularly during the Stalin era after 1929, but those willing and able to adapt could pursue a wide variety of occupations as physicians, engineers, teachers, military officers, industrial managers, government administrators, and so on. Hence, many members of the pre-1917 Russian radical intelligentsia provided a vital component for the new Soviet intelligentsia (in the official usage of that term). One has only to look at the biographies of top party and government officials and professional experts of the 1920s and 1930s (including those in education, research, and industrial administration) to see the strong threads of continuity. The old term intelligentsia was applied to the new Soviet intelligentsia as a group of nonmanual occupational categories because in so many instances the holders of these positions had been revolutionary or reform-minded *intelligenty* before 1917. The term intelligentsia carried a sufficiently positive connotation after 1917 to help legitimize the transition. All of this, of course, carries us far beyond the context of these essays on professional groups in late imperial Russia, but I wanted to point out some of the problems they raise and some of the implications this material has for an understanding of later Soviet history.

A final point I would like to make concerns the nature of the job market for many of these occupations in late imperial Russia. Balzer, Frieden, and others mention the relative scarcity or oversupply at various times of persons qualified for professional positions, and how the job market may have affected issues of professionalization. Frieden supplies the most detailed breakdown for any of these occupational markets; she indicates what percentage of physicians worked for *zemstva*, for the central government, in private practice, and in other types of jobs, the relative status and remuneration of these various categories, and the significance of unemployment, which Balzer also emphasizes. However, for purposes of comparison among professions, it would be useful to have similar data for the other occupations considered, particularly since the structure of job markets and the opportunities they afforded may well have been crucial in terms of attitudes toward professional issues.

A related issue is the extent to which the central government controlled a particular job market and employed its monopoly to stifle professionalization. Does professionalization—and thereby the ability to organize independently to influence social action—tend to vary according to the power of the state to monopolize employment in a particular occupation, or are other factors more important? If the answer to the first part is yes, and I am not sure that it is, then what other channels for exerting influence on social action remain to an occupational group whose autonomy is severely limited in a strongly statist society, a society in which the state has a high level of control over job markets and can punish those who challenge it by denying employment in one's chosen field? The answers to these questions obviously have important implications for understanding the process of social change and stability not only in late imperial Russia but even more so in Soviet history and the history of other socialist societies.

Notes

1. William J. Bouwsma, "Lawyers in Early Modern Culture," *The American Historical Review* 78, no. 2 (April 1973): 303.

2. Harold Perkin, *The Origins of Modern English Society, 1780-1880* (London: Routledge and Kegan Paul, 1969), 252 ff. A subsequent volume continues the case through the twentieth century, *The Rise of Professional Society: England Since 1880* (London: Routledge, 1989).

3. Perkin, *Origins*, 170.

4. Ibid.

5. This theme is made explicit in Perkin's second volume, *Rise of Professional Society*.

6. Alfred J. Rieber, *Merchants and Entrepreneurs in Imperial Russia* (Chapel Hill: University of North Carolina Press, 1982).

7. Thomas C. Owen, *Capitalism and Politics in Russia: A Social History of the Moscow Merchants, 1855-1905* (New York: Cambridge University Press, 1981).

8. Nancy Mandelker Frieden, *Russian Physicians in an Era of Reform and Revolution, 1856-1905* (Princeton, NJ: Princeton University Press, 1981).

9. Ibid., 60.

10. Leopold Haimson, "The Problem of Social Stability in Urban Russia, 1905-1917," *Slavic Review* 23 (December 1964): 619-42, and 24 (March 1965): 1-22.

11. Vera Romanova Leikina-Svirskaia, *Russkaia intelligentsiia v 1900-1917 godakh* (Moscow, 1981).

12. See, for example, S. Fediukin, *Velikii oktiabr' i intelligentsiia* (Moscow, 1975).

13. Barbara Alpern Engel, "Women Medical Students in Russia, 1872-1882," *Journal of Social History* 12 (Spring 1979): 394-414.

3

The Engineering Profession in Tsarist Russia

HARLEY D. BALZER

Engineers in tsarist Russia managed to develop a strong sense of professional identity despite their inability to establish a national professional organization or attain professional autonomy. The engineers' situation of thwarted professionalism contributes to our understanding of the social and political context in which they worked and helps point to the reasons engineers were among the Russian professional groups that adapted relatively successfully to Soviet power. The approach here will be bifocal: The "near" image is a social history of Russian engineers before the revolution, paying particular attention to education and professional activity; but we will periodically raise our gaze, using the "distant" lens to point out aspects of engineers' behavior and situation that became important subsequently.

The crucial forges of a profession are education and professional organizations, and there is a reciprocal relationship between them.[1] In most instances a small group of leading practitioners seeks to institutionalize standards of practice and professional behavior through influence on educational establishments.[2] Once firmly established, the educational institutions exert an important influence on the "collective personality" of the profession, and on the larger society. Criteria for admission to the schools become crucial regulators of social mobility. Graduates' exclusive claims to particular jobs further enforce social stratification. And the worldview internalized by students profoundly influences their subsequent professional behavior.[3]

Early Development of the Engineering Profession

A coterie of leading practitioners intent on fostering engineering professionalism in Russia appeared only after the Crimean War. Before the 1860s a pattern of education and employment that may be described as "ministerial" dominated most specialized fields: an individual was trained in a (usually militarized) special school operated by a government ministry, and after graduating spent his entire career working for that ministry.[4] The Great

Reforms in the 1860s abolished serfdom and precipitated what was for Russia an unprecedented degree of social fluidity—the breaking down of barriers to physical, social, and intellectual movement. This flowering of varied forms facilitated the appearance of engineers with more diverse social and educational backgrounds.[5]

A good example of the new environment is provided by a small mechanics study circle that formed around I.A. Vyshnegradskii at the Petersburg Technical Institute in the early 1870s. The Pentagonal Society (the name apparently came from its five-person membership) played a major role in the development of Russia's engineering profession.[6] Its weekly discussions focused on practical and theoretical developments in applied mechanics, and it was to this group that Vyshnegradskii first read his seminal work on the theory of automatic controls. The other members became leading academics and engineering practitioners. The group included three faculty members at the institute —Viktor L'vovich Kirpichev (1845-1913),[7] Nikolai Pavlovich Petrov (1836-1920),[8] and Aleksandr Parfenevich Borodin (1848-1898)[9]—plus Pavel Vasil'evich Koturnitskii (1844-1913),[10] who was then a promising student. During a career spanning more than three decades, Vyshnegradskii made major contributions in science, education, the economy, and government. He was the most important individual involved in Russian technical education in the 1870s and 1880s. When the activities of his "circle" are added, the impact is even more significant.[11] In their subsequent careers these men sought to revise and expand the Russian system of technical education and to create bonds of community and profession among engineering practitioners.

The members of the Pentagonal Society were representative of Russia's emerging nonministerial engineering professionals. Their diverse backgrounds reflect the flux in Russia society after the Crimean War. They shared a sense of being in the vanguard of the new field of applied mechanics. Each made important scientific and technical contributions, but their subsequent activity went well beyond the realm of science and technology. All of them conducted important technical work for government and private industry. They shared a strong sense of identity as engineering professionals and a belief in engineers' mission to improve the quality of human life. Each was active in establishing engineering societies and journals to pursue these goals. They played key roles in creating new educational institutions which not only increased the number of engineers in Russia but also shifted the training itself to a model more closely resembling their ideal image of an engineer. A theme underlying all of their activity was the need to free Russia from reliance on foreign economic and technical assistance.

The Pentagonal Society members present a contrast to the generation of Russian engineers who preceded them—men predominantly of gentry origin who were educated in ministerial institutes.[12] While each of them began his activity by remaining at an institute to teach and conduct scientific research (the pattern typical of Russian academics), their careers quickly became more complex. They demonstrated an ability to move between private and state activity indicative of Russia's "mixed" economy in the late nineteenth century. Vyshnegradskii consulted for the Artillery Department, other government agencies, and numerous private firms, and became involved in academic administration before his appointment as finance minister. Borodin left teaching shortly after completing his degree as a transport engineer and held various technical posts on several railroads. When the Southwestern Railway was organized, he was offered the position of director but preferred the more technically oriented post of chief engineer. He ran the technical side of the line for twenty-three years before moving to St. Petersburg to work in government and private industry. [13] Petrov taught at the Technical Institute and was a consultant for government agencies and several private firms, most notably the Main Society of Russian Railroads. He became an important official in the Ministry of Communications, chairing the Directorate of State Railroads, and finally left teaching to head the ministry's Engineering Council. He served as assistant minister (1893-96) and was subsequently appointed to the State Council. Kirpichev and Koturnitskii each had a number of consulting positions during their teaching careers. While Koturnitskii remained at the Technical Institute, Kirpichev moved into academic administration, becoming director of the new Khar'kov Technical Institute in 1885. In 1898, Sergei Witte asked him to head another new engineering institute, the Kiev Polytechnicum.

Diverse technical and managerial jobs demonstrated the image these men had of an engineer as someone with a knowledge of theoretical science and the ability to apply that knowledge in varied practical contexts. Borodin wrote numerous articles extolling the virtues of private industrial activity. [14] He expressed unbounded admiration for American technology and the "American engineering spirit," and sought to duplicate the concern for cost and efficiency found in American private enterprise. [15] Petrov, too, was fond of quoting "American" maxims, such as "An engineer must know something about everything and everything about something."[16] Kirpichev predicted a future "golden age" characterized by "general material well-being." He went on to state: "We get to it by the path of technical improvement and invention. We are led to it, directed, shown the way by engineers."[17]

The Pentagonal Society's engineers supported exchange of scientific information and organized collective activity in formal and informal technical societies. Kirpichev was a founder of the South Russian Society of Technologists at Khar'kov, an organization unique in not limiting membership to graduates of a particular institute. It was Russia's first general engineering, as opposed to technical, society. Kirpichev laid the basis for a similar organization at the Kiev Polytechnicum and established a study circle at Petersburg Polytechnicum which continued into the Soviet period as the *kruzhok im. Kirpicheva*.[18] He was also a leader of the Union of Engineers in 1905.[19]

Vyshnegradskii and his circle sought to provide engineering associations with their own publications. Vyshnegradskii established the first scientific periodical at the Petersburg Technical Institute; Koturnitskii founded and edited the Society of Technologists' *Vestnik*; Kirpichev began journals at Khar'kov and Kiev, and also initiated a scientific publication at the Petersburg Polytechnicum. Perhaps the most significant publishing activity was Borodin's. He was one of the founders of *Engineer (Inzhener)*, Russia's first private technical periodical, and served as its editor for a dozen years. The journal was both an example of independent activity and a forum Borodin used to call for such activity. In its pages he discussed his favorite themes: America's technology and engineering spirit, the evils of state operation of railroads, the incompetence of engineers in the Ministry of Communications, and the shortcomings of the institution that trained them.[20]

Any meaningful change in the number and orientation of Russian engineers required changes in the system of higher technical education. Aware of developments in Europe, Vyshnegradskii's circle sought to replace Russia's ministerial model with institutions combining what they believed were the best features of German polytechnicums and the French École Centrale: close ties with industry and a program imparting basic skills that graduates could apply to a broad range of tasks. Their ideal engineer was a generalist possessing sufficient specialized knowledge to cope with diverse economic and technical problems. Vyshnegradskii's associates were active participants in the creation of new institutes emphasizing practical engineering on a polytechnical pattern. Sergei Witte shared many of their views, particularly those regarding the need to develop Russia's economic and entrepreneurial powers and to end foreign influence. Witte was a protégé and a colleague of the Pentagonal Society engineers. His career was intertwined with Vyshnegradskii and Borodin on the Southwestern Railway, with Kirpichev in establishing the Kiev and Petersburg Polytechnical Institutes, and with Vyshnegradskii and Petrov in the St. Petersburg bureaucracy.

The new, industry-oriented technical institutes were intended not just to impart a superior form of engineering education, but also to encourage professional organization and social responsibility. The founders considered formal and informal communication with peers an indispensable element of professional growth. Having worked out their ideas in an informal study circle, these engineers sought to encourage similar groups and orchestrated larger meetings representing engineers' professional interests. They were conscious of the reciprocal relationship between education and profession, and acted to implement their ideas.

Expansion of the School System

The projects first discussed by Vyshnegradskii and his circle produced significant results under the astute political tutelage of Vyshnegradskii's successor as minister of finance, Sergei Witte. Within a six-year period at the turn of the century, Russia's would-be engineering professionals succeeded in doubling the number of Russian engineering institutes and more than trebling the number of students. The new schools were different from existing ministerial institutes, offering training modeled on European polytechnical systems. The courses of instruction were shorter, less encyclopedic, and geared more to practical applications than those at the other ministerial institutes. Characteristically for Russia, the new technical institutes did not replace the existing ones, but rather became parallel and hence rival institutions. A majority of the new schools were located outside the capitals, in regions where economic growth was generating rapid changes. The student body was also different. Even had new schools not been located on the periphery and given a more practical orientation, the geometric increase in numbers alone would have had a "democratizing" effect on the educational system.

Statistics provide eloquent testimony to the expansion of engineering education. In 1895 there were seven technical institutes conferring engineering degrees; by 1902 there were thirteen. The number of students increased from 4,000 in 1895 to 13,000 in 1904 and to more than 20,000 in 1914. On the eve of World War I, more students attended the Petersburg Polytechnical Institute than studied at all Russian higher technical schools at the end of the nineteenth century. Despite disappointing completion rates (one in ten in the 1890s), the enormous increase in the number of students meant an increase in the number of graduate engineers. In 1895 approximately 400 graduated; in 1904 the number was more than 1,000; by 1914 it exceeded 2,000.[21]

Economic Difficulties as a Spur to Professionalization

The appearance of large numbers of engineers with training oriented to practical work in industry was of enormous importance for Russia's economic development, but the full impact came only with renewed economic growth after 1907. The implications for the engineering profession were more immediate and profound. Graduates of the expanded education system began to enter the job market in the years after 1900, when economic difficulties depressed the demand for engineers. The decade before 1905 was also a period of intense politicization among Russia's educated public. Economic and political conditions led engineers to make new demands on professional associations, both for employment-related assistance and for political action.

Table 3.1

Placement Situation of South Russian Society of Technologists

Year	Number Seeking Jobs (Unemployed)	Number Placed
1895-1896	24	4
1897-1898	40	7
1898-1899	30	16
1899-1900	5	10
1900-1901	98	9
1901-1902	76	6
1902-1903	6	5
1908-1909	24	5
1913-1914	27	3

Source: Annual reports in *Izvestiia Iuzhno-russkogo obshchestva tekhnologov.*

One technical society's experience illustrates the growing economic pressures facing engineers. The South Russian Society of Technologists published annual reports describing its efforts to find positions for unemployed members. These data show a significant increase in the number seeking positions after 1900, combined with the organization's declining ability to assist them in finding employment (see Table 3.1). In its report for 1895-96, the first year of operation, the society considered the major problem to be an inability to match candidates with suitable positions. This was attributed to information coming from intermediaries rather than from the employers themselves, and to "the relative ease with which candidate technicians currently find places independent of the society. The work of mechanical technicians is currently much in demand on railroads and in factories, and the demand for them is not being fully met by graduates of higher technical schools."[22] Two years later the society still considered its lack of success a reflection of "mechanical" difficulties resulting from seasonal needs in particular industries and students' being impelled by financial necessity to accept positions immediately after graduation.[23]

The situation deteriorated markedly after 1900. Not only did the number seeking work increase while the society's ability to assist them declined, but the reasons given for the poor performance changed. In its report of 1900/01 the society spoke of "the decline in demand, which is a consequence of the crisis our industry is going through." Similar concerns were expressed in each of the succeeding years through 1905.[24] The market for engineers was declining just as the supply of candidates increased at unprecedented rates.[25]

Russian specialized higher education was already more open to the non-privileged classes than were similar schools in other European countries. Trebling the number of students in technical institutes meant that even more students would be drawn from families for whom four or five years of higher education entailed genuine financial hardship.[26] Such students, if they were diligent and fortunate enough to attain a diploma, might be expected to have been particularly frustrated when their years of work and sacrifice led not to financial security but to a seemingly endless search for work.[27]

Engineers responded to the difficulties by placing more demands on their professional organizations. Employment services may have been the most significant activities for individuals, but for the profession as a whole these efforts were dwarfed by larger group endeavors. Engineering associations established mutual assistance societies and set up insurance plans to assist members. It is hardly a coincidence that membership in most engineering organizations reached its peak in the years around 1905 (see Table 3.2). But perhaps the most important function of professional organizations was to serve as a vehicle for political expression.

1905 and the Growth of Professional Organizations

The Revolution of 1905 was a crucial watershed in the development of Russia's engineering profession. Ferment in Russian political life stimulated an increase in the number of organizations and their membership, encouraged politicization, and brought changes in the nature of engineering associations. Two seemingly contradictory processes were at work. On the one hand, more groups tended to organize on the basis of regional or specialized technical interests, narrowing the scope of their membership (this was particularly true in the case of electrical engineers). At the same time, there was growing consciousness of the need for an all-Russian professional engineering organization.

Prior to 1905 the membership of each Russian technical society was narrowly circumscribed. Most were alumni associations of individual schools, such as the Society of Technologists at Petersburg Technical Institute, the Polytechnical Society at the Moscow Higher Technical School, or the Societies of Mining and Transport Engineers. When new mining and transport schools were opened at the end of the nineteenth century, existing societies suggested that they organize their own separate associations for graduates, rather than creating larger "specialty" organizations. A few groups sought to become local or regional organizations, but even these, for example the South Russian Society of Technologists, were based primarily on a single institute (in this case the Khar'kov Technical Institute). The only technical organization asserting a claim to universality was the Russian Technical

Table 3.2

Membership in Russian Engineering Societies

	South Russian Society of Technologists	Polytechnical Society (Moscow)	Society of Mining Engineers
1886	—	—	204
1887	—	190	242
1888	—	—	253
1889	—	—	271
1890	—	—	188
1891	—	—	250
1892	—	—	257
1893	—	—	257
1894	—	—	277
1895	—	—	224
1896	199	—	247
1897	286	—	190
1898	366	515	298
1899	430	556	288
1900	496	620	278
1901	493	697	275
1902	512	731	415
1903	487	739	615
1904	438	773	560
1905	440	787	471
1906	—	812	363
1907	—	860	326
1908	239	—	389
1909	236	—	341
1910	—	—	280
1911	—	692	219
1912	—	646	—
1913	—	621	—
1914	227	842	—

Source: Annual reports in *Izvestiia Iuzhno-russkogo obshchestva tekhnologov; Politeknicheskoe obshchestvo sostoiashchee pri Moskovskim vysshem teknicheskim uchilishchem, ocherk 40-letiia deiatel'nosti,* 33, 39; and *Izvestiia obshchestva gornykh inzhenerov,* no. 12 (1912): 7.

Society, which was too diverse in membership and too closely tied to the state to express effectively the professional interests of Russian engineers.[28]

Beginning in the 1880s, sporadic attempts were made to establish professional associations based on geographic location or the actual practice of engineering rather than ties to a state-run school. When the journal *Engineer* began publication in 1882, it pointed out the need for a nongovernment professional engineers' organization, a call it repeated a number of times before 1917.[29] In 1894, a young member of the Society of Technologists in St. Petersburg suggested that the group change its organization to admit graduates of all engineering schools, but the membership voted by a margin of two to one that such a step was "premature."[30] Other groups' efforts to establish an independent professional association met resistance from the government, which feared any independent collective activity by its citizens. With the increase in the number of engineers and their collective action in the years before 1905, organizational efforts gained momentum.

While the original impetus for increased organization membership and activity was primarily economic, there were engineers who advocated a greater political role. In 1904 a group of politically aggressive engineers organized one of the first professional unions, the Union of Engineers.[31] In the aftermath of Bloody Sunday (9 January 1905), many engineering associations began to pay more attention to broader political questions, and the Union of Engineers took the lead in seeking to create an all-Russian professional organization.[32]

The Union of Engineers typified the growing politicization of Russian society. It published a declaration blaming social unrest on government support for employers against workers and added its voice to the clamor for political and organizational freedoms. Many older engineering associations followed the union's lead. The *Vestnik* of the Society of Technologists (St. Petersburg) initiated a new "political and economic section" which devoted much of its attention to the labor question, expressing sympathy with workers' demands and criticizing employers' use of lockouts. The Polytechnical Society in Moscow, the South Russian Society of Technologists, and even the elite Society of Mining Engineers also began sympathetic discussion of the labor question.[33]

During the period 1904-6, numerous new associations of technicians and engineers appeared. Moscow was a major center of activity, with several groups seeking to unite the technical personnel of the Central Industrial Region in a regional engineering society, even if an all-Russian organization proved impossible. Plans for an "Assembly of Engineers in Moscow" were drawn up in 1904. Its protocols asserted that engineers working in the same city had just as much common ground for organizing as graduates of individual institutes, and demanded a change in government policy on this issue. Moscow engineers also stressed the need for associations serving engineers in new specialties. Some of the new groups were short-lived, while others kept no records, making it difficult to construct a full list of the various engineers' and technicians' organizations which sprang up in the Moscow region in this period. There were at least a dozen.[34]

Despite a strong desire for unity, neither the Union of Engineers nor any other organization could effectively speak for all Russian engineers, much less all technical personnel. In the highly charged atmosphere of 1905, such an organization was impossible. A number of groups formed to the left of the Union of Engineers, such as the Moscow Union of Technicians. This group, led by Marxist engineer P.V. Tochinskii, was opposed by the much less radical Society for the Mutual Aid of Russian Technicians, which sought to limit organizational activity to aiding needy technical personnel.[35]

The October Manifesto and the general strike exacerbated political differences, and engineers split into groups at various points along the political spectrum. Not all engineers sympathized with even the mildest forms of political activity. L.N. Liubimov, one of the elite transport engineers, recounted having to run for his life after angering a mob by refusing to doff his cap to the "new freedoms."[36] A reaction typical of many engineers was that of E.O. Paton, who sought to immerse himself in technical problems while remaining "neutral" politically.[37] For those engineers who were politically active, an important issue was to define their relationship to workers and employers. This question became even more pressing in 1917.

Continuing Efforts at Professionalization

In contrast to the upsurge in public activity during the years before 1905, the period after 1906 was characterized by a retreat from social and political activism. The government's policies of concession and repression worked —for a while. Individuals evinced much more concern with personal and career issues. Even a committed Bolshevik like Leonid Krasin turned from making revolution to making his fortune.[38] Along with increased concern for careers came a greater consciousness of professional identity. Engineers paid less attention to broad social issues, devoting their energy instead to personal and professional matters. In some cases, this led to discussion of the ways engineers' professional activity was important for all of Russian society, but often personal and material considerations dominated.

After 1905 membership in most Russian engineering associations declined, although the number of such organizations increased (see Table 3.3). The total number of engineers belonging to engineering societies continued to grow.[39] New groups organized on the basis of professional specialization, and increasingly devoted attention to new professional issues.

Evidence for the new awareness of professional identity appears in engineering journals, in other publications, in questions raised at meetings of engineers, and in their conduct in the workplace. Even the Imperial Russian Technical Society's staid journal *Electricity* (*Elektrichestvo)* initiated a new section dealing with "Professional Life."[40] Electrical engineers were among the most active in forming new organizations, and they took a leading role in pressing for creation of national engineering organizations and discussing such professional issues as engineering ethics. The leading role of electrical engineers may reflect the importance of electrical technology as Russia joined the industrial revolution, or it may be attributable to the rapid development of "late starters." Whatever the reason, electrical engineers frequently appear in the forefront of professional activities, and in some cases this activism presaged important contributions in the Soviet era.[41]

Russian electrical engineers sought to organize an All-Russian Conference of Electrical Technologists beginning in the 1880s. The tsarist government typically balked at the idea, but finally permitted a meeting in 1900.[42] The electrical engineers sought to meet biannually thereafter. Having succeeded in establishing an ongoing organization, they believed the next step was a full-fledged All-Russian Electrotechnical Society organized independently of existing institutions. Its goals were to foster economic development through electrification and to defend the professional interests of electrical engineers:

> The chief task of such a society should consist first of all in studying existing Russian electrotechnical projects; preparing material for conferences; collecting statistical information; studying local conditions and peculiarities for supply of electrical energy; working out and regulating norms for using electricity in industry and for expert advice on social issues related to electricity. Further, its tasks must be defense of the economic interests of personnel serving in electrotechnical enterprises and assistance for technicians seeking work.[43]

Electrical engineers played a leading role in discussing engineering ethics. The Fifth All-Russian Electrotechnical Conference in Moscow (1908) approved "in principle" drafting a code dealing with an engineer's relationship to lower-level technical personnel.[44] The discussions quickly became more sophisticated, and an electrical engineer wrote the first Russian monograph discussing engineering ethics.[45]

Much in the manner of Vyshnegradskii's *kruzhok*, Russian electrical engineers based their activity on an idealized image of American engineering and on organizational activity in Germany and the United States. Leaders of Russian engineering groups asserted that American engineers had become concerned with ethics through the influence of educators, and that such concerns had been taken up by their professional organizations.[46] They also continued to extol the virtues of America's "practical" engineers, who represented an approach very different from the formal rationality prevailing in Russia:

Table 3.3

Russian Engineering Societies
(in order of year founded)

Organization	Place and Date Founded	Membership	Publication
Russian Technical Society	St. Petersburg 1866	By invitation	*Zapiski*
Polytechnical Society	Moscow 1877	Moscow Technical Institute	*Biulletin, Vestnik,* and *Trudy*
Organization of Transport Engineers	St. Petersburg 1882	Transport Institute	*Izvestiia*
Society of Technologists	St. Petersburg 1884	Technical Institute	*Vestnik*
Society of Mining Engineers	St. Petersburg 1887	Mining Institute	*Izvestiia*
Electrotechnical Society	St. Petersburg 1892	Electrotechnical Institute	*Electricheskii Vestnik*
Society of Civil Engineers	St. Petersburg 1894	Institute of Civil Engineers	*Izvestiia*
South Russian Society of Technologists	Khar'kov 1895	Khar'kov Technical Institute	*Izvestiia*
Society of Naval Engineers	Kronstadt 1896	Military	*Vestnik*
All-Russian Union of Technicians	St. Petersburg 1905-6	Open	–
Union of Technicians	Moscow 1905	Open	–
Society for the Mutual Aid of Russian Technicians	Moscow 1905	Open	–
Society of Technicians of the Moscow Industrial Region	Moscow 1906	Regional	*Tekhnik*

Organization	Place and Date Founded	Membership	Publication
Society of Military, Naval, and Agricultural Technicians	St. Petersburg 1906	Specialty	–
Khar'kov Society for the Mutual Aid of Electrotech Workers	Khar'kov 1906	Regional	–
All-Russian Air Club	St. Petersburg 1908	Specialty	*Vozdukho-plavatel'*
Circle of Technologists of Moscow Region	Moscow 1908	Regional	*Biulletin*
Society of Electrical Engineers	St. Petersburg 1909	Specialty	*Izvestiia* and *Zapiski*
Society of Electrical Technicians	Moscow 1909	Specialty	*Biulletin*
S-W Society of Electrical Technicians	Kiev 1909	Speciality	–
Society of Siberian Engineers	Tomsk 1909	Tomsk Technical Institute	*Zhurnal*
Moscow Flying Society	Moscow 1910	Specialty	*Biulletin*
Russian Society of Testing Materials	Moscow 1911	Specialty	*Trudy*
Kiev Polytech Society of Engineers and Agronomists	Kiev 1911	Regional	*Biulletin*
Russian Society for Testing Materials	St. Petersburg 1912	Specialty	*Izvestiia*

Source: Compiled by the author from N.G. Filippov, *Nauchno-tekhnicheskie obshchestva Rossii (1866-1917 gg.)* (Moscow, 1976), and from the journals of the various technical societies.

One should not think that the American does not believe in science, in theoretical or practical knowledge; he simply does not believe in papers. . . . A person who can do both intellectual and manual work is valued much more than a person who can do only manual or intellectual work, and a person who, in addition to having experience, knows theory, is valued more highly than someone who is only a practitioner or a theoretician; but in any instance, his value must be demonstrated in practical work, and not on paper, not by a diploma. Similarly, it is not important where or how knowledge and experience were acquired, it only matters that they exist.[47]

Codes of behavior were only part of a long list of professional concerns developed by Russian engineers. They sought to participate in drafting health and safety regulations, to deal with the question of whether an engineer managing a factory should be considered an engineer or an administrator, and to create new professional organizations. In their efforts to establish new professional societies, engineers simultaneously advocated specialized groups and a national association representing the entire profession.

Russian engineering groups constantly referred to European models like the *Verein Deutscher Ingenieure* or to their American counterparts when discussing organization. There was some irony in this, since another primary goal Russian engineers articulated was to decrease the country's reliance on imported technology and to oust foreign personnel from strategic (and lucrative) positions in Russian industry.[48] Soviet writers have gone out of their way to portray foreign capitalist exploitation of tsarist Russia. Even less tendentious sources, however, suggest that foreigners—both individuals from outside the Empire and those from non-Russian areas—occupied a disproportionate number of important positions.[49]

Efforts continued to establish an Empirewide professional organization uniting all Russian engineers. As in the case of the electrical engineers, these projects continued to meet government resistance. Faced with a ban on permanent groups having a general engineering orientation, Russian engineers sought an alternative in trying to arrange a congress of engineers to discuss professional issues. The Pirogov Congresses convened by Russian physicians served as a model, as did the successful All-Russian Electrotechnical Conference.[50] By 1912 discussion of the issue was no longer confined to engineering journals. *Russkii vestnik* asked, "Isn't it time to think seriously not of emphasizing differences but rather of joining together on the basis of cultural and professional interests?" The paper defended its involvement in the matter by noting the social impact of engineers' activity:

Specialists hardly perform their work in a vacuum; they work among the people—in society; every one of them in real activity comes into contact with fundamental national interests. Engineers' knowledge, their training, intellectual level, the conscientiousness with which they perform their work, their relations with workers, millions of whom are under their administration and supervision—all of these are questions of fundamental importance, and society has the right and the duty to seek an answer.[51]

Public prodding, professional interest, and foreign examples all induced Russian engineers to seek a national professional organization. The annual Easter Ball held by Moscow's Polytechnical Society provided an opportunity for informal discussion with colleagues from St. Petersburg and led to formation of an ad hoc organizing committee for a conference. Leading figures in the profession like V.L. Kirpichev and V.I. Grinevetskii endorsed the proposal, and by June 1913 several technical societies had formulated plans and approved a program.[52]

Program for the Congress of Engineers

The program drawn up for the "First All-Russian Congress of Engineers" provides a good summary of engineers' evolving professional concerns and demonstrates the growing complexity of Russia's private economic sector.[53] Issues for discussion were divided into seven categories: scientific-technical questions, professional-legal issues, engineers' economic situation and role in the national economy, social welfare, technical education, a general engineering journal, and an institutional mechanism for periodic congresses. The major issues were discussed in a degree of detail allowing us to see the spectrum of engineers' interests.

The "scientific-technical questions" were couched in the broadest possible terms. As might be expected, these included descriptions of technical and economic conditions in industry, the status of technology, and uniform norms and standards. But they went on to add the "rationalization" of industrial organizations, and the final item was listed as "technical-social questions of municipal and *zemstvo* life." These topics implied a mandate to become involved in all aspects of the enterprises in which engineers were employed and a multitude of issues concerning the communities in which they lived and worked.

In discussing "professional-legal questions," the authors of the program demonstrated a similarly broad range of concerns, while their choice of which elements to stress indicates a highly developed understanding of "bread and butter" issues. Subsections on "the situation of engineers in industry and in society" and "professional ethics" were simply included as topics for discussion. In contrast, "mutual relations between engineers and employers" was broken down into quite specific discussions of the details involved in contractual relations. These issues included basic contract agreements, provisions for consulting work, invention and patent rights, and the implications for engineers of new forms of economic organization such as syndicates and trusts.

Discussion of welfare questions was no less detailed. The authors proposed that the congress explore old-age pensions, disability funds, burial funds, mutual assistance arrangements and family insurance programs. Also on the agenda were mechanisms to assist engineers in finding jobs or moving to more desirable positions, and providing educational opportunities for children of engineers employed away from "cultural centers."

When it came to questions of "the economic situation of engineers and their role in the country's economic development" the program reverted to generalities. The organizers hoped to collect a mass of statistical information about engineers' remuneration and productivity, and to use this in constructing a profile of their profession. But suggestions for aiding Russia's economy did not go beyond "encouraging" engineers to take advantage of Russia's natural resources and to organize enterprises in new branches of industry. There was much more consensus on issues of direct personal or professional concern than on questions about broader national economic priorities.

Education issues indicated a similar reluctance to grapple with difficult questions. T⁷ document does not suggest priorities for technical education or school curricula. Nowhere do the authors attempt to define what it meant to be an engineer, c. to confront the widespread problem of individuals occupying responsible positions without proper education. The program merely states the need to evaluate lower and secondary technical training and focuses on questions involving practical training for beginning engineers. The authors also mention nontechnical skills and continuing education, and propose a survey of personnel serving in Russian industry.

The program for the planned congress is as eloquent in what it omits as in what it includes. On issues of direct economic interest to engineers, the authors were able to present a detailed discussion of common concerns. The level of discourse was quite sophisticated, and the terms of the debate would have been intelligible in (and similar to) discussions in many European or American engineering associations. When the topics involved more general issues of economics and national policy, they were presented in vague and nonprovocative form. An attempt at inclusiveness required that the authors seek the "lowest common denominator" of acceptable discourse.

The draft program was not used for the purpose intended until the autocracy collapsed. Despite (or more likely because of) the success of physicians' Pirogov Congresses, the Interior Ministry would not permit a Congress of Engineers. Proposals to convene in the spring of 1914, in December 1914, and at Easter 1915 were all rejected. [54] The closest Russian engineers came to establishing a broad association was in 1915, when the Society of Technologists in St. Petersburg and the Polytechnic Society in Moscow merged their publications to establish a new journal, *Vestnik inzhenerov*. This was done in the firm belief "that a congress of Russian engineers will be held in the near future."[55] Government hesitation and the worsening military situation made it impossible for such a gathering to convene until after the February Revolution, and an all-Russian Union of Engineers was established only in May 1917.[56]

Proposals for meetings and for all-Russian professional organizations came from acknowledged leaders in the field, and documents like their program for the Congress of Engineers represent the concerns of the most articulate, active, and successful engineering practitioners.[57] While the questions these leaders addressed were issues many engineers aspired to deal with, they were mainly concerns of the elite. The great majority of Russian engineers resembled less the industrial entrepreneurs like N.S. Avdakov or G.F. Glezmer, than the ordinary physician (*srednii vrach*) portrayed by Nancy Frieden.[58] A full history of these "average" practitioners remains to be written. The final portion of this essay sketches the outlines of this history, focusing on the growing diversity within the profession. While clearly demonstrating the pace and sophistication of economic development in Russia, these lines of cleavage also took on a darker meaning in the Soviet era.

Diversity and Cleavages in the Engineering Profession

Calls for an all-Russian organization of engineers masked deep conflicts within the profession. Alongside ministerial institutes with encyclopedic and heavily theoretical curricula, there were polytechnicums emphasizing practical and industrial skills. Young graduates of these schools shared their elders' dislike of the foreign technical personnel who dominated many branches of Russian industry, but they were equally impatient with the older Russian engineers. To the normal generational conflicts were added profound differences in education, socialization, and political outlook—all exacerbated in the hothouse political atmosphere of 1905. A certain percentage of engineers had always chosen the profession for material reasons, and expansion of the educational system increased the number for whom engineering was a source of economic survival while also increasing the competition for desirable jobs. And it should be remembered that a majority of the individuals performing engineering work were *praktiki* who had no advanced degree at all.

Diversity within the engineering profession began in the educational system. The older ministerial institutes (the Transport Institute and to a lesser extent the Mining Institute) maintained strong elitist traditions. Though no longer constituting military corps as in prereform times, they retained much of the "regimental" spirit. Graduates were a select group, destined to occupy top positions in government enterprises and eventually in the upper echelons of their ministries. At times even the students themselves rebelled against this corporatism. In 1901, Transport Institute students refrained from publishing an annual yearbook to protest the "narrow in-group spirit" of transport engineers.[59] More frequently, these students accepted special status as their due. This was particularly true after graduation, when social connections and the "old school tie" could be crucial in obtaining a position.[60]

In the name of specialized knowledge and competence, graduates of the ministerial institutes claimed exclusive rights to government positions. Witte was extremely proud of being the first Russian railroad director who was *not* a transport engineer.[61] Other men managed to break through the barriers, but not many. Those at the top jealously guarded their prerogatives. One account from the late 1890s indicates the way this system functioned. As a young engineer, Evgenii Paton enjoyed some success as a bridge designer, but could not understand why his older colleagues spent so much time on their calculations and projects. An older engineer "explained" that undue haste undermined confidence and might lead to lower fees. Paton's complaint to the ministry was ignored:

> At that time a small group of old engineers in the ministry enjoyed the full monopoly of designing many bridges for roads under construction. The "working out" of designs was organized in grand style. The group had an assortment of ready-made designs of bridges with different spans and offered them to various roads.[62]

If even some of the transport engineers themselves objected to the elitism and questionable practices of their colleagues, we may imagine the attitude of engineers from other schools. Graduates of the St. Petersburg and Moscow technical institutes, and after 1900 those from the new "practical" higher schools, spoke with bitterness about the "gentleman engineers" who received prestigious diplomas without the slightest capacity to perform practical engineering work. Such criticism was voiced by transport engineers themselves throughout the tsarist era. Baron A.I. Del'vig described the institution in the reign of Nicholas I as a place where students graduated without ever "dirtying their hands." N.A. Liubimov made similar statements based on his experiences in the 1880s. After the exciting intellectual atmosphere at Moscow University, he found:

> only dry bureaucratic formalism and almost apathetic attitudes to subjects being taught, and at times even very slight acquaintance with the practical aspects of the subject. From the institute I got nothing but a diploma . . .[63]

Graduates of new industry-oriented institutes had little patience with older engineers lacking applied skills. Many had even less tolerance for the questionable practices that constituted "business as usual" in Russia. Fictional accounts and memoirs abound with descriptions of corrupt contractors, fortunes made through graft, and generally lax morals.[64] An engineer seeking a job where illegal practices would not be the norm faced a particularly difficult task. Garin-Mikhailovskii's fictional hero Tema Kartashev despaired of ever working as an engineer at all. Liubimov's refusal to "play the game" alienated colleagues and damaged his career.[65]

The prevalence of quasi-legal and corrupt practices provided a major impetus for discussions of ethics after 1905. To some extent these discussions were a product of genuine moral revulsion that young engineers imbued with the prevailing culture of student radicalism felt when they examined their elders' behavior. But discussions of ethical standards were also a tactic in the job market and an important aspect of the intensely political struggle for professional leadership. An emphasis on disinterested professionalism in the service of public needs represented a powerful weapon in the hands of new groups. In the United States, concern over business practices and professional ethics was a major factor in the proliferation of engineering organizations representing new specialties. The Russian experience was similar.[66]

Pervasive corruption was attributable less to the salary level of Russian engineers than to the prevailing culture and young engineers' expectations. Industrial development promised enormous fortunes for those with luck or connections. In Baku during the early oil boom, people greeted each other not by saying "hello" but with "is it gushing yet?" Stories of quick wealth from oil encouraged many local secondary school graduates to seek admission to the Mining Institute.[67] Similar fantasies possessed Paton's fellow students at the Transport Institute:

> One of them . . . dreamt aloud of a profitable job in the administration of a railway, of the lucrative position of a chief of a railway division, of well-paying contracts. He hinted directly at an all-powerful relative with important connections. . . . Another . . . was telling breathlessly somebody else's story about adroit road-builders who could "make money out of pure air."[68]

Successful engineers could reap large financial rewards for honest work as well as for dubious activities. V.N. Ipatieff's account of receiving 3,000 rubles for a single consulting job involving two days every two months is famous, but hardly typical.[69] The "stars" of Russian academic and business life could hold a number of academic positions and/or directorships simultaneously. Serving on the boards of corporations while working for the government was not unusual, and such behavior became more common as Russia's economy became more complex. It also raised thorny ethical issues involving conflict of interest.

The range of engineers' legal incomes varied tremendously (see Tables 3.4 and 3.5). For every talented and savvy expert like Ipatieff or entrepreneur like Avdakov, dozens of engineers were barely scraping by on inadequate salaries.

Table 3.4

Representative Starting Salaries for Engineers
(in rubles per year)

1896	**Rubles**
Teacher at technical school	1,200
Chemist in sugar refinery	840-1,200
Assistant chief of railroad depot	1,600
Instructor in distillery	1,800
1914	
Teacher at technical school	1,500
Factory engineer	900
Engineer to supervise steam engines	1,200
Railroad engineer	2,400
Position in factory shop (*tsekh*)	900-1,200
Railroad line engineer	1,200
Director of technical bureau	2,400-3,600
Construction engineer	2,100
Zemstvo engineer	2,400
Teacher of math and physics	2,500
Teacher in railroad technical school	1,700
Director of city electrical station	3,000
Assistant chief of railroad maintenance	1,800-2,400
Mining engineer	3,600

Source: Izvestiia Iuzhno-russkogo obshchestva tekhnologov, no. 4 (1896/97): 44, and no. 1 (1914): 1-12. The salaries for 1896 are those actually received by members placed in positions with the help of the society. The data for 1914 are based on positions listed with the society by employers, only some of which were actually filled at the salaries indicated. None of the salary figures include the value of housing and food allowances or state dwellings, which were perquisites of some positions.

If the rewards of success in private enterprise were enormous, the risks were at least as great. Many engineers preferred to avoid the gamble, opting for government positions which guaranteed salaries and pensions.[70]

Young engineers frequently reported difficulty finding "suitable" positions, yet Russian industry remained woefully short of personnel with higher technical education. The geometric increase in engineering students produced a glut of engineers in some geographic locations and in particular specialties, but did not begin to meet Russia's need for trained personnel. Russia's threefold increase in engineering students in the years 1896-1902 should be

Table 3.5

Reported Annual Income
Members of South Russian Society of Technologists, 1898

More than 6,000 rubles per year	1
4,000 to 6,000	4
3,000 to 4,000	17
2,000 to 3,000	50
1,800 to 2,000	46
1,500 to 1,800	56
1,200 to 1,500	60
Less than 1,200	22
No information	29
Unemployed	5

Source: Izvestiia Iuzhno-russkogo obshchestva tekhnologov, no. 2 (1897/98): 20. These figures represent members who were required to pay a percentage of their annual salary as dues to the organization. This tended to exclude lower-paid or financially troubled individuals. Engineers without permanent employment were exempt from membership dues.

compared to the tenfold increase in engineers in the United States in the decade 1890-1900 and to the enormous expansion in Germany and Hungary in the period before World War I.[71] Many positions which should have been occupied by diplomaed engineers went by default to individuals who learned their skills on the job. The reaction of these *praktiki* to the appearance of institute graduates lacking applied skills was frequently hostile. The metallurgical engineer M.A. Pavlov recounted how a lab technician at his first workplace, fearing competition from a school-educated engineer, put sand in Pavlov's test samples to distort the results.[72]

Some of the *praktiki* were students who had failed to complete courses at technical institutes because of academic or financial difficulties. There were intermittent proposals to accord these individuals some sort of formal status, and in a few cases this was accomplished.[73] It would be valuable to know how many laboratory assistants, technicians, and other middle-level personnel came from the ranks of dropouts. These individuals shared at least some characteristics with the graduate engineers, but also had much in common with the *praktiki* who acquired all their knowledge on the job. The problem of the *praktiki* took on a particularly sharp meaning in the Stalin era, when political leaders sought to reassert the virtues of uneducated specialists.[74] As this discussion makes clear, the conflicts that climaxed in Stalin's Cultural Revolution had a long history.

The best way to examine the career patterns of engineers would be a thorough analysis of the biographies of technical institute graduates. Unfortunately, the availability of institutional anniversary volumes providing biographical information decreases as we approach 1917. There are some thorough publications for individual institutes covering the mid-nineteenth century, and a few that reach to 1905, but very little covering the period 1905-17, which is likely to be the most interesting. Memoirs for this period are also scarce.[75]

Examination of the biographical materials available on graduates of the engineering schools provides overwhelming confirmation of the "ministerial" pattern. This is particularly true of the Transport Institute, and somewhat less the case for the Mining Institute.[76] The more "practical" schools, as we might expect, produced graduates with more diverse career patterns.

The importance of Witte's new polytechnical institutes is underlined when we look at the career patterns of graduates of the Electrotechnical Institute. Given the prominent role of electrical engineers and electricity in Russian industrialization, the institute might have been expected to play an important role in new career paths. Yet the institute, operated by the Ministry of Internal Affairs (MVD), graduated specialists who overwhelmingly remained in the employ of the MVD. Their activity in local urban lighting, electrical supply, telephone, telegraph, tram, and other electrical services provides a good measure of the diffusion of electrical technology in the country. But few of these engineers branched out into private enterprise, at least in the period before 1907. The St. Petersburg and Moscow technical institutes produced far more of the private sector electrical engineers.[77]

Information regarding individuals is both more interesting and riskier to use. Lacking detailed biographical data on a representative sample of engineers, there is a danger of being misled by the experiences of a few individuals. Yet it is important to record the experiences of some of the trailblazers who marked out new paths.

The career of Aleksandr Andreevich Auerbakh demonstrates that among mining engineers new patterns appeared relatively early. Born in 1844, his father was a physician who managed a small family estate and factory while also dispensing medicine. Aleksandr was educated at home till age twelve, when he entered the Corps of Mining Engineers, beginning in the second class. He graduated as a Mining Engineer in 1863. He worked for the government, and tried his hand at prospecting for coal but was unsuccessful. When the corps was reorganized as the Mining Institute, he became a candidate for a faculty position, and after defending his dissertation in 1868 was sent abroad to prepare for a teaching career.

Auerbakh took up his teaching post in 1869, but maintained an interest in commercial activity, using the summers to work for private firms interested in developing coal reserves. In 1871 he resigned his professorial post to work as director of a French concern's coal mines in Russia. In 1876 he left the French firm and returned to St. Petersburg to work in various mining-related activities. He served as consultant to two coal industry firms and soon added additional consulting and technical work. In 1881 he became director of the Bogoslovskii mining district. Five years later, he founded Auerbakh and Co., Russia's first factory for producing mercury.[78]

The career of Vasilii Ivanovich Al'bitskii demonstrates the effects of economic difficulties on some engineers' early training. The son of a priest, Al'bitskii was educated at home until age ten, when he enrolled at the Vladimir Church School. He returned home almost immediately due to the family's economic circumstances, but was permitted to remain on the school's list of students. During the next two years Al'bistkii studied with the village deacon. He returned to school a month and a half prior to his group's *perekhodnyi* exams (given for promotion to the senior grades), which he passed. Once again poverty forced him to live at home and study with the local deacon, and again he was able to assimilate enough of the curriculum to pass his graduation exams.

Al'bitskii entered the Vladimir Seminary, but left after the fourth class to take a position as a tutor for a local family. During this period he studied for the entrance exams for the Petersburg Technical Institute, while "saving money for life in the capital." He survived a precarious first year at the institute and was rewarded with a state stipend in his second year. He graduated first in his class in 1877. Vyshnegradskii invited him to remain at the institute and prepare to become a professor of applied mechanics. He received a special stipend from the Ministry of Finance, spent a year abroad, and began a career as a teacher.[79]

Aleksandr Nikolaevich Bykov was inclined to the art world. His father Nikolai Dmitrievich Bykov left home for St. Petersburg, where he hoped to learn to paint, and spent some time at the Academy of Arts. He received an order to paint a church in one of the large Siberian towns, where he "somehow" (*sluchaino*) acquired shares in a gold mine that soon made him wealthy. He built a house on Vasilevskii Island in the capital and raised a large family. Aleksandr was the youngest, and was torn between the art world he learned from his father and his schoolboy inclination to democratic and populist ideas. He tried the architecture division of the Academy of Arts for a year, but left when one of his professors advised him that an artistic career demanded "all," and that if he had any doubts about his suitability he should try something else.

Against his father's wishes, Aleksandr enrolled in the Technical Institute in 1878, where he was immediately caught up in the populist political activity of the period. Despite his sympathies with the revolutionary wave, he managed to avoid direct involvement and graduated in 1883. His father's death the following year required that he and his brothers deal with the family's affairs, and he took a position at an oil refinery outside Moscow although the work was not to his taste. He spent some time working for a private railroad and in 1889 began service in the Ministry of Finance's factory inspectorate, traveling to Moscow, Tula, Smolensk, Khar'kov, and Riga. In Riga he became heavily involved in politics during 1905-6. His active role in elections to the First Duma led the MVD to demand his removal from government service, and at a minimum from the city. Offered a post in Iaroslavl, he took a cut in pay to go to St. Petersburg, where his political interests remained strong. In 1913 he was elected to the City Duma. Throughout these years he was a prolific writer and an active member of the Russian Technical Society and the Free Economic Society.[80]

Konstantin Alekseevich Zvorykin represents the type of engineer with practical experience who was recruited to teach at the new technical institutes established during Witte's tenure as minister of finance. Born in 1861, Zvorykin attended gymnasia in Vladimir and Moscow, and graduated from the Petersburg Technical Institute in 1884. After military service he worked in factories in Astrakhan, where he helped build the first river steamships. In 1887 he moved to Perm to help supervise construction at I.I. Liubimov's new plant. In 1889 he became an adjunct professor at Khar'kov Technological Institute, and in 1898 was asked to assist in setting up the laboratories at the new Kiev Polytechnical Institute. He became the institute's director in 1904.[81]

Even a cursory examination of the changes in technical career patterns and engineering organizations in the final three decades of the tsarist era provides evidence that must be added to our evaluation of the economic and social processes unfolding at that time. Expansion of the technical education system generated large numbers of graduate specialists with training in new disciplines. Where Russia's earlier industrialization had relied heavily on foreign specialists, after 1905 the great majority of engineers were Russians, even when the investment capital was foreign.[82] These Russian engineers followed career patterns that were far more diverse than those of earlier generations, and engaged in professional activity that reflected a maturing economic environment. Their experience suggests that there is nothing in the Russian soul, psyche, or temperament that precluded the development of a modern industrial system.

Conclusion

By the outbreak of World War I, many Russian engineers had developed a sophisticated professional consciousness. The major barrier to constituting themselves as a profession in the manner of engineers in other Continental nations remained opposition from the tsarist government. Yet, alongside the picture of Russian engineers seeking an all-encompassing professional organization must be set an appreciation of the very real (and changing) tensions within the profession.

While wartime conditions gave the government a rationale for preventing convocation of an All-Russian Congress of Engineers, its handling of the wartime economy also convinced large numbers of engineers that the autocracy was a disaster in economic and technical terms as well as politically.[83]

Following the February Revolution, engineers returned to the professional agenda they had established before the war. They convened an all-Russian congress, sought to establish a unified engineering society, and devoted particular attention to establishing an identity distinct from both workers and management. Although western experience would lead us to expect engineers to be staunch supporters of a "bourgeois" regime, many Russian engineers were quite susceptible to the Bolsheviks' appeals. What there was of a technocratic movement in Russia found allure in an ideology promising rapid economic growth and technical transformation.[84] Some regarded the new regime as an opportunity to settle old grievances, while others saw the Bolsheviks as the only group capable of protecting their property and even their lives in an era of increasing anarchy.[85] Still others believed the Bolsheviks represented the best chance to defeat Russia's enemies.[86] If they did not welcome the Bolsheviks, many engineers were at least willing to give them a chance. Had they known what the new regime would mean for their profession, many—but not all—might have reconsidered.[87]

Notes

1. My formulation is presented in more detail in the Introduction to this volume, 3-6. It owes much to the work of Magali Sarfatti Larson, *The Rise of Professionalism: A Sociological Analysis* (Berkeley: University of California Press, 1977); Steven Brint, *In an Age of Experts: The Changing Role of Professionals in Politics and Public Life* (Princeton, NJ: Princeton University Press, 1994); Eliot Freidson, *Professionalism Reborn: Theory, Prophecy and Policy* (Chicago, IL: University of Chicago Press, 1994); Freidson, *Professional Powers: A Study of the Institutionalization of Formal Knowledge* (Chicago, IL: University of Chicago Press, 1986); and Thomas L. Haskell, ed., *The Authority of Experts: Studies in History and Theory* (Bloomington: Indiana University Press, 1984).

I have also benefited enormously from the growing literature on engineers in Europe and the United States. The most important sources on American engineers are Edwin Layton, *The Revolt of the Engineers* (Cleveland: The Press of Case Western Reserve University, 1971); David F. Noble, *America By Design: Science, Technology and the Rise of Corporate Capitalism* (New York: Alfred A. Knopf, 1977); Monte A. Calvert, *The Mechanical Engineer in America, 1830-1910* (Baltimore, MD: Johns Hopkins University Press, 1967); Daniel H. Calhoun, *The American Civil Engineer, Origins and Conflict* (Cambridge, MA: MIT Press, 1960); and Thomas P. Hughes, *American Genesis: A Century of Invention and Technological Enthusiasm* (New York:

Viking, 1989). On French engineers, see the work of John Hubbel Weiss, *The Making of Technological Man* (Cambridge, MA: MIT Press, 1982); and Weiss, "Bridges and Barriers: Narrowing Access and Changing Structure in the French Engineering Profession, 1800-1850," in *Professions and the French State, 1700-1900,* ed. Gerald L. Geison (Philadelphia: University of Pennsylvania Press, 1984), 15-65; Terry Shinn, *L'École Polytechnique 1794-1914: Savoir scientifique et pouvoir social* (Paris: Presses la fondation nationale des sciences politiques, 1980); and Shinn, "From 'Corps' to 'Profession': The Emergence and Definition of Industrial Engineering in Modern France," in *The Organization of Science and Technology in France, 1808-1914*, eds. Robert Fox and George Weisz (New York: Cambridge University Press, 1980). On Germany, see Kees Gispen, *New Profession, Old Order: Engineers and German Society, 1814-1914* (New York: Cambridge University Press, 1989); Konrad H. Jarausch, *The Unfree Professions: German Lawyers, Teachers and Engineers, 1900-1950* (New York: Oxford University Press, 1990).

2. In the American and British cases, the professionals sought to foster educational institutions. In continental Europe, where the state established and supported the specialized schools, the professionals sought to influence or even gain control of these institutions.

3. The influence of the professional community and corporate enterprise on education is discussed in detail by Noble. On the early development of the Russian engineering profession, see Harley D. Balzer "Educating Engineers: Economic Politics and Technical Training in Tsarist Russia" (Ph.D. diss., University of Pennsylvania, 1980); and Alfred J. Rieber, "Politics and Technology in Eighteenth Century Russia," *Science in Context* 4, no. 2 (Summer 1995): 341-68; and idem, "The Rise of Engineers in Russia," *Cahiers du Monde Russe et Soviétique* 31, no. 4 (Octobre-Décembre 1990): 539-68.

4. My description of the ministerial pattern is derived from Donald W. Green "Industry and the Engineering Ascendancy: A Comparative Study of the American and Russian Engineering Elites, 1870-1920" (Ph.D. diss., University of California at Berkeley, 1972).

5. Ben Eklof, John Bushnell, and Larissa Zakharova, eds., *Russia's Great Reforms* (Bloomington: Indiana University Press, 1994); Harley D. Balzer, "The Origin and Legacy of Russian Professions," paper delivered at conference on "The Great Reforms in Russian History, 1861-1974," University of Pennsylvania, 25-28 May 1989.

6. Vyshnegradskii's *kruzhok*, called the Pentagonal Society, is described in Balzer, "Educating Engineers," 141-53. The group may be instructively compared with early leaders of the American engineering profession (such as John Sweet, Alexander Holley, and Robert Thurston) described by Layton, *The Revolt of the Engineers*, 36 ff., Emil Otto Fritsch and his colleagues who founded the journal *Deutsche Bauzeitung* which generated support for the *technische Hochschule* (Gispen, *New Profession, Old Order,* 91-98), and the founders of the École Centrale portrayed by Weiss in *The Making of Technological Man*, 16-25.

Vyshnegradskii's circle was not the first instance of a small group of specialists taking the initiative to expand technical education. He had himself been recruited in an earlier initiative. Under Finance Minister A.M. Kniazhevich, a small group including mining engineers N.A. Perets and K.F. Butenev, along with E.N. Andreev, oversaw the development of Russia's first serious engineering institutes. They recruited Russian specialists with European experience, including Vyshnegradskii, D.I. Mendeleev, and N.P. Il'in. See Balzer, "Educating Engineers," 25-29, 39-42.

7. The Pentagonal Society is mentioned in several sources, but the only place I have found all five members named is in the second edition of *Bol'shaia sovetskaia entsiklopediia*, vol. 9, 542. The biographies of individual members frequently discuss the existence of the group but do not name all of the participants. On Kirpichev, in addition to entries in the standard encyclopedias, see *Liudi Russkoi nauki* vol. 4, 340-47; and "Viktor L'vovich Kirpichev," in *Vestnik vysshei shkoly*, no. 6 (1959): 59-63. The collection *Illiustrirovannyi sbornik materialov k istorii vozniknoveniia Kievskogo politekhnicheskogo instituta. Pamiati Viktora L'vovicha Kirpicheva* (Kiev, 1914) contains a good biography and also reprints several of Kirpichev's speeches. Also see the obituary, "Pamiati V.L. Kirpicheva," in *Russkaia mysl'*, November 1913, 130-34. There is also a Soviet-era biography, A.A. Chekanov, *Viktor L'vovich Kirpichev, 1845-1913* (Moscow: Nauka, 1982). Chekanov mentions the Pentagonal Society on page 20, noting the role of Borodin and Petrov.

8. For Petrov, see *Liudi Russkoi nauki* vol. 4, 240-46; *Bol'shaia sovetskaia entsiklopediia*, 2nd ed., vol. 32, 599; *Brokhaus Efron* vol. 45, 363-64; and L.I. Gumilevskii, *Russkie inzhenery* (Moscow, 1953), 189-96.

9. Aleksandr Parfenevich Borodin should not be confused with Aleksandr Porfir'evich Borodin, the chemist and composer. On Borodin the engineer, see *Bol'shaia sovetskaia entsiklopediia*, 2nd ed., 592; Gumilevskii, 196-98; and Donald W. Green, "Industrialization and the Engineering Ascendancy: A Comparative Study of the American and Russian Engineering Elites: 1870-1920," (Ph.D. diss., University of California at Berkeley, 1972), 240-43. The fullest biography is S.M. Zhitkov, *Biografii inzhenerov putei soobshcheniia*, 3 vols. (St. Petersburg, 1889-1902) vol. 3, 24-36. Much of Zhitkov's material is a verbatim reprint of the memorial issue of the journal *Inzhener*, no. 4/5 (1898). Borodin's numerous articles in *Inzhener* are an invaluable source.

10. For Koturnitskii, see Voronov, 519; and N.G. Filippov, *Nauchno-tekhnicheskie obshchestva Rossii (1866-1917 gg.)* (Moscow, 1975), 42.

11. The most extensive biography of Vyshnegradskii is in *Liudi Russkoi nauki* vol. 4, 218-26. There are entries in all three editions of the *Bol'shaia sovetskaia entsiklopediia*. The fullest appreciation of Vyshnegradskii's achievements as a scholar is Kirpichev's May 1895 memorial address: V.L. Kirpichev, *Ivan Alekseevich Vyshnegradskii, kak professor i uchenyi* (St. Petersburg, 1895). Also see Gumilevskii, *Russkie inzhenery*, 200-204.

12. Vyshnegradskii was the son of a priest; Petrov and Borodin were from the nobility; and Kirpichev was the grandson of a peasant who had achieved officer's rank during the Napoleonic War. Their educations were highly individualized, with subsequent teaching at the Petersburg Technical Institute being the common thread.

13. Borodin's term as chief engineer included the period during which Witte was director of the Southwestern Railway.

14. Borodin's experience in railroad work led him to views somewhat different from Vyshnegradskii's. He opposed government operation of railroads, asserting that

supervision by government ministries turned good scholars into "*chinovniki* and bunglers." *Inzhener*, no. 19 (1895): 109.

15. For example, see Borodin's series of articles called "Amerikanskie zametki" in *Inzhener*, nos. 7/8, 9, and 12 (1883), and nos. 6 and 9 (1884). No. 6 (1884) dealt with the "marvels" of technical development in America. Russian engineers were not unusual in their tendency toward "Americanism." A number of French engineers demonstrated similar leanings. Theodore Zeldin, *France, 1848-1945: Ambition and Love* (Oxford: Oxford University Press, 1979), 93.

16. N.P. Petrov, *Kakova dolzhna byt' vysshaia tekhnicheskaia shkola* (St. Petersburg, 1897), 2, 5. For an extended treatment of "Americanism" and American influence in Russia, see Hans Rogger "*Amerikanism* and the Economic Development of Russia," *Comparative Studies in Society and History* (July 1981): 382-420. Rogger's emphasis is somewhat different from my own, but I fully agree with his assessment that

> although it was Europe that played by far the largest role in Russian economic development, and before 1914 an almost exclusive one, it was America that furnished the operative values, the imagery, the symbols, and the myths of a superior industrial civilization. . . . (390)

The mythology of America and "Amerikanism" became even stronger in the Soviet period. See Kendall E. Bailes, "The American Connection: Ideology and the Transfer of American Technology to the Soviet Union, 1917-1941," *Comparative Studies in Society and History* (July 1981): 421-48; and Stephen Kotkin, *Magnetic Mountain: Stalinism as a Civilization* (Berkeley: University of California Press, 1995) 125-26, 363.

17. V.L. Kirpichev, *S'ezdy inzhenerov. Rech', skazannom zasluzhnym professorom V.L. Kirpichevym pri otkrytii S'ezda deiatelei po gornomu delu, metallurgii i mashinostroenniu, 17 aprelia 1913 g.* (St. Petersburg, n.d.), 7.

18. *S-Peterburgskii politekhnicheskii institut imperatora Petra velikogo 1902 g.–1952 g.*, 2 vols. (Paris, 1952, 1958), vol. 2, 107.

19. S.D. Kirpichnikov, "L.I. Lutugin i Soiuz Soiuzov," *Byloe* 34, no. 6 (1925): 136; and Filippov, *Nauchno-tekhnicheskie obshchestva Rossii*, 53-54.

20. See the article by Abragamsom on Borodin's work as editor of *Inzhener* in no. 4/5 (1898) 133-38.

21. See Balzer, "Educating Engineers," 401, 469-70.

22. *Izvestiia Iuzhno-russkogo obshchestva tekhnologov* [hereafter *IIuROT*], no. 4 (1896/97): 43.

23. *IIuROT*, no. 2 (1897/98): 21-22.

24. *IIuROT*, no. 2 (1901):18; no. 3 (1902): 35; no. 11 (1903): 177; and no. 11/12 (1905): 163.

25. The Russian engineer glut was cyclical, reflecting the combination of economic downturn and increased numbers of engineers. It differed from the situation in Germany and other Central European nations, where the overproduction of engineers became chronic. As Kees Gispen has noted:

> The shortage of technical personnel anticipated in the 1880s and the excitement about industrialization during the 1890s had produced a boom in technical and engineering education that turned into a bust in the decade preceding

1914. The tremendous supply was absorbed only because large numbers of engineers and other technicians found positions for which they were overqualified, and in which they were underpaid and otherwise treated in accordance with the unmerciful logic of supply and demand. Many worked for years as menial copyists and draftsmen, being paid less than what (skilled) blue-collar workers earned.
Kees Gispen, "Engineers in Wilhelmian Germany: Professionalization, Deprofessionalization, and the Development of Nonacademic Technical Education," in *German Professions, 1800-1950,* eds. Geoffrey Cocks and Konrad Jarausch (New York: Oxford University Press, 1990), 111. Chronic overproduction of engineers in Russia was a Stalinist achievement, perpetuated by his successors.

26. See, for example, the career of V.I. Al'bitskii, described on page 77.

27. This point is suggested, although not documented, by James C. McClelland *Autocrats and Academics: Education, Culture and Society in Tsarist Russia* (Chicago, IL: University of Chicago Press, 1979), 106-7. Even the most rudimentary statistics prove the relative "democracy" of Russian higher schools. In *Russia's Educational Heritage* (Pittsburgh, PA: Carnegie Institute Press, 1950), 290, William E. Johnson provides a table showing that members of the nobility and officials constituted less than one quarter of the student body at five technical institutes in 1914, while the categories "merchants and citizens" and "workers and craftsmen" represented more than 50 percent of the enrollments. This may be compared to the situation in France, where schools like the École Centrale and École Polytechnique admitted far fewer students from the middle and lower classes. See Weiss, *The Making of Technological Man,* 76-77.

28. The Technical Society did play an important role in fostering informal networks and providing opportunities for technical personnel to meet with civic and government leaders. For more on its limited capacity to express professional interests, see Harley D. Balzer "The Imperial Russian Technical Society," *Modern Encyclopedia of Russian and Soviet History* (Gulf Breeze, FL: Academic International Press, 1983) vol. 32, 176-80.

29. *Inzhener,* no. 1/2 (1882): vi; no. 1 (1892): 11.

30. *Tekhnicheskoe obrazovanie,* no. 4 (1897): 347.

31. Kirpichnikov, "L.I. Lutugin," 135-36.

32. Shmuel Galai, *The Liberation Movement in Russia, 1900-1905* (Cambridge: Cambridge University Press, 1973), 234-35; Filippov *Nauchno-tekhnicheskii obshchestva Rossii*; and L.K. Erman, *Intelligentsiia v pervoi russkoi revoliutsii* (Moscow, 1966), 242, 306-7. Erman is not fully reliable. The most comprehensive account of the Union of Unions is by far Jonathan Sanders, "The Union of Unions: Economic, Political and Human Rights Organizations in the 1905 Russian Revolution" (Ph.D. diss., Columbia University, 1985). For a solid overall history, see Abraham Ascher, *The Revolution of 1905: Russia in Disarray* (Stanford, CA: Stanford University Press, 1988).

33. The "political-economic section" of *Vestnik obshchestva tekhnologov,* edited by M.V. Bernatskii, appeared beginning with no. 3 (1905). For an article critical of the lockout see no. 11 (1905): 475-76. There is an editorial endorsing the eight-hour day in no. 3 (1906): 141.

34. *Tekhnicheskii sbornik i vestnik promyshlennosti*, no. 12 (1904), 418-20. For an account of 1905 in Moscow, see Laura Engelstein, *Moscow, 1905: Working-Class Organization and Political Conflict* (Stanford, CA: Stanford University Press, 1982).

35. Ibid.; and Erman, *Intelligentsiia v pervoi russkoi revoliutsii* 156-57, 206-7, and 242.

36. L.N. Liubimov, "Iz zhizni inzhenera putei soobshcheniia," in *Russkaia starina* 157 (March 1914): 584-85.

37. E.O. Paton, *Vospominaniia* (Moscow, 1956), 51-52. Paton was in Kiev. Neutrality may have been somewhat harder to maintain for engineers in the capital cities.

38. Krasin's wife recalled, "Now that business offered better prospects and politics were at a discount, all his energies were concentrated on acquiring the necessary technical knowledge which he hoped later on to apply to the numberless neglected opportunities in his own country." Liubov' Krasina, *Leonid Krasin: His Life and Work* (London, 1929), 40. Timothy Edward O'Connor's recent biography of Krasin emphasizes his break with Lenin and his radical revolutionary stance: "Political reaction at home and organizational defeat abroad, not engineering and familial considerations, were ultimately responsible for Krasin's disassociation from the revolution." O'Connor concurs with Krasina's version for the period after 1911, at least "until more archival maerials become available." *The Engineer of Revolution: L.B. Krasin and the Bolsheviks, 1870-1926* (Boulder, CO: Westview Press, 1992), 114, 126. A survey of students at the Petersburg Technical Institute in 1910 found that political affiliations had moved well to the right of those expressed in 1905, and that students "even" were heard to express anti-Semitism. M.V. Bernatskii, ed., *K kharakteristike sovremennogo studenchestva* (St. Petersburg, 1911).

39. One aspect of organizational membership that has not been adequately investigated is the degree of turnover. Research being conducted by Nathan Brooks on chemical societies indicates a significant level of turnover, in this case replacing university graduates with institute-trained chemists. Brooks's data suggest that we should be alert to similar processes in other scientific and professional associations. I am grateful for his willingness to share this information prior to publication.

40. Starting in 1907, *Elektrichestvo* changed the name of its eleventh section from "Electrical apparatus. State of electrical technology in various countries. Exhibitions and Congresses.," to "Professional Life."

41. Two of the leading figures of the pre-1917 period, M.A. Shatelen and P.S. Osadchii, remained very active after the Bolshevik revolution. See Jonathan Coopersmith, *The Electrification of Russia, 1880-1926* (Ithaca, NY: Cornell University Press, 1992), especially 21-27. On the activism of American electrical engineers, see Layton, *The Revolt of the Engineers*, 26, 38-39, 84-86.

42. M.A. Shatelen, *Russkie elektrotekhniki XIX veka* (Moscow and Leningrad, 1955), 385-86.

43. A.V. Ol'shvang, "On Organizing an 'All-Russian Society of Electrical Technicians,'" *Elektrichestvo*, no. 3 (1909): 122-25.

44. *Elektrichestvo*, no. 2 (1909): 83.

45. P.S. Osadchii, *K voprosu o printsipakh professional'noi etiki inzhenerov* (St. Petersburg, 1911).

46. *Elektrichestvo*, no. 2 (1909): 83.

47. Ibid., 82.

48. V.L. Kirpichev, *S"ezdy inzhenerov* (St. Petersburg, n.d. [1913?]).

49. Shatelen, *Russkie elektrotekhniki XIX veka*, 374-75; M.A. Pavlov, *Vospominaniia metallurga* (Moscow, 1943) 6, 76-77; and the fictional account by Mikhail L. Slonimskii, *Inzhenery* (Leningrad: Sovetskii pisatel', 1971; 1950). Also see Balzer, "Educating Engineers," 367, 423; Heather Hogan, *Forging Revolution: Metalworkers, Managers, and the State in St. Petersburg, 1890-1914* (Bloomington: Indiana University Press, 1993); Susan McCaffray, *The Politics of Industrialization in Tsarist Russia: The Association of Southern Coal and Steel Producers, 1874-1914* (DeKalb: Northern Illinois University Press, 1996); Thomas C. Owen, *Russian Corporate Capitalism from Peter the Great to Perestroika* (New York: Oxford University Press, 1995); and John P. McKay, *Pioneers for Profit: Foreign Entrepreneurship and Russian Industrialization, 1885-1913* (Chicago, IL: University of Chicago Press, 1970).

50. The role of physicians' Pirogov Congresses as a model for engineers to emulate is discussed in *Vestnik manufakturnoi promyshlennosti*, no. 31/7 (1911/12): 1690.

51. Ibid. The public statement that the new engineers' organization had to be independent of existing institutions is particularly striking.

52. Kirpichev, *S"ezdy inzhenerov*; on Grinevetskii's role, see *Inzhener*, no. 7 (1915): 224.

53. From *Izvestiia obshchestva gornykh inzhenerov*, no. 7 (1913): 18-20. A full translation of the program is provided in Balzer, "Educating Engineers," 471-73.

54. *Inzhener*, no. 7 (1915): 224.

55. Ibid., 224-26. The quotation is on page 226.

56. Kendall E. Bailes, *Technology and Society Under Lenin and Stalin* (Princeton, NJ: Princeton University Press, 1978), 42.

57. A striking feature of professionalism is the extent to which leadership falls to individuals who have established credentials as leading educators or practitioners, regardless of their organizational abilities or ability to "represent" most members of the profession.

58. Nancy Mandelker Frieden, *Russian Physicians in an Era of Reform and Revolution, 1856-1905* (Princeton, NJ: Princeton University Press, 1981). For biographies of some of the engineers who became successful entrepreneurs, see Alfred J. Rieber, *Merchants and Entrepreneurs in Imperial Russia* (Chapel Hill: University of North Carolina Press, 1982); and Ruth Amende Roosa, "The Association of Industry and Trade, 1906-1914" (Ph.D. diss., Columbia University, 1967).

59. Stephen P. Timoshenko, *As I Remember* (Princeton, NJ: D. van Nostrand, 1968), 63.

60. Liubimov, "Iz zhizni," February 1914, 354. Also see August 1913, 220, for Liubimov's genuine outrage when a classmate refused to assist him with employment difficulties.

61. S.Iu. Witte, *Vospominaniia* (Moscow: Izdatel'stvo sotsial'no-ekonomichesko i literatury, 1960), vol. 1, 142.

62. Paton, *Vospominaniia*, 30-31. The quotation is on page 31.

63. A.I. Del'vig, *Polveka russkoi zhizni, Vospominaniia 1820-1870* (Moscow, 1930), vol. 1, 91, 293; Liubimov, April 1913, 95. Also see Liubimov, May 1913, 391, for an account of his lack of skills when called upon to conduct actual railroad construction. A similar situation is described in Garin-Mikhailovskii's novel *Inzhenery* (Moscow: Khudozhestvannaiia literatura, 1964), 231, 388-89.

64. See Liubimov, "Iz zhizni"; Paton, *Vospominaniia*; and Garin-Mikhailovski, *Inzhenery*. For a discussion of corruption in the framework of Russia's business climate, see Owen, *Russian Corporate Capitalism*, 66-67.

65. Liubimov, "Iz zhizni," July 1913, 21; and Garin-Mikhailovskii, *Inzhenery*, 233. Vyshnegradskii's simultaneously occupying important government posts and serving on the boards of private companies gave rise to gossip and accusations, but rules about conflict of interest were never really worked out in Russia. The difficulties on this score since the collapse of the USSR represent another problem that cannot be blamed solely on the communist experience, suggesting that it will be difficult to cure.

66. Layton, *The Revolt of the Engineers*, 29, 41. Again, in both countries electrical engineers, as practitioners of the leading technology, played a key role.

67. Pavlov, *Vospominaniia metallurga*, 29-30.

68. Paton, *Vospominaniia*, 25. He goes on to describe one scheme in which contractors on the Trans-Siberian Railroad were to assemble and install bridges using metal supplied by the railroad. Since the contract included large penalties for late delivery, the contractors arranged with the mills to delay shipments, and everyone shared in the proceeds. There are similar accounts in Liubimov, "Iz zhizni," and Garin-Mikhailovskii, *Inzhenery*.

69. V.N. Ipatieff, *Life of a Chemist* (Stanford, CA: Stanford University Press, 1946), 169.

70. In addition to a high degree of job security and the guarantee of a pension, government positions also frequently provided other perquisites, such as housing and food allowances. These arrangements could vary widely and must be taken into account when assessing the relative salaries earned by Russian government employees.

71. Layton, *The Revolt of the Engineers*, 4; Gispen, *New Profession, Old Order*; and Mária M. Kovács, *Liberal Professions and Illiberal Politics: Hungary from the Habsburgs to the Holocaust* (New York: Oxford University Press, 1994). In Russia, a very high percentage of engineers sought to remain in the major cultural centers, particularly the capital cities. There was intense competition for positions in Moscow and St. Petersburg, while enormous regions, particularly Siberia, were desperately short of trained personnel.

72. Pavlov, *Vospominaniia metallurga*, 97.

73. The protracted effort to establish an examination system for the rank "Tekhnik putei soobshcheniia" is described in Balzer, "Educating Engineers," 341-43.

74. Bailes, *Technology and Society*, 306-9 and passim; and his "Stalin and the Making of a New Elite: A Comment" *Slavic Review* 39, no. 2 (June 1980): 286-89.

75. For example, Fenin's excellent account of the southern metallurgical industry, published in Germany, covers only the period up to 1905. A second volume, dealing with the later period, may still exist in manuscript form in archives captured during World War II. A.I. Fenin, *Vospominaniia inzhenera: K istorii obshchestvennogo i khoziastvennogo razvitiia Rossii (1883-1906gg)* (Prague, 1938). This quite rare volume has recently been made available in English: Aleksandr I. Fenin, *Coal and Politics in Imperial Russia: Memoirs of a Russian Mining Engineer*, trans. Alexandre Fediaevsky, ed. Susan P. McCaffray (DeKalb, IL: Northern Illinois University Press, 1990).

76. For the Transport Institute, see S. Zhitkov, ed., *Biografii inzhenerov putei soobshcheniia*, 3 vols. (St. Petersburg, 1893, 1899). On the Mining Institute, see *Spisok lits, okonchivshikh kurs v Gornom Institute s 1847 po 1908 god (po vypuskam)* (St. Petersburg, 1908); and for the early years, *Nauchno-istoricheskii sbornik, izdanyi gornym institutom ko dniu ego stoletnego iubileia 21 oktiabria 1873 goda* (St. Petersburg, 1873).

77. *Avtobiografii okonchivshikh kurs v Elektrotekhnicheskom institute, 1889-1904* (St. Petersburg, 1908). Coopersmith, *The Electrification of Russia*, 25-26. The MVD responsibility for the Electrotechnical Institute seems to have had origins in both the history of technology and political concerns. Electrical technology evolved in part out of telegraphy, which was an MVD responsibility. We would expect the Interior Ministry to pay particular attention to any technology related to communications. They were not willing to cede it to the Ministry of Transportation, which at this time was strongly influenced by the more liberal Ministry of Finance.

78. Pushkinskii dom, f. 377, d. Auerbakh, ll. 2-4 ob.

79. Pushkinskii dom, f. 377, d. Al'bitskii, ll. 7-11 ob.

80. Pushkinskii dom, f. 377, d. Bykov.

81. Pushkinskii dom, f. 377, d. Zvorykin, ll. 1-2.

82. For example, Fenin notes that where there were about ten Russian engineers in the Donbas in 1890; by 1913 the number had grown to several hundred. *Vospominanie inzhenera*, 8.

83. Lewis H. Seigelbaum, *The Politics of Industrial Mobilization in Russia, 1914-1917: A Study of the War-Industries Committees* (New York: St. Martin's Press, 1983).

84. S.V. Utechin discusses Mendeleev's "gradualism" as a Russian variety of technocracy in *Russian Political Thought: A Concise History* (New York, 1964), 183-84. He suggests, "The democratic idea was never particularly attractive to the technical intelligentsia, and the failure of democracy in 1917 must have made even those who had tended toward it doubt the validity of democratic premises and strengthened the elitist tendencies in their thinking." A more nuanced analysis of the technocratic strains among Russian engineers is provided by Alfred Rieber in "The Rise of Engineers in Russia." Rieber emphasizes the influence of French St. Simonianism, imported along with French specialists in the early nineteenth century. He argues that Russian engineers' education and career experiences:

mutually reinforced their collective belief that technology was the solution to social problems. Thus, they came to identify the general welfare with the growth of their influence within the bureaucracy. . . . They believed that the state should take responsibility for planning and developing both communications and natural resources; they remained suspicious of the private sector with its particularist, crassly materialist aims. The dominant values in shaping the ethos of the Russian engineers, internationalism and technocracy, became deeply embedded in the culture. They survived major political upheavals and remained a powerful current in Soviet intellectual life in the late twentieth century. (563)

85. Bailes, *Technology and Society*, 24, which includes reference to Ipatieff's statement that he owed his life to the Bolsheviks, from *Life of a Chemist*, 257.

86. Ipatieff, *Life of a Chemist*, 256-67; and Paton,*Vospominaniia*, 66.

87. For a discussion of the engineering profession in the Soviet period, see Harley Balzer, "Engineers: The Rise and Decline of a Social Myth," in *Science and the Soviet Social Order,* ed. Loren Graham (Cambridge: Harvard University Press, 1990), 141-67; and Olga V. Kryshtanovskaia, *Inzhenery: Stanovlenie i razvitie profession-al'noi gruppy* (Moscow: Nauka, 1989).

4

Politics and Medical
Professionalization After 1905

JOHN F. HUTCHINSON

The years from 1900 to 1907 were a watershed in the history of medical professionalization in Russia. Prior to 1900, community physicians employed by *zemstva* and municipalities led the drive to achieve professional goals. As Nancy Frieden has shown, they sought to establish a national professional association, demanded the right to regulate their own affairs, and preached the doctrine of public service as justification for achieving a special position in society.[1] Their success, though limited, is attributable in part to the fact that they presented a united front, and in part to the political leverage which they were able to exercise. The leverage, in turn, resulted from their growing scientific expertise which, in Frieden's words, "gave substance to the medical experts' claims to authority."[2]

After 1907, the situation changed considerably. There was a good deal less unity among physicians, including community physicians, about both their goals and how to achieve them. Frieden ascribes this fragmentation to the failure of liberal assumptions about Russia's evolution into a constitutional monarchy.[3] Whether the Revolution of 1905 caused this crisis or, as will be argued below, exacerbated tensions which were already apparent among medical professionals by the turn of the century, there is no doubt that the community physicians and their national association, the Pirogov Society of Russian Physicians, lost the virtual monopoly which they had previously enjoyed in speaking for the medical profession.[4]

Another significant development apparent after 1907 is that scientific expertise, while continuing to provide physicians with some political leverage and influence, no longer served primarily to buttress the case of those who sought to free the profession from the tutelage of the state. Within the academic medical community and the senior medical bureaucracy, the idea of the physician as a medical servitor of the state enjoyed a marked revival, resulting in the formulation of plans to bind physicians more closely to the state than to each other. These plans, which reversed the predominant tendencies of the previous forty years, were elaborated by distinguished medical professionals who were broadly sympathetic to the innovations of the bacteriological revolution, but who were convinced that physicians should achieve their professional goals not by struggling for autonomy and popular acceptance but by placing their knowledge and talent at the disposal of the autocratic state.[5] The emergence of a coherent, conservative, alternative mode of medical professionalization is a useful reminder that, although the medical innovations of the nineteenth century made it reasonable for physicians to seek more power in society, they dictated neither the forms which that power should take nor the purposes for which it should be used.

This essay begins with a brief analysis of the impact of the events of 1905-7 on the course of medical professionalization, providing the political and professional context within which a conservative position could begin to take shape. Considerable attention is devoted to the work of G.E. Rein, a pioneer of antisepsis who went from a successful career as a teacher and research scholar in Kiev and St. Petersburg to become both the foremost advocate of state control and the most successful opponent of professional autonomy in Russian medical history. The argument offered here suggests that, thanks to the work of Rein, the tsarist regime was poised in the spring of 1914 for a thorough assault against both the community medical tradition and the faltering drive to professionalize Russian physicians. The outbreak of war spoiled these plans—paradoxically, considering the degree to which wars usually strengthen central governments—and played into the hands of the supporters of professional autonomy. The essay demonstrates the extent to which the argument over state control divided both medical professionals and bureaucrats, while focusing attention on the conflict which existed within the medical profession between academics and practitioners.

Medical Professionalization Before and After 1905

As Nancy Frieden has pointed out, events in the years from 1902 to 1904 were of decisive importance in politicizing Russia's community physicians.[6] As a result, the Pirogov Society openly and vociferously sided with the opposition to the regime during the Revolution of 1905. Temporary though it was, this alliance profoundly altered the course of medical professionalization. First, it effectively destroyed earlier efforts by physicians to achieve an autonomous corporate status similar to that enjoyed by Russian lawyers. Second, it sowed dissension within the Pirogov Society itself, lessening its hitherto unblemished reputation for scientific integrity and civic respectability. Third, the failure of the opposition, coupled with the revival of the government and the conservative gentry in the countryside, caused a severe and prolonged crisis of confidence among the community physicians who had previously considered themselves the natural leaders of the medical profession. Finally, and perhaps most important, the 1905 alliance revealed the potentially subversive nature of the community medical tradition, confirming bureaucrats in their belief that organizations of physicians, like those of other incipient professionals, were untrustworthy unless carefully controlled and policed.

The politicization of Russia's community physicians is demonstrated by the resolutions of the 1904 Pirogov Congress, by the demands of the March 1905 "Cholera Congress," and by the formation of the Union of All-Russian Medical Personnel.[7] Frieden has rightly emphasized the extent to which many community physicians, frustrated by their inability to secure the redress of long-standing grievances, were forced to take political positions in pursuit of professional goals. Nevertheless, such an argument scarcely explains the peculiar combination of zeal, intolerance, and naiveté that characterized the Union of All-Russian Medical Personnel.[8] The union's program assumed that what brought physicians together as medical workers would also bring them together as citizens, that because they all desired the same improvements in public health, they would naturally agree on the political action necessary to achieve them. In other words, it proclaimed the ethical obligations of physicians to society and the political imperatives attendant on them. One of its goals was to engage in the "moral evaluation of the sociopolitical misdemeanors" of all physicians.[9] Moreover, the union wanted to break down distinctions between physicians and other medical personnel. In the effort to ally medical workers with the working class, it was even prepared to countenance the strike as a legitimate political weapon. Clearly, the union's program went much further than was necessary for sober professionals seeking redress of grievances, even in the highly charged atmosphere of 1905. Its radicalism is attributable not merely to the frustration of ordinary community physicians, but to the extraordinary influence at the 1905 Cholera Congress of a minority of radical physicians acting in concert with numerous dissatisfied younger hospital physicians and interns. To be sure, the union did not survive the year 1905; its attempt to organize physicians collapsed along with the revolutionary movement once the regime began to reassert its authority. Nevertheless, this episode was to have long-term consequences of much greater significance than its small contribution to the events of 1905.

The revolutionary militancy of the union stood in stark contrast to earlier efforts to unify Russian physicians. These began in the 1890s under the aegis of the St. Petersburg Physicians Mutual Assistance Society, itself an offshoot of the 1889 Pirogov Congress. The society's aim was to unify physicians into a professional estate (*soslovie*) with legally recognized rights of autonomy and jurisdiction.[10] By 1900, the society had more than a thousand members throughout Russia, and its leaders were discussing its transformation into a corporate professional organization that all physicians could be required by law to join. Evidently, they were attracted by the rights enjoyed by their colleagues in Germany, where Chambers of Physicians were able not only to regulate the medical activity of their members, but also to influence the government's legislation and to represent the professional interests of physicians. The existence in Russia of Councils of the Bar (discussed in Brian Levin-Stankevich's essay in this volume) suggested that the formation of Chambers of Physicians was not an unreasonable goal. The leaders of this campaign were, however, convinced of two desiderata: first, legislation to establish a corporate professional organization must follow—not precede, as it had in the case of the lawyers—the growth of professional estate conscious-ness among physicians; second, reflecting the society's initial concern with ethical and legal problems, there was to be no place in this scheme of things for youthful enthusiasts who sought to pursue material or political goals. Any suggestion of militancy was held to be out of keeping with the obliga-tions of professional responsibility.

Physicians who had worked for a decade to achieve corporate status as a professional estate were appalled and disillusioned by the events of 1905. The ringing declarations of the 1904 and 1905 Pirogov Congresses suggested that political, rather than estate, consciousness was the dominant concern of most community physicians. The formation of the union seemed to suggest that all sense of professional responsibility had been lost. As early as 1902, the president of the St. Petersburg Physicians Mutual Assistance Society warned of the danger of abandoning the cause of professional unity to "adolescents" whose "beautiful words and noble impulses" could destroy the whole endeav-or.[11] The events of 1905 seemed to prove him right. However brief the life of the union, its militant trumpeting undid years of careful work aimed at achieving an accommodation with the tsarist regime, and the supporters of corporate autonomy took years to recover from the shock. In the years to come, they were to blame their radical colleagues for spoiling the possibili-ties for moderate reform.

Disillusionment with the radicals' excursions into opposition politics was not confined to those who had supported the formation of a professional estate. Many physicians believed that it was inappropriate for a medical society or organization of physicians to take positions on political issues.[12] Doubtless some of them felt that the Pirogov Society had abandoned its earlier broad appeal to physicians as men of science and had become a mouth-piece for the most militant group of community physicians, the *zemstvo* sanitary physicians. There were also some who objected, not to the idea of a political alliance, but rather to the cut of the political cloth. Once the regime had published the October Manifesto and was seen to be reforming itself to accommodate the new legislative institutions, a number of physicians took the view that the regime deserved their loyalty and support. This group included some longtime supporters of *zemstvo* medicine and of the Pirogov Society, notably M.Ia. Kapustin. With the formation of political parties in late 1905, physicians were presented with the full spectrum of political loyalties. Although the union's logic argued that physicians should at least support the Kadets, if not revolutionary parties, some found a comfortable home in the moderate Octobrist Party, while others supported rightist and even reactionary parties. This political differentiation demoralized erstwhile supporters of the union and led to recriminations in the medical press about physicians betraying their civic duty and professional obligations.[13]

If the events of 1904-5 exacerbated tensions among physicians, what happened during the succeeding five years showed that earlier attempts to organize the profession had entirely lost their momentum. Nothing whatever was heard from those who had previously supported the formation of a professional estate. At the 1907 Pirogov Congress, held amid the intensifying climate of reaction in the *zemstva*, supporters of the 1905 union made a desperate attempt to rekindle the enthusiasm of the revolutionary period.[14] It was a dismal failure. Deadlocked on whether an organization like the union was still desirable, participants were unable to decide its proper relationship to the Pirogov Society, let alone its political role now that the Duma existed. The committee appointed to resolve these issues dispersed without making any substantive decisions.[15] Stolypin's coup of 3 June 1907 and his subsequent abandonment of plans to reform the *zemstva* were the final blow for the radicals, who had hoped to reorganize the union as a force for popular education and covert political propaganda at the local level. By 1910, when the next Pirogov Congress was held, the political climate had become so inhospitable that further proposals for the organization of the profession were simply shelved. With falling membership and declining revenues, the Pirogov Society was in serious difficulty. Already articles had begun to appear in the medical press suggesting that *zemstvo* medicine, and indeed the whole community medical tradition, was in a state of crisis.[16] Authors variously attributed the crisis to the persecution of third-element employees by conservative *zemstvo* boards, the inability of physicians to establish a powerful national professional organization, and the threat posed to traditional sanitary services by the popularity of laboratory research among younger physicians.

By 1910, in short, Russia's community physicians were in professional and political disarray. In the preceding two decades, three models of professional organization had been advanced—an autonomous professional estate, a union of medical personnel, and a more extensive and inclusive version of the Pirogov Society—but none had drawn sufficient support to unite the profession from within. Estate status was too conservative an approach to satisfy the liberals and radicals; the idea of a union was distasteful to conservatives, while its militancy was offensive to many rank-and-file physicians; the proposal for an "All-Russian" Pirogov Society was too amorphous ever to attract broad support, chiefly because its relationship to existing medical societies was unclear. Like other incipient professional groups in tsarist Russia, community physicians were now in a weaker position vis-à-vis the state than they had been for several decades prior to 1905.

The Government and the Problem of Medical Reform

What conclusions did the government draw from the behavior of physicians during the revolutionary years? Senior bureaucrats in the Ministry of the Interior (MVD), which was largely responsible for medicine and public health in the Empire, were concerned that *zemstvo* medical activities had grown too quickly and without sufficient supervision. Between 1902 and 1904, the central medical agencies of the ministry had been reorganized to provide greater financial and administrative control over the medical and sanitary activities of *zemstva* and municipalities.[17] However, the events of 1904-5 demonstrated that the threat posed by the growth of community medicine was political as well as administrative and would require a political solution. The alliance between the Pirogov Society and the opposition, not to mention the formation of the medical union, suggested that advocates of community medicine were aiming at nothing less than destruction of the existing regime. Given their influence within the profession as a whole, the creation of a professional medical estate with autonomous rights of jurisdiction was now clearly out of the question. Whatever advantages the regime might have derived from establishing Chambers of Physicians on the model of the Councils of the Bar were outweighed by the dangers of creating a legal forum for politically unreliable, even dangerous, community physicians. More than enough had been heard from them already.

Yet however much tsarist bureaucrats were determined to resist the pretensions of the community physicians, a large-scale reform of medical and sanitary affairs could not be postponed indefinitely. Cholera, plague, and other epidemic diseases could not be banished by edict. But effective action was hampered by the proliferation of responsibility among several ministers and departments.[18] Legislative action in other states showed what could be done by governments determined to reduce morbidity and mortality.[19] Reforms on such a scale were probably beyond the abilities of the career bureaucrats who staffed the central medical agencies of Russia's Ministry of the Interior. Within the ranks of the Pirogov Society, there were certainly individuals with the requisite knowledge and imagination, yet for the government to sit down with them in the wake of 1905 was unthinkable. Obviously, a fresh face was called for, but the choices were extremely limited. Whoever undertook the task would have to be unquestionably loyal to the tsarist regime, an innovator but not a radical, with sufficient nerve to battle the *zemstva* and sufficient prestige to confront the community physicians. Merely to shout them down, or force them into silence, was not enough; the government needed to find someone who could disprove their claim that only they had the knowledge, understanding, and dedication to improve public health in Russia.

The Appointment of G.E. Rein

In the fall of 1908, Prime Minister P.A. Stolypin, under pressure from the tsar to curb the ravages of disease and bent on trimming the sails of the *zemstva*, believed that he had found just the man for the job. On 21 November, Professor G.E. Rein of the Imperial Military-Medical Academy was appointed president of the Medical Council of the Ministry of the Interior, with a brief from Stolypin to plan an extensive reform of the Empire's medical and sanitary administration.[20]

One may well ask why Stolypin should have turned to G.E. Rein. Russia's professors, as Samuel Kassow points out in his essay in this volume, typically saw themselves as scholars and teachers whose task was to serve society rather than the autocracy. Nor had medical scientists distinguished themselves in 1905 by their loyalty to the regime. On both counts, however, Rein was an exception; in academic as well as medical circles, he belonged to the minority that was vocal in its support for the tsarist regime. This is not to say that Rein was either a blind reactionary or a sycophant. His career prior to his appointment, as well as his tireless pursuit of the cause of reform in the years which followed, make it clear that he was both a dynamic figure in the evolution of Russian medicine and a thorn in the side of the government. To be sure, he made no secret of his politics; as an Octobrist deputy in the stormy Second Duma, he joined the conservatives in denouncing political terrorism. Nevertheless, he was a prominent figure in St. Petersburg medical circles well before his excursion into Duma politics. Stolypin may have selected Rein primarily because of his energy and his loyalty, but he came to the prime minister's notice only because his peers in university and medical circles had recognized his stature as a scientist, teacher, and organizer.

That Rein had a promising career ahead of him seemed likely when he took the gold medal at the Imperial Medical-Surgical (later Military-Medical) Academy in 1874.[21] After obtaining his M.D. degree and serving at the front in the war against Turkey, he returned to the academy as a *privat-dotsent*. He soon left St. Petersburg again for an extended research trip to western Europe. Most of his time was spent in Strasbourg studying microscopic anatomy and embryology, and in Paris studying histology, but he also visited scientific institutes and clinics elsewhere in France, Germany, and Italy. While in England to attend an international congress of physicians, he familiarized himself with Lister's recently successful antiseptic techniques. Returning to Russia, his further research in the physiology of sex, embryology, and surgical obstetrics gained him the chair of Obstetrics and Gynecology at Kiev University in 1883. He made an immediate impact by insisting on antiseptic surgery; mortality from obstetric operations and childbed fever was dramatically reduced. For seventeen years he remained in Kiev where, in addition to his academic duties, he founded the Kiev Obstetrics and Gynecology Society, edited its *Transactions (Trudy)*, raised money for construction of a new clinic, and attended local, Pirogov, and international congresses. When he left in 1900, it was to return to the capital to occupy the chair of Obstetrics and Women's Diseases at the Imperial Military-Medical Academy.

Rein's career in academic medicine kept him well away from most of the concerns of Russia's community physicians. Where they were disposed to regard the growth of *zemstvo* medicine as the great beneficial innovation of the nineteenth century, Rein thought this place belonged to antiseptic surgery. Although he attended Pirogov congresses, it was not the sections on community medicine which interested him, but those on physiology, surgery, and obstetrics. He was a medical society man, but an organizer of specialists, not of physicians in general. For the legal and material difficulties experienced by his colleagues elsewhere in the profession he showed little sympathy; the practical problems facing *zemstvo* physicians in small rural hospitals he could not comprehend. In Kiev, thanks to private donations, new facilities, and hard work, he had been able to significantly reduce maternal mortality. How could he not be skeptical of physicians who claimed that only sweeping changes in the country's political, economic, and social structure could reduce Russia's high mortality rate? In Rein's view, most of the propagandists of community medicine were little better than merchants of doom.

During the years from 1900 to 1905, the very time when liberal and radical sentiments were growing apace among the community physicians, Rein was settling comfortably into the academic and medical establishment in St. Petersburg. Within a year, he had been elected academician, and in 1905 was chosen an honored professor of the academy. Continuing the work begun in Kiev, he became president of the St. Petersburg Obstetrics and Gynecology Society, edited its journal, and planned the curriculum for the academy's new obstetric clinic. By the time revolution broke out in 1905, he had become a member of several bodies advisory to the government, including the Medical Council of the Ministry of the Interior, the Learned Committee of the Military-Medical Academy, and the Commission to Reform Higher Educational Institutions. While the Pirogov Society was joining ranks with the opposition, Rein was forging closer ties with the tsarist regime.

In addition to his professional life as a scientist and academic, Rein was also a noble landowner. He possessed a substantial estate (3,600 *desiatina*) in Volhynia province. Here again, Rein was atypical; few physicians were nobles, and fewer still had country estates.[22] While about one-fifth of the Empire's physicians were employed by *zemstva* (and numerous others had had *zemstvo* experience at some point in their careers), Rein's contacts with the *zemstvo* were of a different order; he had served as an elected deputy (*glasnyi*). His political outlook thus had more in common with that of his fellow landowners than with that of *zemstvo* physicians and other third-element employees. These facts help to explain why, when Rein ventured into the Second Duma in 1907 as a deputy from Volhynia, he gravitated not to the Kadets, where so many academics and professionals found a congenial home, but to the more conservative Octobrists. A middle-aged noble landowner in an assembly of young radicals, Rein could scarcely have enjoyed his experience as a deputy and took little part in the Duma's proceedings. He made the ritual denunciation of terror, pleaded for an appreciation of the regional disparity of the Empire in devising solutions to the agrarian problem, and provoked the wrath of the left by suggesting that Jews were especially adept at evading military service. He did not stand in the elections to the Third Duma, and when Stolypin invited him to become president of the Medical Council, he seized the opportunity with relish.

Stolypin's invitation, with its implied promise of "big things to come," helped him to work out his own future role in Russian society. Combining his loyalty to the tsar, his penchant for public service, his scientific expertise, and his organizational ability, he would put himself at the disposal of Nicholas II in order to bolster the sagging prestige of the autocracy. By employing the best measures that contemporary science could suggest to reduce mortality and improve living conditions, he would help to defeat the liberals and revolutionaries by proving them wrong. Like the community physicians, Rein was beginning to understand the relationship between politics and public health. As he was to argue in a report submitted to the tsar in 1910, cholera and other epidemics resulted not only in the deaths of hundreds of thousands of people, but also in the waste of financial resources, the destruction of the economy, the loss of international stature, and—perhaps most important—the undermining of the people's trust in their rulers.[23] To be sure, cultural, economic, and educational improvements would in time help to promote public health, but Rein believed that the political situation was too precarious to rely on such long-term measures.

What, then, could a loyal, concerned scientist do? A great deal, according to Rein, who, as a pioneer of antisepsis, easily appreciated the scope that the bacteriological revolution offered for decisive intervention by the state. He began to emphasize the importance of improving drinking water, eliminating impurities from all water supplies, supervising the quality of food products, and improving housing conditions. He was able to make his point forcefully in 1909, when the Medical Council was called upon to deal with a serious outbreak of cholera in St. Petersburg. Rein immediately rushed off abroad to learn about ozone water purifiers and, on his return, persuaded the city administration to install one quickly; as a result, he claimed later, "pathogenic microbes were virtually eliminated from the water that went through it."[24] This event provided him with precisely the sort of example he needed to demonstrate that intervention by the state, employing the latest technology, could achieve dramatic success. Contrasting his own performance with the inactivity of the City Duma, which had allowed the problem of impure water to reach catastrophic proportions, and with the indifference of the Third Duma, Rein was confirmed in his belief that little could be expected from elected bodies. He had also satisfied himself that the so-called experts in community medicine simply did not know what they were talking about.

Rein's growing appreciation of the possibilities for state action was sharpened by his experience during the cholera epidemic in southern Russia in 1910. Pressure from industrialists anxious about falling coal production in the Donets basin forced the government to intervene, and Rein found himself appointed Red Cross Supreme Commissioner in charge of antiepidemic measures. True to form, he dispatched medical "flying squads" to the area, even as he himself prepared to travel south. Once there, he found his efforts hampered by the unwillingness of local authorities—zemstvo and administrative—to take the initiative in a crisis, and by the lack of trained personnel, the unequal allocation of resources, and the traditional preference for piecemeal, temporary measures.

Rein returned to the capital convinced that it was necessary to establish a centralized agency to run public health affairs in Russia. What was required, he argued in reports to the tsar and to Stolypin, was a separate ministry for health and sanitation, which should undertake a thoroughgoing reform of medical and sanitary legislation and implement the necessary changes as quickly as possible.[25] An unspoken but obvious implication was that the new ministry should be headed by Rein himself.

Not surprisingly, Rein's growing aspirations delayed his success. Stolypin was heartily in favor of reasserting state control over the zemstva and recognized the need to revise existing medical legislation, but he did not share Rein's enthusiasm for creating a separate ministry. Rein's proposal necessarily involved seriously reducing the authority of several existing ministries, notably the MVD, and threatened to create a super-ministry to which the MVD might itself be subordinated. With the support of the chief medical inspector and other high-ranking MVD officials, Stolypin insisted that the implications of Rein's proposal should first be discussed within the MVD itself.[26] Because of bureaucratic jealousies and maneuvering, matters were still unresolved when Stolypin was assassinated in 1911. However, with Stolypin out of the way and the unimaginative A.A. Makarov installed as minister of the interior, Rein soon had his way. In March 1912, thanks largely to his continuing good relations with the tsar, he was appointed president of a full interdepartmental commission to review the entire structure and organization of medical and sanitary affairs in the Empire. In the belief that this was his great opportunity to save the Empire from the ravages of disease and the tsar from the machinations of the opposition, Rein enthusiastically set to work.

The Rein Commission and Its Work

Despite the commission's unwieldy size and interdepartmental character, Rein's influence was enormous. He decided in advance the scope and direction of its work, organized its subcommittees, and retained for himself control over the important subcommittee on finance and organization. He personally chaired all of its plenary sessions. For his chief assistant, he chose probably the only person in the Empire who understood the legal complexities of the subject, Dr. N.G. Freiberg, author of the standard compilation of existing medical and sanitary legislation.[27] The subcommittee on sanitary measures was headed by Chief Medical Inspector L.N. Malinovskii. During the earlier discussions within the MVD, Malinovskii had opposed the creation of a separate ministry on the grounds that it was premature, but now he found himself in a subordinate position where he could no longer stem the tide of Rein's influence. In any case his deputy, Dr. N.F. Gamaleia, editor of the influential biweekly *Hygiene and Sanitation (Gigiena i sanitariia)* was a known advocate of centralization and a formidable lobbyist on behalf of state-supported research in bacteriology and epidemiology.[28] The other subcommittees were all chaired by Rein's colleagues on the Medical Council, themselves high-ranking medical bureaucrats and academics.[29] In addition to representatives from no less than fifteen ministries, the Red Cross, and the Imperial Philanthropic Society, the commission included several mayors and town councilors, members of various *zemstvo* boards, a few physicians from provinces lacking *zemstvo* institutions, and representatives of the Moscow Stock Exchange, the mining industry, and the Congress of Representatives of Industry and Trade.[30] With such a large and disparate membership, the real work was done in subcommittee, not at the plenary sessions.

Spokesmen for the community medical tradition were predictably outraged by the absence of formal representation from the Pirogov Society and by what appeared to be a random selection of *zemstvo* representatives.[31] Their immediate conclusion was that Rein was deliberately snubbing those best qualified to advise on the principles of medical, and especially sanitary, reform. To such accusations Rein remained impervious, and it is not difficult to understand why. Explicit participation by the Pirogov Society risked a reiteration of the earlier demands for constitutional reforms as a necessary preliminary to constructive activity; it would also have necessitated sending similar invitations to all other medical societies, thus making the commission even larger than it already was. Co-opting individuals from *zemstva* and municipalities was the normal means by which such commissions operated, and here Rein was simply following precedent. In any case he had no trouble finding individuals ready to serve. As far as expertise was concerned, the subcommittees either included or consulted with recognized medical authorities, whatever their politics, when drawing up specific legislative proposals. An outstanding example of this process was the participation of the distinguished epidemiologist and well-known radical D.K. Zabolotnyi in planning new legislation to deal with epidemics. Rein was prepared to avail himself of scientific expertise, but he was determined not to make the commission a forum for the expression of political opposition to the regime. Suggestions were also made in the Pirogov Society's organ *The Community Physician (Obshchestvennyi vrach)* that commercial and industrial interests would exercise a disproportionate and harmful influence over the commission's work.[32] These appear to have stemmed from the almost hysterical anti-capitalism typical of some *zemstvo* intellectuals. After his experience in southern Russia in 1910, Rein appreciated that the cooperation of business and industry would be an important factor in the eventual success of his reforms. On the other hand, he had no reason to pander to commercial interests, and in fact the commission's recommendations in some areas went much further than representatives of trade and industry would have liked.[33]

The work of the Rein Commission extended over three years. The first full session was held in November 1912; the fifth and last in March 1914. The subcommittees were in almost constant session during this period. The commission resulted in the most extensive proposals for the reform of public health ever produced under the tsarist regime: over forty legislative proposals, twelve of them dealing with sanitation, four with medical assistance, eight with the training and obligations of medical personnel, four with forensic medicine, and fifteen with administrative reorganization at all levels.

The Main Administration for State Health Protection (GUGZ)

The centerpiece of the Rein Commission's work was the proposal to establish a Main Administration for State Health Protection *(Glavnoe upravlenie gosudarstvennogo zdravookhraneniia*, hereafter GUGZ). It was to undertake the overall direction and supervision of medicine, public health, and sanitation throughout the Empire and was to be responsible for shepherding all of the other reforms through the legislative institutions. Although its jurisdiction was not to include military medicine (which would continue under the naval and war ministries), GUGZ was to assume almost complete control of the civil medical sector. Only the medical administration of the Ministry of the Imperial Court was to be exempt from its control. All other ministries, including of course the MVD, were required to submit for approval by GUGZ all measures which touched in any way on matters of public health.

The proposed structure of the new agency indicates the range of the activities it was expected to undertake.[34] Its medical department was to include four divisions: hospitals, medical assistance, pharmacology, and forensic medicine. This would be complemented by a sanitary department with three divisions: sanitation, epidemic disease, and chronic contagious and occupational diseases. A department of general affairs was to include the secretarial and accounting staff, as well as the inspectorate, which would take over the functions previously performed by the administration of the chief medical inspector in the MVD. This department was also assigned responsibility for the publication of a new journal intended to replace the MVD's *Bulletin of Community Hygiene, Forensic and Practical Medicine (Vestnik obshchest-vennoi gigieny, sudebnoi i prakticheskoi meditsiny)*, as well as weekly bulletins concerning epidemic diseases. The learned branch (*uchebnyi otdel*) was to direct education in medicine, pharmacy, and veterinary science, and was to administer those institutions attached directly to the ministry —initially, the Imperial Institute of Experimental Medicine and the St. Petersburg Orthopedic Institute. Also attached to GUGZ were a statistical section, a technical-structural section, a *jurisconsult* section, the existing veterinary administration, and a new state laboratory.

This vast administrative structure was to be guided by three advisory bodies, two of which—the Medical Council and the Veterinary Committee— were to be transferred from the MVD to GUGZ. In addition, a new Main Sanitary Committee was to advise on sanitary measures of statewide significance, and to coordinate relations between the central government and the *zemstva* and municipalities. Unlike the Medical Council and the Veterinary Committee, which were small bodies composed exclusively of scientific experts, the Main Sanitary Committee was to be an enormous (and therefore ineffective?) assembly of bureaucrats and representatives of local government with a membership approaching two hundred. Though not as large as the MVD, GUGZ was obviously meant to be a substantial addition to the St. Petersburg bureaucracy. Several hundred new positions would have been required to bring it to full operation. The potential for interministerial conflict inherent in its broad jurisdiction would soon have demanded a host of additional personnel in the *jurisconsult* section alone.[35]

Naturally GUGZ was not intended to reside just in St. Petersburg. Its authority was to be felt throughout the Empire through the establishment of thirteen regional (*okrug*) medical-sanitary departments, eight of them in European Russia, two in Siberia, and one each in the Far East, Turkestan, and the Caucasus. The commission also proposed to establish medical-sanitary councils at the provincial (*guberniia*) and district (*uezd*) levels, each with their own inspectorates, and new dictrict-level organizations for combating epidemics. GUGZ's jurisdiction was to extend to provinces without *zemstvo* institutions and also to those parts of the Empire under special forms of military authority, such as the Cossack areas. Had all these plans been carried to fruition, agents of GUGZ would doubtless have become as familiar (and probably as contentious) a part of the local scene as the existing agencies of the MVD and the Ministry of Finance, compounding the bureaucratic assault on the countryside.[36]

The Rein Commission and the Medical Profession

Given Rein's plan for GUGZ, it should come as no surprise that many of the commission's proposals were designed to increase substantially the authority of the state over physicians and other medical personnel. Physicians who sought to professionalize Russian medicine—who believed, in other words, that they themselves ought to control admission, education, working conditions, and their relationship to the state and society—found nothing in its proposals which moved them one degree closer to realizing these aspirations. The failure of moderates and radicals alike to build a unified and organized profession in the two decades prior to 1910 left the way clear for a determined effort to thwart the movement towards professionalization. Into this void stepped Rein and his like-minded colleagues from the Medical Council and the university medical faculties, intent on reasserting both the ethic of state service and the primacy of academic over practical medicine. This was nothing less than an attempt to destroy the community medical tradition that had made physicians a force for social criticism and social change in the late nineteenth and early twentieth centuries.

Reassertion of state authority can be seen clearly in the commission's proposals for the reform of medical education.[37] They drew a sharp distinction between medicine as an academic discipline and medicine as a vocation, leaving the former under the control of medical faculties and placing the latter squarely under the control of the state. In place of the existing two-tiered degree structure in which both those who planned to teach and those intending to practice took the same initial degree (*lekar'*), the commission proposed two different paths. Those planning to teach would initially study for the new degree of candidate of medical science, pursuing a longer, broader, and more onerous program than that required for the *lekar'* degree. Then they would proceed to the M.D., which was to become essentially a proof of ability in one particular specialty (e.g., internal medicine, surgery, ophthalmology, etc.). Faculties of medicine were to set the requirements for these degrees and to examine the candidates. Those intending to practice would follow a quite different program. They would work not toward a degree but toward receiving one of three titles (*zvaniia*): that of physician (*vrach*), sanitary physician (*sanitarnyi vrach*), or forensic physician (*sudebnyi vrach*). Although these studies would be pursued within a medical faculty, the courses would be prescribed by the state (i.e., by the learned branch of GUGZ), and students would be examined by specially appointed State Examining Commissions. Henceforth, freedom of inquiry was to be permitted only in academic medicine. Practitioners, especially those who might find employment as community physicians, were to be given the correct (i.e., politically acceptable) view of the tasks of physicians, weaning them from the dangerous notion that the improvement of public health required granting civil and political liberties.

The same trend toward greater state control is apparent in the commission's plans for the expansion of medical research, the collection of statistics, and the development of hygiene education. Besides taking over the Imperial Institute of Experimental Medicine, GUGZ was to establish and run a vaccination institute, an institute of tropical medicine, and (under the aegis of the Medical Council) a state laboratory for research in hygiene, pharmacy, physiological chemistry, forensic medicine, toxicology, and bacteriology. The need for expanded research facilities had been a constant theme in the medical press, but their relatively small growth in the two decades after 1890 had been sponsored almost entirely by the *zemstva*.[38] The commission was thus proposing a substantial shift in the major responsibility for medical research from the local level to the central government. This was equally true of medical statistics, where for years the really significant work had emanated from *zemstvo* sanitary bureaus and from the Pirogov Society. True, the administration of the chief medical inspector published annual reports on public health and medical assistance, but these were of little use as a basis for planning. The statistical section of GUGZ was assigned a much larger role, involving the collection, digestion, and publication of information not only about Russia, but also about foreign states. It was to be concerned not only with morbidity and mortality, but also with antiepidemic measures and medical-sanitary legislation. Most important of all, it was given the power to prescribe "the rules and forms for . . . registration and reporting,"[39] which, together with the supervisory duties of the inspectorate, meant that GUGZ could control the collection and publication of statistics by the sanitary bureaus of *zemstva* and municipalities. Popular hygiene education, another area in which sanitary bureaus and the Pirogov Society had been active, was also accorded a high priority by the commission.[40] It is scarcely surprising that community physicians regarded these recommendations as a plan to emasculate *zemstvo* and municipal sanitary services. Stripped of their role as educators and social reformers, *zemstvo* sanitary physicians would be transformed into local medical policemen.

Most revealing of all were the commission's recommendations on the professional activity of physicians. Whatever differences had divided Russian physicians, there is no doubt that most of them believed that a national professional organization was desirable, that such an organization ought to speak for all physicians, and that it ought to play an important role in the formulation of state policy concerning public health. That they had not been able to find the appropriate form in which to cast the organization does not mean that the idea had been entirely abandoned. Rein and his colleagues on the Medical Council, however, subscribed to a much narrower definition of professionalism, in which physicians were purely and simply practitioners. As practitioners, their activity was sufficiently important to warrant regulation through legislation and state supervision.

Thus the commission understood "the professional activity of physicians" to mean neither more nor less than state regulation of the legal and ethical aspects of medical practice. The subcommittee to which this subject was entrusted concentrated on such matters as illegal practice, medical confidentiality, and the ethical aspects of surgery and anesthesia. Clearly, the intention was to produce a code of ethics which could be enforced on all physicians in state or public service through the inspectorate of GUGZ. But what of the private practitioners who made up approximately one-third of those in practice? How to enforce professional discipline on those outside state service was a serious problem. For advice on this problem as well as on the particulars of the code, the commission turned to several medical societies, although the Pirogov Society itself was once again ignored.

At this point, supporters of corporate autonomy for the profession began to make their opinions heard. The St. Petersburg Physicians Mutual Assistance Society revived its campaign for creation of an autonomous medical estate. In 1902, it had taken the position that state action should follow, not precede, the growth of "estate consciousness" among physicians. In 1912, the society argued for immediate state action. Its president, Dr. K.P. Sulima, medical inspector of the City of St. Petersburg, urged the commission to recommend the establishment of an autonomous corporate organization modeled on the German and Austrian Chambers of Physicians.[41]

Not surprisingly, Sulima's proposal ran into heavy opposition in the Rein Commission, especially in the plenary sessions where ministerial representatives and provincial governors spoke out against creation of an autonomous medical estate. Influenced no doubt by memories of 1905, the commission flatly rejected Sulima's proposal on the grounds that "an organization of physicians with rights of jurisdiction, and with the right of raising questions of state significance . . . is, in the interests of the state, inadmissible."[42] The commission wanted to encourage physicians to confine their professional interests to such matters as salaries, pensions, trust funds, and refresher courses, leaving matters of high policy to GUGZ. If they wished to advance other professional interests, they would have to do so through medical societies organized under the 1906 laws for unions and associations, and thus subject to the double scrutiny of GUGZ and the MVD. Rather shrewdly, the commission had drawn a sharp line between physicians' medical activities, which were so important that they demanded regulation, and their other professional activities, in which the state allegedly had no interest.

Nevertheless, the problem of disciplining private practitioners remained. To deal with it, the commission devised an ingenious solution based on a severely truncated version of the Sulima proposal. It recommended the creation of much smaller Councils of Physicians (*sovety vrachei*), the jurisdiction of which would be confined exclusively to private practice.[43] These councils were quite unlike their German and Austrian namesakes; they did not represent all physicians, dealt only with private practice, and had no power to speak for the whole profession on broad issues of policy. Like the Councils of the Bar, the Councils of Physicians were designed to ensure that practitioners operating outside the state service were still subject to state authority.

With the completion of the commission's work in the spring of 1914, the tsarist regime was poised for a thoroughgoing reform of public health. It claimed its objectives were entirely apolitical: the reduction of morbidity and mortality coupled with the improvement of medical and sanitary services. There can be no doubt, however, that the implementation of these proposals would have had political consequences most satisfactory for the government, ending with the destruction of the community medical tradition and the virtual integration of community physicians into a state medical service controlled by GUGZ. In fact, the commission's proposals went even further; they constituted a determined counterattack on the ideals espoused by supporters of medical professionalization. They restricted to a minimum opportunities for physicians to act as a unified group in society. They reduced physicians to the status of mere practitioners whose every move was supervised by agencies of the state. They prescribed the legal and ethical obligations of physicians and established a new institutional framework through which to police them. They made a concerted attempt to put the state in control of the development of medical knowledge. Had the commission's proposals been fully implemented, the relationship between physicians and the state would have been set back half a century.

The Impact of World War I

Wars normally increase the powers of central governments. In theory, therefore, a centralizer such as Rein should have had everything to gain from the
outbreak of hostilities in August 1914. Indeed, his own reaction was to plead
for the immediate establishment of GUGZ, regardless of whatever temporary
measures were required to cope with the army's medical needs. Tsarist Russia
did not, however, conform to the norm. Within months, the authority of the
civil government had almost ground to a halt. Effective power devolved to the
army at the front and the voluntary organizations in the rear. This phenomenon has been examined at length elsewhere;[44] for our purposes it is necessary
to note its consequences for Rein's reform plans. These were dramatic. To
Rein's dismay, the war continually provided more scope to the community
physicians, while he himself was virtually paralyzed.

Thanks to the unpreparedness of the army's medical corps, the duration of
the war, and the tendency of corps commanders to rely on the voluntary
organizations, the community physicians enjoyed a windfall opportunity to
reorganize and rejuvenate themselves. The All-Russian Union of *Zemstva*
soon became, in the words of one historian, "one of the most important
medical offices in Russia,"[45] and the All-Russian Union of Towns was not
far behind. Rein found himself an unwilling spectator as community physicians, reorganizing themselves in the departments and bureaus of the voluntary organizations, resumed the very drive toward professionalization that he
had worked so diligently to abort. He had not reckoned on a war that quickly
outstripped the capacities of the regime and provided the professional intelligentsia, especially the community physicians, with fresh opportunities to
extend their influence at the national and local levels.

Precisely how the war would upset Rein's plans was not, of course, immediately apparent. His first concern was to secure the approval of the Council
of Ministers, so that the legislation to establish GUGZ could be sent to the
legislative institutions.[46] The new minister of the interior, N.A. Maklakov,
was by no means as sympathetic as his predecessor had been, and Rein had to
call upon the tsar's support in order to have the GUGZ proposal discussed in
the council in September 1914. Between those who, like Maklakov, opposed
the creation of a super-ministry and those who simply thought the measure
untimely, support was neither unanimous nor enthusiastic. In the end, the
council approved the measure in principle, but decided to postpone sending
the legislation to the Duma until the war was over.

Still confident of the tsar's support, Rein appealed to Nicholas to override
the ministerial decision and establish GUGZ by means of Article 87, which
provided for the enactment of emergency measures when the Duma was not in
session. This the tsar might have done had it not been for the opposition of

Prince A.P. Oldenburg, head of the Red Cross and director of the Sanitary Evacuation Branch of the army. This new agency had been created by the tsar himself in the early days of the war in an attempt to redress the glaring deficiencies of the army's medical-sanitary inspectorate. By the summer of 1915, Oldenburg's branch had become heavily dependent on the voluntary organizations for the evacuation of wounded, the provision of hospital facilities in the rear, and countless other forms of medical and sanitary assistance.[47] Oldenburg adamantly opposed the creation of GUGZ, knowing full well that Rein's plans could cause chaos in the medical work of the voluntary organizations. Under pressure from Oldenburg, the tsar, who in any case had more important issues than GUGZ to deal with in the summer of 1915, withdrew his support. Rein was fobbed off with an appointment to the State Council.[48]

Yet this was neither the end of GUGZ nor of Rein's career. Within a year, Nicholas changed his mind again. Over Oldenburg's objections, the nucleus of GUGZ was established under Article 87, and Rein was named main administrator for State Health Protection (*Glavroupravliaiushchii gosudarstvennogo zdravookhraneniia*).[49] Presumably the tsar had become convinced by late 1916 that the voluntary organizations constituted a real political threat to the regime and that their activities must be curbed, whatever temporary dislocation this might cause the army.[50] Doubtless Rein took every opportunity to blame the uncontrolled growth of the voluntary organizations on the decision to delay the establishment of GUGZ. Having put an end to the negotiations between his ministers and the Duma's Progressive Bloc for the creation of a "ministry of public confidence," Nicholas must have felt it his duty to take the lead himself in curbing the pretensions of the voluntary organizations. Rein's new ministry was ideally suited to this purpose. Prince Oldenburg grudgingly consented, on the condition that he see every legislative proposal produced by GUGZ before it went to the Duma.[51]

Rein barely had time to be fitted for the uniform appropriate to his new position when he was overtaken by events. When the Duma reconvened in early 1917, it soon became apparent that it would refuse to ratify the establishment of GUGZ. Although objections centered on the use of Article 87, many deputies feared that Rein's intention was to emasculate the voluntary organizations. They turned a deaf ear to Rein's protestation that the *zemstva* had no more to fear from GUGZ than from the introduction of compulsory primary education a few years previously. To avoid a confrontation in the Tauride Palace, Rein withdrew the bill. Days later, the regime collapsed and Rein, like other ministers of the tsar, found himself arrested and held for interrogation. Despite all his far-reaching plans, he had found time during GUGZ's brief life to issue only one pronouncement, which concerned the trade in saccharin. The mountain had labored, and had indeed brought forth a mouse.

For Russia's community physicians, the consequences of the war were utterly different. During the prewar years, it appeared to be only a matter of time before they were tied to the apron strings of Rein's new ministry. By 1915, thanks to the army's lack of preparation, the military prowess of the Germans, and the desperate plight of Russian commanders in the field, they enjoyed a freedom of action which, while not unrestricted, was much greater than they could have expected had GUGZ been established before the war broke out.

The rapid growth of the voluntary organizations and of their medical bureaus has been ably discussed in the work of William Gleason.[52] Their activities can be seen not only in the context of the liberal movement in wartime Russia, but also—in the case of the medical bureaus—against the background of the prewar conflicts among physicians. Many of those who joined the medical and sanitary bureaus of the voluntary organizations had sympathized with the 1905 alliance between the Pirogov Society and the opposition. Having lived through the years of crisis, disarray, and despondency which characterized community medicine after 1905, they plunged into war work with the specter of the Rein Commission hanging over them. No more than Rein could they have foreseen the enormous role that the war would carve out for them, and indeed for the first several months they were wholly occupied with the day-to-day problems of sick and wounded soldiers and refugees. Nevertheless, once they realized the possibilities that had opened up, they were determined to make the most of them.

By the summer of 1915, it had dawned on those directing the medical work of the voluntary organizations that what was at stake was not only the provision of assistance to the army, but the larger question of the postwar reorganization of medical and sanitary affairs. Would it be directed by conservative centralizers such as Rein or by the community physicians themselves? Eagerly they seized upon every opportunity to extend their authority not only to the front, but throughout the country.[53] From its prewar doldrums, the Pirogov Society sprang back to life, organizing conferences of epidemic prevention, bacteriology, urban sanitation, tuberculosis, venereal disease, alcoholism, and mental illness.[54] Acting on the recommendations of these conferences, the medical staffs of the two unions drew up vast programs of vaccinations, urban sanitary improvements, and other preventive measures.[55] Local committees of the voluntary organizations drew upon wider social participation than had the zemstva and town dumas, so that community physicians were able to use these bodies to enhance their positions as professional experts, while at the same time pressing for a broadened zemstvo and municipal franchise.[56] By late 1916, the unions' sanitary bureaus had worked out the nucleus of an extensive reform program and had created an institutional framework to put it into effect. Rein, recognizing what was afoot, played upon these developments in urging the tsar to put him in control of GUGZ.

Needless to say, the community physicians were as surprised as Rein at the speed of the monarchy's collapse, but unlike him, they were in a position to exert considerable leverage. The institutional structure of the unions, both central and local, as well as their importance to the war effort, provided reform-minded community physicians with the opportunity to influence the Provisional Government. Days after the tsar's abdication, a high-powered delegation of community physicians was in Petrograd, beginning the work of ensuring that they, and they alone, would design and carry out the long overdue reform of medicine and public health in revolutionary Russia.[57]

Conclusion

Rein and his commission deserve a place in this book not because of what they achieved, but because of what they represent. The role of the Russian state in creating professions is incontestable; so also is the fact that, at a certain point, most of these professions, or at least groups within them, turned against the state and attempted to take control of their own affairs. Thus it is easy—perhaps too easy—to see the last decades of the tsarist period as a contest between the bureaucracy, anxious at all costs to preserve its authority, and new professional groups, intent on achieving corporate autonomy. Certainly this is part of the story. What gets lost in such a simple, dualistic formulation of the conflict is demonstrated by Rein's career and the work of his commission.

Had it not been for the outbreak of war, Rein might have succeeded in establishing a powerful ministry committed to the expansion of medical research, the improvement of medical education, and the maintenance of professional standards in the healing arts, headed by a physician with a distinguished record of professional accomplishment. This is scarcely evidence that the tsarist regime was inveterately hostile to all forms of professionalism. By the same token, the opinions of Rein and his colleagues show that some of Russia's most distinguished medical scientists believed that the future of medicine lay in working with, not against, the state. Nineteenth-century Russian physicians owed a great deal to the state. As Nancy Frieden has pointed out, "they deviated from their usual mode of accommodation" when they ventured into radical policies in 1905.[58] But deviate they did, and the community physicians who led the way compromised themselves not only before a regime that expected loyalty, but also before their colleagues who expected greater professional responsibility. Thus it is possible to see in the work of the Rein Commission a fresh attempt to find an accommodation between physicians and the tsarist regime—a limited and controlled professionalism, unacceptable to the community physicians, but one with which both the regime and the majority of physicians could live.

Obviously, Rein was not an advocate of professionalization, as understood by spokesmen for the Pirogov Society. He shared neither their faith in *zemstvo* medicine as a force for constructive social change nor their insistent belief in the virtues of decentralization. That the future of medicine and public health should be left to the unsupervised deliberations of country practitioners, many of them populists and radicals, was in his view sheer nonsense. They had demonstrated their political unreliability in 1905. With a landowner's fear of revolution, an academic's snobbishness about mere practitioners, and a conservative's distrust of elected bodies, Rein was an inveterate opponent of the domination of Russian medicine by community physicians.

Yet Rein was a professional in a more limited sense, and he did share many of the attributes of professionalism. In the first place, he believed in the authority of knowledge. He spent much of his life in the creation and diffusion of knowledge: in the laboratory, in the lecture hall, in learned journals, and at the meetings and conferences of medical societies. His own research work in the clinics of Kiev and St. Petersburg, his international contacts, and his experience as president of the Medical Council, all convinced him that the latest scientific knowledge could make his country healthier and its people less barbaric and more productive. This conviction he shared with other medical professionals. What separated him from the community physicians was that he saw no inherent conflict between the authority of knowledge and the authority of office.[59] Second, Rein shared the frustration of all professionals that the pace of change in Russia was so slow. By 1910, he knew what he wanted to do and had won the tsar's support, yet he had to put up with Stolypin's delaying tactics, the ponderous mechanism of an interdepartmental commission, and then further delays occasioned by the war. His complaint during the prewar period was not the typical professional's "all the wrong people are in charge," but rather that no one was in charge, and that he ought to be. It was the wartime growth of the voluntary organizations that threatened to put the wrong people in charge. Rein never lost his conviction that *zemstvo* medicine, for all its achievements, was as much an obstacle to the creation of a unified public health policy as was the proliferation of responsibility for medical affairs among so many government departments. Third, Rein believed it was his professional duty to influence government policy. Though frequently labeled a careerist by his enemies, Rein was in fact a missionary in his own cause—that of persuading the regime that an institution such as GUGZ was crucial to its survival. Like his opponents among the community physicians, Rein believed that social change must depend upon harnessing modern medical knowledge, but where his conception of the future was based on strengthening the autocracy, theirs was based on weakening it.

Rein's career raises questions about the relationship between the bacteriological revolution and medical professionalization. Following Eliot Freidson's emphasis on the medical accomplishments of the nineteenth century, Nancy Frieden has argued that, in the wake of these revolutionary advances, Russian physicians became less dependent on the state and began to seek an autonomous position in society.[60] Yet in Rein's case we have a pioneer of medical innovation who rejected professional autonomy and instead worked to make physicians more dependent on the state. This surely underlines the crucial importance of the institutional setting in any discussion of scientific imperatives. Rein and his colleagues lived their professional lives in the universities and the high bureaucracy, far from the everyday realities of *zemstvo* service. Thus the same medical advances that turned community physicians into advocates of decentralization could cause some research scientists to become convinced centralists. In the Russian context, the bacteriological revolution not only fortified the professional aspirations of community physicians, but also became a vehicle through which the academic medical community, in partnership with the state, could reassert its authority over the development of medicine and its relationship to Russian society.[61]

In the case of medical reform, it is misleading to assume that the bureaucrats were on one side and the medical professionals on the other. Supporters and opponents of greater state control can be found in both camps. Admittedly, most of the bureaucrats who opposed the establishment of GUGZ did so not out of concern for its consequences for medicine, but because they feared the emasculation of the MVD. By the same token, most of the medical professionals who supported it were academics who saw it as their best hope for influencing the future development of Russian medicine. But the very existence of these interest groups should alert us to the complex problems involved in modifying the traditions of tsarist government so as to incorporate the growing expertise of professionals. In the case of medicine, the best chance for an accommodation seemed to lie in the regime granting substantial power to the academic wing of the profession on the condition that it undertake to regulate the practitioners in the best interests of the state. What of the regime's relations with other professions? Perhaps, in addition to looking for the equivalent of activist *zemstvo* physicians among engineers, lawyers, teachers, and psychiatrists, we might also find loyal professionals who opposed the struggle for corporate autonomy.

Notes

Much of the material in this essay was incorporated, in a slightly different form, into chapter four of my book *Politics and Public Health in Revolutionary Russia 1890-1918*, published in 1990 by The Johns Hopkins University Press, which granted permission for the use of this copyright material. Also of relevance are: John F.

Hutchinson, "Tsarist Russia and the Bacteriological Revolution," *Journal of the History of Medicine and Allied Sciences* 40 (1985): 420-39; idem, "Russian Physicians and Medical Politics in the Revolution of 1917," *Canadian Bulletin of Medical History* 3 (1986): 153-65; idem, "Who Killed Cock Robin? An Inquiry into the Death of Zemstvo Medicine" in *Health and Society in Revolutionary Russia*, eds. Susan Gross Solomon and John F. Hutchinson (Bloomington: Indiana University Press, 1990), 3-26.

1. On the growth of professional aspirations and organizations among Russian physicians between the Crimean War and the Revolution of 1905, see Nancy Mandelker Frieden, *Russian Physicians in an Era of Reform and Revolution, 1856-1905* (Princeton, NJ: Princeton University Press, 1981).

2. Ibid., 107.

3. Ibid., 320.

4. On the conflict among Russian physicians over the forms and goals of professional organizations, see John F. Hutchinson, "Society, Corporation or Union? Russian Physicians and the Struggle for Professional Unity (1890-1913)," *Jahrbucher fur Geschichte Osteuropas*, Band 30 (1982), Heft 1, 37-53. See also Peter F. Krug, "Russian Public Physicians and Revolution: The Pirogov Society, 1917-20," (Ph.D. diss., University of Wisconsin–Madison, 1979), especially chapter 2,   38-65.

5. It appears that a similar development took place within the academic profession as a whole. For a fuller discussion, see Samuel Kassow's essay in this volume.

6. See Frieden, *Russian Physicians*, 231-311.

7. In addition to Frieden's book and my own work cited above, see Jonathan Sanders, "The Union of Unions: Political, Economic, Professional and Human Rights Organizations in the 1905 Revolution," (Ph.D. diss., Columbia University, 1983) for the participation of the All-Russian Union of Medical Personnel in the Union of Unions. On the radicalization of the medical staffs of psychiatric hospitals, see Julie V. Brown, "The Professionalization of Russian Psychiatry: 1857-1911" (Ph.D. diss., University of Pennsylvania, 1981), 344-61.

8. For a fuller discussion, see Hutchinson, "Russian Physicians," 44-47.

9. Its program is analyzed in detail in G.I. Dembo, "Voprosy vrachebnogo byta na X Pirogovskom s"ezde," *Vestnik Sanktpeterburgskogo vrachebnogo obshchestva vzaimnoi pomoshchi,* vyp. 15-16 (1907), 27. (hereafter *Vestnik SVOVP*).

10. For a fuller discussion, see Hutchinson, "Russian Physicians," 40-44.

11. M.N. Nizhegorodtsev, "Sanktpeterburgskoe vrachebnoe obshchestvo vzaimnoi pomoshchi i russkoe vrachebnoe soslovie," *Vestnik SVOVP*, vyp. 1 (1902), 13.

12. Again, a similar position was taken by some professors who argued that the academy ought to be above politics. See Samuel Kassow's essay in this volume.

13. S.I. Mitskevich, *Zapiski obshchestva russkikh vrachei v pamiat' N.I. Pirogova*, no. 12 (1906): 331-40. (hereafter *Zhurnal ORVP*).

14. On the gentry reaction in the *zemstva*, see Roberta Thompson Manning, *The Crisis of the Old Order in Russia: Gentry and Government* (Princeton, NJ: Princeton University Press, 1982).

15. For a fuller discussion, see Hutchinson, "Russian Physicians," 48-49.

16. See, for example, the exchange between G.I. Berdichevskii and S.N. Igumnov, *Zhurnal ORVP*, no. 1 (1908): 5-27; no. 3, 283-96; also M.M. Gran', "Sposobny li vrachi k ob"edineniiu?" *Vrachebnaia gazeta*, no. 6 (1909): 178-84; no. 7, 208-15.

17. These changes, and the thinking which led to them, are discussed in Frieden, *Russian Physicians*, 286-92.

18. Although the Ministry of the Interior retained the lion's share of responsibility for civil medicine, eight other ministries had medical responsibilities, ranging from the extensive establishments of the War Ministry and the court to the small sections of the Ministry of Finance which were concerned with sanitation on the railways and the health of the border police. For a succinct discussion, see Mitskevich, *Zapiski vracha-obshchestvennika, 1888-1918 gg.* (Moscow-Leningrad: Medgiz, 1940), 139.

19. For a convenient summary of public health organization in the major European states at the end of the nineteenth century, see Albert Palmberg, *A Treatise on Public Health and Its Applications in Different European Countries*, trans. Arthur Newsholme (London: S. Sonnenschein & Co., 1895).

20. The history and functions of the Medical Council are described in A.I. Moiseev, *Meditsinkii sovet ministerstva vnutrennykh del': Kratkii istoricheskii ocherk* (St. Petersburg, 1913).

21. The biographical sketch which follows is based upon information from his memoirs. G.E. Rein, *Iz perezhitogo 1907-1918*, 2 vols. (Berlin, n.d. [1936?]).

22. Only 5.4 percent of the 147 government physicians in Nancy Frieden's archive sample for 1902 were children of hereditary nobles. Frieden, *Russian Physicians*, 337.

23. Rein, *Iz perezhitogo*, vol. 1, 72.

24. Ibid., 59.

25. Rein's account of these events, including the full text of his report to the tsar dated 12 October 1910, may be found in *Iz perezhitogo*, vol. 1, 65-73.

26. This gave rise to the special conference headed by Senator S.E. Kryzhanovskii; for an account of its proceedings, see Rein, *Iz perezhitogo*, vol. 1, 91-103.

27. N.G. Freiberg, *Vrachebno-sanitarnoe zakonodatel'stvo v Rossii*, 2nd ed. (St. Petersburg, 1908).

28. On Gamaleia's place in the history of Russian medicine, see L.Ia. Skorokhodov, *Materialy po istorii meditsinskoi mikrobiologii v dorevoliutsionnoi Rossii* (Moscow, 1948). His memoirs, covering only the late nineteenth century, may be found in volume 5 of his *Sobranie sochinenii*, 5 vols. (Moscow, 1953).

29. Professor N.A. Veliaminov, chief medical inspector of the court, chaired the subcommittee on medical assistance and charity; Professor E.A. Neznamov, director of the Medical-Sanitary Department of the Ministry of Public Instruction, chaired the subcommittee on medical education; and Ia.A. Pliushchevskii-Pliushchik, principal medical legal advisor to the MVD, chaired the subcommittee on forensic medicine.

30. For the composition of the commission by name and office, see Rein, *Iz perezhitogo*, vol. 1, 175-79.

31. See, for example, the comments of A.S. Durnovo, "Sovremennaia zhizn' i narodnoe zdravie II," *Obshchestvennyi vrach*, no. 10 (1912): 1218-24.

32. Ibid., 1220.

33. See the complaints of an anonymous writer in *Promyshlennost' i torgovlia*, no. 21 (1913): 402-3.

34. The draft statute, entitled "Osnovnye polozheniia glavnogo Upravleniia Gosudarstvennogo Zdravookhraneniia," may be found in Rein, *Iz perezhitogo*, vol. 1, 227-37. It was given final approval at the commission's meeting of 27 May 1913; see *Obshchii zhurnal*, 50-60, of the incomplete collection of papers of the Rein Commission in the possession of the National Library of Medicine, catalogued as *Russia. Mezhduvedomstvennaia komissiia po peresmotru vrachebno-sanitarnogo zakonodatel'stva. Sbornik.* (hereafter *Sbornik*).

35. On the role of the *jurisconsult* in the MVD, see Daniel T. Orlovsky, *The Limits of Reform: The Ministry of Internal Affairs in Imperial Russia, 1802-1881* (Cambridge: Harvard University Press, 1981), 80-84.

36. On the intrusion of the central bureaucracy into the Russian countryside, see George L. Yaney, *The Systematization of Russian Government* (Urbana, IL: University of Illinois Press, 1973).

37. For a brief description, see Rein, *Iz perezhitogo*, vol. 1, 242-43.

38. The strengths of *zemstvo* medical and sanitary research lay in epidemic prevention, occupational mortality, and the sanitary condition of the laboring population. For a general survey, see P.E. Zabliudovskii, *Istoriia otechestvennoi meditsiny, chast' I, period do 1917 goda*, (Moscow, 1960).

39. Rein, *Iz perezhitogo*, vol. 1, 234.

40. On the involvement of *zemstvo* physicians in the collection of medical statistics and the promotion of hygiene education, see Frieden, *Russian Physicians*, especially 96-104, 179-99.

41. For a fuller discussion, see Hutchinson, "Russian Physicians," 50-51. The details of Sulima's proposal are in "Ob organizatsii vrachei v soslovie s pravami iurisdiktsii," *Obshchestvennyi vrach*, no. 7 (1913): 814-25.

42. Sulima, "Ob organizatsii," 825. Rein skirts around the rejection in his memoirs, *Iz perezhitogo*, vol. 1, 209, 243. On the role of the governors in voicing opposition to the proposal, see *Sbornik*, no. 7, *Obshchii zhurnal*, 20 and 22 May 1913, 33, 42; *Russkoe slovo*, 14 September 1913, 7.

43. For details, see Rein, *Iz perezhitogo*, vol. 1, 244.

44. On the civil power exercised by the army, see Daniel W. Graf, "The Reign of the Generals: Military Government in Western Russia, 1914-1915" (Ph.D. diss., University of Nebraska, 1972). For a thorough analysis of the work of the voluntary organizations, see William E. Gleason, "The All-Russian Union of Towns and the All-Russian Union of *Zemstva* in World War I: 1914-1917" (Ph.D. diss., Indiana University, 1972), especially chapter 3, "Medical Operations on the Homefront," 33-55, and chapter 6, "The Health Crises," 107-37. Gleason has summarized his

findings concerning the Union of *Zemstva* in "The All-Russian Union of *Zemstva* and World War I," in *The Zemstvo in Russia: An Experiment in Local Self-Government,* eds. Terence Emmons and Wayne S. Vucinich (New York: Cambridge University Press, 1982), 365-82.

45. Gleason, "The All-Russian Union of Towns and the All-Russian Union of *Zemstva* in World War I," 49.

46. This account of the war period is based on Rein's memoirs, *Iz perezhitogo,* vol. 1, 49-133, 190-221; also on his testimony before the Investigating Commission of the Provincial Government in *Padenie tsarskogo rezhima,* ed. P.E. Shchegolev, vol. 5 (Moscow-Leningrad, 1926), 1-31.

47. These are described in detail in Paul P. Gronsky and Nicholas J. Astrov, *The War and the Russian Government* (New Haven: Yale University Press, 1929), 198-219, 242-52. See also the two chapters of Gleason's dissertation cited in note 44.

48. On the political crisis in the summer of 1915, see Michael F. Hamm, "The Progressive Bloc of Russia's Fourth State Duma" (Ph.D. diss., Indiana University, 1971).

49. Nicholas II agreed to the appointment of Rein and to the establishment of the central council and learned branch of GUGZ, with effect from 1 September 1916. Rein, *Iz perezhitogo,* vol. 2, 88.

50. This is not to say that the political threat was real. Gleason argues persuasively that the two unions failed to exert as much political pressure as they might have done. "The All-Russian Union of Towns and the All-Russian Union of *Zemstva* in World War I: 1914-1917," 245-70. For a quite different view of the role of the voluntary organizations, see George Katkov, *Russia 1917: The February Revolution* (New York: Harper & Row, 1967).

51. Rein, *Iz perezhitogo,* vol. 2, 132.

52. See note 44.

53. See, for example, the increasingly ambitious plans of the Sanitary Bureau of the Union of Towns: N.F. Nikolaevskii, "Obzor organizatsii i deitel'nosti sanitarnogo otdela glavnogo komiteta soiuza gorodov," *Vrachebno-sanitarnyi vestnik,* no. 1-2 (1917): 73-87.

54. For a description of the wartime activities of leading members of the Pirogov Society, see Krug, "Russian Public Physicians," 66-93.

55. On the extensive plans of the unions, see in addition to Nikolaevskii (cited in note 53), Z.P. Solov'ev, "Itogi vrachebno-sanitarnoi deiatel'nosti zemskogo soiuza i ee dal'neishie shagi," *Obshchestvennyi vrach,* no. 7 (1916): 363-73; for the development of local organs of the Union of Towns, "Soveshchanie chlenov sanitarno-tekhnicheskikh biuro soiuza gorodov (12-15 November 1916)," *Izvestiia vserossiiskogo soiuza gorodov,* no. 38 (1916): 115-51.

56. On the struggle for local reform, see William E. Gleason, "The All-Russian Union of Towns and the Politics of Urban Reform in Tsarist Russia," *Russian Review,* no. 3 (1976): 290-302.

57. See A.N. Merkulov's report to a joint meeting of physicians employed by the voluntary organizations, municipal and *zemstvo* physicians in Moscow on 23 March 1917 in *Vrachebno-sanitarnyi vestnik,* no. 1-2 (1917): 101-2.

58. Frieden, *Russian Physicians,* 316.

59. For an elaboration of this sense of conflict, acute among Russian psychiatrists, see Julie Brown's essay in this volume.

60. Frieden, *Russian Physicians*, 52. For Freidson's argument, see *Profession of Medicine: A Study of the Sociology of Applied Knowledge* (New York: Dodd-Mead, 1970).

61. That it continued to do so after the Bolshevik revolution can be seen in the speed with which scientists such as D.K. Zabolotnyi, L.A. Tarasevich, and P.N. Diatroptov went to work for the new regime. Admittedly, they were radicals while Rein was a conservative, but this only underlines the fact that the political differences within the academic medical community were in the long run less significant than the divisions which separated the creators of knowledge from the practitioners.

5

Professionalism and Politics: The Russian Feldsher Movement, 1891-1918

Samuel C. Ramer

One of the most striking characteristics of Russian society at the turn of the century was an almost frenzied proliferation of private organizations of all descriptions, from philanthropic and cultural societies to labor unions and political parties. By no means all of these private associations were new. The tradition of forming organizations independent of direct state control had a long, if frustrating, history in Russia. On the eve of the Revolution of 1905, however, the number of private associations in existence was greater than ever before, and the impulse toward organization, for whatever purposes, was spreading rapidly through all ranks of Russian society. The highly charged political atmosphere of the time gave such free associations an enormous civic significance, even when their aims or activities were not explicitly political. In the very chaos of their congresses and publications, in their conflicts with the government as well as their internecine strife, one can sense the emergence, at least in urban Russia, of an embryonic civil society.[1]

Aside from political parties, the most prominent organizations to appear during this period were unions whose membership was drawn from one or another occupational group. Of these, the most politically significant were the trade unions formed by urban workers and the professional unions established by physicians, lawyers, academics, and other representatives of the learned professions. The reasons these two types of occupational unions tended to dominate political life during the Revolution of 1905 are readily apparent. The strike movement among industrial workers was at the very heart of the revolution itself, and the Marxist parties in particular viewed the working class as the most promising vehicle of social revolution. The leaders of the various professional unions, on the other hand, were highly visible organizers of the liberation movement. What they lacked in numbers they made up in their prolific writing on all aspects of public life and their intense belief in their historic mission as leaders of a free and liberal Russia. Drawn from the cream of educated society, they were the embodiment of the liberal intelligentsia in Russia.[2]

The well-established tradition of considering the labor movement and the professional intelligentsia as clearly separate groups is certainly justified by the two groups' radically different perceptions of their own identities.[3] The tendency to juxtapose them nevertheless obscures the fact that, in a number of important respects, there was no clear line of demarcation between the heterogeneous labor movement on the one hand and the diverse intelligentsia on the other. When we look at the unions that these groups formed, for example, we do not find a clear division into two distinct and readily identifiable kinds of organization, but a spectrum of organizations with differing but comparable aims which sprang up to represent everyone from unskilled workers at one extreme to the learned professions at the other.[4]

The usefulness of viewing the labor movement and the professional intelligentsia as parts of an organizational continuum is particularly clear when one contemplates the numerous intermediate occupations whose members were neither industrial laborers nor professionals in the fullest sense of the word, such as schoolteachers, feldshers, midwives, pharmacists, bookkeepers, and office workers. Contemporaries referred to those engaged in such occupations as the "semi-intelligentsia," a term which recognizes their kinship to the intelligentsia while emphasizing the limited nature of their skills, training, and overall cultural attainments. Given the imprecision of the term "intelligentsia," and more particularly the extent to which it was a self-defining concept, it is simpler to consider these groups as a part, however humble, of the intelligentsia. Certainly they saw themselves in this way. Moreover, this is how they were viewed by the majority of the population in a predominately illiterate society.[5]

The professional unions established by intermediate occupational groups tended to combine the pretensions and self-perception of the intelligentsia with many of the goals, and even tactics, of trade unions. Feldshers and midwives, who began to organize in the 1890s to defend what they described as their "corporate" interests, constitute a particularly good example of the activities and mentality of these intermediate occupational groups.[6] This essay analyzes the efforts they made to improve their professional and social status during a revolutionary era.[7]

The Creation of a Feldsher Professional Movement

There were approximately 23,000 civilian feldshers practicing in Russia in 1907.[8] With several hundred feldshers in almost every province, the feldsher was a familiar figure. While many feldshers worked in urban hospitals, factories, mines, schools, or even on railroad lines, most (about two-thirds) lived and worked in the countryside. Ideally, such rural feldshers worked in a clinic under a physician's direct supervision. In practice, however, many were assigned to remote feldsher stations where a physician visited periodically to assist them and supervise their practice. These visits were infrequent and hurried, so that for all practical purposes many feldshers were on their own.

The nature of feldshers' training varied considerably. Many, particularly the *rotnye* feldshers who were retired army medics, had only the most superficial formal training. The stereotype of the feldsher as an ignorant, unsavory, and usually alcoholic older man owed much to these *rotnye* feldshers' overall crudeness and genuine inadequacy as healers. Despite their shortcomings, *rotnye* feldshers continued to play an important role in rural medicine well into the 1930s.

Alongside the *rotnye* feldshers, however, there was a rapidly growing corps of feldshers and feldsher-midwives, many of them urban women with extensive gymnasium education, who had graduated from a three- or four-year feldsher school such as those pioneered by the *zemstvo*.[9] Thus, by the early twentieth century, feldshers (and feldsher-midwives) comprised an occupation whose members had quite diverse training and qualifications. Many were praised by the physicians with whom they served as skilled and dedicated assistants. Such individual recognition, however, did not substantially alter the popular image of feldshers as ignorant, avaricious, and addicted to the bottle.

Prior to the 1880s, the superficial character of feldsher training did little to give even the graduates of feldsher schools (*shkol'nye* feldshers) a sense of professional identity. Their geographic dispersal and consequent isolation from colleagues muted whatever sense of occupational identity and professional solidarity they might otherwise have developed. A movement to organize feldshers in order to improve their professional position required a critical mass of better-educated feldshers who believed (1) that their training and the nature of their service entitled them to better professional and social status and (2) that feldshers could achieve such increased status through organization and publicity. A sufficiently large body of such professionally conscious feldshers only began to emerge in the 1880s.

For the most part these were *shkol'nye* feldshers, so that for the first time there was a significant number of feldshers with more than a functional level of literacy.[10] The *shkol'nye* feldshers' relative youth (few were over thirty), their more extensive training, and the service ideals they acquired in school made them less willing to accept the low social status and servile relationship to physicians that had been the feldsher's traditional lot. They did not challenge physicians' superior expertise, but actively sought greater respect and appreciation for their role as trained assistants. Physicians' frequent insensitivity to their feelings, coupled with their ongoing public disparagement of feldshers' abilities, was one reason that the feldsher movement as it took shape in the 1890s was profoundly hostile to physicians.

A professional movement of feldshers with shared goals and perceptions first appeared in the 1890s. The catalyst for this movement was the appearance in 1891 of a biweekly journal entitled *Feldsher*. Edited by Dr. Boris Oks, an enterprising publisher as well as physician, *Feldsher* elicited an outpouring of letters from feldshers all over the Empire. In these letters, feldshers portrayed themselves as dedicated laborers whom society, and physicians in particular, had exploited, abused, and unjustly maligned. By regularly printing such letters, Oks created a cathartic outlet for the resentment which feldshers had nourished for years in isolation and encouraged the formation of an organized community to combat the causes of this resentment. *Feldsher's* role as a forum to protest grievances and debate professional questions quickly surpassed its initial primary function of disseminating medical knowledge among feldshers.[11]

In *Feldsher's* pages one can observe how an inchoate and previously inarticulate occupational group acquired a voice and a sense of collective identity. The historian is struck by the passion of feldsher letters, as well as by their imploring urgency and sense of newly awakened hope. Oks noted this at the time, writing that while the enthusiastic response to the journal gratified its editors, "the hopes which its appearance have raised among feldshers frightened us and continue to frighten us."[12]

Feldsher quickly became the communication center of a feldsher professional movement, a position it held without challenge until 1905. It fostered the creation of an increasing number of local feldsher societies in the 1890s and helped to coordinate their activities. By reprinting the debates which took place in these societies, it gave local meetings a national resonance. In its pages an increasingly articulate elite of feldshers from throughout the Empire could compare their problems and begin to hammer out a consensus.

Feldsher Goals

The general nature of feldshers' professional goals was clearly defined by the turn of the century in the charters that local feldsher societies drew up and in the articles and letters that individual feldshers wrote. Mutual aid (the establishment of retirement or social security funds) was the only purpose for which the state would permit feldshers to organize, and it occupied a genuinely prominent position in the activities of all feldsher societies before 1905.[13] But mutual aid was only the lowest common denominator of a nascent professional group whose members were frequently in dire straits. Once organized, local feldsher societies defined a broader variety of substantive goals related to their professional activity.

The first was improvement of feldshers' material existence and the related goal of increasing public understanding of the difficult conditions feldshers endured on the job. In their articles and letters, feldshers complained unceasingly about their wages and working conditions. They worked long hours, treating patients in clinics or hospitals and traveling torturous miles on horseback or in peasant carts to attend emergency cases. The overall shortage of medical personnel and the needs of the population made it impossible to limit or even regulate these hours. It was not unusual for a feldsher to work a long day, travel through the night to treat a distant patient, and return without sleep in the morning to find ambulatory patients awaiting care.[14] Disease being no respecter of the Sabbath, feldshers were also without holidays or vacations. Limited budgets often forced feldshers at independent points to receive patients in their own peasant cabins, thus exposing their families to the same infectious diseases that were a constant risk in their work.

In return for their tiring and hazardous labor, feldshers were paid between twenty and thirty rubles a month, only one-quarter to one-fifth the salary of a *zemstvo* physician. Survival on such an income was difficult, particularly for those with families. Most feldshers had no property or income beyond their salaries. Those serving at independent posts could (and did) supplement their salaries by accepting gifts in kind from patients, but the practice violated *zemstvo* medical principles, earned them a reputation for extortion, and undermined feldsher claims for greater prestige and status. Finally, the feldshers' low salaries made them almost totally dependent upon their superiors; even brief unemployment threatened financial ruin. Given feldshers' marginal economic existence and unremittingly exhausting routine, these classic trade-union issues would always have a prominent place in their discussions.[15]

A second set of demands recognized feldshers' need to improve their own professional qualifications. *Feldsher* writers repeatedly insisted upon the need for reforms in feldsher education (the inclusion of obstetrics as a required course for male feldshers, for example), urged that refresher courses be established, and asked that qualified feldshers be allowed to enter medical school.[16] Tsarist administrators resisted this demand to the last, insisting that only graduates of classical gymnasia had a sufficiently broad general education to serve as physicians.

Feldshers Versus Physicians: The Issue of "Feldsherism"

The most basic feature of the feldsher movement was a yearning for greater professional recognition, social status, and respect. This manifested itself most clearly in feldsher protests about the arbitrary way in which physicians and hiring authorities treated them. Feldshers were almost defined as a group by their common resentment of physicians; they resented the brusque attitude many physicians adopted toward them, and even more so the slights, insults, and even physical beatings which physicians occasionally handed out. They were particularly offended when physicians asked them to perform the tasks of personal servants or treated them more generally as social inferiors.

The difficult and often emergency conditions under which physicians worked left little time to consider the feldsher's amour propre. The patient's welfare was the physician's first concern, and any mistakes or slowness on the feldsher's part understandably evoked an impatient and sometimes angry response.[17] This being understood, however, the fact remains that physicians were often insensitive to feldshers' feelings. As a prominent physician acknowledged, the feldsher's position could be made unbearable by the physician's "lack of tact" or by his refusal "to recognize the male or female feldsher who is subordinate to him as an intelligent comrade, often one with broader social interests than the physician himself."[18]

To feldshers, the most important source of antagonism between physicians and feldshers was the virtually unlimited authority physicians possessed in dealing with them. Feldshers argued that this authority should be restricted to purely medical matters and asked for the kind of due process in dismissal proceedings that would give them a modicum of job security. Finally, they wanted their professional rights spelled out more clearly.

As it was, the law gave the feldsher no explicit rights vis-à-vis the physician, requiring them instead to obey the physician without question (*besprekoslovno*). Physicians frequently possessed the authority to fire feldshers outright, and even in those cases in which the *zemstvo* or other hiring authority reserved the right of review, the physician's recommendation of dismissal was rarely challenged. This kind of total dependence, frequently on one individual, created an open field for arbitrariness. When physicians ordered feldshers to perform personal tasks unconnected with medicine, for example, most complied for fear of losing their jobs.

This deferential and essentially patriarchal relationship between physicians and feldshers had been traditional in Russia. To some extent it was based on the physician's superior training and the nature of their cooperative activity, in which the physician was the final authority. But it derived additional strength from the disparity in the two groups' cultural attributes and social origins. Physicians were drawn mainly from the urban sector of Russian society. Many were from the upper classes, and the majority, who were either priests' children or *raznochintsy*, were able to transcend their nonaristocratic origins through higher education and identification with an intelligentsia which valued ideals and ability more than social origin.[19]

Feldshers were usually of common, and very often rural, origin. The typical relationship between physicians and feldshers at the turn of the century was much as Chekhov described it: the feldsher removed his hat in the physician's presence; he answered "yes, sir!" to the physician's familiar (*ty*) address; and willingly or grudgingly he performed personal tasks for the physician such as cleaning his clothes or shining his boots. It appears that *rotnye* feldshers, inured to the discipline of the army, were more willing to assume this lackey status than were *shkol'nye* feldshers. Contributors to *Feldsher*, most of whom were *shkol'nye* feldshers, objected to this kind of relationship and charged physicians as a group with retaining caste attitudes no longer acceptable in the 1890s.

Another problem that troubled feldshers was the legal ambiguity of the independent practice that their jobs often demanded. The law specified that feldshers could practice only under a physician's direct supervision. Despite this, rural feldshers were frequently assigned to isolated clinics, miles from the nearest physician. A physician's periodic visits maintained the fiction of supervision, but the impossibility of summoning the physician on short notice meant that many feldshers were independent practitioners. Physicians regularly denounced this independent feldsher practice, which was known as "feldsherism."

Given the shortage of rural physicians and the Empire's vast expanses, this kind of independent feldsher practice seemed unavoidable for the foreseeable future. Feldshers urged physicians to recognize publicly the valuable role that isolated feldshers played, rather than continually denouncing feldsherism or emphasizing that it was a "necessary evil." Most important, feldshers demanded that such independent practice, to which they were regularly assigned, be explicitly sanctioned by law.[20]

Physicians were unwilling to sanction feldsherism for a variety of reasons. Some maintained that independent feldsher care was worse than no care at all.[21] Most physicians feared that even the provisional acceptance of feldshers as adequate rural practitioners might lead district governments to replace physicians with the cheaper feldshers. Physicians and medical administrators alike preferred to tolerate feldsherism in practice without formally recognizing it as legitimate.[22]

The persistent and acrimonious public debate over feldsherism suggests that it was a more critical issue to all concerned than it appears. It was troubling to feldshers for two reasons. First, under existing laws independent rural practice, even when officially sponsored, had a quasi-legal character at best. More important, the word "feldsherism" itself, coined as a pejorative for independent feldsher practice, inevitably suggested a blanket condemnation of all feldsher practice, thus bringing the legitimacy of the feldsher's very existence into question. Nor was this interpretation far-fetched or paranoid, as the Soviet effort to eliminate feldshers in the 1920s would show.[23] Feldshers were not simply trying to improve their professional position; they were struggling to establish an undisputed place for themselves in the firmament of existing occupations. No one speaks of schoolteachers or librarians as a "temporary necessity" or "unavoidable evil," but this is precisely the terminology applied to feldshers in the debate over feldsherism. It does much to explain the feldsher community's bitterness toward physicians.[24]

Fundamentally, the more educated feldshers felt ambivalent toward physicians. They had internalized a professional ideal whose model was the physician. They envied physicians' knowledge, their professional consciousness, their social position, organizational abilities, and role as "enlighteners." They never claimed that the feldsher should be the physician's professional equal, but they desperately wanted the legitimacy and importance of their auxiliary role to be recognized. Only physicians had the professional competence to offer this recognition.

Finally, and perhaps most important, feldshers sought to improve their standing in society. The quest for what Max Weber called "social honor" permeated all of their activities. Activists in the feldsher professional movement were particularly conscious of the fact that their social status was unlikely to improve as long as their pay was low, their legal position insecure, and their professional qualifications both diverse and, in many cases, genuinely inadequate for the tasks they were asked to perform.[25]

Professionalism and Politics: The Revolution of 1905

Feldshers' political views were neither unified nor easily categorized. They had no uniform or clearly enunciated political vision, and for the period before 1905 we have no record at all of what most of them actually thought about national political issues. Their extensive complaints about their lot as feldshers, however, provide a basis for some estimate of their general political outlook.

Prior to 1905, rank-and-file civilian feldshers, including the leaders of the feldsher professional movement, showed only a muted concern for the national political issues on which physicians and physicians' organizations were so outspoken. Censorship and the rules governing the activities in which feldsher societies could engage were partly responsible for this. Most feldshers, however, seem to have assumed that, whatever its defects, the existing social and political order in Russia was a stable entity, unlikely to change except in its details. The goal of the organized feldsher movement was therefore less to transform this order than to improve the feldsher's place in it. Physicians loomed as the main barrier to this improvement, and it was consequently physicians—not the social or political order—who were the chief targets of feldsher resentment and protest.

The fact that feldshers were not primarily concerned with national political issues does not mean that they had no political vision at all. The very nature

of their complaints indicates that they had internalized an essentially democratic value system which was radically at variance with the prevailing norms
of Russia's caste society (and closely attuned to the values of the radical
intelligentsia). Many sources of feldsher discontent, particularly those involving a perceived offense to feldshers' personal dignity, invited a broader and
often radical critique of Russian society. This tie between feldshers' professional woes and the potential for broader political criticism was one that
feldshers clearly recognized.[26]

Feldshers' reticence on political questions ended abruptly in 1905. The
deepening revolutionary crisis in the months following Bloody Sunday
created opportunities for freer political expression and more organized political activity, and many feldshers understandably wanted to participate in the
national transformation that seemed imminent. Like physicians and other
professionals, many individual feldshers joined political parties; others participated to varying degrees in revolutionary activities. For their outspoken
views and general political "unreliability," many of these politically active
feldshers were arrested and dismissed from their posts. The journal of the
Pirogov Society published their names and fates along with those of physicians and other medical personnel who suffered from political repression in
1905.[27]

The intrusion of politics into almost all spheres of life in 1905 raised the
question of whether professional societies, as opposed to individual professionals, should take stands on political issues that did not involve their
professional competence. The professional unions in the liberation movement, which were primarily political organizations aimed at the overthrow of
the autocracy, argued that the transformation of Russia's political structure
was a prerequisite to solving more narrowly defined professional problems. In
the radicalized atmosphere of 1905, most professionals believed that their
societies should contribute to the larger political discussion. However, not all
shared this view.

Dr. Oks, for one, thought it would be "ridiculous, fruitless, and harmful"
to discuss "general political questions concerning the state" in *Feldsher*. His
argument, which he was able to enforce in the pages of his own journal, was
that a professional association should only concern itself with professional
issues. Colleagues with opposing political views, he insisted, should still be
able to cooperate with one another in professional affairs. If professional
societies were to endorse political goals, he argued, the basis for this cooperation would be undermined and ultimately destroyed.[28]

Oks's apolitical stance overlooked the extent to which political commitment had become a touchstone of professional maturity in Russia. In the
revolutionary atmosphere of 1905, his argument angered the many feldshers
who wanted to use feldsher societies as a political weapon. They watched as

others, physicians in particular, put the professional authority of their associations behind a variety of revolutionary demands. They wanted to do the same, and Oks's inflexibility on this issue (feldsher critics emphasized his ox-like qualities) did much to destroy his authority in their eyes.

The energetic and politically outspoken Voronezh feldsher society emerged in 1905 as the organizer and political leader of the scattered feldsher community. Its members rejected Oks's tutelage and took the lead in expressing feldsher views on the burning questions of the day. They joined with representatives of other local feldsher societies to create the first national feldsher organization. By January 1906, they had launched their own national feldsher journal.[29] Their spirited political and organizational activity deserves special attention.

Anxious to become involved in the larger political discussion, the Voronezh feldsher society welcomed Nicholas II's *ukaz* of 18 February 1905, which invited private individuals and institutions to submit "ideas and suggestions" to him concerning "improvements in the state organization and betterment of the people's existence."[30] Intended as a conciliatory gesture, this *ukaz* elicited a flood of political demands from hundreds of radicalized organizations. On 26 February, in a virtually immediate response to the tsar's invitation, the Voronezh feldsher society unanimously adopted a series of almost exclusively political demands.

Describing themselves as "physicians of the common people, who know their needs better than anything else,"[31] the Voronezh feldshers first called for an end to repressive measures such as the use of armed troops against unarmed crowds of civilians and the "reinforced security" legislation which gave the state broad powers of arbitrary arrest and detention. In this regard they also demanded a reduction in the numbers of police, the transfer of control over police to *zemstvo* and municipal governments, and the immediate release of all persons imprisoned for political or religious reasons.[32]

Their chief political demands were for a constituent assembly to be elected by direct and secret ballot without regard for estate, property qualifications, sex, nationality, or religion, and for the introduction of classic political freedoms: freedom of speech and press, freedom of unions and assembly, freedom of movement, freedom of religion and the separation of church and state, the inviolability of person and dwelling, the election of local judges and mandatory jury trials in all cases, and equality of all before the law.

If the Voronezh feldshers did not mention such issues as the eight-hour day, adequate wages, workers' insurance, or the right to strike, their petition nevertheless demanded far-reaching economic and administrative reforms: the immediate abolition of redemption payments, the reduction of indirect taxes and the introduction of an income tax, the immediate fixing of rent taxes on land "to prevent rural unrest," the creation of the small *zemstvo* unit, expansion of *zemstvo* and municipal governments' competence, and the introduction of compulsory universal education at state expense.[33]

Although the Voronezh feldshers' stated demands were almost exclusively political, some were directly related to public health. For example, they urged an end to the pharmacists' monopoly, freedom for medical personnel to conduct public classes on medical problems, the abolition of temporary rules on combatting epidemics, the transfer of public health entirely to public institutions, the hiring of medical personnel without administrative approval, and lastly, "in view of the approaching cholera," an end to the war. One should note that no demands in the petition advanced any exclusively feldsher claims; moreover, nothing at all was said about the feldshers' professional status.[34]

In addition to submitting this petition to the Council of Ministers and the provincial *zemstvo* assembly, the Voronezh feldshers circulated their demands to other feldsher societies and sought to mobilize their support. Some feldsher societies did not respond to this effort; others replied that their societies lacked the standing to address these kinds of questions. The Ekaterinoslav feldsher society, however, passed an equivalent petition.[35]

The Voronezh feldshers' demands were at once radical and commonplace in the spring of 1905. Many were derivative in their very wording. The influence of Gapon and the general program of the liberation movement is clear; the Pirogov Society would advocate similar positions at its "Cholera Congress" in March 1905. That their demands were not unique should not diminish their significance. The Voronezh feldshers' petition and the efforts they made to organize support are evidence that as early as February 1905 many feldshers had acquired a civic consciousness as feldshers which made speaking out on national political issues a "moral duty."[36] Moreover, they had acquired the confidence to participate and even lead others in political struggle.

The Voronezh feldshers' concern for national political issues in no way displaced their desire to improve the feldsher's professional position. If anything, political and professional activism seemed to have gone hand in hand. Both the Voronezh and Ekaterinoslav feldshers argued that a national feldsher organization was necessary in order to achieve real improvements in the feldsher's position. Attempts to unite local societies in a national organization had been made earlier (in 1892 and 1898), but the state had always refused to allow national meetings. To feldshers in Voronezh and Ekaterinoslav, at least, 1905 looked like the right time to try again.

Because of their own provincial location, both Voronezh and Ekaterinoslav feldsher societies thought it preferable for the feldsher societies of St. Petersburg or Moscow to take the lead in forming a national organization. They each asked the St. Petersburg society to host a conference of delegates from local feldsher societies, but it refused, citing the circumstances of 1905 as "untimely."[37] The Moscow feldsher society was more accommodating, and the first delegates' conference met there in April 1905.

This founding conference convened twenty-three feldshers representing sixteen local feldsher societies.[38] It was the first time that feldshers from many areas and societies had ever discussed their professional problems face to face, and negotiations over what form a national organization would take lasted four days. At the conference's conclusion on 28 April, the assembled delegates recommended the creation of a national Union of Societies of Physicians' Assistants. (The term "physician's assistants" [*pomoshchniki vracha*] simultaneously made room for midwives and excluded *rotnye* feldshers). They also agreed that this Union of Societies should have its own journal and should convene a national congress as quickly as possible. A national congress was necessary if feldshers were to win public support for their professional goals. Equally important, delegates argued, only a national congress would enable physicians' assistants to acquire "an upbringing [*vospitanie*] as citizens and develop skills in public activity."[39]

Finally, the delegates' conference concluded with a resolution that only the passage of broad political reforms would make it possible to improve the feldsher's position. The delegates' closing statement insisted that no decent medical system could be created without fundamental social, political, and economic reforms, including the abolition of estate privileges and the protection of the working class. The link between political change and professional improvement was made in this closing statement, which substantially reiterated the February political demands of the Voronezh feldshers, adding only insistence on the right to strike.[40]

After several additional planning conferences, the Union of Societies of Physicians' Assistants was formally established in July 1906. At the end of 1906, it began to publish the journal *Feldsherskii vestnik*. In response to the creation of the Union of Societies, Dr. Oks established his own national feldsher society, known as the Organization of Russian Feldshers (ORF), which sponsored the continued publication of *Feldsher*. During the decade after 1905, there were thus two rival national organizations of feldshers and midwives, each with its own journal. These two national organizations engaged in a good deal of petty infighting, much of which involved resentment of Oks's personality, his political conservatism, and what his rivals perceived as his paternalism. ORF never acquired the same national appeal as the Union of Societies and was finally absorbed into it when Oks retired in 1916.

During 1905, feldshers did not formally identify themselves with any single political party. P.A. Kalinin, who was a participant, writes that most feldsher organizations in 1905 pursued a political program similar to that of the Kadets.[41] E.I. Rodionova also stresses the "caution and restraint" of their political demands. Given the sympathy with much of the Kadet program that can be seen in the Voronezh feldshers' original petition, it is important to note that the Union of Societies also had close ties to the *Trudoviki* and the Social Democrats, whom it described as the "true defenders of the working class."[42] This identification with moderate socialist parties and the general cause of "the working people," without any detailed discussion of party programs, would also characterize the feldsher movement in 1917.

Cultivating Recognition:
The Russian Feldsher Movement, 1906-17

In the atmosphere of political reaction following 1905, even the politically engaged feldsher leadership withdrew from articulate political involvement to a narrower concern for professional questions. Feldshers' professional goals between 1906 and 1917 were much the same as they had been during the 1890s. In the period following 1905, however, feldshers developed more sophisticated tactics with which to reach these goals.

The intensity of feldsher organizational activity after the creation of the Union of Societies of Physicians' Assistants was greater than it had been before 1905. The Union of Societies itself gave feldshers a national platform from which to advance their professional claims. No forum was more effective in bringing their collective demands to society's attention than the national congresses that the Union of Societies organized between 1907 and 1912. Attendance at these national congresses was impressive given the size of the country and feldshers' meager salaries. About 500 attended the congress held in Moscow in 1907. In 1909, there were 466 at the Kiev congress. In St. Petersburg in 1912, there were 286.[43] The papers given at these congresses, which were subsequently published,[44] stimulated discussion both in feldsher journals and local feldsher societies.

Feldsher congresses on the provincial and district level complemented these national meetings. The national and local congresses became the most important tool feldshers had for strengthening organizational ties, refining goals, and debating tactics. They were instrumental in raising the professional consciousness of rank-and-file civilian feldshers. The personal ties that were made or renewed at such congresses reaffirmed the notion of a professional community among feldshers and midwives who often worked in isolation from their peers. In such an organized setting, whose arrangement required extensive planning and cooperation, even the less professionally conscious feldshers could sense that the group to which they belonged was a vital one that contributed to the public life of the nation.

Feldsher activists also urged that feldshers be included as full participants in the provincial and district sanitary councils that began to appear at the turn of the century. They were anxious for feldshers to be heard on issues that directly affected them, but they also believed that feldshers' everyday experience gave them valuable insights on more general medical issues. Inclusion in these councils would enhance their social and professional status as well, since it required physicians to recognize, at least implicitly, that feldshers and midwives were not lackeys, but conscientious partners committed to improving public health. A growing number of local sanitary councils included feldshers in the period immediately before and after 1905, and feldshers urged that such participation be made more general.[45]

The most prestigious forum to which feldshers sought entrance after 1905 was the Pirogov Society of Russian Physicians. Leaders of the feldsher movement asked that delegates from local feldsher societies be admitted to all sessions of the Pirogov congresses. In the immediate wake of the Revolution of 1905, when the democratic ethos among the intelligentsia was at its highest, physicians responded to this feldsher request with some sympathy. At the Tenth Congress of the Pirogov Society in Moscow in 1907, for example, seventeen feldshers attended as representatives of eleven local feldsher societies. They read four papers, all related to aspects of feldsher practice, and many physicians went out of their way to welcome their contributions.[46]

At subsequent congresses, however, leaders of the Pirogov Society refused to admit anything beyond a token feldsher delegation. Feldshers regarded this rejection—particularly after their initial participation in 1907—as yet another manifestation of physicians' "caste mentality." They argued that delegates from all feldsher societies should be admitted (with speaking and voting rights) to the Pirogov congresses, and particularly to all panels on social medicine or the everyday problems of medical personnel. Pirogov organizers rejected this on the grounds that the panels on social medicine were already overcrowded without admitting "feldshers, midwives, dentists, pharmacists, and so on." They did agree to admit a limited number of feldshers, but only as experts on feldsher problems.[47]

In addition to taking part in strictly medical councils, feldsher leaders sought to bring their professional grievances before a larger public by lobbying with the Duma. The Union of Societies of Physicians' Assistants, for example, sponsored the preparation of lengthy reports—what we would call "white papers"—on issues such as feldsher education and the legal position of paramedical personnel, and submitted these reports directly to the Duma. In these white papers they documented their complaints, argued the need for change, and tried to provide legislators with reform suggestions which would satisfy their own demands and still be defensible in medical terms.[48] Through this kind of lobbying, which took advantage of the political opportunities that emerged in the post-1905 period, the Union of Societies of Physicians' Assistants emerged as an aggressive representative of feldsher interests.

Finally, feldsher leaders recognized that they would have to transform their own community in a number of ways if they were to improve their professional status. This involved not only improving feldsher education, which their congresses emphasized, but setting up licensing procedures to transform the feldsher community from one with widely divergent and often inadequate abilities into one with acceptable and reasonably uniform qualifications. To this end they sought to formalize the distinction between themselves and *rotnye* feldshers by denying *rotnye* feldshers membership in their societies and by cultivating the title of "physician's assistant" for themselves, a term which avoided the disdain and lack of esteem associated with the very word "feldsher."[49]

The feldsher movement after 1905 was almost exclusively preoccupied with feldshers' own problems. However, feldsher leaders understood that feldshers would have to exhibit a certain degree of civic commitment in order to achieve even their narrow professional goals. This civic commitment might be only a manifest and informed concern for issues of public health that transcended feldshers' own immediate problems. Indifference to such broader questions would make it difficult for the state or educated society to take their professional pretensions seriously. Only a demonstrated interest in all aspects of public health could justify feldsher claims that they deserved to be considered as real partners with physicians.[50]

Although they did not advocate any specific political goals in the period between 1906 and 1917, the leaders of the feldsher movement believed that feldshers should not isolate themselves from the broader social and political problems of the day. Here again feldsher leaders, at least implicitly, identified with physicians, and particularly with the tradition of civic commitment which characterized the Pirogov Society.[51]

The Russian Feldsher Movement and the 1917 Revolution

The collapse of the tsarist regime in February 1917 ushered in an ongoing renegotiation of the social contract in Russia. As a group with significant personal and professional grievances under the old regime, feldshers naturally wanted to make their voices heard as a new social contract was written. Their mania for professional organization in 1917 dwarfed what they had previously achieved. More than 300 new societies for civilian *shkol'nye* feldshers appeared in 1917 alone, compared to the 54 societies that had existed before.[52] Most of these local and provincial societies joined the All-Russian Union of Unions of Physicians' Assistants, the new name given to the Union of Societies of Physicians' Assistants.

After the February Revolution, *rotnye* feldshers also formed a national organization. The number of *rotnye* feldshers had grown rapidly during the war, so that there were over 75,000 of them in 1917. Most were of peasant origin. Throughout 1917 most of them were on active duty in the army. Both their numbers and the politicized atmosphere within the army encouraged organization. In June 1917, the first national congress of *rotnye* feldshers created the All-Russian Union of Physicians' Assistants (*lekarskikh pomoshchnikov*), which had a membership of 80,000 by 1918.[53] An additional union sprang up in 1918 to represent *rotnye* feldshers employed by the railroad.[54]

The *rotnye* feldsher unions put out their own journals in which they argued the case for giving *rotnye* feldshers more recognition and professional rights.[55] They resented *shkol'nye* feldshers for their refusal to include *rotnye* feldshers in their societies, and made no effort to work with the *shkol'nye* feldshers' Union of Unions. Relations between these two types of feldshers thus continued to be strained even after they joined with others in 1919 to form a single union for all health workers.[56]

The revolutionary atmosphere of 1917 held forth the promise that *shkol'nye* and *rotnye* feldshers alike might be able to improve their place in society. On a purely professional level, they could reasonably hope to achieve many of the goals their movement had worked for, from better working conditions and a firmly acknowledged place in the medical system to the possibility of upward professional mobility. It is also important to recall what the revolutionary premises that dominated political debate in 1917 promised feldshers on a more personal level. They were part of a lower middle class of educated people who sought respect, recognition, and a responsible role within a new society. The egalitarian rhetoric of 1917 seemed to promise all of that. Feldshers could only welcome such an environment, which would enhance their authority and prestige.

The attitude of feldsher organizations toward political involvement in 1917 was somewhat different than it had been in 1905. The Voronezh feldshers advanced political demands in 1905 that were both more explicit and more militantly worded than feldsher political rhetoric in 1917. They were anxious to join others in fighting an autocratic regime whose powers were as yet intact. In 1917, with the tsarist regime gone, leaders of the Union of Unions of Physicians' Assistants were primarily concerned with improving *shkol'nye* feldshers' professional (and social) position. They were certainly not indifferent to politics, but they tended to assume that the outstanding political questions would be resolved in the forthcoming Constituent Assembly.

The political stance of most feldsher leaders in 1917 was that of moderate socialists. In their formal statements they expressed enthusiasm for such general categories as revolution, democracy, and socialism, but there is no indication that they fully understood the differences between socialist parties.

In mid-1917, for example, the Union of Unions insisted that it stood "outside parties," but went on to state that "the socialist parties" were its "ideological representatives."[57] Throughout 1917 they supported the Provisional Government and urged all socialist parties to unify their tactics.[58]

Despite their commitment to "socialism,"*shkol'nye* feldsher leaders were stunned and outraged by the Bolshevik seizure of power in October. The editors of *Feldsherskii vestnik* immediately denounced the coup in terms that would have been acceptable to Mensheviks and Socialist Revolutionaries alike. In the editors' view, Russia clearly lacked the economic and cultural prerequisites for socialism. Any effort to create socialism overnight, they argued, could only succeed by imposing economic and social solutions on an unwilling population. Such an effort would inevitably involve tremendous violence and bloodshed, and the end result would be a centralized dictatorship based on force.[59]

Many *shkol'nye* feldshers opposed the October Revolution, evidently agreeing with *Feldsherskii vestnik*'s analysis, but a large number welcomed it, as did the majority of *rotnye* feldshers.[60] These feldshers shared the general sense of exhilaration that Bolshevik supporters experienced after October and hoped to find a place for themselves within the new medical system. Those who intended to remain feldshers thought that the Bolsheviks, whose ideology embraced the underdog, would value their labor and treat them with respect. The egalitarian ethos of the early Soviet period made the achievement of equal wages with physicians and some real authority in the workplace seem like realistic possibilities. These prospects, understandably attractive to feldshers, posed a challenge to the exclusive competence that physicians had traditionally been granted in medical matters.

This challenge was reinforced by early Bolshevik policies toward labor unions. In 1918, for example, the Commissariat of Labor began to organize a large industrial union, called *Vsemediksantrud*, which included all "medical workers"—from physicians, feldshers, and midwives to nurses, sanitary personnel, carpenters, and cooks. Physicians would have been a small minority in this enormous industrial union. *Vsemediksantrud* became the organizational center of the "feldsher challenge," as Peter Krug has called feldsher efforts to exploit the egalitarian atmosphere of the time in order to improve their place vis-à-vis physicians.[61] Individual *shkol'nye* feldshers played a leading role in the union's organization. In October 1918, the Union of Unions of Physicians' Assistants dissolved itself and entered *Vsemediksantrud*.[62] *Rotnye* feldshers and sanitary personnel followed suit, sensing that this large labor union offered the best chance to improve their own positions.[63]

Physicians were hostile to the syndicalist vision implicit in *Vsemediksantrud*'s organization. Whatever their differences with the Pirogov physicians,

Lenin and N.A. Semashko, the first commissar of public health, were equally opposed to the idea of a Soviet medical system founded on syndicalist principles. As long as he could secure their political neutrality, Lenin was anxious to use what few technical specialists the country had, including physicians, and he believed that the first trait that the Bolsheviks had to seek in medical practitioners was expertise, even if this meant overlooking problems of social class for the moment. The Bolsheviks' ultimate rejection of the "feldsher challenge" in 1919 helped persuade the initially recalcitrant Pirogov physicians to play an active role in the Soviet health system.[64]

The Soviet Regime and the Organized Feldsher Movement

Given the struggle that feldshers waged for almost thirty years to improve their social and professional status, it seems appropriate to ask how they fared under the Soviet regime. Two positive changes should be noted at the outset. First, the Bolsheviks opened the medical faculties to feldshers and encouraged *shkol'nye* feldshers to requalify themselves as physicians.[65] This reduction in admissions standards, which defined physicians more narrowly as technical specialists, was based on the regime's sense that it was urgent to expand the corps of competent physicians rapidly in order to improve the delivery of health care. But it also created a path of upward professional mobility for feldshers. Taking advantage of this new opportunity was difficult in practice, particularly for older feldshers with families, but the feldsher's position ceased to be a professional dead end.

Second, the egalitarian spirit which characterized the early years of the Soviet regime favored the recognition of feldshers' worth, if not as medical practitioners, then at least as human beings. Most striking, however, is the extent to which feldshers were exempted from this general enthusiasm for the lower classes. They lacked the social cachet of being workers, and their professional conflicts with physicians continued unabated. When the Soviet regime contemplated the organization of a health care system, its primary consideration had to be how to provide the best care for the broad masses of the population, not how to satisfy the longings of feldshers for professional and social recognition.

The most important step that the Soviet regime took regarding the feldsher, however, was its decision to abolish the feldsher's position entirely.[66] Leading Soviet health administrators were as hostile to feldsher practice as the most outspoken *zemstvo* physicians had been. As early as 1918 they announced their intention of eliminating the feldsher's position altogether. Initially, however, they recognized that it would not be possible to do this as long as the conditions which had justified feldsher practice before 1917 continued to exist.

In 1922, however, after a highly publicized debate on auxiliary medical education, the Commissariat of Enlightenment moved to end feldsher training altogether, allowing those already in practice to fulfill whatever temporary demands there might be for feldsher care. The advocates of this position were convinced that newly trained physicians and nurses would soon make the feldsher superfluous, even in the countryside. The decision was quickly implemented, so that by 1924 feldsher training had almost entirely ceased.

In marking the feldsher for extinction, the Soviet authorities undermined the hopes that feldshers had nourished for decades that their position as a physician's assistant would one day be legitimized and appreciated. The suspension of feldsher training deprived even practicing feldshers of whatever sense of professional esteem they had been able to sustain. In a strictly professional sense, the Bolshevik regime brought about the ultimate nightmare for feldshers qua feldshers; it decreed them unworthy of existence and attempted to abolish their practice in all contexts. This effort ultimately failed, since the regime could never supply the countryside with enough physicians, and feldsher training was resumed in the 1930s. But no professional movement comparable to that which feldshers mounted between 1890 and 1917 reappeared in the Soviet era.

Why was the early Soviet verdict on feldsher practice so severe? This brings us to the question of what it was about the nature of the feldsher's position which made the achievement of professional recognition so difficult. Feldshers were, to begin with, a classic "semiprofession," that is, an occupational group lacking in one or more of the traits required for society to grant full professional status.[67] Feldshers lacked two traits considered vital in the definition of a profession. They did not have exclusive mastery of an esoteric and socially vital body of knowledge, nor did they have autonomy over their own practice. By definition, they stood in the physician's shadow.

But this does not account for the peculiarity of the feldshers' dilemma, since they never claimed or sought full recognition as professionals. What they hoped to achieve was a greater recognition of their undisputed skills and labor. The reason they failed even here was because of the historical confusion over their role. Although they were trained as physicians' assistants, in practice they had often worked as physicians and continued to do so. The notion of the feldsher as "the physician of the common people" was hardly a notion of the remote past. Early Soviet physicians sought to eliminate this confusion by training larger numbers of physicians and replacing the feldsher with the nurse.[68]

The everyday position of the more than 25,000 feldshers who remained in practice during the 1920s was trying and bleak. Very few of the material demands that the feldsher movement had articulated over the years were satisfied in the early Soviet period. Practicing feldshers' wages and social status remained low; their dependence upon arbitrary local authorities was much the same as it had always been; the poverty of the countryside throughout much of the 1920s (and certainly the 1930s) made their working conditions, if anything, more difficult; finally, the massive unemployment affecting much of urban Russia in the 1920s made their situation even more precarious.[69]

There was very little that the Bolsheviks could have done about any of these problems in the short run. Moreover, it is difficult to speak about a unified Bolshevik policy in the everyday administration of public health, since so much depended upon local decisions, including those of local physicians. Suffice it to say that the legacy of war, revolution, and civil war made the feldsher's professional existence in the 1920s even more trying than it had been before 1914. *Shkol'nye* feldshers often found it difficult to compete with the demobilized *rotnye* feldshers, many of whom had returned to their own villages. Attempts to reduce the number of independent feldsher points drove many better-trained feldshers from their jobs, often without putting anything in their place.

Given the deterioration of the feldshers' position that took place during the 1920s, the decision feldshers made in 1918 to abandon their own professional societies in favor of the larger, faceless *Vsemediksantrud* in 1918 takes on a different significance. The creation of *Vsemediksantrud* and the simultaneous liquidation of local and national societies deprived feldshers of vital, authentic, and free associations which were meaningful to all participants, and did so without providing much of a substantive nature in return.

Conclusion

In assessing the significance of feldsher organizations, and particularly the Union of Unions of Physicians' Assistants, one has to reflect for a moment on the peculiar position feldshers occupied in Russian society. They were marginal people in many respects. Their education, limited as it was, had cut them off from their humble social origins without integrating them into any other social strata. A large proportion of them worked in remote areas. In general, they had few close ties with the population they served, and were equally isolated from the local intelligentsia.

The various feldsher societies, with their periodic congresses and publications, thus fulfilled an important social function for feldshers and midwives, even when they did not achieve all the goals they had set for themselves. They fostered the development of a professional identity and consciousness among paramedical personnel and endowed their work with significance at a time when many physicians argued it was worthless. Moreover, one is struck by the large number of feldshers who realized a kind of civic existence within these societies, devoting all of their spare time to some aspect of feldsher organization. Finally, feldsher societies provided their members with a haven of understanding in a world either unsympathetic or indifferent to their problems. No wonder that feldshers consistently used the word "family" to refer to their collective existence. As P.A. Kalinin remarked after visiting a congress of feldshers in Poltava in 1913, "I saw a rather numerous family of more than 150 people. Not a meeting of feldshers and feldsheritsas, but precisely a *family*, inspired by their public work and nourished by common interests . . ."[70]

Vsemediksantrud destroyed this free and spontaneous professional activity among feldshers, with its organizational roots at the local level. When it failed to improve the substantive conditions in which feldshers worked, it is small surprise that feldshers began to exhibit what was denounced as a "guild" mentality,[71] which was in fact a longing for the specific set of organizations which had at least articulated their aspirations.

Notes

I would like to thank the Kennan Institute of Advanced Russian Studies, the National Endowment for the Humanities, the International Research and Exchanges Board, the Fulbright-Hays Fellowship program and the Tulane University Committee on Research for their generous support in the writing of this article.

1. On the variety of these burgeoning voluntary associations, see Jacob Walkin, *The Rise of Democracy in Pre-Revolutionary Russia* (New York: Frederick A. Praeger, 1962), 121-52. See also Joseph Bradley, "Voluntary Associations, Civic Culture, and *Obshchestvennost'* in Moscow," in *Between Tsar and People: Educated Society and the Quest for Public Identity in Late Imperial Russia*, eds. Edith W. Clowes, Samuel D. Kassow, and James L. West (Princeton, NJ: Princeton University Press, 1991), 131-48.

2. On the liberal intelligentsia and 1905 see Shmuel Galai, *The Liberation Movement in Russia, 1900-1905* (Cambridge: Cambridge University Press, 1973); Terence Emmons, "Russia's Banquet Campaign," *California Slavic Studies* 10 (1977): 45-86; idem., *The Formation of Political Parties and the First National Elections in Russia* (Cambridge: Harvard University Press, 1983), chaps. 1-2; K.F. Shatsillo, *Russkii liberalizm nakanune revoliutsii 1905-1907 gg.* (Moscow, 1985); A.D. Stepanskii, "Liberal'naia intelligentsiia v obshchestvennom dvizhenii Rossii na rubezhe XIX-XX vv.," *Istoricheskie zapiski*, vol. 109 (Moscow, 1983): 64-94; and V.V. Leontovich, *Istoriia liberalizma v Rossii, 1762-1914*, trans. Irina Ilovaiskaia (Paris: YMCA Press, 1980), 360-438.

3. How perceptions of social identity evolved during this period is a problem which needs more investigation. For a beginning, see Leopold H. Haimson, "The Problem of Social Identities in Early Twentieth-Century Russia," *Slavic Review* 47, no. 1 (Spring 1988): 1-20, and the ensuing comments by William G. Rosenberg and Alfred J. Rieber.

4. On the diversity of the urban working class in Russia, see Victoria E. Bonnell, *Roots of Rebellion: Workers' Politics and Organizations in St. Petersburg and Moscow, 1900-1914* (Berkeley: University of California Press, 1983), chap. 1, and idem., "Urban Working-Class Life in Early Twentieth-Century Russia: Some Problems and Patterns," *Russian History* 8, pt. 3 (1981): 360-78. For statistics on the

composition of the intelligentsia at the turn of the century, see L.K. Erman, "Sostav intelligentsii v Rossii v kontse XIX i nachale XX v." *Istoriia SSSR* 7, no. 1 (January-February 1963): 161-77 and idem., *Intelligentsiia v pervoi russkoi revoliutsii* (Moscow, 1966), 7-33.

5. For studies of the professional intelligentsia which include these middling groups see Erman, *Intelligentsiia*; V.R. Leikina-Svirskaia, *Intelligentsiia v Rossii vo vtoroi polovine XIX veka* (Moscow, 1971); idem., *Russkaia intelligentsiia v 1900-1917 godakh* (Moscow, 1981); and N.M. Pirumova, *Zemskaia intelligentsiia i ee rol' v obshchestvennoi bor'be do nachala XX v.* (Moscow, 1986).

6. For studies of comparable intermediate occupations see Jeffrey Brooks, "The Zemstvo and the Education of the People," in *The Zemstvo in Russia: An Experiment in Local Self-Government*, eds. Terence Emmons and Wayne S. Vucinich (Cambridge: Cambridge University Press, 1982), 243-78; Mary Schaeffer Conroy, *In Health and Sickness: Pharmacy, Pharmacists, and the Pharmaceutical Industry in Late Imperial and Early Soviet Russia* (Boulder, CO: East European Monographs, 1994); Ben Eklof, *Russian Peasant Schools: Officialdom, Village Culture, and Popular Pedagogy* (Berkeley: University of California Press, 1986), part II; idem., "The Village and the Outsider: The Rural Teacher in Russia, 1864-1914," *Slavic and European Education Review* 1 (1979): 1-19; Christine Ruane, *Gender, Class, and the Professionalization of Russian City Teachers, 1860-1914* (Pittsburgh, PA: University of Pittsburgh Press, 1994); Jonathan Sanders, "Drugs and Revolution: Moscow Pharmacists in the First Russian Revolution," *Russian Review* 44, no. 4 (October 1985): 351-77; Scott Seregny, "Revolutionary Strategies in the Russian Countryside: Rural Teachers and the Socialist Revolutionary Party on the Eve of 1905," *Russian Review* 44, no. 3 (July 1985): 221-38; idem., *Russian Teachers and Peasant Revolution: The Politics of Education in 1905* (Bloomington: Indiana University Press, 1989).

7. Feldsher societies included midwives, but the organizers and driving force of these societies were feldshers or feldsher-midwives. The societies were almost exclusively devoted to the problems of feldshers and feldsher-midwives.

8. *Otchet o sostoianii narodnogo zdraviia i organizatsii vrachebnoi pomoshchi v Rossii za 1907 god* (St. Petersburg, 1909), 91-92.

9. Samuel C. Ramer, "The Transformation of the Russian Feldsher," in *Imperial Russia, 1700-1917: State, Society, Opposition. Essays in Honor of Marc Raeff*, eds. Ezra Mendelsohn and Marshall S. Shatz (DeKalb, IL: Northern Illinois University Press, 1988), 136-60.

10. By 1891 there were 21 male feldsher schools and 11 female feldsher schools with 241 and 134 graduates, respectively, in that year. *Otchet meditsinskogo departamenta Ministerstva vnutrennykh del za 1891 god* (St. Petersburg, 1894), 272-73. Women were first allowed to practice as feldshers in 1871 and would become an increasingly significant portion of the *shkol'nye* feldshers. L.F. Ragozin, ed., *Svod uzakonenii i rasporiazhenii pravitel'stva po vrachebnoi i sanitarnoi chasti v Imperii*, 3 vols. (St. Petersburg: 1895-98), I, 218. On the social dimension of improvement in feldsher training see Samuel C. Ramer, "Transformation."

11. For Oks's original intentions in publishing *Feldsher*, see Boris Oks, "Po povodu izdaniia 'Feldshera'," *Feldsher* 1, no. 1 (1891): 10-11. The need for a feldsher journal that would improve feldshers' medical skills and present a more positive

image of the feldsher was noted as early as the mid 1870s in an anonymous feldsher contribution to *Zdorov'e* 2, no. 44 (August 1876): 363. See also E—v. [I.V. Egorov], "Po voprosu ob izdanii populiarnogo periodicheskogo organa dlia feldsherov," *Zdorov'e* 2, no. 51 (November 1876): 490-93 and no. 52 (December 1876): 511-14.

12. Oks writing in afterward to *Feldsher* 1, no. 24 (1891): 313.

13. The emphasis upon mutual aid is clear in the title of the first feldsher society, established in Odessa in 1882: Obshchestvo shkol'nykh feldsherov "Samopomoshch'" [The "Self-help" Society of *Shkol'nye* Feldshers]. E.I. Rodionova, *Ocherki istorii professional'nogo dvizheniia meditsinskikh rabotnikov* (Moscow, 1962), 36.

14. For a memoir recounting such experiences see Anna A., "Na zemskoi sluzhbe: Iz zapisok feldsheritsy," *Vestnik Evropy* 6, no. 12 (December 1890): 549-93.

15. For a survey of articles on these kinds of problems see A.V. Pedanenko, "Obzor statei i korrespondentsii o bytovykh usloviiakh i deiatel'nosti feldsherov, pomeshchennykh v gazete 'Feldsher' s 1891-go po 1900-y god," *Feldsherskii sbornik: po povodu desiatiletiia gazety "Feldsher,"* comp. B.A. Oks (St. Petersburg, 1903): 1-64.

16. See, for example, "Soiuz obshchestv pomoshchnikov vrachei," *S"ezd po reforme feldsherskogo i akusherskogo obrazovaniia v Moskve (2-6 ianvaria, 1911 g.)* (Moscow, 1911); V.P. Popov, "Obzor statei po voprosu o povtoritel'nykh kursakh dlia feldsherov," *Feldsherskii sbornik,* 113-43; G.P. Zadera, *Pravo feldsherov i feldsherits na vyshee meditsinskoe obrazovanie* (St. Petersburg, 1907).

17. For the classic fictional portrayal of a physician's frustration with his feldsher, see Chekhov's story "Nepriiatnost'," in Anton Chekhov, *Sobranie sochinenii v dvenadtsati tomakh* (Moscow, 1963), vol. 6, 113-32.

18. V. Chenykaev, *Feldsher* 6, no. 3 (1896): 85.

19. For a social profile of physicians, see Nancy M. Frieden, *Russian Physicians in an Era of Reform and Revolution, 1856-1905* (Princeton, NJ: Princeton University Press, 1981), chapter 9.

20. See, for example, A.A. Gorbachevich, *Samostoiatel'naia deiatel'nost' feldsherov i neobkhodimost' ee uzakoneniia* (St. Petersburg, 1907).

21. See, for example, I.I. Molleson, *Zemskaia meditsina* (Kazan', 1871), 22.

22. For a prominent negative evaluation of feldsherism by a physician, see M.Ia. Kapustin, *Osnovnye voprosy zemskoi meditsiny* (St. Petersburg, 1889), 28-41.

23. See Samuel C. Ramer, "Feldshers and Rural Health Care in the Early Soviet Period," in *Health and Society in Revolutionary Russia,* eds. Susan Gross Solomon and John H. Hutchinson, (Bloomington: Indiana University Press, 1990), 121-45.

24. The response to Dr. G.M. Gertsenshtein's qualified endorsement of feldsherism at the Fifth Congress of the Pirogov Society gives some idea of just how much passion the issue could provoke. See G.M. Gertsenshtein, "Zemstvo i feldsherizm," *Trudy V-go s"ezda obshchestva russkikh vrachei v pamiat' N.I. Pirogova,* vol. 2 (St. Petersburg, 1894): 591-618.

25. The drive for recognition by society is a dominant theme in all feldsher writings. For an example of this, see feldsher R. Tsiurupa's letter in *Feldsher* 14, no. 23 (1904): 707-8.

26. Commenting on the Moscow feldsher society's 1900 application to publish its own journal, for example, Sergei Zubatov wrote that sanctioning such a forum for feldshers to discuss their professional position would inevitably draw the society "into the field of politics." Gosudarstvennyi arkhiv rossiisskoi federatsii, f. 63, op. 20, d. 224/900, l. 4, quoted in A.V. Ushakov, *Revoliutsionnoe dvizhenie demokraticheskoi intelligentsii v Rossii, 1895-1904* (Moscow, 1976), 44.

27. Pirogov Society records indicated that 1,064 medical personnel suffered from some form of repression in 1905. Of these, a little more than 250 were feldshers or feldsher-midwives. Most were arrested or fired; however, 10 were killed, 9 were beaten or wounded, 19 were exiled, 1 was sentenced to a disciplinary battalion, and 1 died in prison. "Repressii po otnosheniiu k meditsinskomu personalu," *Feldsherskii vestnik* 1-2 (December 1906): 58.

28. B.A. Oks, "Pro doma sua," *Feldsher* 15, no. 14 (1905): 430-34.

29. The Voronezh feldshers took over the existing journal *Meditsinskaia beseda* on 1 January 1906. In September 1906, they changed its name to *Pomoshchnik vracha*. In late 1906, *Pomoshchnik vracha* was shut down by the tsarist administration. Its editor, Dr. A.S. Kraevskii, was arrested and expelled from Voronezh. After a month the journal reappeared under the title *Lekarskii pomoshchnik* and lasted for three years, eventually closing for financial reasons. Kalinin, *Profdvizhenie*, 151.

30. Abraham Ascher, *The Revolution of 1905: Russia in Disarray* (Stanford, CA: Stanford University Press, 1988), 113.

31. "Otchet o deiatel'nosti Voronezhskogo obshchestva pomoshchnikova vrachei za 1905 god," *Pomoshchnik vracha* 10 (1906): 263.

32. Ibid., 264.

33. Ibid.

34. Ibid., 263-64.

35. Ibid., 264-65.

36. Ibid., 263.

37. Ibid., 269.

38. Feldshers at this first conference came from Odessa, Moscow, St. Petersburg, Kazan', Novocherkassk, Ekaterinoslav, Saratov, Samara, Chernigov, Kiev, Kostroma, Kursk, Tambov, Irkutsk, Voronezh, and Elisavetgrad. Ibid., 273.

39. Ibid., 274-75.

40. Ibid., 278.

41. Kalinin, *Profdvizhenie*, 21.

42. Rodionova, *Ocherki istorii professional'nogo dvizheniia meditsinskikh rabotnikov*, 57.

43. Kalinin, *Profdvizhenie*, 41.

44. *Trudy pervogo Vserossiiskogo s"ezda feldsherov, feldsherits i akusherok s 20-go po 25-oe ianvaria 1907 goda v g. Moskve* (Moscow, 1907); *Trudy vtorogo Vserossiiskogo s"ezda feldsherov, feldsherits, i akusherok s 10-go po 17-oe iiunia 1909 goda v g. Kieve* (Moscow, 1909); *Trudy tret'ego Vserossiiskogo s"ezda feldsherov, feldsherits i akusherok s 21-go po 27-oe iiunia 1912 goda v S-Peterburge* (Moscow, 1913).

45. P.A. Kalinin, "Doklad obshchemu sobraniiu Saratovskogo feldsherskogo obshchestva ob uchastii delegatov ot feldsherov v sanitarnykh sovetakh i v soveshchaniiakh vrachei," *Vrachebno-sanitarnaia khronika Saratovskoi gubernii* 5-6 (May-June 1903): 229-31. For one physician's opposition to such feldsher representation, see S. Igumnov, "Feldsherizm i sanitarnye sovety," *Vrachebnaia khronika Khar'kovskoi gubernii* 10, no. 9 (September 1906): 485-89.

46. Kalinin, *Profdvizhenie*, 29-34.

47. For the Pirogov Society's review of this problem in 1913, see *Doklady i kommissii XII-mu Pirogovskomu s"ezdu vrachei (S.-Peterburg, 29 maia - 6 iiunia 1913 g.)* (Moscow, 1913), 26-27.

48. See, for example, *O pravovom polozhenii i obrazovanii feldsherov i feld-sherits v Rossii. Sbornik materialov dlia chlenov Gosudarstvennoi Dumy* (Moscow, 1917).

49. On the conflict between *shkol'nye* and *rotnye* feldshers, see Samuel C. Ramer, "Who Was the Russian Feldsher?" *Bulletin of the History of Medicine* 50 (1976): 213-25.

50. For an argument that feldsher organizations should have more general goals than improving the feldsher's lot, see G. Kovalenko, "Zadachi i tseli feldshersko-akusherskoi organizatsii," *Feldsherskii vestnik* 8, no. 1 (1913): 13-22.

51. Ibid.

52. *Dvenadsatyi delegatskii s"ezd Vserossiiskogo soiuza soiuzov pomoshch-nikov vrachei (8-14 maia n. st. 1918 g.)* (Moscow 1918), 5-6. P.A. Kalinin records only 279 new societies for 1917, bringing the total number of feldsher societies at the end of 1917 to 327. Kalinin, *Profdvizhenie*, 49.

53. A. Aluf, *Kratkaia istoriia professional'nogo dvizheniia medrabotnikov*, 3d ed. (Moscow, 1927), 46-47.

54. *Vserossiiskii soiuz zh.-d. rotnykh feldsherov.*

55. The All-Russian Union of Physicians' Assistants published *Izvestiia Vse-rossiiskogo soiuza lekarskikh pomoshchnikov* until 1918. The All-Russian Union of Railroad *Rotnye* Feldshers published the *Vestnik zh.-d. feldsherov* briefly in 1918.

56. Kalinin, *Profdvizhenie*, 50.

57. *Odinadtsatoe sobranie delegatov Vserossiiskogo Soiuza soiuzov pomoshch-nikov vrachei (30 aprelia-4 maia 1917 g.). Rezoliutsii* (Moscow, 1917), 3.

58. Ibid.

59. N. Popov, "1917-y god," *Feldsherskii vestnik* 2, nos. 47-48 (15-23 December 1917): 586-87.

60. Peter F. Krug, "Russian Public Physicians and Revolution: The Pirogov Society, 1917-1920" (Ph.D. diss., University of Wisconsin-Madison, 1979), 238.

61. For an excellent discussion of this "feldsher challenge" to physicians' exclusive medical authority, see Krug, "Russian Public Physicians," chap. 8.

62. "Nasha pozitsiia," *Feldsherskii vestnik* 12, nos. 41-44 (1-23 November 1918): 422-26.

63. Aluf, *Kratkaia istoriia*, 57.

64. On Lenin's attitude to the technical intelligentsia, see Kendall E. Bailes, *Technology and Society Under Lenin and Stalin: Origins of the Soviet Technical Intelligentsia, 1917-1941* (Princeton, NJ: Princeton University Press, 1978), chap. 2.

65. *Dekrety sovetskoi vlasti,* vol. 3 (Moscow, 1964), 141; L.F. Raukhvarger, "Zavershenie medobrazovaniia feldsherov," in *Pervyi Vserossiiskii s"ezd po meditsinskomu obrazovaniiu,* ed. L.F. Raukhvarger (Moscow, 1920), 36, 71.

66. For a discussion of this decision, see Samuel C. Ramer, "Feldshers and Rural Health Care in the Early Soviet Period."

67. For a review of semiprofessions and their problems, see Amitai Etzioni, ed., *Semi-Professions and Their Organization: Teachers, Nurses, Social Workers* (New York: The Free Press, 1969).

68. L.F. Raukhvarger, "Feldsherskie shkoly," in *Pervyi Vserossiiskii s"ezd po meditsinskomu obrazovaniiu,* ed. L.F. Raukhvarger (Moscow, 1920), 36.

69. On the causes of this unemployment among physicians and feldshers and measures proposed to deal with it see "Po bezrabotitse sredi medpersonala i merakh bor'by s nei," *Shestoi Vsesoiuznyi s"ezd Medsantrud (3-12 iiunia 1926 g.): Rezoliutsiia i postanovleniia,* 2nd ed. (Moscow, 1926), 70-74.

70. "Tri dnia v Ukraine," *Feldsherskii vestnik* 8, no. 25 (1913): 793-94.

71. *Shestoi Vsesoiuznyi s"ezd Medsantrud,* 70.

6

Professionalization and Radicalization: Russian Psychiatrists Respond to 1905

Julie V. Brown

The dominant profession stands in an entirely different structural relationship to the division of labor than does the subordinate profession.

—Eliot Freidson, 1970

The administration of the mental hospital should be shared not only by all physicians but by support personnel as well.

—D.A. Amenitskii, 1910

The first decade of the twentieth century was pivotal for many professional groups in Russia, including the Empire's relatively small (less than 600 members in 1908) psychiatric profession. At the turn of the century, leaders of the profession were absorbed by their efforts to gain control over mental institutions and to force official recognition of psychiatrists' judgment in all matters pertaining to the diagnosis and management of insanity. Although the obstacles to professionalization were enormous and the profession was torn by internal dissension, the prevailing mood was one of optimism. By the eve of World War I, however, the situation had changed dramatically. Great numbers of Russian psychiatrists were united in open hostility to the tsarist government. Calls for professional autonomy had given way to demands for radical reform of society. Solicitation of central government and *zemstvo* support for the profession's claims to unique and valuable expertise had been supplanted by charges that both agencies were causes of the problem psychiatrists sought to ameliorate.

The events that culminated in the political disaffection of Russian psychiatrists were numerous and complex.[1] This essay focuses upon one important dimension of that process and demonstrates how the broader political struggles in Russian society impinged upon psychiatrists' efforts to resolve what

143

they had regarded as an internal professional dispute. The intrusion of extraprofessional actors into the debate both changed its nature and increased the stakes. The ultimate result was that many members of the profession felt compelled to declare allegiance either to their employers or to colleagues whom they had earlier opposed. In this instance psychiatrists opted for professional solidarity. Ironically, their newfound unanimity involved adherence to a vision of the internal administrative order of the asylum that threatened to undermine the profession's position of dominance in the psychiatric hospital.

In the late nineteenth century, the first generation of psychiatrists had endorsed the concentration of formal authority within mental institutions in the hands of one physician-director.[2] However, in the early years of the twentieth century, a new generation of psychiatric professionals, convinced of the superiority of their qualifications and ideologically opposed to autocratic rule, demanded that the rigidly hierarchical administrative structure of the mental hospital be eliminated. In its stead they sought to establish a democratic system based upon the principles of individual equality and professional self-regulation. Their term for this new regime was "collective administration" (*kollegial'noe upravlenie*).

In the format initially proposed, authority would be shared by all physicians on the staff of an institution. However, during the strike-ridden months of late 1905 and 1906, other occupational groups within asylums made similar demands for a share in the administration of the institution. The most radical psychiatrists were active participants—on occasion even leaders—of these protests. More conservative members of the profession were appalled by the disorders and continued to insist upon the inviolability of the hospital's autocratic structure.

For the majority of psychiatrists (including most of the leaders of the profession), the issues were not so clear-cut. They had joined with the hospital proletariat, as well as other groups in society, in calling for the introduction into Russia of participatory government. However, the demand by the hospital workers that mental institutions be governed according to those same principles represented a direct threat to their professional authority. Bothered by what appeared to be a contradiction between their beliefs in political equality and professional privilege, psychiatrists went to great lengths to justify their claims to professional superiority.

In the immediate post-1905 era, most psychiatrists instituted some form of collective administration in their institutions. A few of the most "progressive" ones admitted representatives of nonphysician groups into the decision-making processes of the hospital. They did so on a very limited scale and in more than a few instances with the consent of the local self-governments, or *zemstva*, under whose auspices most mental institutions had been placed after the Great Reforms of the 1860s.

Over the course of the next several years, increasingly conservative *zemstvo* officials and provincial administrators attempted in increments to re-establish the asylum's autocratic regime. Many psychiatrists had been less than enthusiastic about the "democratization" of the mental hospital; however, they interpreted these and other simultaneous actions as intolerable efforts to undermine their authority. Many youthful members of the profession responded by adopting a more radical posture. Their behavior made officials more suspicious of psychiatrists, resulting in additional measures to control the activities of the profession. There ensued a cycle of protest and repression culminating in the political disaffection of much of the profession and its insistence that mental institutions be governed by all of those who worked within their walls.

Emergence of the Autocratic Asylum

The first formal gathering of Russian psychiatrists took place in 1887. Organizers of the meeting hoped to provide psychiatrists with an opportunity to solve the most serious problems facing them. Those problems were not theoretical or scientific but rather involved practical organizational and administrative concerns. Members of the profession unanimously endorsed a resolution advocating that mental institutions be directed by one specially trained physician to whom all other hospital employees would be subordinate.[3] This shared conviction regarding the centrality of the asylum medical director derived in large part from the concept of "moral treatment" which dominated the thinking of nineteenth-century psychiatrists. The basic tenets of moral treatment were summarized by a prominent historian of American psychiatry:

> moral treatment meant kind, individualized care in a small hospital; resort to occupational therapy, religious exercises, amusements and games; repudiation in large measure of all threats of physical violence; and only infrequent application of mechanical restraints. . . . Along with a rationale for care and treatment went a fairly elaborate vision of the structure of the ideal mental hospital. There was a general agreement that hospitals should remain small (250 or less); that superintendents should have complete control of the medical, moral and dietetic treatment, and that all staff, professional and supporting, should remain under the unfettered control of the superintendent.[4]

Support of Russian psychiatrists for asylum autocracy was also fostered by the peculiar set of problems the profession faced during its early decades. As was true of its parent, the Russian medical profession, the emergence of a native psychiatric profession was almost entirely the result of government initiative.[5] Prompted to action by a combination of idealism regarding the curability of insanity and amorphous fear of urban disorders, the government under Nicholas I (1825-55) decided to construct a network of regional asylums (*okruzhnye lechebnitsy*) under the auspices of the Medical Department of the Ministry of Internal Affairs.[6] Inspired by western models, these were to be therapeutic institutions designed to care for those with acute forms of insanity (believed to be the most treatable), and the patients were to be under the supervision of medically trained specialists in insanity.

The governmental reformers soon discovered to their dismay that there were few such specialists to be found on Russian soil.[7] Having legislated into existence a system of institutions to treat the insane, the government then set about to arrange for the creation of a cadre of specialists with whom to staff them. The first regional asylum was located in Kazan', largely because of the presence there of a university to train psychiatrists.[8] The government's concern with the dearth of specialists was also a primary consideration in the decision to establish a department of psychiatry at the Medical-Surgical Academy in St. Petersburg in 1857.[9]

In the years immediately following establishment of the *zemstva*, the Ministry of Internal Affairs abandoned the regional asylum project and shifted responsibility for care of the insane to the *zemstva*. When they proved reluctant to assume the burden, the central government insisted. Senate rulings issued in the mid 1870s required that the *zemstva* provide asylum space to all comers, even if doing so necessitated expanding existing facilities or acquiring new ones.[10] At that point, *zemstvo* mental institutions consisted principally of aging asylums inherited from the prereform-era provincial Departments of Public Welfare. Most were quite small and in serious disrepair. Moreover, in the years after emancipation of the serfs, demand for asylum space increased at a rapid rate, a trend which gave no indication of abating.[11]

Not surprisingly, the Senate rulings produced panic among *zemstvo* officials and led to a massive outpouring of protest. The result was a promise by the Ministry of Internal Affairs in 1879 to provide significant financial aid for new construction of mental institutions. Assured of rapid reimbursement, many *zemstva* sprang into action in the early 1880s. Old facilities were renovated, new ones were begun, and asylum populations continued to rise.[12]

Most *zemstva* were slower to perceive a need for psychiatric expertise than for expanded facilities to house the insane, doubtless due to the fact that only the asylums had been mandated from above.[13] Still, practical necessity dictated that someone be in charge of the burgeoning institutions, and the "enlightened" public of the time was increasingly of the opinion that the insane were "ill" and should be ministered to by a physician. Consequently, most *zemstvo* mental institutions came early on to be staffed by medical personnel. A few *zemstvo* executive boards sought specially trained psychiatrists to staff their asylums. Most, however, utilized any available medical talent. By far the most common pattern was to place the mental institution under the administrative jurisdiction of the provincial somatic hospital.[14] By the end of the decade, the majority of *zemstvo* mental institutions included on their staffs a physician who laid claim to the title of psychiatrist. In some instances the claim was justified in terms of formal training in a university program at St. Petersburg or Kazan' (or less often, training abroad); in others, accumulated years of practical experience within the asylum underlay claims to special expertise.

Psychiatrists increasingly protested their administrative subordination to nonpsychiatric institutions, demanding complete autonomy for the asylum and the removal of nonspecialist physicians from positions of authority over the mentally disturbed. Even psychiatrists employed by autonomous mental institutions were frequently forced to share authority with a nonspecialist. Most asylums were governed jointly by a medical director and a lay supervisor (*smotritel'*). *Zemstvo* executive boards often explicitly stated that the authority of the *smotritel'* surpassed that of the chief medical officer. Psychiatrists considered subordination to nonspecialist physicians an affront to their professional status.

Consequently, a central concern of psychiatrists in the 1880s and 1890s was to wrest power from those nonpsychiatrists with whom they were forced to share it. [15] The ideology of moral treatment was particularly useful in this regard, providing the Russian profession with a western, "scientific" rationale for their insistence upon complete and autonomous control over mental institutions. In addition, in their struggle with the *zemstva,* it was more effective for Russian psychiatrists to argue that control over psychiatric institutions should be concentrated in the hands of one highly qualified individual who could be easily identified and held accountable rather than in the hands of an amorphous collective administration. During this era, the number of psychiatrists working in any given institution was generally quite small. In hospitals employing only one psychiatrist, collective administration had no meaning. In those employing several, one individual was often clearly distinguishable by virtue of formal training or asylum experience. Under the circumstances, his "juniors" would have been less likely to question the legitimacy of his superior status and greater responsibility.

There were exceptions to the predominant pattern of hospital administration. The charter of the Kazan' Regional Asylum, for example, as early as 1888 provided for a Council of Physicians (*sovet vrachei*) which was to discuss all aspects of the operation of the institution. Each regular (*shtatnyi*) member of the medical staff participated in the meetings of the council, and each had an equal vote. [16] Nonetheless, the extent to which real authority was shared in the Kazan' institution was by all accounts quite small. Final authority rested with the institution's director, who alone answered to the Ministry of Internal Affairs. This was a state of affairs that psychiatric physicians regarded as right and proper. Commented one in the late 1880s, "The difference between the director of a psychiatric hospital and an intern (*ordinator*) is one of the same order of magnitude as that between a boss and a hired hand."[17]

By the turn of the century, the number of trained psychiatrists employed by the *zemstva* had increased substantially, and the medical press began to report conflicts between the directors of psychiatric asylums and younger staff members. In areas as remote from each other as Khar'kov, Ufa, and St. Petersburg, serious clashes occurred between junior and senior physicians.[18] The number of such confrontations increased steadily after the turn of the century. The youthful practitioners protested that the bureaucratic organization of the psychiatric hospital was incompatible with the ideals of collegiality and cooperation, which they had been socialized to regard as inherent in the notion of "profession" and hence central to the medical practice of psychiatry. In each instance of conflict the catalyst was somewhat different, yet the disputes were consistently defined in terms of the unjustifiable subordination of junior staff members to directors who were superior to them neither in terms of the quality of their professional training nor by virtue of any extraordinary personal attributes. That the *zemstva* generally sided with the senior physicians against their younger colleagues heightened the latter's sense of frustration and outrage.[19]

The growing concern of young psychiatrists with the unequal distribution of power in psychiatric institutions was first expressed at meetings of the Pirogov Society of Russian Physicians in the early years of the twentieth century. At its Ninth Congress in St. Petersburg, the society's section on nervous and mental diseases passed a resolution supporting the principle of collective administration for psychiatric institutions. Proponents of collective administration hoped to minimize or eliminate inequalities among physicians. The resolution called for replacing the existing hierarchical organization of medical staffs with councils of peers, thereby making the psychiatrists within an institution a true "fraternity of equals."[20]

The strong feelings of newer members of the profession about their subordination were based on more than a heightened sense of their own personal worth and professional capabilities. Asylum directors were frequently political appointees, many of whom lacked appropriate qualifications for the position and/or abused their privileges to the detriment of patients and staff alike.[21] Such instances were foremost in the minds of those who joined in the discussions in 1905, as is indicated by the following comments:

> Not a week passes without word reaching us of new and scandalous conflicts between directors and interns which occurred solely because of attempts by the latter to protect the basic human rights of the patients . . .

> What does one need with laws if one is friendly with the judges? I am reminded of the sad incident at the hospital in Smolensk. All of the interns there were forced to leave because of the horrible way in which the director treated the

patients. The director is still there now. Why? Because "he knew the judges." He knew the governor, and he also knew the head of the zemstvo executive board.[22]

Widespread perception of a problem is suggested by the fact that when participants at the Second Congress of Psychiatrists in Kiev in 1905 appointed a committee to draft a resolution on institutional administration, they insisted that at least half of its membership consist of junior interns (*mladshie ordinatory*), the ones "who especially suffered because of the lack of regulations."[23] The resolution, written by the committee and approved by the conference as a whole, spelled out clearly what collective administration was to mean in practice. It also called for institutional and professional autonomy, laying particular emphasis on the psychiatrists' right to participate in personnel decisions involving their professional colleagues.[24]

The campaign to restructure the internal organization of the asylum reached its zenith in 1905 and 1906, and much of the rhetorical language in which it was couched reflected the broader political concerns of those involved.[25] In the eyes of the new generation of psychiatrists, the asylum was the larger society in microcosm. Those values and organizational principles that dominated Russian society and against which they were raising their voices in protest were central to the functioning of the Empire's psychiatric institutions. The administrative structure of those institutions, they alleged, was rigidly hierarchical, with power concentrated at the top and exploitation rampant.

Although few public objections were raised to the concept of collective administration at the Kiev meeting, the idea was far from universally accepted. Discussions of the subject at meetings of the St. Petersburg Society of Psychiatrists, for example, revealed continued opposition to the demands of junior physicians for an equal role in the administration of the hospital. Some objected that the concept remained untested and that it had failed in other contexts. One senior psychiatrist defended the institutional hierarchy by means of an analogy between the battleground and the hospital: "In Austria during the war the army was commanded collectively. As a result the Austrians lost every single battle."[26] In other instances, serious objections to collective administration were raised only after eager junior interns returned home from the Second Conference of Russian Psychiatrists and attempted to implement the resolutions passed in Kiev.[27] Nonetheless, before significant change could take place, the focus of the discussion shifted as other hospital workers began actively asserting their own right to a larger role in the governance of the institutions.

The Asylum in Turmoil

The first major confrontation involving the nonprofessional personnel of a psychiatric hospital began within weeks of the close of the Second Conference of Russian Psychiatrists in August 1905, in the midst of one of the stormiest years in Russia's history. While a full recounting of Empirewide unrest is impossible, detailed information about a few specific instances involving psychiatric hospitals provides some of the flavor of these months. One of the first recorded confrontations took place at the Hospital of St. Nicholas the Miracle Worker in St. Petersburg during the tempestuous days preceding issuance of the October Manifesto. The hospital was notorious as a place of danger for staff and patients alike. The building that housed the Hospital of St. Nicholas had been constructed in 1852 as a special psychiatric wing of the central St. Petersburg correctional institution. In 1872 it was administratively separated from the prison and transferred to the municipal government. While a part of the prison system, it emphasized restraint rather than humane treatment. Yet by all accounts, conditions in the institution worsened after its transfer to the city. The number of inmates rose dramatically, the facility fell into disrepair, and the salaries of physicians and other staff members were reduced. The building was designed to accommodate a maximum of 300 patients. By the early years of the twentieth century, the patient population had reached a staggering 1,200, and those unfortunate individuals whose fate it was to spend a portion of their lives there slept crowded together on decrepit benches and chairs.[28]

Political meetings at the institution, involving both patients and staff, began as early as May Day 1905. The first serious disturbances took place in mid October of that year, while the institution's chief physician was abroad.[29] A central figure in the drama was G.Ia. Troshin, a senior intern who had helped to organize the Union of Hospital Workers. On 15 October, Troshin called a meeting of the medical staff at which he presented a resolution calling for autonomy for the hospital and cessation of all dealings with the central government. Troshin urged that the current chief physician, N.N. Reformatskii, be removed and a new one elected by all hospital personnel by means of a "universal, direct, equal, and secret" ballot. The new chief physician would, according to Troshin's plan, perform only administrative functions. All decisions concerning the hospital order and patient care would be made by a committee comprised of all physicians employed by the hospital. Those present at the meeting agreed to reconvene two days later to discuss the proposal further and to put the question of institutional autonomy to a vote.

The second meeting was attended by the staff physicians, a representative of the city medical administration, and a group of hospital workers. The hospital workers entered the room en masse in the company of Dr. Troshin. The participation of an "outside" element in what was to have been a meeting of physicians had not been anticipated by the city official. He began to chat with the workers but did his best to postpone any voting until a more auspicious moment. Nonetheless, in the ensuing semichaos a vote was taken, with the majority of those present supporting Troshin's proposal.

The hospital workers interpreted the presence of a municipal representative at the time of the vote as indicating that the city government sanctioned their actions. They began to hold regular meetings at which they formulated a set of economic demands and continued to discuss the general question of institutional autonomy and their own future role in the administration of the hospital. Informal leadership of the workers was assumed by Troshin and by the hospital's *smotritel'*. The workers expected a quick and positive reaction from the city to their demands. What came instead were efforts to control what municipal officials clearly regarded as a potentially explosive situation.

By the end of the year, the atmosphere in the hospital had become extremely tense. Some attributed the rising level of agitation among the workers to the underground efforts of radical groups; others cited the workers' frustration that the city had imposed repressive measures rather than following through with promised improvements. In early January 1906, violence erupted. An angry mob of workers gathered outside Reformatskii's office, demanding that he leave the hospital. When the chief physician failed to respond, the mob broke into his office, surrounded him, and carted him from the building in a wheelbarrow.[30] The workers then began to release some of the prisoners (including "political" ones) who were incarcerated in the institution.

Both the police and the army were called to the scene, and the situation was brought back under control. Armed guards were stationed in the hospital and twenty-six workers placed under arrest. Troshin was fired, and criminal charges were filed against him for the violence perpetrated against Reformatskii. Charges were also filed against the arrested workers, and most were subsequently convicted. The workers were given prison sentences ranging from six to eight months. Troshin received a sentence of sixteen months.

In mid November 1905, a scenario strikingly similar to what took place at the Hospital of St. Nicholas was played out in the Ukrainian city of Khar'kov.[31] Protesting their working conditions, the workers of the Khar'kov *zemstvo* psychiatric hospital at Saburovaia Dacha prepared a set of demands for presentation to the provincial executive board. On 17 November the workers gave their petition to the hospital's director, Pavel Iakobii, with instructions that he pass it on to the board. As Iakobii talked with the workers in the hospital kitchen, tensions mounted. Finally, one of the workers demanded that the director leave the premises. As Iakobii headed for the exit, he was surrounded, thrown into a wheelbarrow, and carried from the hospital. The workers then carted him around the hospital grounds amidst jeers and whistles. When the crowd was finally persuaded that the director had endured enough, it turned to "more important matters."

After Iakobii's departure, the workers decided to convene a "constituent assembly." The newly formed assembly promptly organized a representative government to run the hospital. The workers elected two delegations of six persons each (six paraprofessional workers and six unskilled workers) and asked that the hospital physicians select six of their number to join the workers' representatives. The eighteen persons so chosen were to form a united delegation which would comprise the hospital administration. The psychiatrists agreed to accept the workers' proposal and elected six representatives. However, they insisted that their cooperation was temporary. In the long run they wanted the hospital to be governed by a council composed of all physicians with representatives of both paraprofessional and unskilled workers.

The following day (18 November), the full delegation convened and selected a committee to inform the *zemstvo* executive board of the events that had transpired and seek its sanction. A 19 November meeting was attended by the delegation, the provincial executive board, and representatives of a *zemstvo* commission that had recently been organized to consider the reorganization of psychiatric care for the province. At that meeting the executive board agreed to major concessions. It increased workers' salaries and reached an agreement with the united delegation regarding hiring and dismissal procedures for all hospital personnel. The board also promised to raise the issues of autonomy and collective administration at the next meeting of the provincial assembly. Finally, it agreed not to prosecute any of the workers for their part in bringing about the demise of the old hospital regime.

In March 1906, the provincial assembly approved collective administration for the hospital. Nominal authority was given to the physicians collectively. The assembly also approved the formal participation of the workers in a newly formed Hospital Council (*bol'nichnyi sovet*) which was to address all serious problems faced by the hospital. However, in June the workers formulated a new set of demands and threatened to strike unless the *zemstvo* officials agreed to negotiate with them. When the officials balked, the workers made good their threat. On 27 June they left their assigned posts. The strike lasted only two and a half hours, since troops were promptly called to the scene to restore order. Twenty-nine persons were fired by the *zemstvo* for participating in the disorders.

The parallels between the incidents in Khar'kov and St. Petersburg are striking. Both occurred in large institutions with particularly bad reputations. (One psychiatrist remarked of Saburovaia Dacha that the best thing that could be done for Khar'kov's mentally ill citizens would be to burn it to the ground.)[32] Both institutions had histories of conflicts between junior and senior physicians.[33] Each of the incidents resulted in the ignominious departure of the hospital's senior medical officer and an effort to democratize the administration of the institution. In each instance, a relatively youthful psychiatrist was at the center of the controversy. In St. Petersburg the doctor held responsible for the violence was Troshin. In Khar'kov P.P. Tutyshkin was arrested and charged with instigating the incident. The individuals involved and many of their colleagues insisted that involvement in political activities was perfectly legal according to the October Manifesto. Their supporters insisted that neither Troshin nor Tutyshkin was guilty of more than the "crime" of propagandizing the ideas of collective administration and institutional autonomy which their professional colleagues had overwhelmingly approved only a few months before at the Second Conference of Russian Psychiatrists.

As similar as the two incidents were, their outcomes were very different. Whereas in St. Petersburg the city government came down with an iron hand, effectively returning the hospital to police control, in Khar'kov the *zemstvo* acceded to many of the workers' demands. Most of those fired at the time of the strike were subsequently rehired, and the new administrative structure of the hospital was left intact. Although Tutyshkin was not permitted to return to his old position at Saburovaia Dacha, the charges filed against him were dropped long before the case could come to trial. Troshin went to prison. Tutyshkin soon found a new position at Kostiuzhenskaia Psychiatric Hospital in Bessarabia.[34]

Response to 1905:
Political Equality and Professional Privilege

The incidents in Khar'kov and St. Petersburg, along with analogous ones in other cities, made a significant impression on the psychiatric profession.[35] Some of its members were deeply disturbed by the intrusion of politics into the inner sanctum of the psychiatric hospital. As one commented:

> The political contest goes on in many arenas: the press, the factories, public meetings, the state Duma, even the streets. Surely, its chances of success will not be lessened if it remains outside of institutions for the mad. In ancient Greece, as you all know, a criminal was never apprehended while he was inside a temple. The jurisdiction of the law terminated at the door of the temple. Let us likewise stop revolutionary agitation at the door of the psychiatric institution.[36]

Many psychiatrists were also distressed by the concessions that were made to the nonprofessional personnel of those institutions. They saw the indignities suffered by Reformatskii and Iakobii as seriously undermining the professional authority of psychiatrists. They reiterated their concern that the medical policies of the hospital not be directed by semiliterate workers and expressed the conviction that the real concern of those workers was not political but economic. Those who gave in to their political demands, the critics maintained, not only threatened the welfare of psychiatrists' patients, but they did so for naught. All that the workers really cared about were their salaries and their working conditions. Those economic grievances, which most acknowledged were legitimate, could be satisfied without compromising the formal structure of authority within the hospital and the welfare of the patients.

Other psychiatrists were pleased by the steps taken to democratize administration of the asylum and applauded the actions of those psychiatric physicians who had taken leading roles. They insisted that the political concerns of the workers were legitimate, since the structure of the mental hospital was a reflection of some of the worst and most repressive features of the tsarist regime. In the words of one:

> It is not right to simplify the issue by attributing the protests in the psychiatric hospital to the workers' attempts to improve their material conditions.
> One of the primary reasons why the "liberation movement" had such a pronounced effect on psychiatric hospitals is the moldy old system which predominates within them. The despotic features of our outdated political system are strikingly similar to the despotic regimes which govern our psychiatric hospitals.[37]

According to this view, individuals such as Iakobii and Reformatskii were not owed special apologies. The attacks against them had not been personal but symbolic.[38]

Psychiatrists were less divided over political issues than professional ones, although the two were, of course, interrelated. For the most radical members of the profession, the elimination of political inequality implied the elimination of professional privilege as well. At the opposite extreme were those who insisted that the broader political struggle be kept entirely separate from professional concerns. According to the latter view, analogies between the political structure of Russian society and that of the asylum were meaningless and counterproductive.

Most members of the profession were painfully aware that the turmoil in the psychiatric hospital was inextricably bound up with the broader political struggle in which they were actively engaged. Having joined with the hospital proletariat in the demand that Russia be governed by a constituent assembly, psychiatrists were placed in a particularly awkward position when the workers demanded a similar government for their mutual workplace. The principle of universal and equal suffrage was one that most psychiatrists advocated for the Empire as a whole; however, support for the workers' position within the smaller confines of the asylum carried with it the implication that each hospital employee was equally capable of making responsible decisions about hospital affairs. To accept that principle would have been tantamount to denying their professional superiority. Having devoted much of the previous quarter century to the effort to gain official acknowledgment of their claims to superior knowledge and expertise, they were understandably reluctant to abandon the struggle so readily.

Psychiatrists continued to grapple with the problem of reconciling their advocacy of democratic rule in society with their support for oligarchic rule in the hospital. In the spring of 1906 they were provided with a particularly apt public forum in which to compare their views. Amidst the turmoil at Saburovaia Dacha, the provincial executive board's commission on psychiatric care invited a group of prominent psychiatrists from throughout the Empire to attend a conference in Khar'kov on psychiatric hospital administration. The invitations to the conference stressed that the executive board was concerned about the recent changes in the administration of Saburovaia Dacha and wished to know the experts' opinion as to the best form of hospital administration.

Zemstvo officials asked that the experts clarify the meaning of the terms "hospital autonomy" and "collective administration," inquiring specifically whether participation by nonprofessional personnel was necessary or desirable. The visiting psychiatrists were also asked whether Saburovaia Dacha should continue to have a "senior physician," and if so, what the rights and responsibilities associated with the post should be. Each of the invited experts was given the opportunity to express his personal opinion, after which the floor was opened to discussion. After discussion of each subject, the participants formulated a statement summarizing their views.

The conference proceedings provide a concise and clear summary of the views of many principal spokesmen for the profession.[39] Although there were disagreements among those congregated in Khar'kov, the specialists reached a consensus on most issues. They concluded that institutions like Saburovaia Dacha should continue to have a senior medical officer appointed by the *zemstvo* executive board in consultation with experts. That individual would direct the hospital in conjunction with a board of physicians (*kollegiia vrachei*). The experts concluded further that the nonprofessional workers in the hospital should be given only a limited administrative role:

> To turn over the management of the hospital to a corporation of workers or a group of asylum employees of differing categories is in theory an incorrect approach and in practice impossible to achieve. . . . However, in the interest of fairness and expediency and because it has proven necessary to protect them from capriciousness, the workers should be guaranteed representation in the Council when their interests are directly involved.[40]

The conclusions reached by the experts in Khar'kov were quite moderate, leaving the professional integrity of psychiatrists securely intact. Still, the events of preceding months had clearly made an impression on the collective psyche of the profession. The experts not only advocated that formal authority be shared by all members of the medical staff of an institution, but they discussed the possibility that nonprofessional workers might share in it as well. Several of those involved in the conference eagerly propagated that view.[41] Opinions expressed by those who participated in the conference in Khar'kov provide a striking contrast to the views espoused by leaders of the profession a few years earlier.

The participants at the Khar'kov conference clearly felt the need to justify in their own minds and for the benefit of their more radical peers their support for an institutional authority structure and a professional role that was taken for granted in most other contexts. In the effort to do so, they presented elaborate arguments in defense of the thesis that a hospital is not a "society." In particular, they argued that all individuals and social groups within the hospital were oriented toward one common goal—curing patients. Since success in that enterprise depended upon the application of specific scientific knowledge, the very logic of the endeavor dictated that authority rest in the hands of those with requisite technical skills. Those experts were, of course, the psychiatric physicians. As if oblivious to the events of preceding months, the psychiatrists also contended that those considerations of class which were so important in the larger society were subordinated within the hospital context to the welfare of the patients.

> Revolution in a state is one thing; in a hospital it is quite another. As correct as it is to demand that the principle of democratization be realized in the governance of a society, it is equally incorrect to demand that within hospitals. What we are witnessing is a mental aberration. Special educational backgrounds are not necessary for those who participate in the governance of a society.[42]

Finally, the psychiatrists resorted to the older and more familiar argument that the workers in Russia's mental institutions were exceptionally poorly qualified. Because of their ignorance and cultural backwardness, so the argument went, the workers could hardly be expected to make informed decisions on either patient care or hospital administration. This skepticism as to the capabilities of workers notwithstanding, psychiatrists were forced to acknowledge that workers did in practice make important decisions regarding patient care and hospital management. Most institutions employed few physicians. As a result, the majority of the day-to-day decisions were made by nonprofessional workers. As early as 1883, one psychiatrist commented acerbically that within the asylum, "the attendant is tsar."[43] Psychiatrists expressed little reluctance to share the governance of Russian society with "pretentious semiliterates";[44] however, they were adamant that the reins of the psychiatric hospital be kept beyond the reach of those same individuals.

> I am not an opponent of democratization, but I do oppose a medical democracy. I am against rule by ignoramuses, especially in our society. Despite the extent of democratization and the respect for legal principles which one finds in

England and America, one does not find in those societies (or anywhere else) that the hospital workers have the rights which our workers are now demanding.[45]

The majority of psychiatrists clearly hoped in those years to reconcile their political convictions with their professional self-interest. Since the espousal of collective administration involving only psychiatric physicians represented a concession to their political convictions, which posed little or no threat to their professional self-interest, most were willing to go along with the idea. Still, there was a significant and vocal minority advocating a more radical view. Typical of these individuals was a contingent of youthful psychiatrists in the St. Petersburg Society of Hospital Physicians who resolved, in contradistinction to their professional "superiors," that all asylum employees should participate in the administration of the institution. They based their decision on two considerations: that even unskilled workers could make a positive contribution to hospital management, and that the Russian masses needed experience in decision making, since they had been denied it at all levels of society in the past.[46] At the opposite end of the professional and political spectrum were those who continued to defend the old asylum order. While their numbers were perhaps smaller, they were still very much in evidence.

Over the course of the next half decade, the weight of professional opinion shifted significantly in the direction of further democratization of the asylum. This was far less a result of positive experiences with collective administration than a response to external pressure exerted by increasingly uncooperative (and in some cases, politically reactionary) *zemstva* and the central government.

Autocracy Triumphs over Collective Administration: The Disaffection of Psychiatrists (1906-11)

The cooperativeness of *zemstvo* assemblies, evidenced in Khar'kov in 1905, renewed psychiatrists' hope in the ability of the two groups to work together. Buoyed by events in Khar'kov, many psychiatrists envisioned a new era of mutual effort that would witness great progress in the development of organized care for the insane and that would be associated with greater decision-making power for psychiatrists.

Beginning in 1905, psychiatrists throughout the Empire started, with tacit approval of the *zemstva*, to democratize the provincial mental institutions. In most instances the changes involved introduction of physicians' councils and reduction or even elimination of distinctions of seniority among the members of the medical staff. In some areas, "progressive" psychiatrists began to admit nonprofessional workers into the governance of their institutions, albeit on a limited scale. In 1906, for example, the support personnel in Voronezh were invited into the psychiatric hospital's council (*sovet*) "on the basis of active and equal participation in decisions regarding all hospital matters."[47] Similar steps were taken in Saratov, Moscow, and other locales as well.[48]

However, psychiatrists' momentary optimism regarding their future with the *zemstva* was soon "drowned in a wave of political reaction."[49] The first signs came with systematic efforts by the central government's provincial representatives, and increasingly by the *zemstva* as well, to eliminate nonprofessional workers from the administrative organs of asylums. In Saratov, the *zemstvo* executive board justified such action on the grounds that it had earlier been pressured into unwise decisions by the disorders of 1905.[50] In most other instances no effort whatsoever was made to justify the decision. Even Saburovaia Dacha was moved by the shifting winds; in 1908, the Khar'kov provincial assembly arbitrarily removed all nonprofessional representatives from the institution's Hospital Council.[51]

Psychiatrists at the institutions involved tended to be among the most politically active members of the profession, and they protested what they regarded as retrogressive measures. Their protests often resulted in their being forced to resign and occasionally in their exile or imprisonment, thereby adding more "victims" to the growing numbers of those prosecuted in relation to incidents involving political prisoners.[52] In 1906, for example, the governor of Moscow province ordered the firing of a prominent psychiatrist and director of the *zemstvo* psychiatric hospital, V.I. Iakovenko, along with other members of the medical staff. Iakovenko resigned before the order could be carried out, but another psychiatrist employed at the institution, Dr. Lebedev, was arrested and placed in prison, where he soon died of typhus.[53] That same year another prominent psychiatrist, Dr. A.A. Govseev, was imprisoned and threatened with exile to Arkhangel'sk. In 1907 the director of the provincial psychiatric hospital in Voronezh, N.A. Vyrubov, was fired and exiled from the province. A psychiatrist at the Nizhnii Novgorod institution for the insane (Liakhovo), Dr. Fal'k, suffered a similar fate.[54]

Even those psychiatrists who disagreed with the professional and political activities of their more outspoken colleagues objected to the treatment accorded their professional associates. Professional journals provided a detailed chronicle of repressive actions taken against psychiatrists during these years. As the list grew longer, the inclination on the part of the spokesmen for the profession to defend their "progressive" colleagues became more pronounced. Their defense increasingly involved the vindication of collective administration, the cause for which many of their associates were suffering, including the format which gave a significant role to nonprofessional workers.

At the Tenth Congress of the Pirogov Society in 1907, the section on nervous and mental diseases passed a resolution calling for the inclusion of nonprofessional personnel in organs established to administer hospitals collectively.[55] The issue headed the agenda of the Third Conference of Russian Psychiatrists in late 1909, at which a resolution was approved "recognizing the absolute necessity of basing the hospital order upon the principles of autonomy and collective administration, . . . [including] as soon as possible . . . representatives of the hospital support personnel in the activities of those collective institutions which *direct the affairs of the hospital*."[56]

As the first decade of the century drew to a close, the distance between the perceptions of the psychiatric profession and those of officials at all levels had grown wider still. In case after case, asylum charters were revoked by *zemstva*, many of whose leaders refused to allow nonprofessionals to have a voice in asylum affairs and insisted that any collective administration by medical personnel be eliminated. The Saratov, Tver, and Kursk provincial *zemstva* formally reinstituted hierarchical administrative systems within their provincial mental hospitals and declared that "ultimate" authority rested with the director.[57] In 1908 the Moscow provincial *zemstvo* executive board refused even to accept annual reports from an institution's director because they had been co-signed by other physicians and representatives of the support staff.[58] In 1909 the Kursk provincial executive board approved a new charter for the provincial asylum that not only reaffirmed the "absolute" authority of the director but also called for a representative of the executive board to live on the hospital grounds to supervise the goings-on there.[59] These actions infuriated the psychiatric profession, causing it to question its future under the existing regime. As he chronicled these events, N.A. Vyrubov, editor of the journal *Contemporary Psychiatry*, mused:

> The thought inevitably comes to mind that some time in the near future the *zemtsy* will have mastered psychiatry to such an extent that they will no longer need doctors and will replace the physicians with members of the executive board.[60]

Collectively, the effect appears to have been to persuade an increasing number of the profession's members to endorse more "radical" positions. Only a few psychiatrists—mostly directors of *zemstvo* asylums—dared as late as 1909 to defend the actions of the local self-governments and the concept of administrative hierarchy. In the words of one,

> the individual who is held responsible should be the one to have executive power. Since the majority of zemstvo assemblies clearly wish to have a single accountable person at the head of the hospital (and, in particular, one whom they trust), it seems to me that for the time being the best approach is an accountable directorate.[61]

The opinion of the majority was that such individuals were guilty of unpardonable collusion with the *zemstva* in the persecution of their colleagues.

They were severely chastised for placing extraprofessional ties above their obligations to their professional comrades.[62] The strength of feeling on the subject is attested to by the unanimous passage of a supplementary resolution at the 1909 conference emphasizing the necessity for institutional autonomy and collective administration.[63]

By 1911, when the first meeting of the Russian Union of Psychiatrists and Neuropathologists took place, the few remaining critics of collective administration had been silenced by the loud outpouring of protests against the policies of the *zemstva* and central government alike. In addition, there was near universal support among psychiatrists for the inclusion of nonprofessional personnel in the administration of the mental hospital.[64] The arguments offered in 1911 in support of "democratization" suggest that many psychiatrists considered all employees of the asylum to have common interests overriding differences of background and training and thought the hospital proletariat made a significant contribution to patient care.[65] P.P. Kashchenko, director of the St. Petersburg *zemstvo* provincial psychiatric hospital, summarized these feelings when he insisted that the nurses, attendants, orderlies, and maids in the asylum were psychiatrists' "coworkers and collaborators" rather than their "servants or assistants."[66]

A central defining characteristic of a profession is its autonomy, which "is sustained by the *dominance* of its expertise in the division of labor."[67] The position advocated by Russian psychiatrists in 1911 with respect to their relationship to support personnel in the hospital appears to have threatened their professional dominance. However, espousing that view was little more than a symbolic gesture of protest against outside efforts to compromise their autonomy. Each of the profession's many employers had left no doubt in the minds of psychiatrists that it was they (i.e., the *zemstva* and the tsarist bureaucracy) who would dictate asylum policy regarding both administration and medical matters. Despite near universal advocacy by psychiatrists, none of those agencies was willing to sanction the "democratization" of psychiatric institutions.

> Our employees boldly attempt to restrict the introduction of "collective administration" in mental institutions. Not only the central government but the organs of local self-government as well regard it as an encroachment upon their executive prerogatives. We cannot name so much as one institution in which the principle as it was spelled out in discussions at our conferences has been formally approved and put into practice.[68]

Psychiatrists' inability to influence the administrative order of the asylum was only one of several significant setbacks suffered by the profession during those years. In the post-1905 era the government effectively placed many psychiatric asylums under police control. Shackles and armed guards became a common sight in those institutions of "healing," and psychiatrists' efforts to have them removed were consistently rebuffed. Acquiescing to the "realities of Russian life," psychiatrists abdicated responsibility for the "dangerous" insane and surrendered them to the control of tsarist prison institutions.[69] Meanwhile, the fiscally strapped *zemstva* were increasingly approving plans which would remove most of the "harmless" insane from expensive provincial psychiatric hospitals. Some sought to disperse them among the smaller district somatic hospitals; others were of the opinion that the patients should be returned to the peasant hearths from which most of them had earlier been removed. Both of these proposals involved the transfer of primary responsibility for the insane to nonpsychiatrists. The profession responded by promoting an alternative program of extramural psychiatric care (referred to as the *patronage familial*) under which they would be able to retain a measure of control over the situation.[70] However, this attempt met with only limited success.

By the eve of World War I, much of the psychiatric profession was outspoken in its opposition to the tsarist regime. The hostility was expressed in numerous ways—some overtly political, others only indirectly so. Many members of the profession were drawn into the revolutionary movement, and psychiatric hospitals became centers of underground political activity.[71] Their distaste for the political regime and disapproval of the socioeconomic structure that it supported were also reflected in their "scientific" theories as to the etiology and presumedly increasing incidence of insanity in Russia.[72]

Conclusion

All professions are dependent upon the state, as "it is by the interaction between formal agents or agencies of the occupation and officials of the state that the occupation's control over its work is established and shaped."[73] However, the dependence of Russian psychiatrists upon state patronage was particularly great. As employer to the vast majority of psychiatrists, the government not only determined how many psychiatrists would be needed, but also controlled the quality of their working conditions and was the source of legitimation of their claims to professional status. Psychiatrists' dependence on the state was compounded by their inability to demonstrate empirically the technical expertise they professed to possess. The theoretical models propounded by psychiatrists remained vague, and practitioners were unable to treat the insane with any measurable degree of success. As a result, the "scientific" theories elaborated by psychiatrists continued to reflect, on the one hand, the asylum's role in society, and on the other, the profession's perception of its own role in the institution.[74] In that sense, psychiatry's subordination to the state was cognitive as well as economic and political.

This extraordinary dependence made the psychiatric profession extremely vulnerable to changes in government policy. The events of the post-1905 era suggested strongly to many psychiatrists that the priorities of the existing regime left them with little future to contemplate. They had responded to the new institutional arrangements which were thrust upon them by attempting to redefine their role. That endeavor was largely unsuccessful. Indeed, their efforts at accommodation led them to espouse positions that were inimical to the interests of the profession and morally or professionally repugnant to much of its membership. That psychiatrists declared their independence from the state and increasingly chose to cast their lot with those who advocated its overthrow would seem to indicate that they had concluded they had nothing to lose from the downfall of the existing regime and indeed that its perpetuation placed the survival of the profession in doubt. Awareness of their exceptional dependence upon state patronage is suggested by the fact that they were one of the first professional groups to support the Bolshevik regime which assumed control in the fall of 1917.[75]

Notes

1. They are analyzed in Julie V. Brown, "The Professionalization of Russian Psychiatry: 1857-1922" (Ph.D. diss., University of Pennsylvania, 1981).

2. *Trudy pervogo s"ezda otechestvennykh psikhiatrov proiskhodivshogo v Moskve s 5 po 11 ianvaria 1887 g.* (St. Petersburg, 1887), 334.

3. Ibid.

4. G.N. Grob, *Mental Institutions in America: Social Policy to 1875* (New York: Free Press, 1973), 168-70.

5. Nancy M. Frieden, *Russian Physicians in an Era of Reform and Revolution, 1865-1905* (Princeton, NJ: Princeton University Press, 1981).

6. The factors which brought about this new concern with the construction of asylums are discussed in detail in Brown, chapter 2.

7. Most of the existing asylums were under the auspices of the Department of Public Welfare and were staffed by nonmedical personnel, frequently retired soldiers. The few "psychiatrists" in Russia prior to midcentury were employed by several elite institutions in Moscow and St. Petersburg.

8. I.R. Pasternatskii, "K voprosu o domakh umalishennykh v Rossii," *Trudy 1887*, 845; A.M. Shereshevskii, "Istoriia sozdaniia okruzhnykh psikhiatricheskikh bol'nits v Rossii," *Zhurnal nevropatologii i psikhiatrii im. S.S. Korsakova* (1978): 433.

9. F.S. Tekut'ev, *Istoricheskii ocherk kafedry i kliniki dushevnykh i nervnykh boleznei pri imperatorskoi voenno-meditsinskoi akademii* (St. Petersburg, 1898), 78-79.

10. The government's principal concern was that it be able quickly to remove "dangerous" persons from society. The rulings are discussed in N. Kamenev, "Meditsinskii otchet po psikhiatricheskomu otdeleniiu bol'nitsy Tul'skogo gubernskogo

zemstva s 1-go ianvaria po 1-e ianvaria 1897 goda," *Voprosy nervno-psikhicheskoi meditsiny* 2, no. 4 (1897): 538-92.

11. Prior to the emancipation of the serfs, many *prikaz* asylums had been half empty. During the last half of the century, asylum populations skyrocketed throughout the Empire. The reasons for the increase are complex. I have argued elsewhere that the crucial factor was a change in the manner in which the peasantry utilized the institutions rather than a change in rates of mental disorders. See Julie V. Brown, "Peasant Survival Strategies in Late Imperial Russia: The Social Uses of the Mental Hospital," *Social Problems* 34 (1987): 311-29.

12. The central government did provide a great deal of money for subsidies during the 1880s; however, it did not nearly cover the costs incurred by the *zemstva*. By the 1890s, the subsidy money dried up as the Ministry of Internal Affairs resurrected the provincial asylum concept. *Zemstvo* costs continued to escalate.

13. Despite its protestations to the contrary, the central government continued to behave as if the asylum were a "police" institution rather than a "medical" one. Much of the medical profession was skeptical regarding the validity and/or necessity of psychiatric expertise as well. Brown, "Professionalization."

14. Initially, the medical director of the somatic hospital had full responsibility for the psychiatric department. This was the situation depicted in Anton Chekhov's story, "Ward 6." However, as the number of asylum inmates increased, additional medical personnel were hired specifically to manage them. The authority of these new physicians almost always remained subject to that of the hospital director. As of 1900, only twelve *zemstvo* psychiatric asylums were independent and under the direction of a psychiatrist. E.A. Ossipoff et al., *La medecine du zemstvo en Russie* (Moscow, 1900).

15. This was clearly evident at the First Conference of Russian Psychiatrists. The most strongly worded resolution of the conference was on the subject of institutional autonomy. The resolution is cited in Brown, "Professionalization," 128.

16. The supervisor (*smotritel'*) also had a vote on matters relating to the economic management of the institution. The charter even provided for limited participation in institutional decision making by the most senior of the nonprofessional personnel, the *nadziratel'* and *nadziratel'nitsa*. D.A. Amenitskii, "Istoricheskii ocherk vnutrennego upraveleniia v obshchestvenno-psikhiatricheskikh uchrezhdeniiakh," *Sovremennaia psikhiatriia* 4 (1910): 349-456.

17. P.A. Arkhangel'skii, *Otchet po osmotru russkikh psikhiatricheskikh zavedenii* (Moscow, 1887).

18. See *Nevrologicheskii vestnik* 6 (1898): 250 and *Nevrologicheskii vestnik* 8 (1900): 228.

19. Turnover among junior staff physicians of psychiatric institutions was notoriously high. Many psychiatrists protested that this discouraged young physicians from entering the profession. See, for example, V.F. Chizh, "O vnutrennei organizatsii zavedenii dlia dushevno-bol'nykh," *Vestnik klinicheskoi i sudebnoi psikhiatrii i nevropatologii* 9 (1891): 1-45.

20. Obshchestvo russkikh vrachei, *S"ezd IX: Trudy deviatogo s"ezda* (St. Petersburg, 1904).

21. The complaint was voiced by other physicians as well. See Frieden, 337.

22. *Trudy 1905*, 99-103. Similar accusations were made within the American psychiatric community as well. See, for example, Ruth B. Caplan, *Psychiatry and the Community in Nineteenth-Century America* (New York: Basic Books, Inc., 1969), 204-5.

23. *Trudy 1905*, 106.

24. Ibid., 107.

25. The effort to "democratize" was widely felt during those years. Even the St. Petersburg Society of Psychiatrists was affected by it. A group of youthful members attempted to restructure that organization: to eliminate what they dubbed its "bureaucratic centralism" and replace it with a council (*sovet*), the membership of which would change at regular intervals. See *Nevrologicheskii vestnik* 8 (1905): 152.

26. The speaker did not specify which war he had in mind. The rejoinder to that comment by a defender of collective administration was: "During the Manchurian War we didn't have 'collective' command, and we still lost every single battle." *Obozrenie psikhiatrii, nevrologii i eksperimental'noi psikhologii* 10 (1905): 777; and *Zhurnal nevropatologii i psikhiatrii im. S.S. Korsakova* 7 (1907): 1204-5.

27. A prime example was the psychiatric clinic of Moscow University. In 1906, V.P. Serbskii, the clinic's director, fought a bitter battle with the junior staff members of that institution over how much administrative authority should be shared. Serbskii insisted upon his own right to virtual dictatorial rule. The other psychiatric staff members (with one exception) all resigned in protest against his policies. See *Nevrologicheskii vestnik* 14 (1907): 143-44; and A.G. Gerish, *P.B. Gannushkin* (Moscow, 1975), 25-26.

28. *Trudy pervogo s"ezda russkogo soiuza pskihiatrov i nevropatologov sozvannogo v Moskve v pamiat' S.S. Korsakova 4–11/IX 1911 g.* (Moscow, 1914), 664. See also, O.A. Chechott, *K razvitiiu prizreniia dushevno-bol'nykh s-peterburgskim gorodskim upravleniem 1884-1912* (St. Petersburg, 1914).

29. The account of the events at the Hospital of St. Nicholas is based upon reports in *Obozrenie psikhiatrii, nevrologii i eksperimental'noi psikhologii, Zhurnal nevropatologii i psikhiatrii im. S.S. Korsakova*, and *Nevrologicheskii vestnik* during 1905-8. The journalistic accounts differ slightly as to the details of what transpired, but the outline of events is clear.

30. In this troubled era, demonstrations occurred at many types of institutions. The ubiquitous wheelbarrow became a standard means by which demonstrators transported human cargo from the premises.

31. The following account of the events at Saburovaia Dacha is based upon reports in *Obozrenie psikhiatrii, nevrologii i eksperimental'noi psikhologii* for 1905-6; N.M. Zelenskii, *150 let Saburovoi dachi* (Kiev, 1946); and A.G. Ianovskii, "P.P. Tutyshkin—Vrach, Uchenyi, Revoliutsioner," *Zhurnal nevropatologii i psikhiatrii im. S.S. Korsakova* 74 (1974): 1411-15.

32. The remark was attributed to Bazhenov. See *Trudy tret'ego s"ezda otechestvennykh psikhiatrov* (St. Petersburg, 1911), 94.

33. The earlier conflict at the Hospital of St. Nicholas had been settled amicably. The incident at Saburovaia Dacha culminated in the resignation of the institution's director, N.V. Krainskii. See *Nevrologicheskii vestnik* 6 (1898): 250.

34. Ianovskii argues that Tutyshkin was not rehired because of his political activities. He contends that Tutyshkin was imprisoned briefly in December 1905, after he had been caught hiding revolutionaries in the hospital. Tutyshkin very soon lost the position in Bessarabia as well, due to his involvement in an incident similar to the one at Khar'kov. For Tutyshkin's account of the events in Bessarabia, see P.P. Tutyshkin, "Opyt provedeniia v zhizn' postanovlenii vtorogo s"ezda otechestvennykh psikhiatrov v g. Kieve ob avtonomno-kollegial'nom upravlenii psikhiatricheskikh uchrezdhenii," *Trudy tret'ego s"ezda*, 79-88.

35. While the two incidents recounted above were the most widely publicized, they were by no means the only ones. For a summary of similar events, see the discussions of the St. Petersburg Society of Psychiatrists during 1906. *Protokoly zasedanii obshchestva psikhiatrov v s-peterburge za 1906* (St. Petersburg, 1907); and P.A. Ostankov, "Vrachebnyi stroi psikhiatricheskikh bol'nits," *Obozrenie psikhiatrii, nevrologii i eksperimental'noi psikhologii* 12 (1907): 606-24.

36. *Protokoly*, 22-23. The subject was discussed by the members of the St. Petersburg Society of Psychiatrists at virtually every one of its meetings during 1906.

37. Ibid., 24.

38. Ibid., 22.

39. The minutes of the conference were reported in *Vrachebnaia khronika Khar'kovskoi gubernii* 12 (1906).

40. Ibid., 72-78.

41. One of the dissenters was V.I. Iakovenko, director of the Moscow *zemstvo* provincial psychiatric hospital, who insisted that nonprofessional workers could and should be included in asylum administrative organs. He based his contention on his own experience. Ibid., 64.

42. Ibid., 65.

43. This seems to be a universal characteristic of public mental institutions throughout the western world, a fact which has suggested to many observers that the primary function of such institutions is social control rather than healing. M.E. Lion, "Iz otchetov o sostoianii otdeleniia dushevno-bol'nykh," *Arkhiv psikhiatrii, nevrologii i sudebnoi psikhopatologii* 1 (1883): 206-16, 211-12.

44. *Vrachebnaia khronika khar'kovskoi gubernii*, 62.

45. Ibid., 63.

46. Amenitskii, "Istoricheskii ocherk," 445.

47. *Sovremennaia psikhiatriia* 2 (1908): 244.

48. *Obozrenie psikhiatrii, nevrologii i eksperimental'noi psikhologii* 11 (1906) and *Vrachebnaia khronika*.

49. Stanilovskii in a discussion at the Third Conference of Russian Psychiatrists. *Trudy tret'ego s"ezda*, 166.

50. *Obozrenie psikhiatrii, nevrologii i eksperimental'noi psikhologii* 11(1906).

51. The political reaction during this era was, of course, a generalized one. In Khar'kov after 1905, the composition of the *zemstvo* assembly changed significantly. T.I. Iudin, "Tri goda deistviia pravil kollegial'nogo upravleniia v Khar'kovskoi gubernskoi zemskoi bol'nitse," *Trudy tret'ego s"ezda*, 88-94. The reversals at Saburovaia Dacha provoked a bitter discussion at the 1909 meeting of psychiatrists.

52. See Brown, "Professionalization," 277-92. The journal of the Pirogov Society of Russian Physicians listed thirteen psychiatrists who were either fired or otherwise punished by the authorities in 1906 alone.

53. *Obozrenie psikhiatrii, nevrologii i eksperimental'noi psikhologii* 11 (1906): 79. The Moscow governor also complained that the *zemstvo* psychiatric hospital was an illegal center of political activity.

54. *Protokoly*, 12; *Zhurnal nevropatologii i psikhiatrii im. S.S. Korsakova* 7 (1907): 1008; and T.I. Iudin, *Ocherki istorii otechestvennoi psikhiatrii* (Moscow, 1951), 316.

55. The passage of the resolution followed a presentation by Tutyshkin on the subject of collective administration.

56. *Trudy tret'ego s"ezda*, 108-9. (Emphasis added.)

57. *Obozrenie psikiatrii, nevrologii i eksperimental'noi psikhologii* 11 (1906).

58. *Sovremennaia psikhiatriia*, II: 574, 1908.

59. N.A. Vyrubov, "Na ocherednyia temy obshchestvennoi psikhiatrii. Bol'nichnyi ustav i sovremennoe zemstvo," *Sovremennaia psikhiatriia* 3 (1909): 183-87.

60. Ibid., 186.

61. *Trudy tret'ego s"ezda*, 103-5.

62. Ibid., 97.

63. Ibid., 686.

64. Only one participant at the First Conference of the Russian Union of Psychiatrists and Neuropathologists, V.N. Ergol'skii, opposed the inclusion of support personnel. He did so on familiar grounds: "We all know how uncultured and unsatisfactory these workers are." *Trudy tret'ego s"ezda*, 143.

65. Ibid., 742-48.

66. Ibid., 452.

67. Eliot Freidson, *Professional Dominance: The Social Structure of Medical Care* (New York: Atherton Press, 1970), 136.

68. N.A. Vyrubov and S.S. Sergievskii, "Osnovnye polozheniia k ustavu psikhiatricheskoi bol'nitsy," *Trudy 1911*, 724-36.

69. Brown, "Professionalization," 288-92.

70. Julie V. Brown, "A Sociohistorical Perspective on Deinstitutionalization: The Case of Late Imperial Russia," *Research in Law, Deviance and Social Control* 7 (1985): 167-88. This concept originated in the West and drew much of its support from observations of the Belgian community of Gheel.

71. Saburovaia Dacha in Khar'kov was a prime example. Its staff held political meetings and published illegal literature at the institution. On occasion, fugitive revolutionaries were sheltered within its walls. Similar activities went on at Liakhovo Psychiatric Colony near Nizhnii Novgorod. The private asylum in Moscow, Krasnosel'skaia Lechebnitsa, was used after 1905 to hide illegal literature and weapons and for political meetings. Contemporary journalistic accounts strongly suggest that the staffs of a number of institutions were similarly engaged.

72. Julie V. Brown, "Revolution and Psychosis: The Mixing of Science and Politics in Russian Psychiatric Medicine, 1905-13," *Russian Review* 46 (1987): 283-302.

73. Eliot Freidson, *Profession of Medicine* (New York: Dodd and Mead, 1970), 23-24.

74. This continues to be true today. See, for example, Charles Rosenberg, "The Crisis in Psychiatry Legitimacy," in *American Psychiatry Past, Present and Future*, ed. George Kriegman et al. (Charlottesville: University Press of Virginia, 1975).

75. See J.V. Brown, "Psychiatrists and the State in Tsarist Russia," in *Social Control and the State*, ed. Stanley Cohen and Andrew Scull (Oxford: M. Robertson, 1983), 283, 286-87.

7

Professional Activism and Association Among Russian Teachers, 1864-1905

Scott J. Seregny

The Revolution of 1905 drew most strata of Russian society into politics and politicized the professions. Teachers, particularly those in rural primary schools, were in the forefront of the liberation movement, organizing an All-Russian Union of Teachers with overt political aims. They were among the most militant of professionals represented in the Union of Unions. Rural teachers proved to be highly critical of the existing social and political order and became involved in popular political mobilization through peasant unions, new political parties, and elections to the State Duma. Teachers' activism during 1905-7 was unprecedented, catching many contemporaries by surprise.

The political activization of teachers during the revolution was conditioned, quite naturally, by the dynamics of the revolutionary situation itself, specifically, the disarray at all levels of administration, pressure from educated society for teachers to assume a political role in the village, and not least, pressure "from below," from local peasant communities toward a similar end.[1] The roots of teacher radicalism, however, must be sought in the development of the profession in preceding decades, in the efforts of teachers to define collectively their role within the larger context of Russian educational and social development. In approaching this task Russian teachers faced fundamental contradictions in their professional status. Ultimately, it was through attempts to resolve these contradictions that increasing numbers of rural teachers were transformed into opponents of the old regime.

Teachers' Status in Tsarist Russia

The generally low status of teachers in primary schools has been noted by observers of modern professions. Teachers tend to exhibit a relatively low degree of professionalization compared to members of the "pure" professions such as medicine and are sometimes referred to as "marginal," or "semiprofessional." Their status is conditioned and characterized by a number of factors: low pay, increasing feminization, modest social backgrounds, large numbers, high rates of turnover (lesser commitment), subordinate status within a bureaucratic framework, and lack of autonomy. These are mutually reinforcing; for example, there appears to be some correlation between predomination of women in a profession and its subordinate status. All tend to reinforce teachers' low prestige within society at large.[2]

Society's perception of the social value of a given occupation is crucial in the progress of its members toward professional status. Public recognition of the indispensability of services provided strongly influences an occupation's status and its bargaining power vis-à-vis society (or important elites, including political power holders), e.g., in demands for autonomy or input into decision making and administration. Lacking an esoteric knowledge base (or services considered by society to be of sufficient importance, such as medicine or the military), teachers historically have not enjoyed much power. Herein lies the key to the low status of teaching as a profession. As British sociologist J.A. Jackson writes, "teaching is the most profoundly contaminated (secularized) profession because with the rise of mass education its mystique is compromised by the fact that in general the tasks it performs are within the competency of all who have been taught themselves and since those on whom it practices are children, many of these functions are substitutes for parental roles in any case."[3]

To one degree or another, these generic traits of teaching apply to rural teachers in Russia, although certain features appeared hypertrophied there. Meager formal qualifications were severely aggravated by rural isolation and cultural deprivation upon arrival at the school. Subordination was extreme, not only to local school boards, state inspectors, and zemstvo employers, but to a host of rural officials. Teachers lacked even the right of self-defense before school boards in disciplinary matters. Restrictions on professional association, including social intercourse, were draconian even by Russian standards.[4]

Yet this is an essentially static picture, revealing little about the development of the teaching profession in Russia, the history of professional association and consciousness, or even the resolution of problems of status and identity. These were shaped in the interactions between teachers on the one hand, and state and society on the other. Russian society was largely peasant and unschooled, quite different from the country of mass education described by Jackson, where low status inevitably accrues to "teachers in primary schools to which *everyone goes* to learn *what everyone knows*."[5] The imperatives and dilemmas involved in educating Russian peasant society had yet to be agreed upon, and this lack of consensus (in fact, conflict) strongly influenced the nascent teaching profession. The successes and failures of the

Russian teachers' movement were, to be sure, conditioned by the limits of professionalization that seem generic to teaching as an occupation. But they were also influenced by Russian realities: the imperatives of modernization, government policies, conflict between state and society, and the intractability of specific social and political institutions.

Of crucial significance was the position of educated Russian society (*obshchestvo*). By the turn of the century, key elements of society (e.g., the *zemstva*) came to attach a special, urgent significance to the education of the rural masses (*narod*) and fostered an image of the teacher's role that went well beyond the confines of the classroom and the task of imparting the "three Rs" to peasant children. Progressive society projected an image of the teacher as a "cultural pioneer" and "public activist" fulfilling a mission of crucial importance in the country's social, economic, and even political development. Society's perception of the teacher as the advance guard in a multifaceted "enlightenment" campaign among the *narod* enhanced the potential (and actual) status of teachers, while influencing the growth of a professional movement and the rapid rise in corporate consciousness among teachers during the decade before the Revolution of 1905.

Teachers' internalization of this ideal image was central to the movement, providing the basis for claims to legitimacy as a profession with certain rights and prestige; the ideal also underlay teachers' opposition to the old regime. To the degree that they aspired to the ideal of "cultural pioneer," which was laden with a strong populist ethic of service and sacrifice, teachers would struggle for radical improvements in their professional status (which they argued were essential to the fulfillment of their role as cultural agents among the "dark" masses), as well as for public recognition as "experts" enjoying some measure of autonomy.

The fundamental contradiction between the ideal of the rural teacher —working against formidable odds to bridge the gulf between educated society and the *narod*—and the harsh realities of isolation and cultural deprivation was a source of increasingly militant professional activism for many. The perception that the Russian government was to a large degree responsible for perpetuating this contradiction ensured that the nascent teachers' movement would embrace other visions of the future, whether liberal or revolutionary, and would advance a program in which professional and political demands were inextricably linked. As with other Russian professionals, but in no case more powerfully than among teachers, political opposition arose from the contradiction between the ideal image of their role in Russia's transformation, which they had internalized, and the realities of traditional power, privilege, and bureaucratic control. As teachers groped toward self-definition, they became increasingly aware that their interests could not be accommodated either by autocracy and unrestrained bureaucratic rule or by the gentry-dominated and undemocratic institutions of local self-government, the *zemstva*.

This essay examines the history of teachers' association and professional activism in Russia from the period of the Great Reforms of the 1860s to 1905, tracing those specifically Russian factors that stimulated the growth of professional consciousness or thwarted teachers' aims, as well as those barriers to professionalization generic to teaching. In both contexts, specific and generic, comparisons will be drawn with *zemstvo* medicine, the other major branch of *zemstvo* services, which teachers consciously adopted as a model. The discussion is broken down into two periods divided by a major watershed in Russian development, the famine and cholera of 1891-93. While the beginnings of teachers' association were evident during the initial decades of the *zemstvo* school, a sufficiently compelling professional identity and ethos, supporting a professional movement, took shape only in the wake of the crisis of the early 1890s.

Teachers' Association Before 1890

Contrary to the claims of liberal Russian historiography, the period before 1890 did not witness a massive or sustained commitment on the part of the new *zemstvo* institutions to public education. During the postreform era, the number of schools increased, and a modest cadre of teachers developed. In 1880 a government census counted 22,770 rural schools in 60 provinces of European Russia (including Poland and the Baltics) with 24,389 teachers (19,511 men and 4,878 women).[6] Much of this achievement was recorded under the auspices of the *zemstva*—within the 34 *zemstvo* provinces there were between 9,000 and 10,000 *zemstvo* schools—although not necessarily by means of local self-government.[7] An inordinate share of the burden for public education was borne directly by peasant communes rather than defrayed through general *zemstvo* revenues.[8] For the gentry landowners who dominated *zemstvo* affairs, the prevailing view was that primary schooling was first and foremost the concern of the peasants whose children would directly benefit.[9] Schooling was viewed as neither an urgent nor a national imperative, and it did not transcend narrow estate (*soslovie*) interests.

Nevertheless, the foundations of the *zemstvo* school system were laid during this period, and the first cadre of "professional" teachers recruited—professional in the sense that teaching was performed by persons who considered it a career, unlike the assorted clerics, retired soldiers, seminary dropouts, and literate peasants who approached teaching more as a supplementary "craft" and remained common figures in rural schools as late as 1870.[10] Two things can be said about the growth of the profession in this period: qualifications improved and with the beginnings of association an incipient professional consciousness was evident.

From the outset, *zemstva* faced the problem of finding adequately prepared teachers to staff their schools, and teacher training consumed the lion's share of *zemstvo* education budgets during this period. Sources of recruitment, however, were limited. Normal schools—both state and *zemstvo*-run teachers' seminaries—were few in number, with small graduating classes. By 1880 some sixty training schools had been established Empirewide, but these could not come close to meeting the demand for personnel (in fact, the number of seminaries would not be appreciably increased until 1910).[11] Meanwhile, *zemstva* were forced to recruit from a variety of sources: secondary school dropouts, graduates of women's secondary institutions (gymnasia, progymnasia, and diocesan schools), and frequently persons possessing nothing more than three or four years of elementary schooling. Many of these new teachers were woefully deficient in terms of pedagogical preparation and suffered from serious gaps in basic general knowledge. Some had not yet mastered basic literacy.[12]

The task faced by *zemstva* in attempting to upgrade and standardize qualifications was immense. To alleviate the situation, *zemstva* began in the late 1860s to organize short-term courses during the summer months for teachers already in the schools. The aim of these courses was to supplement teachers' often meager fund of general knowledge, demonstrate teaching methods and, if possible, keep teachers abreast of advances in pedagogical theory and practice. A wide range of gatherings was held during the early 1870s, tailored to fit the needs of a given audience. Among these were local teachers' congresses (*s"ezdy*) at which more experienced teachers played an active role, discussing with *zemstvo* and school officials a host of issues connected with operating the schools. Resolutions of these congresses—on curricula, popular libraries, and textbooks—were sometimes considered by *zemstvo* assemblies and incorporated into *zemstvo* policy.[13]

For the rural teachers these gatherings were of crucial professional and psychological importance. Cultural deprivation and isolation were perhaps the most salient aspects of the Russian teacher's existence, more insidious than even the economic insecurity and low juridical status under which teachers labored throughout this period. Cultural deprivation was understandable in a context in which schools and literacy were only beginning to penetrate a rural society just emerging from serfdom. Yet the dearth of cultural amenities, measured in terms of access to reading materials and contact with educated society,[14] confronted teachers with the ever present danger of sinking into the "uncultured" morass of rural life where, as teachers put it, they were "condemned to grow ignorant and dull, to become wild."[15]

Perilously high rates of turnover plagued the Russian teaching profession because of poor pay, subordinate status, and cultural despair. The summer courses and congresses helped fill this void. Here teachers had a chance to meet and exchange experiences with colleagues and with members of intelligent society, providing psychological gratification (in terms of feeling oneself to be an important agent in society's mission to enlighten the masses and an object of society's concern) and instilling a sense of corporate solidarity. Describing these gatherings, teachers often used the term "holiday" (*prazdnik*), and said the benefits were more than practical or intellectual, but even "spiritual" (*dukhovnye*).[16] The educator N.F. Bunakov, who lectured at courses during the 1870s, underscored their significance:

> The zemstvo viewed the teacher's congresses as one of the most effective and comparatively speedy means of improving teaching personnel and the level of teaching in zemstvo schools, the number of which was growing each year. The congresses not only illuminated the pedagogical understanding of teachers, acquainted them with proper methods of instruction, but also raised their spirits, inspired and united them, scattered as they were throughout the remote villages, deprived of any contact with the cultured world, with intelligent people, and with each other.[17]

In short, teachers' courses and congresses filled a variety of needs and were held with increased frequency in provincial and district (*uezd*) towns during the early 1870s.[18] But the government soon intervened. Faced with the revolutionary movement "to the people" of 1873, the government of Tsar Alexander II proved responsive to Minister of Education D.A. Tolstoi's argument for a more active state role in primary schooling and increased supervision over instruction. Fear of radical influences in the schools was an important factor in framing a new school statute in 1874, which enhanced the role of both the gentry and the government inspectorate in supervision.[19]

It was within this climate that the government moved to limit *zemstvo* initiative in the area of teacher association. By rules of 5 August 1875, teachers' courses were placed squarely under official control, with *zemstva* retaining little more than the obligation to fund them. The content of the courses was strictly limited to pedagogical topics.[20] The result was a sharp decline in courses after that date.[21] Furthermore, the rules of 1875 had a stifling effect on the broader form of teachers' association, the congresses, which, except for a brief period under the relatively liberal ministry of Baron A.P. Nikolai at the beginning of the 1880s, were no longer sanctioned and were banned altogether in 1885.[22]

Official motivation is not difficult to determine. Rural teachers had in the 1870s been conspicuous participants in the revolutionary movement; many became teachers calculating that this was a sure way of making contact with the peasantry.[23] From this time dates the official view of the teacher as a potential threat to the social order.

The government's dilemma was clear, and it would shape official policy on teachers until the end of the old regime. The state had committed itself to mass education, within limits to be sure; at the same time, it sought to protect peasant society from pernicious influences which, in the official view, emanated from urban, educated society. It can be argued that a major function of the provincial administration was to guard the frontier separating urban from rural society. Teachers, unlike most other *intelligenty*, had crossed that border by virtue of their occupation. The problem was then one of controlling the impact of these "outsiders" on peasant society. Government supervision (*nadzor*) was insufficient; the inspector was often responsible for as many as 100 schools spread over an immense area.[24] Instead, in order to neutralize the teachers' potential as mediators between society and the masses, the government—with significant shifts, as we will see—pursued a twofold strategy: first, closely screening candidates for teaching posts (while removing personnel at the slightest hint or rumor of "unreliability," either "moral" or "political"), and second, isolating teachers from society. The latter was accomplished by strictly monitoring teachers' access to reading materials, by administrative subordination, by heavy-handed supervision even over teachers' social lives, and by restrictions on teachers' associations.

Official policy on teachers' association in Russia contrasted with that of other European countries. For example, in France during the early Third Republic, the Ministry of Education under Jules Ferry heartily endorsed periodic teachers' congresses as a means to promote professional solidarity and combat the debilitating effects of isolation.[25] While acknowledging foreign developments, Russian teachers sought professional models closer to home.

For Russian teachers, the mid 1870s ushered in a long period of dissociation, all but erasing the gains of previous years. The extent of teachers' isolation was evident from a survey conducted by the Moscow Committee of Literacy in 1894-95 which found that of those teaching in rural schools, only a small handful had ever attended a professional gathering, not surprising given the high rate of turnover that characterized the profession.[26] The sense of isolation and despair was reinforced by complacency and inactivity on the part of the *zemstva* in the field of education during the "quiet" decade.[27]

This period is often referred to (and sometimes romanticized) as one of "small deeds." Many individuals, no doubt, did perform herculean cultural work at this time, but for teachers collectively it was a period of malaise and crisis. According to one teacher, a general despondency reigned among his fellows during the 1880s, aggravated by rumors that *zemstvo* schools would soon be turned over to Holy Synod management. Books were impossible to obtain, and teachers spent their free time playing cards or drinking.

> With what zeal, with what genuine commitment to make ourselves useful, did many of us first approach [teaching]. Regrettably, all these good intentions, due to the conditions in which we were forced to live, very often shattered. Even those teachers who were most dedicated to the school, having lost their health, enduring so many spiritual trials, and not seeing in the future any [recompense] for their difficult work, finally abandoned the school and sought more gratifying work.[28]

According to the Ministry of Education, many teachers did actually leave to assume the new rural police post (*uriadnik*).[29] In a letter of 1888, the writer Gleb Uspenskii underscored the isolation and despair that had overcome the profession after the promising beginnings of the 1870s.

> . . . now the teacher is left to pine alone with his textbook; he notes down [the pupil's] absence from classes, but to state that the boy was absent because of his father's drunkenness, and further to explain why he became a drunkard (as such transpired at the previous congresses), now there is none of this. A lively observation of popular needs, which is instructive for public activists and which ties them together, is now lacking.[30]

To sum up, the isolation and cultural deprivation that resulted from natural conditions, low pay (teachers rarely had money to spend on reading material), and the like, were strongly reinforced by official policy and public neglect. A basic contradiction in the rural teacher's position—that of a would-be culture bearer cut off from educated society and the higher culture—was thus perpetuated.

Various responses from teachers were possible. Many merely vegetated in the countryside and remained intellectually stunted, barely equipped to combat illiteracy in the classroom, let alone act as viable cultural agents within the community at large. Accounts of the period attest that such types were common and remained so through 1905.[31] Flight was another option. Turnover remained high, especially during the period from 1895 to 1900, when droves of male teachers reportedly left to assume the more lucrative and less subordinate posts of operators of Finance Minister Sergei Witte's new state liquor monopoly.[32] Professional activism, aimed at resolving the contradictions in teachers' status, was a third possibility. The first two responses dominated the period of "quiet" and remained strong in its aftermath. The third—professional association and struggle—was feasible in the new climate after the early 1890s, which was marked by a renewed public commitment to mass education that generated an ethos of the teacher as "cultural pioneer" and provided material and moral support for teachers' efforts.

A Decade of Professional Activism, 1894-1904

When famine and cholera ravaged Russia in the early 1890s, educated Russians were shocked to read lurid reports from the provinces describing violence against medical relief workers and other evidence of popular ignorance. Like no other disaster since defeat in the Crimean War (1853-55), the famine and cholera laid bare Russia's backwardness. "Cholera riots" and mass hunger dramatically revealed the depths of economic backwardness and the gulf of ignorance, hostility, and superstition separating educated and privileged society from the "dark" *narod*. The experience convinced wide sectors of society and government that "enlightenment" was crucial to Russia's social stability, economic progress, and peaceful reform. The crisis of the early 1890s sparked unprecedented public interest in education, just as it led to an upsurge of public activism and optimism in other areas.[33]

Nowhere was this reaction more apparent than in the renewed *zemstvo* education campaign of the following decade. The period after the famine saw a sharp increase in *zemstvo* education budgets.[34] Renewed commitment to education by *zemstva* was reflected in the growth of the school network (in the period 1894-1902 the number of *zemstvo* schools rose by 5,568, compared to 3,046 for the preceding eighteen years);[35] increased assumption by *zemstva* of maintenance costs (e.g., teachers' salaries and classroom materials) from peasant communes;[36] and a flurry of discussion about new programs in adult education, expansion of curricula, and the possibility of achieving universal schooling. While considerable diversity of opinion continued about how much and what kind of education was appropriate for the peasantry, public education was now viewed within the *zemstvo* milieu as a national task, transcending class interests.

The famine and cholera also prompted a rediscovery of the all-but-forgotten rural teacher. Commenting on an incident in which a woman suspected of sorcery was nearly torn to pieces by an enraged crowd at the height of the cholera epidemic in 1892, the educator V.P. Ostrogorskii asked: "Schoolteacher, where are you? Answer."[37] As if echoing this plea, a number of studies were undertaken by the Moscow Committee of Literacy, *zemstva*, and others to determine the physiognomy and status of those teaching in Russia's schools. All data pointed to a profession in crisis.[38] The information that teachers provided concerning their own educational qualifications, access to cultural commodities, material and legal status, and overall occupational satisfaction had to be disturbing to those who saw education as the path to Russia's salvation. The findings of the Moscow Committee and other materials cast considerable doubt on the teacher's potential as a cultural force in the countryside. As V.A. Gol'tsev, who helped compile the committee's data, put it:

> The conclusions of many teachers amount to the fact that unsavory conditions, of both school buildings and teachers' lodgings, lack of books and teaching aids, the pitiful material status of teachers, all conspire to sap his energy, prevent him from rising to the height of his calling and rendering to the population the benefits which could be achieved under better conditions.[39]

The "teacher question," another educator wrote in 1897, could no longer be avoided.

> . . . after heated articles and reports concerning the universal significance of public education, after repeated assertions that the might of Prussia was consolidated not by the army, but by the modest labors of the inconspicuous schoolteacher, that the future belongs to that state which possesses the best schools, it has become impossible to ignore the half-starved existence of the teacher, his nearly complete estrangement from the intelligentsia, his extremely precarious legal status.[40]

It was clear, reasoned this commentator, that the "soul" of the school was the teacher and that this soul was in peril. Any doubts on this score were soon dispelled by reports of teachers leaving en masse for jobs in the state liquor monopoly. As *zemstvo* activists saw it, the task at hand was to arrest this flight and provide the school system with adequately prepared and committed personnel.

Only meager gains were made in improving teachers' material conditions before 1905. The large numbers that have tended to characterize teaching as a profession, coupled with pressure to increase recruitment, have made it difficult to substantially improve salaries.[41] In Russia, the decade before 1905 was one of rapid growth and, in light of the Ministry of Education's unwillingness to provide subsidies to increase salaries, little progress was made in this area. According to the Moscow Committee of Literacy survey, in 33 provinces male teachers' salaries in the mid 1890s averaged 270 rubles per year, and those for women 252 rubles.[42] Some *zemstva* did seek to make improvements, but the record was extremely uneven. Replying to a questionnaire from the local teachers' mutual-aid society in 1904, a teacher from Simbirsk province remarked that a majority of teachers received "from 50 to 70 kopecks a day, that is, as much as is earned by an unskilled common laborer (*chernorabochii*) on a winter day in central Russia."[43] All data indicate that teachers' budgets were strained to the limit and that life for a married teacher with a family was often impossible.

Material improvements came slowly. Instead, the main thrust of *zemstvo* efforts to aid teachers was in the area of professional association and satisfaction of cultural demands. From the mid 1890s, various *zemstva* attempted to meet rural teachers' thirst for reading materials by setting up "teachers' libraries" and, after 1900, subsidizing subscriptions to periodicals, both general and pedagogical. *Zemstvo* activists also helped establish and fund teachers' mutual-aid societies (*obshchestva vzaimopomoshchi*), which proliferated in the period after 1894. While restricted by government statute to providing emergency material aid, the mutual-aid societies attempted with some success to expand their functions to encompass cultural needs and served teachers as incipient corporate organizations. As the only permanent legal associations tolerated by the government, they contributed to the growth of solidarity and professional consciousness before 1905. The Teachers' Union of 1905, in fact, grew out of the mutual-aid societies.[44]

As in the 1870s, in the late 1890s *zemstva* began to organize summer teachers' courses, which played an immense role in instilling a new ethos among teachers as idealistic cultural activists. Teachers internalized an enhanced image of their role in the countryside as agents who would spearhead society's mission to "enlighten," and in some cases "liberate," the peasant masses. That the government defined their role in much narrower terms set the more activist teachers on a collision course with the old regime. In addition, their growing self-confidence led to inevitable demands for a larger role in the formulation of education policies and to their questioning of the traditional, class-based prerogatives of local self-government.

For the *zemstva* the imperatives behind a resurrection of the teachers' summer courses were compelling. As in the 1870s, teachers in the 1890s were still recruited from a wide variety of institutions, and the credentials that many brought to the rural school left much to be desired. Even graduates of teachers' seminaries, while well versed in teaching methods and the pedagogical "tightrope walking" (*ekvilibristika*) demanded by simultaneous work with three grades of pupils (one of them illiterate), often suffered from basic gaps in general knowledge.[45] Qualifications of others were still lower, particularly graduates from women's diocesan schools, who in many provinces constituted some forty percent of female teachers at a time when the profession was undergoing steady feminization. Moreover, given the recruitment pressures of this period, *zemstvo* statistics began to reveal a relative decline in teachers' formal qualifications.[46] *Zemstva* were also compelled to recognize the insidious effects of isolation and cultural deprivation on the morale and effectiveness of teachers, whatever their educational credentials.[47]

Furthermore, *zemstvo* activists expected more of teachers after the crisis of the early 1890s. This was especially true of liberal *zemstvo* men who set policy during this period, particularly at the provincial level.[48] In their scenario, the rural teacher would serve as an all-purpose cultural agent and community activist, initiating adult education programs, acting as a local figure of authority who could counter the influence of the local cleric, and integrating peasant society with the dominant culture. As the Viatka *zemstvo* put it, "the zemstvo school must not only impart simple literacy, but also widen the intellectual horizons of its pupils so that, upon graduation, they will want to continue acquiring knowledge." Teachers should be able to answer a variety of peasant queries, explain the "significance of important phenomena of nature and major public [*obshchestvennye*] events." Only through "intensive intellectual labor," the *zemstvo* argued, could teachers expand their own intellectual horizons and then help raise the cultural level of the masses.[49]

Along with renewed *zemstvo* interest in the summer courses came a relaxation in the government's position on teachers' association. The Ministry of Education was forced to admit that the profession was in a state of crisis. Unwilling to allocate the funds necessary to increase the number of candidates trained in normal schools or to increase teachers' salaries, the government was apparently willing to make other concessions to ameliorate their status.[50] In addition, the government felt reasonably confident concerning the rural social order and the potential of teachers to disrupt it. Commenting that the administration had never doubted the value of teachers' gatherings, a ministry spokesman pointed out that it had previously been forced to restrict them given the "anarchist" movement of the 1870s and 1880s. The situation was now different. Moreover, teachers now constituted a more "reliable and steady professional class" than in previous decades, when many "dropouts" and casual elements had entered the profession.[51]

The restrictive rules of 1875 remained on the books, and the procedure for obtaining official sanction to hold courses was often quite arbitrary, occasioning constant complaints from *zemstva* and teachers. Nonetheless, after a long hiatus, summer courses were held with increased frequency after 1896. Nine provincial *zemstva* were permitted to organize courses (lasting from four to six weeks) in the summer of 1897. In Tambov, courses had not been held for twenty-three years; only one teacher, sixty years old, had experienced the gatherings of the 1870s. The local *zemstvo* nominated 80 teachers to take part; 168 showed up, many travelling to Tambov at their own expense, some from other provinces.[52] *Zemstva* sponsored eleven courses in 1898, twelve in 1899, eighteen in 1900, and twenty-two in 1901.[53] Everywhere teacher response was phenomenal. Courses organized by the Kursk *zemstvo* in 1899 attracted more than 300 teachers from twenty-three provinces, many spending their last kopecks to make the trip.[54]

More significantly, the courses were expanded after 1899 to include a wide range of "general-educational" subjects: natural science, hygiene, history, elementary psychology, Russian literature, and basic legal knowledge. The emphasis was not so much on sharpening teaching skills as expanding teachers' general knowledge. *Zemstvo* activists and educators argued that most teachers already had a good grasp of method.[55]

The expanded courses corresponded to the wider role that many *zemstvo* activists, educators, and teachers were projecting for the rural teacher within the peasant community. Success in adult education and possibly the whole mission of the *zemstva* in the countryside could well hinge upon expansion of the intellectual horizons of the teacher. It was considered axiomatic, for example, that preventive medicine and sanitation programs had to be founded on a bedrock of enlightenment.[56] How could the teacher assume a position of authority in the village if he or she was unable to respond to a variety of queries posed by peasants? This was how liberal *zemstvo* activists reasoned; after all, the teacher was the primary agent of *zemstvo* policy in the village. Those teachers who aspired to the wider role of "public activists" concurred; and for these teachers the *zemstvo* summer courses compared very favorably with the stale curriculum of state teachers' seminaries, which, to quote a report submitted by teachers to the Novotorzhok (Tver) *zemstvo* assembly, could not yield a "genuine zemstvo worker."[57] This phrase contained a strong ideological, idealist element and was commonly juxtaposed with a different type: the teacher who approached his vocation as a "craftsman" (*remeslennik*), limiting his activity to teaching the "three Rs" and not aspiring to a wider role in the community.

Clearly, this ethos was part of the pervasive spirit that propelled society after the crisis of the early 1890s. During the subsequent education drive, many young people entered the teaching profession precisely with this wider role in mind. But it was also shaped and internalized by teachers at the summer courses where rural teachers met with colleagues, *zemstvo* activists, leading educators and representatives of the liberal and radical intelligentsia, particularly other third-element employees.[58]

V.K. Burtsev, a teacher from Iaroslavl' province, recalled that in 1898 at the first courses held there in some time, teachers seemed tentative, as if waking from a deep sleep. At courses in 1900, however, the mood was more "militant." Those attending were generally younger than the auditors of 1898 (due, no doubt, to heavy recruitment) and were more susceptible to liberal and "red" influences. Teachers feverishly discussed plans for expansion of the school program from three to four years, adult education programs, and the like. Burtsev noted a significant advance in professional consciousness, measured in part by teachers' plans to organize on a firmer basis through the establishment of a mutual-aid society.[59]

The Saratov provincial *zemstvo* sponsored teachers' courses every summer from 1897 to 1901 (from 1899 with "general-educational" subjects) and later surveyed teacher-participants. The response was overwhelmingly positive. Aside from the benefits that they received from acquiring knowledge and skills, many respondents cited the invaluable opportunity to exchange experiences with their comrades in the profession. As one auditor (*kursant*) replied, the "courses raised the energy of teachers through contact with their comrades, serving to reinvigorate them after a long winter of solitary labor, after such an isolated experience." Still others remarked that the courses instilled a consciousness of the teacher's ideological ties with "society," with the "zemstvo's mission" (*zemskoe delo*) and with "zemstvo people." The crucial issue of contact with educated society was repeatedly stressed by the Saratov teachers:

> I see great value in mutual intercourse between a large number of teachers and in the sympathy evidenced by zemstvo activists and educators toward the school

and teacher. Seeing such a multitude of people who have sacrificed themselves for the good of the school, seeing the concern of zemstvo activists for this same school, the teacher is renewed and departs for his village reinstilled with commitment and reinvigorated.

Only since 1897 [the first year that courses were held in Saratov] has the teacher of Saratov province looked upon himself as a personality who possesses a tie with the government and with the zemstvo, and only from this time has he understood that the enlightened stratum of Russia is concerned about him, and this fact has significantly contributed to an uplifting of his moral spirit.[60]

Participants in courses elsewhere had similar responses. All underscore the role of these gatherings in shaping a common identity among teachers, a process of professional socialization that compensated somewhat for the absence of a common formal educational experience. Increasing numbers of teachers internalized an image of themselves as the advance guard of society's enlightenment campaign to bridge the gulf separating it from the "dark" masses. Psychologically, it was a gratifying image, a powerful antidote to the difficult working conditions teachers faced. Activist teachers would accept material deprivation, seemingly a vital element in the image of the "cultural pioneer."[61] But isolation from society and other teachers and cultural deprivation were not acceptable, inasmuch as they struck at the very core of the teacher's self-image as an agent of enlightenment. Accordingly, issues of cultural replenishment and association, rather than those of an economic nature, headed the list of teachers' professional demands around the turn of the century, and it was fundamentally over these issues that teachers would clash with the government.

Despite its apparent relaxation of policy on teachers' association, the government's attitude toward mass education remained ambivalent. Schooling for the peasantry was endorsed, but cautiously and certainly not with the sense of urgent commitment that characterized society's approach after the famine and cholera. Tsar Nicholas II summed up this attitude in 1898 when, in response to unprecedented increases in zemstvo education outlays, he wrote: "How many times have I said there is no need to hurry in this matter."[62] As it was, public education rapidly became a political issue between the state and opposition-minded elements in society, centered mainly around the zemstva.[63]

Official wariness of rural teachers' potential for destabilizing peasant society remained fundamentally unchanged, particularly within the Ministry of Interior (MVD), despite the recent relaxation of rules on association. As MVD agents who carried out an audit of the Moscow zemstvo put it, it was the teacher's task to teach children the ABCs, "not to enlighten the surrounding milieu."[64] The notion that the teacher was a potential security risk, whose contacts with society had to be closely monitored, was never abandoned; hence the continuation of close bureaucratic supervision, limits on teachers' access to reading material, and on the activities of the teachers' mutual-aid societies. As for the summer courses, it was soon apparent that they had merely been tolerated. In St. Petersburg the balance soon shifted from concern for the obvious practical needs of the school system for qualified personnel to preoccupation with security and the rural social order. The view of the teacher as an actual threat to that order was again resurgent.

In 1901, and especially in 1902, the MVD began to receive disquieting reports from governors and local police of teachers' revolutionary sympathies and activities. Local officials pointed out that rural teachers, men in particular, were susceptible to radical propaganda and were easily convinced that it was the government that was primarily responsible for their economic status, isolation, and cultural deprivation. [65] Such analyses of the causes of teacher radicalism were not far off the mark. There were reports of agitation conducted at the summer courses, and revolutionary organizations, the Socialist Revolutionary (SR) Party in particular, utilized the gatherings to recruit teachers as rural propagandists. These efforts came to fruition in 1903 when an illegal SR-affiliated Teachers' Union was established to coordinate party work among rural teachers. [66]

All of these official reports were received and evaluated against the backdrop of a mounting revolutionary movement, growing liberal opposition, and most important, the unsettling agrarian movement of spring 1902 in Ukraine. In mid-1903, Minister of Interior V.K. Plehve told a gathering of marshals of the nobility that the main conduit of "sedition" in the countryside was none other than the *zemstvo* teacher. [67] The result was a sharp drop in the number of courses sanctioned by the authorities after the summer of 1902, despite growing interest in the gatherings on the part of both *zemstva* and teachers. [68]

Official policy on teachers' association reflects quite well the Russian government's basic dilemma in educating the masses: to educate the peasantry (within limits to be sure) while protecting the school and teacher from what were seen as dangerous currents within educated, urban society. For teachers, particularly after the early 1890s, these aims were essentially irreconcilable. If the school was to serve as an oasis of culture within the "dark" countryside, if the teacher was to play the role of cultural agent among the peasantry, neither school nor teacher could reasonably be cut off from the higher culture. Of course, there were other obstacles to teachers' fulfillment of this role which have to be evaluated within the context of teacher-community relations and teachers' status as "outsiders" in the peasant community. [69] Teachers argued that if they were properly equipped and given sufficient latitude to work in the countryside, the social and cultural barriers separating them from the people would eventually dissolve.

Here was the underlying premise of the emerging professional consciousness of Russian teachers and the basis of teachers' political radicalism. Given

Russian realities, professional and political activism were necessarily linked. Official neglect, which contrasted so dramatically with public concern, coupled with specific policies that perpetuated teachers' isolation, was a powerful source of radicalization for many teachers. The vacillating nature of official policy (e.g., on the summer courses), which was inherent in the state's ambivalent approach to public education, served only to aggravate the situation at a time of growing consciousness and rising expectations among teachers. This was clear during the Christmas recess of 1902-3, when a national Congress of Representatives of Teachers' Mutual-Aid Societies, hesitantly sanctioned by the government, met in Moscow. Despite official efforts to limit discussion to narrow material and pedagogical issues, the congress's proceedings constituted a wholesale indictment of government policy in education generally and toward the teaching profession in particular.[70]

The Issue of Third-Element Input: The Teacher as Expert

In terms of sheer numbers and the fundamental function they performed, teachers constituted the most significant component of the *zemstvo* intelligentsia, the so-called third element. Rural teachers stood at the cutting edge of *zemstvo* efforts to transform peasant society, yet they were far from being passive executors of *zemstvo* policy. Just as teachers' growing self-consciousness in the decade before 1905 contributed to mounting dissatisfaction with the autocratic political and social order, it also generated teachers' demands for some measure of influence, if only consultative, in the formulation of *zemstvo* educational policies.

The logic behind teachers' demands for democratization of *zemstvo* decision making was compelling, and there were grounds to hope for their realization. First, the *zemstva* in recent years had been solicitous of teachers' professional needs, in sharp contrast to the government. Second, both the range and complexity of *zemstvo* education services (number of schools, new adult education programs, libraries, etc.) had increased dramatically by the turn of the century. Effective control over these operations, not to mention simple receipt of information about far-flung *zemstvo* schools, was beyond the physical capacity of *zemstvo* deputies, particularly the managing *zemstvo* board (*uprava*). Above all, there could be no substitute for the kind of qualitative, firsthand observations by the teacher in the village, a point made by Uspenskii during the late 1880s, which had even more validity in the following decade. Rational economy alone dictated a wider role for teaching personnel when questions affecting rural education were discussed.

Finally, there was precedent. Teachers had made substantive contributions to discussions on various issues at the local congresses of the late 1870s and early 1880s. More important, *zemstvo* medicine provided a model in which doctors, through regular professional congresses and representation on collegial medical councils (*sovety*), came to exert a profound effect on *zemstvo* medicine. The result, averred the educator N.V. Chekhov, was that Russia could boast the only free system of medical services in the world.[71] A brief look at the successes of *zemstvo* physicians in this area underscores the advantages these professionals possessed in comparison with teachers who, by the turn of the century, aspired to a comparable measure of autonomy. As we will see, it was a combination of specific Russian realities, among which the position of the government again loomed large, and factors apparently common to teaching as a profession that thwarted teachers' efforts.

Medical association in Russia enjoyed a happier fate in the postreform period than did teachers' association. Regular congresses of doctors from the 1870s developed into an indispensable component in the formulation and implementation of innovations in *zemstvo* medicine, particularly measures geared toward making services more accessible to the population at large. Doctors' congresses were sanctioned, often grudgingly, by the "second element" (the property-owning *zemstvo* electorate) and by the government. *Zemstvo* assemblies did not always accede to the recommendations of their physician-employees, and the reaction of the 1880s took its toll on medicine. Still, medical congresses were held fairly frequently, ensuring a good degree of third-element input into *zemstvo* policy and uniting the medical profession.[72] Physician input was further augmented through the medical councils, which won the right to make their opinions known to the *zemstvo* assemblies and in some cases influenced appointments of doctors and physicians' assistants. There were many cases of conflict between the propertyowning, "enfranchised" (*tsenzovye*) *zemstvo* men and their employees; nevertheless, collegial medical organization gradually received wide acceptance. By 1890, medical *sovety* had been established in 165 (46 percent) of district *zemstva*, and by 1898 in 231 (65 percent).[73]

Similar developments in education were stifled at birth. Teachers would never achieve the rights of association and limited autonomy won by their medical colleagues, and for several reasons. First, from the government's standpoint, the dispensing of medical services lacked the same political-security aspect that was involved in the delicate business of educating the *narod*. *Zemstvo* doctors were also suspected of harboring oppositional sympathies, but they posed less of a security threat by virtue of the nature of the services they provided and the simple fact that there were considerably fewer doctors working in the countryside.

Second, illiteracy and educational underdevelopment did not appear, at least in the 1880s, to pose the same urgent threat to the old regime or to members of the privileged classes that the problem of chronic epidemics did. It took a high degree of sophistication to recognize that peasant ignorance might, in the long run, pose a greater danger than epidemics to the values, institutions, and "culture" of educated society, as well as to the property of the upper classes and the interests of the state. In this sense alone, *zemstvo* doctors, through their monopoly over expert knowledge, stood in a comparably favorable bargaining position vis-à-vis their *zemstvo* employers.[74] Also, there was no real alternative to *zemstvo* medicine in the Russian countryside, and the role of *zemstvo* doctors was grudgingly accepted by *zemstvo* conservatives who, in the case of education, always touted the alternative of cheap and safe church-run schools.

Finally, within the gentry-dominated *zemstva*, there persisted the view that teachers were incompetent to discuss educational issues with their *zemstvo* "masters" (*khoziaeva*) and incapable of making any contribution to *zemstvo* policy formulation. Teaching was viewed as a less "expert" field than medicine. Anyone could teach basic subjects; in fact, too much education might be harmful for teachers, making them dissatisfied with their modest station. Such arguments were common before the 1890s and seemed to have some validity given teachers' meager educational credentials and cultural deprivation. Moreover, they were strongly reinforced by social distance, as teachers were increasingly recruited from the peasantry in the case of men, and from the clerical estate in the case of women. Increasing feminization of the profession, especially pronounced during the education drive of the 1890s, had to affect attitudes within the male-dominated *zemstva*.[75] The consequences were soon evident in teachers' efforts to emulate their third-element brethren in medicine and other fields.

In 1899 the Ministry of Education revoked the 1885 ban on teachers' congresses and issued a new set of rules to regulate them. *Zemstva* could sponsor the meetings, but the state school inspector was given near dictatorial powers over the proceedings. Congresses were limited to the district level, the government fearing larger gatherings, and the rights of teacher-participants were narrowly circumscribed.[76] Nevertheless, teachers were given the opportunity to articulate their own needs as professionals and those of the schools. In the opinion of one teacher, they had been granted "half a voice," which was certainly better than none.[77] And when given the opportunity, they certainly utilized it. This is clear from the discussions that took place at the first congress held under the new rules in Moscow district in August 1901. Teachers, drawing from direct experience in the school and community, contributed to discussion on a wide variety of topics, demonstrating that in *zemstvo* education, just as in medicine or agronomy, employee-specialists had something to contribute.[78]

Similarly auspicious beginnings marked initial *zemstvo* experimentation with teacher representation on collegial organs modeled after the medical councils. Teacher interest in such experimentation had been evident in discussions within the mutual-aid societies and at the summer courses, and was encouraged by liberal *zemstvo* men. One of the first such experiments, made by the Saratov district *zemstvo* in 1901, was hailed in the liberal press as a "step forward."[79] Twenty teachers were invited to participate in discussions with *zemstvo* men, where they gave a good accounting of themselves, demonstrating maturity and competence in the issues discussed. The *zemstvo* teachers provided valuable, firsthand information on various subjects: peasant receptivity to specific *zemstvo* projects, particularly recent innovations in adult education; the vexing problem of peasant household labor demands on their children and their deleterious effect on school attendance; curricula; and other questions, for instance, the personal techniques that teachers employed to spark peasant interest in Sunday public readings.[80] In short, teachers were not seeking control over education or professional autonomy, but merely a regular forum through which to express their grievances, opinions, and aspirations. Both local teachers' congresses and participation in *zemstvo* collegial organs seemed to provide such a forum. On the eve of 1905, teachers, through petitions and resolutions of their mutual-aid societies, expressed the desire that such forms of association be extensively applied and that official restrictions be relaxed. In such hopes they were bitterly disappointed.

Teachers' congresses, though sanctioned by the rules of 1899, never were organized on a regular basis. In the period 1901-5, congresses were held in only a handful of districts throughout the country (no more than five annually among 350 districts with *zemstvo* institutions).[81] The teachers of Moscow district did not convene again until 1914. At the time, *zemstvo* liberals blamed the government for this failure, citing the restrictive rules of 1899. There was some truth to this, and in some cases, local authorities refused to sanction teachers' congresses, pointing to security considerations.[82]

Yet the fact remains that in the overwhelming majority of district *zemstvo* assemblies, the idea of sponsoring teachers' congresses was never seriously entertained.[83] This is not surprising when one considers that liberal forces (always a minority) tended to be concentrated in the provincial *zemstvo* assemblies. In the districts, where more conservative gentry opinion predominated, the notion that the lowly teacher could have no advice to offer his superiors was quite prevalent. In the backward district *zemstva*, the spirit of the 1880s—in fact the ethos of the days of serfdom—was still pervasive. The case of Vladimir province is instructive. In the ten years after publication of the 1899 rules, only one district congress was held (in Aleksandrov in 1901). In the remaining districts, congresses were never held and only in one (Kovrov, a liberal stronghold before 1905) were funds allocated for the purpose, although the government failed to sanction the meeting.[84] For teachers throughout Russia, the salient point was that few congresses were held, despite surveys demonstrating overwhelming teacher interest.[85] A similar fate befell the initial attempts to involve teachers in collegial school councils. These tended to be restricted to a handful of district *zemstva* with strong contingents of liberal deputies.[86]

That *zemstvo* teachers would eventually aspire to some measure of input in policy making was natural, both as a byproduct of their growing identity as cultural activists and for very practical reasons. Who better understood the myriad problems involved in educating a peasant society? That the average *zemstvo* man was not prepared to accept the teacher as an "expert" probably says less about the generic traits of teaching as a profession (though these were apparent, as the comparison with *zemstvo* medicine indicates) than the deeply conservative attitudes and jealously guarded prerogatives of traditional institutions in the Russian countryside. At one time or another, it should be noted, the *zemstvo* second element lashed out at what it saw as the pretensions of its employees in other fields as well, such as medicine and statistics.

Conclusion

Among Russian teachers, a growing sense of corporate identity led to radicalization and ultimately to open political opposition during the decades before 1905. This was particularly the case after the early 1890s when the profession not only swelled with new recruits but also gained a new and powerful professional identity, that of "cultural pioneers" laboring for the benefit of the masses and for Russia's progress in general. Official policy on education, fraught with contradictions, tended to run counter to teachers' growing aspirations. This was especially true in the area of teachers' efforts to break out of the debilitating circle of cultural deprivation and rural isolation by forming professional associations and forging links with educated Russian society. Government moves to thwart these efforts bred deep resentment, and fluctuations in government policy, so expressive of its basic dilemma in the field of public education, only served to inflame the situation. When the promising movement to organize summer courses stalled after 1902, for example, teachers were bitter. One teacher from Nizhegorod province remarked in 1904, "If it is now considered possible to organize popular universities for common workers, then it is all the more necessary to give teachers in public schools the opportunity to expand their knowledge."[87] Reality was depressingly clear. Not only did rural teachers often earn less than urban laborers, but they also had less access to cultural amenities.

The government must bear much of the blame for this situation. Unqualified official support for teachers' association was not forthcoming until Ignat'ev's tenure in the Ministry of Education during World War I.[88] And yet, despite all their accomplishments in the field of education, the *zemstva* must also share some of the responsibility. This is demonstrated by the fate of local teachers' congresses, a potentially significant form of association which would have granted teachers some collective voice (if only consultative) in *zemstvo* decision making and the status, at least, of junior partners in the task of popular enlightenment. The failure of *zemstvo* collegial organs in education only serves to underscore the point. As public education became an increasingly complex affair, institutionalized teacher input was a logical development. And there was strong precedent in other fields, namely, *zemstvo* medicine. But logic in this case ran up against deep-seated social prejudices within the gentry-dominated *zemstva* toward lower status employees like teachers. In this case, *zemstvo* indifference and hostility toward teachers' professional association dovetailed nicely with government suspicion.

By 1905 many teachers had come to the conclusion that the problems and contradictions inherent in their status—and satisfaction of their growing professional aspirations—could not be resolved within the narrow limits prescribed by the government and tolerated by the *zemstva*. As a result, during the Revolution of 1905 many would join illegal political organizations—above all, the All-Russian Union of Teachers—which opposed both the old regime (autocracy and bureaucracy) and the undemocratic character of local self-government.

Notes

Research for this essay was supported by grants from the International Research and Exchanges Board and from the Fulbright-Hays program.

1. For teachers' activities during 1905, particularly the All-Russian Union of Teachers, see Scott J. Seregny, *Russian Teachers and Peasant Revolution: The Politics of Education in 1905* (Bloomington: Indiana University Press, 1989), chapters 6-9. For brief surveys of the union, see Ronald H. Hayashida, "The Unionization of Russian Teachers, 1905-1908: An Interest Group Under the Autocracy," *Slavic and European Review*, no. 2 (1981): 1-16; and V.R. Leikina-Svirskaia, *Russkaia intelligentsiia v 1900-1917 godakh* (Moscow, 1981), 68-73.

2. See T. Leggatt, "Teaching as a Profession," in *Professions and Professionalization,* ed. J.A. Jackson (Cambridge: Cambridge University Press, 1970), 153-78; and Amitai Etzioni, ed., *The Semi-Professions and Their Organization: Teachers, Nurses and Social Workers* (New York: Free Press, 1969), especially the preface.

3. J.A. Jackson, "Professions and Professionalization—Editorial Introduction," in *Professions*, ed. Jackson, 14.

4. For brief treatment of teachers' administrative position, see Jeffrey Brooks, "The Zemstvo and the Education of the People," in *The Zemstvo in Russia: An Experiment in Local Self-Government*, eds. Terence Emmons and Wayne S. Vucinich (Cambridge: Cambridge University Press, 1982), 258-261; and Ben Eklof, *Russian Peasant Schools: Officialdom, Village Culture and Popular Pedagogy, 1861-1914* (Berkeley: University of California Press, 1986), chapters 2 and 5.

5. Jackson, "Professions," 11.

6. G. Fal'bork and V. Charnoluskii, "Nachal'noe narodnoe obrazovanie," *Entsiklopedicheskii slovar' Brokgauza-Efrona*, 86 vols. (St. Petersburg, 1890-1907), 40: 761; and L.K. Erman, "Sostav intelligentsii v Rossii v kontse XIX i nachale XX v.," *Istoriia SSSR*, no. 1 (1963): 175.

7. In the thirty-four *zemstvo* provinces and the Don Region in 1880, there were some 10,300 *zemstvo* teachers in 9,138 schools, accounting for nearly 70 percent of all rural schools in these provinces. E.G. Kornilov, "Zemskaia demokraticheskaia intelligentsiia 70-kh godov XIX veka," in *Voprosy obshchestvennogo i sotsial'no-ekonomicheskogo razvitiia Rossii v XVIII-XIX vekakh* (Riazan', 1974), 94-95.

8. B.B. Veselovskii, *Istoriia zemstva za sorok let*, 4 vols. (St. Petersburg, 1909-11), 1: 485; and Eklof, *Russian Peasant Schools*, chapter 3.

9. Ibid., 1: 474, 514-15; and N.M. Pirumova, "Zemskaia intelligentsiia v 70-80-e gody XIX v.," *Istoricheskie zapiski* 106 (1981), 130.

10. V. Kolpenskii, "Sel'skaia shkola posle krest'ianskoi reformy," *Arkhiv istorii truda v Rossii*, no. 5 (1922): 45.

11. On the teachers' seminaries, see V. Akimov, "Zemskaia rabota po podgotovke narodnykh uchitelei," *Zhurnal ministerstva narodnogo prosveshcheniia*, no. 6 (1915): 151-59.

12. Pirumova, "Zemskaia intelligentsiia," 140-41; and Seregny, *Russian Teachers*, chapter 3.

13. N.A. Feliksov, "Pedagogicheskie kursy i s"ezdy," *Russkaia mysl'*, no. 10 (1896): 38-41; and E.A. Zviagintsev, *Polveka zemskoi deiatel'nosti po narodnomu obrazovaniiu*, 2nd ed. (Moscow, 1917), 19-22.

14. Teachers' lack of access to reading materials was a serious problem throughout the period under review. Many read little or nothing. For example, of 604 schools surveyed in Tambov province in 1901-2, 109 teachers declared that they had no access to any books whatsoever. In Moscow province in 1899, of 478 teachers replying to a *zemstvo* questionnaire, 150 claimed that they owned no books and did not subscribe to periodicals; 38 of these replied that they never read anything besides materials used in the classroom. Mirovich, "Obrazovatel'nye stremleniia uchitelia i lektsii v provintsii," *Zhurnal dlia vsekh*, no. 5 (1905): 302; and V.V. Petrov, ed., *Voprosy narodnogo obrazovaniia v Moskovskoi gubernii*, 4 vols. (Moscow, 1897-1901), 2: 45.

15. Feliksov, "Pedagogicheskie kursy," *Russkaia mysl'*, no. 11 (1896): 37.

16. M.F. Superanskii, *Nachal'naia narodnaia shkola v Simbirskoi gubernii: Istoriko-statisticheskii ocherk* (Simbirsk, 1906), 200.

17. N.F. Bunakov, "Kak ia stal i perestal byt' uchitelim uchitelei," *Izbrannye pedagogicheskie sobraniia* (Moscow, 1953), 341.

18. Estimates vary, but it is clear that during the period 1867-74 teachers' gatherings were held frequently in provincial and district towns. According to one Soviet source, at least 200 congresses were held before 1874. By another count, they were held in forty-four locales in 1871, fifty-five in 1872 and sixty-three in 1873. See Kornilov, "Zemskaia demokraticheskaia intelligentsiia," 109; and E.A. Zviagintsev, ed., *Voprosy i nuzhdy narodnogo uchitel'stva*, Sbornik 1 (Moscow, 1909), 18.

19. See Allen Sinel, "Educating the Russian Peasantry: The Elementary School Reforms of Count Dmitri Tolstoi," *Slavic Review* 27, no. 1 (1968): 55-56.

20. Zviagintsev, *Voprosy i nuzhdy*, 18-19; and V. Farmakovskii, "S"ezdy uchitelei narodnykh uchilishch prezhde i teper'," *Zhurnal ministerstva narodnogo prosveshcheniia*, no. 12, section 4 (1900): 76.

21. Zviagintsev, *Voprosy i nuzhdy*, 19.

22. O.N. Smirnov, "Zemstvo i biurokratiia v dele narodnogo obrazovaniia," *Russkaia shkola*, no. 12 (1906): 20.

23. According to the calculations of a Soviet historian, some 350 *zemstvo* teachers were implicated in the revolutionary movement. E.G. Kornilov, "Zemskie uchitelia v revoliutsionnom dvizhenii 70-kh gg. XIX v.," *Uchenye zapiski Moskovskogo gosudarstvennogo pedagogicheskogo instituta im. V.I. Lenina*, 439 (Moscow, 1971), 132. Numerous cases are recounted in B.G. Mikhailov, "Revoliutsionnaia propaganda sredi krest'ian na Evropeiskom Severe Rossii v 70-e gody XIX v.," *Istoricheskie zapiski*, 106 (1981): 348-68.

24. In the *zemstvo* provinces, the inspectorate staff remained nearly static from 1870 to 1900 and was not appreciably increased until after the Revolution of 1905. E.A. Zviagintsev, *Inspektsiia narodnykh uchilishch* (Moscow, 1914), 8-9; and Eklof, *Russian Peasant Schools*, 126-38.

25. Peter V. Meyers, "The French 'Instituteur' 1830-1914: A Study in Professional Formation" (Ph.D. diss., Rutgers University, 1972), 156.

26. See, for example, V. Gol'tsev, "O polozhenii uchashchikh v shkolakh Vladimirskoi gubernii," *Obrazovanie*, no. 4 (1897): 11.

27. On this shift, see Veselovskii, *Istoriia*, 1: 488-90.

28. P. Shesternin, "Iz vospominanii sel'skogo uchitelia," *Obrazovanie*, no. 9 (1898): 114, 116.

29. Ministerstvo narodnogo prosveshcheniia, *Izvlechenie iz vsepoddanneishogo otcheta ministra narodnogo prosveshcheniia za 1900 god* (St. Petersburg, 1902), 552-53.

30. Cited in *Russkie vedomosti, 1863-1913: Sbornik statei* (Moscow, 1913), 246.

31. See, for example, K.Ch., "Sel'skii uchitel'," *Russkoe bogatstvo*, no. 4, section 2 (1898): 6.

32. "Khronika vnutrennei zhizni," *Russkoe bogatstvo*, no. 4, section 2 (1900): 186-88.

33. On the general effect of the famine, see Alan K. Wildman, *The Making of a Workers' Revolution: Russian Social Democracy, 1891-1903* (Chicago, IL: University of Chicago Press, 1967), chapter 1. For education, see Allen Sinel, "The Campaign for Universal Primary Education in Russia, 1890-1904," *Jahrbucher fur Geschichte Osteuropas*, Band 30, heft 4 (1982): 481-507.

34. Veselovskii, *Istoriia*, 1: 567-68, provides the following figures (in thousands of rubles averaged for one province): up to 1871 (8.5 thousand rubles); 1871-80 (12.6); 1881-90 (5.9); 1891-95 (11.8); 1895-1901 (38.2); 1902-3 (41.6). See also Brooks, "The Zemstvo and Education," 263-64.

35. Veselovskii, *Istoriia*, 1: 475-76; 3: 389.

36. Ibid., 1: 467-68, 473, 527-33, 540-41.

37. Cited in V.V. Kir'iakov, *Shag za shagom: k istorii ob'edineniia narodnykh uchitelei: Iz lichnykh vospominanii i perezhivanii* (Moscow, 1914), 32.

38. Survey results from the Moscow Committee were compiled and published under the general title "K voprosu o polozhenii uchashchikh v narodnoi shkole," in *Russkaia mysl'*, no. 6, section 2 (1897): 82-94; no. 12, section 2, 61-78; no. 9, section 2 (1898): 189-212, and in the source cited in note 26. Much of this material is summarized in L.N. Blinov, "Narodyi uchitel' v Rossii," in *Vseobshchee obrazovanie v Rossii: Sbornik statei*, ed. D.I. Shakhovskoi (Moscow, 1902), 63-84.

39. Gol'tsev, "O polozhenii uchashchikh," 16.

40. N.A. Skvortsov, "Nazrevshii vopros (polozhenie narodnykh uchitelei i uchitel'nits)," *Obrazovanie*, no. 2, section 2 (1897): 19. The "lesson of Sedan" was a favorite of Russians interested in public education (the reference is to Bismarck's alleged statement that it was Prussia's school system that was primarily responsible for the military victory over France).

41. Leggatt, "Teaching as a Profession," 162.

42. Blinov, "Narodnyi uchitel'," 75.

43. M.F. Superanskii, *Byt uchashchikh v nachal'nykh shkolakh Simbirskoi gubernii* (Simbirsk, 1905), 4.

44. V. Murinov, "Obshchestva vzaimnogo vspomoshchestvovaniia uchashchim i uchivshim," in *Vseobshchee obrazovanie v Rossii*, ed. D.I. Shakhovskoi (Moscow, 1902), 85-98.

45. V.B., "K voprosu o podgotovke narodnogo uchitelia," *Obrazovanie*, no. 4 (1902): 98-100; and Blinov, "Narodnyi uchitel'," 69-70.

46. On declining qualifications, see N. Bratchikov, "Uchebno-vospitatel'naia chast' v nachal'noi shkole," *Russkaia shkola*, no. 2 (1909): 118-120; and I. Iakhontov, "Uchitel'skie kursy, s"ezdy i sobraniia," *Vestnik Novgorodskogo zemstva*, no. 11 (1905): 32.

47. For example, the Kursk provincial *zemstvo* (in 1896), which began to organize summer courses annually beginning in 1897. *Tekushchaia shkol'naia statistika Kurskogo gub. zemstva: god odinnadtsatyi 1906-1907 uchebn. god*, part 1 (Kursk, 1908), 75-76.

48. For a discussion of the ascendancy of the liberals in the *zemstva* out of all proportion to their numerical strength, see Roberta Thompson Manning, "Zemstvo and Revolution: The Onset of the Gentry Reaction, 1905-1907," in *The Politics of Rural Russia, 1905-1914*, ed. Leopold H. Haimson (Bloomington: Indiana University Press, 1979), 30-36.

49. Rossiiskii gosudarstvennyi istoricheskii arkhiv (hereafter RGIA), f. 733, op. 173, d. 127, 11.74-74 ob.

50. According to ministry figures, for example, more than one-third of those occupying vacant teaching posts in 1899 lacked specialized or adequate general educations (i.e., normal school or complete secondary). S.V. Rozhdestvenskii, *Istoricheskii obzor deiatel'nosti ministerstva narodnogo prosveshcheniia, 1802-1902* (St. Petersburg, 1902), 723.

51. Farmakovskii, "S"ezdy uchitelei," 79.

52. V. Shcherba, "Uchitel'skie kursy i pravila o kursakh," *Vestnik Evropy*, no. 5 (1902): 775.

53. A. Lotkin, "Uchitel'skie kursy i s"ezdy," *Vestnik vospitaniia*, no. 6, section 2 (1904): 77-78.

54. A. Nechaev, "Pamiati zemskikh obshcheobrazovatel'nykh kursov dlia narodnykh uchitelei," *Rus'*, no. 162, 19 July 1905, 5. A kind of high point in the movement to organize courses came in 1902 when four or five thousand teachers attended an education exhibition and courses organized by the Kursk *zemstvo*.

55. In discussing projected courses for 1902, the Vladimir *zemstvo* assembly concluded that "today teachers in the majority of cases have a satisfactory pedagogical preparation and are little interested in narrow pedagogical courses and regard them lukewarmly and formalistically." *Russkaia shkola*, no. 7-8, section 2 (1903): 100.

56. See Nancy M. Frieden, *Russian Physicians in an Era of Reform and Revolution, 1856-1905* (Princeton, NJ: Princeton University Press, 1981), chapter 6.

57. V.B., "K voprosu o podgotovke," 100-1; and F.Ch., "Otgoloski uchitel'skikh s"ezdov, kursov i soveshchanii," *Vestnik vospitaniia*, no. 9, section 2 (1901): 90-91.

58. Lectures were given at the courses by scholars of national repute, who usually donated their services free of charge (e.g., in history, S.F. Platonov and the young Marxist historians M.N. Pokrovskii and N.A. Rozhkov).

59. V.K. Burtsev, "Professional'no-politicheskoe dvizhenie Iaroslavskogo uchitel'stva za 20 let (1898-1917 gody)," MS in Gosudarstvennyi arkhiv rossiiskoi federatsii, f. 6862, op. 1, d. 21, l. 271. In many cases the mutual-aid societies grew out of discussions among teachers and others at the courses.

60. The Saratov responses are cited in V. Denisov, "Znachenie uchitel'skikh kursov po otzyvam zemskikh uchitelei," *Obrazovanie*, no. 7, section 2 (1904): 42-47. For similar material, see G.I. Sergeev, *Narodnaia shkola v Nizhegorodskom uezde* (Nizhnii Novgorod, 1905), 36; and V.A. Samsonov, *Byt uchashchikh Novgorodskoi gubernii* (Novgorod, 1907), 87-88.

61. One has a sense that this was reinforced by the heavy influx of young (early twenties), unmarried teachers (without families to support), who tended to downplay material issues.

62. *Svod vysochaishikh otmetok po vsepoddanneishim otchetam za 1898 g. gubernatorov, voennykh gubernatorov i gradonachal'nikov* (St. Petersburg, 1901), 44.

63. A number of measures were enacted during the 1890s and generally interpreted as attempts to limit *zemstvo* prerogatives in education (e.g., making land captains ex officio members of local school boards and the 1900 law limiting annual increases in *zemstvo* budgets to 3 percent). For a full discussion of these and other measures, see Seregny, *Russian Teachers*, chapter 2.

64. N.A. Zinov'ev, ed., *Otchet po revizii zemskikh uchrezhdenii Moskovskoi gubernii*, 3 vols. (St. Petersburg, 1904), 1: 276-77.

65. For example, see the report of the governor of Saratov province for 1902. *Svod vysochaishikh otmetok po vsepoddanneishim otchetam za 1902 g.* (St. Petersburg, 1905), 42-43.

66. On the efforts of the Socialist Revolutionary Party among teachers, specifically the party-affiliated, illegal Teachers' Union, see Scott J. Seregny, "Revolutionary Strategies in the Russian Countryside: Rural Teachers and the Socialist Revolutionary Party on the Eve of 1905," *Russian Review* 44 (1985): 221-38.

67. *Osvobozhdenie*, no. 11 (35), 12 November (25), 1903, 194-95.

68. Lotkin, "Uchitel'skie kursy," 78; and O. Smirnov, "O narodnykh uchit eliakh," *Syn otechestva*, no. 124, 12 July 1905, 1-2. After the high point of 1901 (twenty-two provincial courses), the number of courses sanctioned by the government dropped off as follows: 1902 (eighteen), 1903 (seven) and 1904 (no more than four). In 1903, petitions by eleven *zemstva* to hold courses (most of the expanded "general-educational" type) were rejected. All petitions to hold courses in the summer of 1905 were turned down.

69. See Ben Eklof, "The Village and the Outsider: The Rural Teacher in Russia, 1864-1914," *Slavic and European Education Review*, no. 1 (1979): 1-19; and Eklof, *Russian Peasant Schools*, chapter 8.

70. On the Moscow Congress, see Seregny, *Russian Teachers,* chapter 4. The proceedings are published as *Trudy 1-go vserossiiskogo s"ezda predstavitelei obshchestv vspomoshchestvovaniia litsam uchitel'skogo zvaniia,* ed. V.M. Evteev, 2 vols. (Moscow, 1907).

71. N.V. Chekhov, "Uezdnye uchilishchnye komissii," *Russkaia shkola*, no. 9 (1906): 104-5.

72. On local medical congresses, see Samuel C. Ramer, "The Zemstvo and Public Health," in *Zemstvo in Russia,* eds. Emmons and Vucinich, 287-89; Kornilov, "Zemskaia demokraticheskaia intelligentsiia," 101-5; Pirumova, "Zemskaia intelligentsiia," 132-38; Veselovskii, *Istoriia,* 1: 300-305; and D.N. Zhbankov, *O deiatel'nosti sanitarnykh biuro i obshchestvenno-sanitarnykh uchrezhdenii v zemskoi Rossii: kratkii istoricheskii obzor* (Moscow, 1910), 8-13. According to Zhbankov, doctors' congresses were held fairly frequently during this period as well as later: seventy during the 1870s; ninety-six during the 1880s; ninety-four in the 1890s, and sixty-eight during the 1900s.

73. Veselovskii, *Istoriia,* 1: 308-9; 3: 395; I.D. Strashun, "Polveka zemskoi meditsiny (1864-1914)," in *Ocherki istorii russkoi obshchestvennoi meditsiny (k stoletiiu zemskoi meditsiny): Sbornik statei,* ed. P.I. Kaliu (Moscow, 1965), 51; and Ramer, "The Zemstvo and Public Health," 300.

74. This point is made by Z.G. Frenkel', "Osnovnoi nerazreshennyi vopros zemskoi meditsiny," in *Iubileinyi zemskii sbornik: 1864-1914,* eds. B.B. Veselovskii and Z.G. Frenkel' (Moscow, 1914), 412-13.

75. *Zemstvo* landowners also often viewed physicians as social inferiors. See Frieden, *Russian Physicians,* 209-10, and S.I. Mitskevich, *Zapiski vracha-obshchestvennika (1888-1918),* 2nd ed. (Moscow, 1969), 78.

76. To be precise, the congresses were limited to the inspectoral district (*raion*), usually one or two districts. For the rules (issued 26 November 1899), see V.P. Vakhterov, et al., *Narodnoe obrazovanie v Rossii* in *Narodnaia entsiklopediia nauchnykh i prikladnykh znanii,* vol. 10 (Moscow, 1911), 159-60.

77. Kir'iakov, *Shag za shagom,* 51-52.

78. On the Moscow congress of 1901, see V. Kir'iakov, "S"ezd uchitelei Moskovskogo uezdnogo zemstva," *Russkoe bogatstvo*, no. 1, section 2 (1902): 229-56.

79. A.V. Panov, "Shag vpered: zasedanie uchilishchnoi komissii Saratovskogo uezdnogo zemstva pri uchastii uchitelei," *Obrazovanie*, no. 12, section 2 (1901): 31-42.

80. *Zhurnaly uchilishchnoi komissii Saratovskogo uezdnogo zemstva pri uchastii gg. uchashchikh zemsko-obshchestvennykh uchilishch Saratovskogo uezda* (Saratov, 1901).

81. Lotkin, "Uchitesl'skie kursy," 77-78; and Akimov, "Zemskaia rabota," 131-33.

82. For example, reports of the governor of Novgorod province. RGIA, f. 733, op. 175, d. 77, ll. 361, 362 ob., 370, 370 ob..

83. For example, in 1904 of 243 district *zemstva* for which information is available, only 12 passed resolutions to fund teachers' congresses. V.I. Charnoluskii, comp., *Ezhegodnik narodnoi shkoly* (Moscow, 1908), 244.

84. *Polozhenie narodnogo obrazovaniia vo Vladimirskoi gubernii po izsledovaniiam 1910 goda*, vyp. 2 (Vladimir-na-Kliazme, n.d.), 46.

85. Samsonov, *Byt uchashchikh*, 82.

86. For details, see Seregny, *Russian Teachers*, chapter 5.

87. Sergeev, *Narodnaia shkola*, 36.

88. I. Stepnoi (I.S. Samokhvalov), "Zhivotvoriashchii dukh," *Dlia narodnogo uchitelia*, no. 5 (1915): 2-3.

8

Professionalism Among University Professors

Samuel Kassow

What most distinguished the Russian university professor from other professionals was an inherent tension between his identity as an independent scholar, loyal to a specific discipline, and his relationship to a complex and highly fragile institution—the university—for which he felt primary responsibility and over which he had insufficient control. This tension emerged in the subtle but crucial difference between two major professional goals: academic freedom and scientific freedom. As Walter Metzger points out,

> academic freedom is the ideology of a profession-across-the-disciplines, the profession created out of the common circumstance of an academic appointment in a college or university and of the common duties and anxieties that this entails; scientific freedom is the ideology of the diverse professions-in-the-discipline, the professions based on regularized advance of knowledge in distinctive fields.[1]

Between 1880 and 1917 two parallel developments epitomized the conflict between alternative forms of professional identity. The steady growth in membership and activity of learned societies signified increasing professional confidence in the ability of Russian scholarship to reach the highest international standards.[2] Indeed, when one remembers the *lex Arons* in Germany or gross violations of academic freedom in the United States,[3] and when one considers that Russian professors fired from state universities could teach at other ministries' institutes and work in learned societies, then it can be argued that the conditions of Russian life were at least moderately conducive to scholarship, even when compared to those in more "advanced" countries. It was not in scholarship but in defining their relationship to the state and the nature of their professional identity that Russian professors faced their most serious challenge. The contrast between growing scientific self-confidence and humiliating state tutelage, epitomized by the 1884 University Statute, intensified as time went on.

The issue of state tutelage was complicated by lack of an economic base capable of supporting a real alternative to state-financed higher education. This confronted the professoriate with two interrelated problems. The first was deciding whether the professor was really a civil servant or an independent professional. The second was the issue of how to defend professional rights in case of state attack.

Except for the short-lived Academic Union of 1905-6, the Russian professoriate never created a nationwide professional organization. The focal point of the professors' scholarly identity was the learned society, while cross-disciplinary identity centered on the faculty council. Yet even here there was a strong conservative minority that argued for the primacy of individual departments in university governance. The attitude toward faculty council powers was a basic litmus test of "liberalism" and "conservatism" within the profession.[4] Liberals argued that a strong faculty council signified not only belief in the "unity of science" but the professoriate's dedication to the principle that the university was more than the sum of its parts, that there was in fact a profession-across-the-disciplines with common interests centered on the universities. Yet the lack of interest in a Russian equivalent of the American Association of University Professors showed that the Russian professor saw himself as fundamentally different from other professionals. As Professor Vladimir Sergeevich put it in a 1905 article, what made professors different was that they were "above-average" people.[5] Such an attitude was hardly conducive to unionization or even to the formation of a strong national organization that could defend professional rights.

This essay discusses the profession-across-the-disciplines and focuses on the Russian university professoriate's fight to attain the professional goal of academic freedom. It argues that defining the obstacles to academic freedom proved much easier than deciding what academic freedom actually meant; that the professoriate's "professional ideology" depended on a vision of consensus between academics, government officials, and students on what the university should be; that this consensus, given the complex nature of the Russian universities, did not exist; and finally, that the almost hopeless tactical situation of the professoriate severely hampered its chances of attaining professional goals. On the eve of World War I, relations between the Russian government and the professoriate were worse than at any time since the reign of Nicholas I. Tsarist Russia produced great scholars and scientists but failed to develop a stable university system or a satisfied academic profession.

Tension in the Universities

Russian universities, like those in other countries, were highly complex entities answering to multiple constituencies and called on to perform a variety of difficult and often conflicting functions. In many countries, the period 1880-1914 saw some painful redefinitions of the proper relationship between the universities and society. Russian universities shared in this groping for new relationships.

By defining the universities as "teaching institutions" (*uchebnye uchrezhdeniia*), the 1884 University Statute reminded the professoriate that the government saw them mainly as training mills for the professions and the civil service. Most of the professoriate sought a redefinition of the universities as "scientific-teaching institutions" (*ucheno-uchebnye uchrezhdeniia*), a concept emphasizing the essential interrelationship of scholarship, research, and teaching. The difference was important and served as the fundamental rationale for the professoriate's struggle for greater professional rights. Professors who taught and trained future civil servants had a hard time arguing why the government should not treat them like employees, but professors who devoted their lives to pure research, which in turn was the only guarantee of effective teaching, could make a much stronger argument for academic freedom and university "autonomy." Strictly avoiding all "practical" or "applied" courses, the universities would instill a respect for free research and thus provide the nation with independent, critical, and dedicated civil servants and professionals.[6] It followed that the universities, rather than specialized institutes, should be the linchpin of the nation's higher educational system.[7] Universities based on science would become, the liberal professoriate hoped, the driving force behind government policies serving the interests of the nation as a whole rather than those of separate social groups;[8] moreover, they would pave the way for the gradual democratization of Russia while avoiding the pitfalls of revolution from below. Many liberal professors believed that the university was an essentially "democratic" institution, not because the senior faculty saw junior faculty and students as equals but because the universities were scientific institutions based on meritocratic principles.[9]

A major obstacle to recognition of the professoriate's professional demands was the student problem. As Walter Metzger pointed out in his study of academic freedom in the United States, what really made the importation of German *Lehr-* and *Lernfreiheit* impossible in America was the totally different nature of the American student subculture.[10] In Russia the tensions were much greater. The Russian universities were incubators of a unique student subculture, a funnel through which passed thousands of provincial youth, often poor but having little in common with the *narod* and even less with the ruling elite. They joined a proud new fraternity, the *studenchestvo*, and then left to become teachers, doctors, lawyers, and in a few cases, embittered revolutionaries. The student movement was a way of protesting without making a more extreme commitment to the revolutionary movement. It reflected the concern many students felt about taking their fathers' places as ineffectual "Chekhovian heroes," impotent minor civil servants or provincial doctors, vaguely unhappy about the autocratic system but too timid to do anything but compromise.

The professoriate, counseling students to "take the long view" and show restraint in the face of government repression, was a convenient target for the students. Professorial moderation embodied the hypocrisy of Russian liberalism—the pursuit of self-serving ends disguised by the rhetoric of lofty ideals. That many students saw a little of their future selves here only added to their bitterness. The students attacked what they regarded as professors' cowardice and unwillingness to support student demonstrations.

The professoriate's definition of the university and its own professional role left it open to criticism. There was a wide gap between the professional "ideology" and the reality of Russian university life. In theory, students went to a Humboldtian university, where they eagerly listened to the lectures of eminent scholars and honed their characters by learning the methodology of, and respect for, pure academic research. But in fact most students went to the university for jobs, not to become scholars. Students often had little idea of what jobs they wanted and therefore only vague and often contradictory expectations of what their university education should give them. Furthermore, the political elite of the country still included a large proportion of nonuniversity graduates; unlike Germany, the universities had failed to win the conspicuous support of the government.[11] In short, there was no clear link between students' education and the assurance of stepping into gratifying and powerful roles. The professoriate, with its own professional interests at stake, was giving the students a nonpractical "elite," rather than an "expert," education.[12] But the kind of elite that the professoriate wanted was not in fact running the country. The professor himself was caught in the middle, a symbol of the gap between ideals and reality.

To add to the tensions between professors and students, the faculty-student ratio steadily worsened between 1880 and 1914.[13] Excellent teaching was the exception rather than the rule.[14] The university examination system encouraged rote memorization rather than extensive independent research.[15] But many professors suspected that calls for better teaching and more direct supervision of students' work masked an attempt to turn them into "high school teachers."[16] Frustrated by the student problem, the professoriate tended to blame unrest in the universities on the government's treatment of the academic profession, pointing to Germany as an example of how government respect for professors led to good relations between faculty and students.[17]

Forced to answer so many varied demands, Russia's universities needed some semblance of consensus about their underlying role and purpose, a consensus about what they could and could not do. In the last years of the Romanov dynasty, achieving such a consensus proved to be an elusive goal. In a time of serious political uncertainty and underlying cultural conflict, the universities became painfully vulnerable to disruption and were easy targets for attack from all directions. To the Right, they symbolized a "secular humanist" attack on Russian traditional values, an ally of the liberals and the revolutionary parties.[18] At the same time, many students saw them as irrelevant, especially in a time of political turmoil. The very ideology of the autocracy, with its heavy emphasis on public order, gave educational institutions an exaggerated political importance; the government had a hard time dismissing student demonstrations with a wink and a smile. Rather than achieving internal peace and outside acknowledgment that they were to be spared the nation's political battles, the universities became lightning rods for discontent.

Professors and the 1884 University Statute

In theory, academics formed a privileged profession. They not only communicated knowledge but also created it. Their power to grant university degrees represented a basic standard for entry into other professions. In their "Comparative Study of Academic Freedom and Student Politics," Joseph Ben-David and Randall Collins define four general institutional arrangements of professional freedom: monopoly rights over the performance of certain functions; maintenance of the profession's own standards of talent and erudition; authority of the professional community over the ethical conduct of its members; and strict limitation of the professional's contractual obligation toward clients/employers to performing only those services approved by the profession. The authors conclude that "if professions were to be ordered on a scale according to how fully they realize these conditions academics would come out on top."[19]

Yet if the status of the Russian university professoriate were judged by the letter of the 1884 University Statute, this sanguine appraisal of professional status would be open to serious question. A conscious effort to assert state control over the universities, the statute gave the decisive say in faculty appointments and rectorships not to the faculty councils but to the Ministry of Education.[20] Furthermore, the faculty councils lost all jurisdiction over student discipline and could communicate with the minister of education only through the local educational curator.[21]

The State Council had warned Tsar Alexander III that the university statute would not work, and it was right.[22] By 1900 many of its provisions had lapsed: state graduation examinations meant little, ministerial interference in professorial appointments had become a rarity, and the professoriate was even being asked to take a role in student discipline.[23] The statute was a stark failure, a symbol of the inability of the state to regulate institutions as complex as the universities.

Yet the statute remained in force until 1917, its provisions a constant threat that could be applied or removed depending on the politics of the moment. Complicating the legal position of the academic profession was widespread confusion between the Temporary Rules of 27 August 1905 and the statute. The professors thought that the 1905 rules replaced the statute; the government disagreed. In short, the position of the academic profession in tsarist Russia rested on legal quicksand. Achieving a suitable legal relationship between the government and the universities became a major goal of the Russian academic profession. It was never achieved.

Another reason that the 1884 statute was so disturbing was its reminder that professional arguments cut both ways. Most professors agreed that the worst ministers of education turned out to be their ex-colleagues (e.g., Bogolepov, Schwartz, and Kasso). These ministers, representing a significant minority of the professoriate, believed that it was not the government that was violating professional norms but rather the majority of their colleagues who engaged in "politicking," "pandering to students," "lowering standards," and so on. They viewed the state as an essential protector against the potential tyranny of their colleagues, just as the statute was a professionally honest document which tried to combine the best of German *Lehrfreiheit*, high standards, and service to the state.[24]

Conservatives as well as liberals could use arguments of professional integrity. The complexity of the university and the tension among scholarship, teaching, and institutional responsibility combined to provide an intellectual opening for a coherent counter to the dominant professional ideology. There were many professors ready to defend the statute, despite its many problems.

One obvious problem connected with formalizing relations between government and universities in an all-inclusive written statute was that it made quick response to changing circumstances rather difficult. The professoriate wanted higher salaries and increased state expenditures for higher education. Although the Ministry of Education was sympathetic, little changed, in part due to Ministry of Finance opposition and in part because the government could always postpone the matter pending overall revision of the university statute. Full professors earned 3,000 rubles plus honoraria, associate (extraordinary) professors 2,000 rubles plus honoraria. These salaries had not changed since 1863 and were much less than those of other civil servants in the same grade.[25]

Unlike other elites (such as members of the State Council), few professors had a nonuniversity education.[26] A significant percentage had earned degrees from either Moscow or St. Petersburg universities.[27] Candidates for a professorial position had to steer a grueling course. To become a professor one had to be recommended by one's university, manage a risky relationship with one's advisor, and work as an underpaid *privat-dotsent* until a position became vacant.[28] Of eighty-five students being groomed for academic posts at Moscow University in 1908, thirty-four received scholarships averaging 500 rubles yearly while fifty-one got nothing at all.[29] The dropout rate was high; about half of all those preparing for academic careers left the profession within two years of beginning graduate study.

The social profile of the professoriate on the eve of World War I showed some interesting differences from that of the student body (keeping in mind the limitations of estate [sòslovie] categories as scholarly tools). In 1913, only 20.3 percent of the professoriate came from the petty bourgeoisie (meshchanstvo), merchantry (kupechestvo), peasantry (krest'ianstvo), and honored citizens (pochetnoe grazhdanstvo) as opposed to 45.7 percent of the students in the universities. The percentage of nobles ranged from 46.2 for historians and 48.1 for mathematicians down to 29.3 for medical faculty. It was not a rich profession; 83.5 percent of the professoriate owned neither landed property nor a house. The profession was becoming more religiously homogenous: 75.7 percent of faculty over the age of sixty-five were Russian Orthodox, but this proportion increased to 86 percent of those aged thirty-five to fifty-four.[30]

One of the greatest obstacles to an academic career was the controversial requirement that associate (extraordinary) and ordinary professors have two research degrees—a master's and a doctorate. Because of the limited financial support given candidates for academic posts, there were fewer qualified professors than there were chairs. In 1908, for example, out of a total of 474 chairs in the Russian universities, 115 were "vacant," that is, filled by professors teaching beyond the normal retirement age or by those without requisite degrees.[31] As demands increased for more subjects to be taught in the universities, constraints on the number of legally qualified professors became a growing problem. Especially in the two central universities, the junior faculty assumed a critical share of the teaching load but failed to gain the power or the pay to which they felt entitled. The junior faculty became an additional source of tension in the universities, and its impact was felt in 1905.

A student strike in 1899 set off a series of student disturbances that forced the government to reconsider the 1884 statute and gave the professoriate some leverage to seek its own professional goals. Between 1899 and the outbreak of the Revolution of 1905, the government granted the professoriate several concessions, but they were halfhearted and short-lived. Most important, the concessions were motivated by one essentially utilitarian consideration: stopping student unrest by enlisting the cooperation of the professoriate. The faculty council wanted basic reform of the universities; the government wanted peace and quiet.

A commission headed by Vannovskii investigated the causes of the 1899 student strike and stressed its apolitical character, linking student unrest to abnormalities in the structure of Russian higher education.[32] The government responded with promises of dormitories, directives for more seminar work, and instructions to the professoriate to establish closer relationships with the students and to take a greater interest in their work.[33] The 1884 statute had minimized student-faculty contact; now the Ministry of Education asked the professors to provide "moral guidance" to the students.

Hopes ran high that the government would finally abrogate the 1884 statute. In April 1901, the tsar appointed Vannovskii to be minister of education with an explicit mandate to prepare basic reforms. At this point most students agreed with their professors that attaining their respective goals was possible within the framework of the autocracy—a new statute for the professors, freedom of organization and assembly for the *studenchestvo*. Yet by 1902 most students, and by 1905 most professors, had become convinced that it was no longer possible to separate the issues of corporate and political reform.

The government raised everyone's hopes in 1901 and then beat a confused and hasty retreat. Right after his appointment, Vannovskii asked the faculty councils to respond to a long questionnaire outlining possible directions for university reform. Barred since 1884 from conducting most important university business, the faculty councils jumped at the chance to tell the Ministry of Education what they wanted. The replies to the questionnaire were basically similar; the professors wanted the right to elect their own rectors, control over student discipline, higher salaries, abolition of the honorarium, more faculty power in making new appointments, and replacement of the moribund state examination system.[34]

Nothing came of the Vannovskii questionnaire. Ministry of Education efforts to promote greater student-faculty contact and allow the students more organizational privileges ran into the opposition of the Ministry of the Interior, which feared that the government would lose control over the universities. One promising initiative, a joint faculty-student committee at Moscow University to discuss student grievances, quickly foundered due to the government's second thoughts. Its chairman, Professor P.G. Vinogradov, emigrated in disgust, while the Okhrana complained that the government had lost another great opportunity to pacify the universities.[35] In November 1901 Vannovskii issued new rules on student organization which fell far short of professors' and students' expectations. As the faculty councils predicted, a new student strike erupted, and hundreds of students were arrested. A hapless Vannovskii resigned.

Between 1902 and 1904, the government continued a confused policy combining toughness and halfhearted concessions to the professoriate. The Ministry of the Interior assumed a much more important role in framing higher educational policy. Under V.K. Plehve the government began to limit the relative professional freedom enjoyed by professors at educational institutions not attached to the Ministry of Education.[36] But this attempt at regimentation backfired, as the nonuniversity professoriate shared their university colleagues' growing sense of resentment and frustration.[37]

Even before Bloody Sunday (9 January 1905), the professoriate was slipping onto a collision course with the government. Between 1901 and 1904, the autocracy had admitted the unworkability of the 1884 statute, solicited faculty council opinions, raised hopes, and allowed disciplinary courts; but it then vitiated these efforts with hasty retreats and sporadic repression. The government was caught between its recognition that the statute was not working and its fear of losing control if it gave the professors and students more autonomy.

The professional and political dilemmas of the professoriate intensified during the Revolution of 1905. As the authority of the autocracy tottered, professors were under mounting pressure to make a commitment as a profession to the liberation movement. Here professors faced a real problem. Many supported the liberation movement as individuals, but harbored grave doubts about the wisdom of forming a professional union or jeopardizing in any way the view that the university should be "above politics." Furthermore, there was the well-founded concern for the university's vulnerability to political crosscurrents. This ambivalence was accentuated by their belief that professors were different from other professionals and that expressions of professional identity should not go beyond the faculty council. A national professional organization transcending the faculty council could well threaten their special status as independent scholars.

At the same time, there were strong pressures pushing the professoriate toward professional union and political commitment, pressures reflecting both idealistic conviction and self-interest. Many professors began to ask if they could afford to sit on the sidelines during a time of national renewal. The professoriate knew that it had to win the respect of the *studenchestvo* and the educated public in order to realize its claim to academic freedom and control of the universities. Professors began to realize that they might be jeopardizing their professional interests by not making a corporate commitment to the liberation movement.[38] The pressure mounted when the press, benefiting from the relative freedom of 1904-5, began to demand that the professoriate take a professional stand. In an important and telling break with the "university-above-politics" tradition, Peter Struve's *Osvobozhdenie* urged liberals to take a friendlier attitude toward the student movement and recognize the political uses of the universities.[39] *Nashi dni* published a blunt lead article demanding that the professoriate tell the Russian public whether they saw themselves as government hirelings (*chinovniki*) or as members of the Russian liberation movement.[40]

By the end of 1904, some leading professors were calling on their colleagues to organize. V.I. Vernadskii declared that the time for "inner emigration" had passed; it was time to form an academic union and realize the connection between political reform and professional rights.[41] Khar'kov's N.A. Gredeskul publicly admitted that the professoriate's traditional hostility to student protest may have been a mistake. After all, Gredeskul pointed out, the students had been right in 1899, and their teachers had been wrong; there were times when one could not enjoy freedom without some sort of a struggle.[42] At about the same time, Ivan Grevs published an article brilliantly dissecting his colleagues' "professional ideology" and warning that it would not work in the present crisis.[43] Grevs stated bluntly that he and his colleagues should admit the truth; while they meant well, their corporate passivity and fecklessness had become part of the problem. The professors had lost the students' respect and had allowed the government to use them for its own purposes. Unless the professoriate gained more respect, restoring stable university life was impossible.

Responses by the professoriate to the challenge of 1905 proceeded on two levels. The first was within the legal structure of relationships between the faculty councils, the relevant ministries, and the government. The second was the technically illegal and unofficial Academic Union. Between January and August 1905, there was a clear congruence between the resolutions of the faculty councils and those of the Academic Union, reflecting a degree of professional consensus that outweighed large, conservative groups within the universities. But after the 6 August rescript on the Bulygin Duma and the 27 August Temporary Rules on university governance, the academic profession underwent a trying period of polarization. As soon as the government changed course and showed some flexibility, tensions within the academic profession overwhelmed the fragile unity that marked the first half of the year. After August 1905, the faculty councils and the Academic Union began to go in different directions, largely because of growing strain between the senior faculty and a de facto coalition of junior faculty and students who demanded "democratization of the universities" and a more explicit institutional commitment to the nation's political life.

The Academic Union

Years later, V.I. Vernadskii wrote that in 1905 the professors had been "unwilling politicians." The record of the Academic Union certainly supports Vernadskii's claim. When the Union of Liberation asked Professor A.A. Brandt of the St. Petersburg Electrotechnical Institute to form a professors' union and draw up a political statement, Brandt accepted the charge, but with some significant and telling reservations. Even at the beginning of 1905,

Brandt later recalled, many professors feared that it was too late for a constitution in Russia. ("They [feared] . . . that a constitution in 1905 could lead . . . [to a] . . . social rather than a political revolution."[44]) But despite his misgivings, Brandt assembled a group to draw up a political statement (the "Declaration of the 342") which became the basic charter of the Academic Union. It was eventually signed by 1,650 senior and junior faculty—more than half the profession.[45]

The declaration complained that the government had reduced the professors to the status of petty bureaucrats and had undermined their prestige; neglect of education had sapped the nation's security and strength. Academic freedom was "incompatible with the existing system of government in Russia." Not partial reforms, but only a "fundamental transformation of the present system" would satisfy the academic profession.[46]

The Academic Union was the most moderate of the professional unions in 1905. It refused to pass resolutions calling for a constituent assembly. Nor did the professors join the Union of Liberation in demanding suffrage for women, the eight-hour day, or the transfer of land to the peasants. On academic matters, the First Congress of the Academic Union (March 1905) resolved that teaching in "repressive conditions" was "morally impossible" and demanded that future reforms of higher education be worked out by a "popular representative body" rather than by the bureaucracy. But the first congress did little to spell out the specifics of these reforms. Using an ambiguous phrase which reflected an analogous decision by the faculty councils, the Academic Union held open the possibility of a return to the classroom even before the attainment of satisfactory political reforms if the faculty councils were granted "temporary powers."[47]

The "temporary powers" phrase exposed the latent cracks in the Academic Union. Many members, especially junior faculty, saw it as a possible escape hatch from recent political and moral commitments not to teach until the attainment of political freedom. At a meeting of Moscow professors, Vernadskii explained the union's position by distinguishing between "temporary powers" (which he defined) and "academic freedom" (which he did not).[48] The first strongly resembled what the government would actually grant in August—permission for the faculty councils to elect rectors and assume responsibility for student discipline and internal affairs in the university. That was different, Vernadskii emphasized, from academic freedom, which required more basic political reforms. Some professors objected that if they assumed responsibility for student discipline before Russia had achieved political freedom, they might be falling into a trap. Student disorders would continue, but the faculty, rather than the government, would bear the onus of dealing with them. Vernadskii's response reflected the professors' sense that they were different from other professionals:

> We professors are in a special position. When we discuss events we cannot do
> so solely in our role as Russian citizens. We must also act as the guardian of
> science and education. . . . Our first duty is not to let the VUZy suffer during this
> period of social upheaval.[49]

The notion of a "special position" set the Russian professoriate apart
during 1904-6. A review of leading academics' published articles at the time
conveys the impression that the professoriate was "fighting on all fronts."
Articles by academics like P.G. Vinogradov, E.N. Trubetskoi, and V.I.
Vernadskii contain common themes which emerge as major elements of
"professorial liberalism." There was a clear mistrust of mass revolution and a
strong hope that the government would see reason and collaborate with the
educated classes to forestall popular upheaval. Vinogradov, for example,
expressed a clear preference for "1848" over "1789."[50] Another theme was the
clear line the professors drew between themselves and the "intelligentsia."[51]
Russia needed people who were disciplined, competent, and efficient; people
who knew their jobs and did them well. The "intelligentsia" was too lazy and
intolerant to see this.

Professors made a clear distinction between the autocracy and the nation,
and in so doing defined a major task of the universities: to strengthen the
nation by creating a patriotic professional class.[52] There was no patience for
the defeatism which marked the attitude of many educated Russians during the
Russo-Japanese War. The universities would train citizens to understand the
importance of a civic culture and to shoulder the burden of overcoming social
differences. In short, the universities were essential to the rise of a strong,
unified, and "democratic" Russia. Since they were so important, universities
could not be jeopardized by direct involvement in politics.

The combative mood that marked the Declaration of the 342 faded quickly.
By July, Vernadskii could write in *Russkie vedomosti* that "the professors'
strike was not an act of political protest . . . it was forced on the professoriate. . . . [N]o possible political gain could compensate for the academic
loss which has occurred."[53] According to Vernadskii, the professors had been
forced to choose between the "police" and "revolutionary terror." Here was a
clear hint that the leadership of the Academic Union was looking for a compromise with the government. Vernadskii called on the government to change
the "administrative structure of the universities by decree."

The government obliged on 27 August, and the Second Congress of the
Academic Union which was then in session resolved to accept the Temporary
Rules and return to the classroom.[54] The congress also tried to maintain the
momentum for professional cohesion by calling on the professoriate to
establish alternatives to state universities and boycott institutions where
colleagues had been arrested or illegally discharged. Unlike other professional
unions, the Academic Union took this occasion to make a carefully worded

endorsement of the Bulygin Duma. But signs of the Academic Union's imminent demise began to emerge at its second congress. The union failed to agree on such key issues as the position of students and junior faculty in university governance or the role of the universities in Russia's ongoing political crisis.

It was with a feeling of wary relief that the professoriate accepted the 27 August rules. Many professors believed that a more liberal university statute was just a matter of time. Meanwhile, they hoped that the students would end their strike, work hard, and listen to their teachers. But it took only two weeks to disabuse the professors of these hopes. The absence of a law allowing popular assembly and the hospitality of the students led to numerous popular meetings in the universities in September and October. These in turn provoked attacks by right-wing thugs and sparked bitter disagreements between faculty councils and students. Professors pleaded with the government to allow freedom of assembly and with the students to save the universities by keeping nonstudents out of the buildings. Once again the professors were caught in the middle. Students attacked the professors for cowardice, while the government blamed them for the chaos in the universities. The junior faculty sided mostly with the students, supporting their argument that in such an extraordinary political situation the universities had to stay open and serve as a popular forum.[55] At the same time, junior faculty pressed their claim for a greater role in university governance.

In a last ditch effort to save the universities, many faculty councils voted to close them. This, they argued, was better than the prospect of pitched battles among police, students, and rightist gangs. But closing the universities only exacerbated relations with students and junior faculty who pointed out, with ample justification, that closing the universities dealt a severe blow to the liberation and labor movements by eliminating relatively secure meeting points. An exasperated Moscow University faculty council responded with a declaration echoing the feelings of most of the senior faculty.

> The participation of the university as such in the political struggle is impermissible. . . . [T]he very nature of political activity is incompatible with the nature, purposes and spirit of the university. . . . [T]he university should unite people on the basis of scientific and educational interests and direct them to the service of science and enlightenment. . . . But such a union is possible only on the basis of academic interests. . . . [I]t would collapse immediately as soon as politics were introduced. . . . [T]he university can and should, as long as it does not stray from its primary purpose, serve the cause of freedom. By struggling for the freedom of science and teaching and for the principle of academic autonomy . . . the university serves the cause of freedom and progress.[56]

By autumn, the shock of revolution had forced the professoriate back to the "professional ideology" that Grevs had attacked in the spring. The universities reopened only in September 1906. Two entire academic years were lost.

The traumatic experience of September and October 1905 prompted a searching reevaluation of the role of the academic profession and its relationship to the state. The revolution reminded professors that the university was vulnerable and that their own authority was fragile. Not only the students, but even the junior faculty refused to recognize the senior faculty's claims to undisputed primacy in university governance. These events reinforced the professoriate's fear of confrontation politics and led to polarization within the Academic Union. Many senior faculty left the union, which thereafter reflected the influence of junior and nonuniversity faculty.

Cleavages and Polarization

The polarization of the academic profession was epitomized by decisions at two simultaneous conferences in January 1906: a conference of elected faculty delegates called by the new, liberal minister of education, I.I. Tolstoi, and the Third Congress of the Academic Union.

Although its draft statute never became law, the Tolstoi Conference was a major landmark in the history of the Russian academic profession. For the first time, freely elected members of the professoriate could meet and draft a model university statute with the support of a sympathetic minister of education. But the conference also showed that it was much easier for the professors to unite against the old statute than to agree on the details of a new one.[57] Intense debates marked the proceedings.

The conference called for an elective curriculum to replace the existing restrictive system, and after long and acrimonious discussion, voted to ease entry into the profession by abolishing the requirement for two research degrees. The conference restored the *shtatnye dotsenty*, abolished by the 1884 statute, and recommended much higher salaries for both junior and senior faculty. It also voted down any restrictions on admission to the professoriate and the student body based on religion, nationality, or gender. The delegates also included faculty disciplinary courts in the draft statute. In another liberal move, the conference decided to end the privileged position of the classical gymnasia; graduates of all secondary schools would be eligible to enter the universities, and at sharply reduced fees. As expected, the delegates voted to abolish the requirement that faculty councils communicate with the ministry of education through the curators, but they could not agree to recommend the abolition of the legal privileges connected with the university diploma.

The issue of junior faculty rights produced one of the most serious arguments at the conference. A small liberal bloc proposed allowing elected delegates from the junior faculty to enjoy voting rights at faculty council meetings. But this proposal attracted only seven votes. As before, the junior faculty had no right to participate in or vote at faculty council meetings.[58]

The Tolstoi Conference represented the high point of the professoriate's struggle for state recognition of its professional goals. Its draft charter outlined a university where professors, not the junior faculty or students, would rule. By endorsing the principle of state supervision, the professoriate showed again that it preferred working with, rather than against, the government—especially when the latter showed even slight signs of respecting its professional aspirations. But if the senior faculty displayed a preference for an elitist model of university governance, they also demonstrated a commitment to a university admissions policy free of religious or gender discrimination.

The conference showed that the professoriate was going beyond foreign models in charting a uniquely Russian system of university governance. The clearest example was its insistence, following sharp debate, on the central role of the faculty council rather than the department in university governance. It was the faculty council that was to constitute the touchstone of the Russian professor's sense of professional identity.

At the same time that the Tolstoi Conference was meeting, the Academic Union held its third congress, which drafted a very different university statute and demonstrated that the short-lived unity of early 1905 was giving way to deepening professional polarization.[59] The union's statute gave junior faculty an equal vote in the faculty councils, stated that the professor was not a civil servant, and abolished the Ministry of Education's veto power over appointments. In a clear departure from the Tolstoi Conference's draft statute, the Academic Union refused to define the universities as state institutions.[60]

But by this time the Academic Union was on its last legs. Stung by their experience in the fall, apprehensive about junior faculty demands, and encouraged by the Tolstoi Conference, senior faculty no longer saw much need for a separate national professional organization. Speakers at the congress pleaded with the profession not to drop its guard. It was too early to trust the government, they argued, and Russia's professors still needed a strong Academic Union. But the sense of urgency which led to the Declaration of the 342 and spawned the cross-disciplinary and professional union now gave way to a deep rift in the profession. In an article in *Vestnik vospitaniia,* P.D. Sakulin, then a junior faculty member at Moscow University and a leading member of the Academic Union, accused the delegates at the Tolstoi Conference of having betrayed the ideals that moved the profession the previous year.[61]

In his short tenure as minister, Tolstoi implemented by circular many of the articles in the Tolstoi Conference's draft statute. As the conference ended, he promised the departing delegates he would present the draft statute to the new Duma as soon as possible. He stated that he agreed with the faculty consensus that in issuing the 27 August rules, the government had signaled the death of the 1884 statute. Therefore, until the Duma could adopt a new statute, he would meet the major demands of the professoriate. His circulars lifted admissions restrictions on seminary students and on the graduates of realgymnasia applying to universities. Even after Tolstoi's dismissal, the faculty councils were able to use the 27 August rules for a year to abolish Jewish quotas, admit women, and establish an elective system. When the universities reopened in September 1906, there were twice as many students as before, largely a result of these liberal policies.[62] But there were clouds on the horizon. Tolstoi's tenure was short, and the new prime minister, P.A. Stolypin, had little trust in the academic community.

Just when the professoriate thought that a new relationship with the state had begun, Stolypin taught it some hard lessons in the realities of power. Unwilling to exempt the universities from his pacification program or distinguish between the radical rhetoric of the student movement and the actual threat it posed to the government, Stolypin reverted to the traditional policy of judging the universities by the single issue of student unrest. To make matters worse for the professoriate, the extreme Right had designated the universities, along with the Jews, as major targets.[63] Stolypin, himself vulnerable to attacks from that direction, quickly moved to abolish many of the privileges the universities had gained in 1905. His letters to Gurliand, the editor of *Rossiia*, showed his deep suspicion of the professoriate, which he identified with the Kadet Party.[64] In fairness, the prime minister did not see himself as an enemy of higher education.[65] He merely wanted the professors to act like loyal civil servants who obeyed the government and kept the students in line.

Stolypin's ministers of education—von Kaufman, Schwartz, and Kasso —worked closely with the prime minister in formulating university policy. His dismissal of von Kaufmann (for "softness") in January 1908 clearly indicated what kind of policy Stolypin wanted. Von Kaufman's successor, Schwartz, himself a former professor, drafted a startling memorandum to the prime minister accusing the professoriate of disloyalty to the government and of undertaking deliberate sabotage of the universities in order to turn them into hotbeds of antistate activity.[66] Stolypin agreed with Schwartz's analysis and told *Rossiia* to use it as a guide for its editorial line on the universities.[67]

Schwartz rescinded the relaxation of university admissions requirements, scrapped the Tolstoi Conference project, and introduced a university statute in the Duma that the Moscow and St. Petersburg faculty councils pronounced worse than the 1884 statute.[68] All teaching staff had to acknowledge their civil service status and sign a disclaimer denying membership in antigovernment organizations (including the Kadet Party).[69] Schwartz also won Senate endorsement of his interpretation of the 27 August rules; far from granting any kind of autonomy to the professors, the rules merely made them responsible for keeping the students in order. If the students did not behave, the government reserved the right to return to the status quo ante. In September

1908, the students responded with a nationwide strike. The professors, fearful of jeopardizing support for the profession in the Octobrist-dominated Third Duma, condemned the students' action.

Once again the professoriate was in the middle. While students accused the professors of cowardice, the government argued that the professors were hiding behind the student strike to wring concessions from the state. At least one curator, Sokolovskii of the Khar'kov educational district, agreed with the students' argument that the student movement, not the professoriate, had won the universities their post-1905 gains.

In many respects, therefore, the professional situation of the professoriate was worse after 1908 than it had been in the dark days before 1905. Then, at least, there had been reason to hope for a change in state policy. That hope was now gone, especially when Schwartz's successor, Kasso, declared in 1911 that the 1884 statute was working well and that there was no need to replace it. Another reason that the professoriate's situation worsened was that the Revolution of 1905 and its aftermath led to a conspicuous polarization within the senior faculty, and after 1907, the provincial universities saw an almost total breakdown of professional solidarity. Right-wing professors worked with local military governors and the Ministry of Education to purge more liberal and progressive colleagues who had led the faculty councils in 1905. By 1911, rightist professors were even holding national meetings.

Relations between the senior faculty and the government grew even worse in 1911, when one-third of the Moscow University faculty resigned to protest Stolypin's firing of the university's rector and two prorectors. The crisis began when Stolypin issued a circular (11 January 1911) banning all student meetings on school premises and directing the police to enter the campuses and break up the meetings even before receiving an invitation from the faculty councils to do so. The circular also directed the faculty councils to call in the police at the first sign of trouble.[70] The shocked professors immediately realized that the government was rescinding the last shred of power left them under the 27 August rules, but they complied with Stolypin's *diktat*, even as the students launched a bitter nationwide strike. Normal academic life collapsed as professors had to lecture under the fixed bayonets of military guards.

Unable to cope with the spreading chaos, the rector, assistant rector, and prorector (Manuilov, Menzbir, and Minakov) of Moscow University resigned their administrative posts but not their professorships. Stolypin stunned the entire academic profession by ordering that they be fired from their academic posts as well. The prime minister warned the professoriate that he would not tolerate "political demonstrations" by "state employees." By the end of February, twenty-five full professors and seventy-four assistant professors had resigned from the university.[71] Many of those who resigned managed to find positions in the independent Shaniavskii University, the Moscow Commercial Institute, or other higher-education institutions not attached to the Ministry of Education.[72] The government did not interfere with these appointments. Nor were there resignations from other universities to protest Stolypin's actions. Other professors sympathized with their Moscow colleagues, but they suspected that a mass resignation was exactly what the government wanted.[73]

One contemporary observer, Nikolai Iordanskii, saw the Moscow University crisis as the epitome of the "entire liberal tragedy."[74] Certainly the Moscow professors who resigned cast a plague on both houses—the government and the students. Professor Evgenii Trubetskoi told the readers of *Rech'* that during any period of political confrontation, "the university should enjoy the same status as a Red Cross hospital on the battlefield and should not be shot at from either side. . . . We resigned . . . because neither side respected the neutrality of the university."[75]

The 1911-14 period saw the nadir of relations between the academic profession and the government. One example was unprecedented interference by the Ministry of Education in professorial appointments. Between 1907 and 1909, the ministry followed the recommendations of faculty councils in appointments of professors on all but five occasions. But in 1911, the ministry made twenty-one appointments conflicting with the wishes of faculty councils, and in 1913 this occurred thirteen times.[76]

Kasso dealt ruthlessly with professors who questioned his policies. A favorite tactic was to transfer professors from central to provincial universities, where local authorities were less hesitant to employ the police powers granted them by the 1881 special decrees. In turn, conservative professors were sent to the central universities, where they either had to teach under police guard or stop lecturing altogether in the face of student opposition. The purge continued until the beginning of World War I.[77]

Kasso also insulted the professional competence of the professoriate by recommending reinstitution of a foreign seminar system to train future professors.[78] And in another slap at his profession, he endorsed the government's clear preference for specialized technical institutes rather than universities in the nation's higher educational system.[79]

Conclusion

By 1914, two seemingly contradictory developments marked the position of Russian university professors. Their professional status as scholars-across-the-disciplines reflected the general crisis of the state universities. On the other hand they were much more secure in their status as scholars-within-the-disciplines. Growing international recognition of Russian scientific achievement made the gap between the two forms of professional identity even more glaring.[80] The policies of the Ministry of Education did much to further discredit the prestige of the autocracy among wide sections of the educated public already repelled by incidents like the anti-Semitic scapegoatism of the Beilis trial and the growing role of Rasputin at court. Nor did the ministry achieve its major aim, the elimination of student unrest in the country.

There was, however, a silver lining in the crisis of the state universities. Contributions by private philanthropists, as well as the efforts of such ministries as Finance and Trade and Industry, were laying the foundations for more diversity in Russian higher education and also forcing the professoriate to re-examine its idea of what the university should be. Especially important in this regard was Moscow's Shaniavskii University. In curriculum, governance, and definition of aims, it represented the beginnings of a significant reappraisal of the Humboldtian idea of an elite university. Relations between students and professors at Shaniavskii were excellent. Another sign of growing professional receptivity to new ideas was the founding of Tashkent University in 1915. Regarded as supplements to existing universities rather than substitutes for them, these institutions nonetheless represented a new trend toward educational diversity.[81]

The state was always willing to recognize the professor as a teacher and a scholar. The conciliatory policies of Tolstoi and Ignat'ev showed that real dialogue, even mutual understanding, was possible. But what the state failed to do was to institutionalize university autonomy and recognize the permanence of a professional identity that linked professors-across-the-disciplines in a relationship of shared responsibility for university governance and structural safeguards of academic freedom. That it did not do so is another example of how the government's "ideology of order" crippled its political vision and undercut its ability to govern a rapidly changing society.

Neither the government nor the professoriate could find a satisfactory answer to the third part of the "university question"—student unrest. The student movement vitiated professors' attempts to achieve professional goals, even as the senior faculty hoped that the problem would disappear once Russia reached a certain level of cultural and political development. In the meantime, the universities were central points where many of the tensions generated by the clash of official paternalism, the struggle for professional autonomy, and the insecurities of the Russian student body converged in a pattern of misunderstanding and confrontation.

Notes

1. Walter P. Metzger, "Academic Freedom and Scientific Freedom," *Daedalus* (Spring 1978): 107.

2. On learned societies, see Alexander Vucinich, *Science in Russian Culture,* vol. 2 (Palo Alto, CA: Stanford University Press, 1970), 204-9; and V.R. Leikina-

Svirskaia, *Russkaia intelligentsiia v 1900-1917 godakh* (Moscow: 1981), 91-92. One of the best expositions of the dichotomy between state interference and the growing confidence of the professoriate can be found in V.I. Vernadskii's "1911 god v istorii russkoi umstvennoi kul'tury," *Ezhegodnik gazety Rech' za 1911 g.* (St. Petersburg, 1912).

3. The *lex Arons* was a law that restricted appointment of faculty members who were Social Democrats at Prussian universities.

4. While the professoriate was regarded by the public, the students, and the government as basically a "liberal" profession, it was in fact torn by sharp divisions between conservatives and liberals, especially in the provincial universities after 1905. Three of the most conservative (and hated) ministers of education were ex-professors. Nevertheless, there is some justification for talking in terms of the "professoriate" and even characterizing its basic political physiognomy as being in the "moderate liberal camp." Newspapers ranging from *Rossiia* to *Rech'* to *Pravda* used this label, as did P.A. Stolypin, who saw the professoriate as a wing of the Kadet Party. After 1906, the professoriate elected its own representatives to the State Council, and those deputies were mostly in the "left" or "center" wing of the council. More than half the profession signed the "Declaration of the 342," the manifesto of the Academic Union. Most important, we have ample evidence of collective faculty sentiment in dozens of faculty council resolutions, petitions, responses to government questionnaires, and so on.

5. Vladimir Sergeevich, "Germanskie universitety i nashi," *Vestnik Evropy*, no. 3 (1905): 59.

6. For example, see Boris Chicherin's statement that moral education rested on exposure to scientific research, quoted in G.A. Dzanshiev, *Epokha velikikh reform* (Moscow, 1900), 265-67. On the role of the universities in educating the civil service, see P.G. Vinogradov, "Uchebnoe delo v nashikh universitetakh," *Vestnik Evropy*, no. 10 (1901).

7. As early as 1862, Professor Andreevskii argued that "science . . . can develop only in the universities . . ." The best and most explicit defense of this premise is V.I. Vernadskii's "Vysshaia shkola v Rossii," *Ezhegodnik gazety Rech'* (St. Petersburg, 1914).

8. This happened often. Examples of "scholarship in the nation's service" were: Muromtsev's work on legal codification, Chuprov's on transport economics, Ianzhul's on factory legislation, Ozerov's on tax law, Kliuchevskii's and Tagantsev's memoranda on the historical background of Russian legislative institutions, and Mendeleev's on Russian natural resources.

9. E.N. Trubetskoi, "K nachalu uchebnogo goda," *Moskovskii ezhenedel'nik*, no. 34 (1907).

10. Metzger, "Academic Freedom," 96. *Lehr-* and *Lernfreiheit* refer to the German ideal of academic freedom: the freedom to teach as one sees fit and the freedom to study where one wishes.

11. A.S. Famintsyn, "Nakanune universitetskoi reformy," *Mir bozhii* (January 1903); V.I. Guerrier, "Nauka i gosudarstvo," *Vestnik Evropy* (October 1876) are good sources for the application of the idea of the Humboldtian university to Russia. On the students' motives for going to universities, see A.T. Fortunatov, "Zachem liudi idut v

vysshuiu shkolu," *Po voprosam nauchnoi shkoly* (Moscow, 1916), 35-48. The 1897 edition of *Al'manakh sovremennykh russkikh gosudarstvennykh deiatel'ei* lists eighty-four persons who were members of the State Council, ministers, or department heads. Of these only twenty-two were university graduates. For a complaint about insufficient state support of higher education, and especially universities, see D.I. Bagalei, "Ekonomicheskoe polozhenie nashykh universitetov," *Vestnik Evropy* (January 1914).

12. I have borrowed the notion of "elite" and "expert" universities from a highly suggestive theoretical article by Joseph Ben-David and Randall Collins, "A Comparative Study of Academic Freedom and Student Politics," in *Student Politics*, ed. S.M. Lipset (New York: Basic Books, 1967), 148-95. "Elite" universities did not try to give their graduates practical training; "expert" universities did. The authors also distinguish between model and nonmodel systems. In the former, the universities train graduates for positions and responsibilities which have clear models in the wider society. In the latter, universities "are created by a traditional, or at any rate uneducated elite for the purpose of eventually reforming themselves or increasing their efficiency through training new and better qualified people of a kind that do not yet exist in the country."

13. Student enrollments in Russia's universities increased from 12,033 in 1885 to 34,538 in 1912-13. Neither teaching staff nor scholarship aid kept pace. This was an especially acute problem in the central universities.

14. Mark Vishniak, *Dan' proshlomu* (New York, 1954), 47; N.I. Astrov, *Vospominaniia* (Paris, 1941), 191; and S.P. Mel'gunov, *Vospominaniia i dnevniki* (Paris, 1964), 79-81.

15. A good discussion of the bad effects of the examination system is in Sergei Zhivogo, "Chevo nedostaet v universitete nashim budushchim iuristam," *Russkaia mysl'* (October 1902).

16. This was especially true after 1899 when the Ministry of Education decided that better teaching and more seminars would be a useful antidote to student unrest. For a typical article in the controversy about the relationship of the lecture system of teaching to academic freedom, see N. Kazanskii, "Eshche o prepodavanii na iuridicheskikh fakul'tetakh," *Zhurnal Ministerstva narodnogo prosveshcheniia*, no. 1 (1901).

17. In his Tatianin Day speech of January 1904, Professor Sergei Trubetskoi appealed to the Russian educated public to look to the example of Germany, "where no possible political or social upheaval could upset the consensus that the universities were inviolable and independent." *Russkie vedomosti*, 12 January 1904.

18. One example of a vast right-wing, anti-university literature is Vladimir Purishkevich, *Materialy po voprosu o razlozhenii universitetov* (St. Petersburg, 1914).

19. Ben-David and Collins, "Comparative Study of Academic Freedom," 149-50.

20. For an analysis of the statute, see B.B. Glinskii, "Universitetskie ustavy," *Istoricheskii vestnik*, no. 1 (1900), 2; G.I. Shchetinina, *Universitety v Rossii i ustav 1884 goda* (Moscow, 1976); Silke Spieler, *Autonomie oder Reglementierung* (Koln, 1981). As Ben-David and Collins point out, a distinctive feature of "elite-non-model

universities" is their need for a statute clearly defining their relationship to the state.

21. In a contradictory move designed to apply the principles of German *Lehrfreiheit* to Russia and at the same time force the professors to teach what the state wanted, the statute established a state examination system, an honorarium for professors based on course enrollments, and a new teaching category, *privat-dotsenty*, to compete with professors and force them to keep up to standard. For an attack on these attempts to apply certain features of the German university system out of context, see Vinogradov's "Uchebnoe delo." As he pointed out, there were not enough professors or strong universities for real *Lehrfreiheit*; the dependence of *privat-dotsenty* on their senior protectors ruled out any real competition; the combination of the honorarium system with required courses created gross inequities in professors' pay and tended to demoralize the profession.

22. Gosudarstvennyi sovet, *Otchet za 1884 god* (St. Petersburg, 1884), 231-392.

23. Between 1884 and 1888, the ministry did conduct a limited purge of the teaching staff which affected M.M. Kovalevskii, S.M. Muromtsev, O.F. Miller, and I.I. Ditaatin. Afterwards, and until 1899, ministerial interference became rarer. See B. Buzeskul, *Istoriia Khar'kovskovo universiteta pri deistvii ustava 1884 goda*, (Khar'kov, 1905). Also, T. Zelinskii, "Universitetskii vopros v 1906 godu," *Zhurnal Ministerstva narodnogo prosveshcheniia*, no. 8 (1906). But Bogolepov's unceremonious firing of professors, as Zelinskii pointed out, demonstrated that the staff was legally vulnerable.

24. See A.N. Schwartz's memorandum to Stolypin, Rossiiskii gosudarstvennyi istoricheskii arkhiv (hereafter RGIA), f. 733, op. 226, d. 137, 1. 16.

25. On salaries, see Bagalei, "Ekonomicheskoe polozhenie nashykh universitetov," *Vestnik Evropy* (January 1914);" and Imperatorskii Moskovskii universitet, *Suzhdeniia soveta imperatorskogo Moskovskogo universiteta* (Moscow, 1901), 64-68.

26. This is based on analysis of the Ministry of Education's 1902 and 1913 service lists.

27. Ibid.

28. A good book echoing the complaints of the junior faculty is N. Kol'tsov, *K universitetskomu voprosu* (Moscow, 1909). But in light of the staffing constraints of the statute and the reluctance of the government to increase expenditures on the universities, the *privat-dotsenty* assumed growing importance, especially in the central universities. In 1912 there were 649 *privat-dotsenty*, 350 of whom taught in either St. Petersburg or Moscow universities. This compares to about 630 ordinary and associate professors.

29. Ibid., 5.

30. See note 25.

31. *Otchet* of the Ministry of Education for 1908.

32. The full text of the Vannovskii report is in RGIA, f. 733, op. 151, d. 244.

33. See Imperatorskii Moskovskii Universitet, *Suzhdeniia*, 42-43.

34. One point of disagreement among various faculty councils concerned the rights and privileges connected with a university degree. Some councils wanted the

government to cease awarding ranks to graduates on the grounds that students would then come to the universities to pursue pure learning rather than to seek civil service privileges or military exemptions. But the St. Petersburg faculty warned against pushing the ideology of pure learning too far. Students still needed incentives to seek higher education, and the country still needed an educated civil service. Ibid., 42-75. For the responses of other faculty councils to Vannovskii's questionnaire, see RGIA, f. 733, op. 226, d. 96.

35. Gosudarstvennyi arkhiv rossiisskoi federatsii (hereafter GARF), f. 124, po. 10, ed. kh. 442, 1901, 1. 33.

36. Up to this time, the nonuniversity professoriate had had a much easier relationship with the government. On this issue and on Plehve's crackdown on the Mining Institute, see E.N. Trubetskoi, "Ministerstvo narodnogo prosveshcheniia i kul'turnaia rabota," *Moskovskii ezhenedel'nik*, 3 June 1908; *Konovalovskii konflikt* (St. Petersburg, 1905); and "Razgrom Khar'kovskogo tekhnicheskogo instituta," *Osvobozhdenie*, 7/20 September 1904.

37. One concession that backfired was the government's 1902 decision to allow faculty courts to handle student disciplinary matters. Almost as soon as the courts began their work, the government began questioning the "leniency" of their verdicts. Once again, frustrated faculty councils had to ask themselves whether any kind of professional security was possible without more general political reforms. In December 1903, the Moscow faculty council, in direct defiance of the 1884 statute, protested the constant interference in student disciplinary procedures and threatened to disband the court. In February 1904, the faculty court at Khar'kov University resigned en masse. The tsar responded by appointing a former army general, V.G. Glazov, to become minister of education with explicit orders to "clean house, starting with the professors. There are some decent ones but very few." The general, who made a conscientious effort to master his job, issued a circular authorizing state-appointed rectors to ignore the disciplinary courts in cases of "mass disorders." "Dva razgovora: Iz dnevnikov V.G. Glazova," *Dela i dni*, no. 1 (1920).

38. A good discussion of this point is S.E. Savich's "Zabastovka v vysshikh uchebnykh zavedeniakh," *Pravo*, no. 11 (1905).

39. P.B. Struve, "Chto zh teper'?" *Osvobozhdenie*, 7/20 September 1904. For a bitter attack on this article, see V.A. Maklakov, *Vlast' i obshchestvennost' na zakate staroi Rossii* (Paris, 1936), 183-87.

40. *Nashi dni*, 24 December 1904.

41. "O professorskom s"ezde," *Nashi dni*, 20 December 1904.

42. "Rol' universiteta v obshchestvennom dvizhenii," *Pravo*, no. 40 (1905).

43. "Zabytaia nauka i unizhennoe zvanie," *Nashi dni*, 28 December 1904.

44. A.A. Brandt, *List'ia pozheltelye* (Belgrade, 1930), 26.

45. S.D. Kirpichnikov, *Soiuz soiuzov* (St. Petersburg, 1906), 20. By August, the union had 550 members in St. Petersburg, 400 in Moscow, 111 in Kiev, 112 in Khar'kov, 72 in Odessa, 41 in Warsaw, 100 in Tomsk, and 49 in Dorpat. Membership included faculty in all institutions of higher education. The local chapters of the union had wide autonomy.

46. I have used part of Alexander Vucinich's translation.

47. *Russkie vedomosti*, 30 March 1905.

48. RGIA, f. 733, op. 152, d. 173, 1. 359.

49. Ibid.

50. "Politicheskie pis'ma," *Russkie vedomosti*, 5 August 1905.

51. Ibid.; M.M. Kovalevskii, *La crise russe* (Paris, 1906); Trubetskoi, "K nachalu uchebnogo goda"; Olga Trubetskaia, *Kniaz' S.N. Trubetskoi* (New York, 1953). Lenin used Vinogradov's article to bolster his point that the bourgeoisie (and "its most learned section, the professors") ". . . do not want a revolution."

52. V.I. Vernadskii's letter to S.N. Trubetskoi, February 1904, published in *Kniaz' S.N. Trubetskoi*, 74.

53. "Tri zabastovki," *Russkie vedomosti*, 5 July 1905.

54. A good record of the proceedings was kept by P.N. Sakulin and is found in Rukopisnyi otdel Rossiiskoi gosudarstvennoi biblioteky, f. 264, p. 41, ed. kh. 21.

55. As an example, see the declaration of the St. Petersburg junior faculty published in *Russkie vedomosti*, 10 September 1905, and the declaration of the junior medical faculty of Moscow University, *Russkie vedomosti*, 3 November 1905.

56. *Russkie vedomosti*, 8 November 1905.

57. The most controversial issues at the conference were: procedures for appointing faculty, whether professors were civil servants or professionals, criteria for university admissions, the relationship of the universities to the state, the rights of junior faculty, professional prerequisites for a teaching career, student rights and disciplinary procedures, and the relationship between faculty councils and the various faculty departments. The discussion of the Tolstoi Conference is based on the transcript of the deliberations in RGIA, f. 733, op. 226, d. 121. Also Tolstoi's unpublished memoirs in Gosudarstvennaia publichnaia biblioteka im. Saltykova-Shchedrina. Otdel rukopisei, f. 781, ed. kh. 568.

58. RGIA, f. 733, op. 226, d. 121.

59. For the proceedings of the Third Congress, see *Tret'ii delegatskii s"ezd akademicheskogo soiuza* (St. Petersburg, 1906). For a caustic comparison of the two statutes, see the pro-Academic Union piece by P.N. Sakulin, "Novyi proekt universitetskogo ustava," *Vestnik vospitaniia*, no. 4 (1906).

60. Ibid.

61. Ibid.

62. For the text of the various circulars, see RGIA, f. 733, op. 152, d. 195. One important circular granted permission for students to go to any university they chose, rather than the one attached to their educational district. On student-faculty relations in 1906-8, see my *Students, Professors and the State in Tsarist Russia* (Berkeley: University of California Press, 1989). For a sober but upbeat assessment of the 1906-8 period in the universities, see Ivan Grevs, "Stroitel'stvo i razrushenie v nashei vysshei shkole," *Pravo*, nos. 29, 31 (1908). This was a defense of the professors' claim that more faculty rights constituted the best way to fight student unrest.

63. In a New Year's Day article in 1908, Vernadskii warned that the major question facing the universities was whether Stolypin would be "strong enough to resist the pressure from the extreme Right . . ." *Rech'*, 1 January 1908.

64. RGIA, f. 1662, op. 1, d. 86.

65. For example, in 1907 Stolypin opposed those in the Council of Ministers who argued against the establishment of any new universities in Russia. *Osobyi zhurnal soveta ministrov ob osnovanii novogo v Rossii universiteta*, 10 and 13 April 1907.

66. RGIA, f. 733, op. 226, ed. kh. 137, l. 16.

67. RGIA, f. 1662, op. 1, d. 86.

68. For a full critical discussion of Schwartz's draft statute, see *Vestnik vospitaniia*, no. 8 (1908).

69. RGIA, f. 733, op. 154, d. 192. The faculty most directly affected were those who signed the Vyborg Manifesto: Muromtsev, Shershenovich, Novgorodtsev, and Petrazhitskii. They signed the disclaimer.

70. GARF, f. 102, d. 12, ed. kh. 59 lb, l. 30.

71. A full list of those resigning is found in Vernadskii's, "1911 god . . ." According to the 6 February 1911 edition of *Russkie vedomosti*, 5 percent of the senior faculty of the history-philosophy department, 40 percent of the natural sciences senior faculty, 21 percent of the juridical, and 22 percent of the medical senior faculty resigned. Of the 69 *privat-dotsenty* on the natural sciences faculty, 36 resigned. Figures for the other faculties are: medical, 18 of 124; juridical, 16 of 38; and historical, 9 of 39.

72. M.M. Novikov, *Ot Moskvy do N'iu Iorka* (Moscow, 1952), 94-100; and Spevanskii, *Krizis*, 182-83.

73. V.R. Leikina-Svirskaia, "Iz istorii bor'by Peterburgskogo universiteta s ministerstvom Kasso," *Vestnik Leningradskogo universiteta*, no. 4 (1947).

74. Iordanskii, "Otsy i deti."

75. *Rech'*, 23 February 1911.

76. V.P. Iakovlev, "Politika samoderzhaviia v universitetskom voprose" (Kand. diss., Leningrad University, 1970), 197.

77. *Vestnik vospitaniia*, no. 3 (1914).

78. For discussion of the project by the Council of Ministers, see RGIA, f. 733, op. 155, d. 201. In October 1911 the Academy of Sciences declared that Kasso's proposal represented a "needless abasement of the dignity of Russian science." *Rech'*, 16 October 1911.

79. In February 1912 the tsar issued the following guidelines to the Council of Ministers on higher education policy: "I think Russia needs higher technical schools and *even more so*, intermediate technical and agricultural schools, but the already existing universities are sufficient. Take this resolution to be my guiding order." See the *Osobyi zhurnal* of the council for 9 February 1912.

80. V.I. Vernadskii, "Vysshaia shkola."

81. A.A. Kizevetter, *Na rubezhe dvukh stoletii* (Prague, 1932); and N. Speranskii, *Krizis*, 147-48. On Tashkent University and the concept of a new type of university for Russia, see Novikov, 197-202.

9

The Transfer of Legal Technology and Culture: Law Professionals in Tsarist Russia

Brian L. Levin-Stankevich

The nineteenth-century Russian juridical literature could easily lead one to conclude that convergence of the Russian and the European civil law systems was proceeding apace. The legal treatises, the memoirs of jurists, and even the laws are couched in a language derived from Roman law and treat issues then commonplace in Europe and England. Russian jurists were themselves quite aware of this community with the West. Jurists entering into the world of the prerevolutionary Russian legal professional discovered a familiar and comfortable culture.

As with much in Russia's past and present, however, appearances can be deceiving. The juridical literature of nineteenth-century Russia represented only one part of the world of Russian law—a part reformed along European lines in 1864 and comprising civil, commercial, and some criminal law. Apart from this reformed sector of law, there existed administrative tribunals, military field courts-martial, arbitrary detention and exile, administrative-judicial satraps (the land captains), and a variety of boards and committees that resolved disputes by exercising discretionary and arbitrary authority, very often without regard for the "rights" of individuals. In this "traditional" part of the Russian legal world, the jurist was not welcome. Even less welcome were the jurist's intellectual assumptions.

Working quite apart from the traditional legal world, the jurist was confined to the reformed part of the Russian legal system. This segregation of law into private (reformed) and public (traditional) law jurisdictions significantly affected the ability of the jurist to become a professional. The jurist could never claim a monopoly over the knowledge base of his profession (the law) because much of that knowledge base was beyond his control. Yet the appearance of being a western-style professional was significant for Russian jurists.

The first part of this essay examines the transformation of Russian law—the legal professional's knowledge base—and the effect of this transformation on the legal occupations as they emerged following the Judicial Reform of 1864. The second section examines the Russian legal occupations after 1864 to determine the extent to which they meet criteria often used to define a profession. The third part explores an alternative definition of the Russian legal profession based on the extent to which "professionalization" had occurred in the Russian legal occupations and the degree to which the paths followed by Russia's legal professionals and their European counterparts converged.

Reform of the Legal System

The Russian Judicial Reform of 1864 involved two elements basic to professionalization of the legal occupations. The first was the development of a technically complex knowledge base to which an occupational group could lay exclusive claim and on which a profession could be built. The second was the creation of training facilities and a corps of experts schooled in the knowledge base but lacking the formal attributes of a modern profession, namely, formal organization, external recognition, autonomy and self-regulation.[1]

The transformation of Russian law was the sine qua non for development of the legal profession. Most of the population was subject to locally effective customary law, the repositories of which were the village elders, and district notables and landlords. At the same time, much of Russian law was inaccessible. The national or common law, such as it existed, was an aggregate of statutes and rule-decisions, many of which were unpublished, obsolete, or contradictory.[2] Often the national law could be articulated and applied in the settlement of disputes only through the great pains of chancellery clerks identifying literally applicable rules rather than general legal principles from which specific norms might be deduced.

The national laws reflected a system of distributive justice. Each social stratum (*soslovie*) possessed differentiated legal rights. There was no unified system of national courts to apply a common law. Court systems served the nobility, the townspeople, the merchants, and the state officials. Judicial functions were in many situations adjunct to administrative functions. Judges in the national court systems were former administrators or soldiers, lacking formal training in law. Procedures were inconsistent between courts and were often referred to as "chancellery mysteries." With so much imprecision in the substantive law and inconsistency in procedures and jurisdictions, "legal" expenses were more efficiently utilized in bribing a chancellery clerk (the only "expert" in the law) who could influence a court decision by citing favorable or unfavorable statutes or rule-decisions than for hiring an "attorney" who, working outside of the court, would himself not know the laws or rule-decisions applicable to his client's case and who could not operate on any assumptions of predictability or certainty of outcome.[3]

Those who worked in the law courts of early nineteenth-century Russia appeared to be as diverse as the laws and the adjudicative processes. There were no prerequisite qualifications for employment as judges, clerks, prosecutors, or attorneys. Fictional accounts and memoirs of the early nineteenth century attested to widespread disdain for these occupations. Autocrats, partly sharing this popular disdain for the legal occupations and partly fearing that the development of a corps of professional lawyers would create an organized center for the expression of social and political discontent, did little to encourage the growth of expertise or the improvement of status in the legal occupations.[4] But in the reform era, the autocracy could not avoid the improvement and modernization of the laws and legal procedures. These measures, in turn, brought into being a formal legal profession.

Through the seventeenth and eighteenth centuries, the obligation-based (public law) definition of a legal person was superseded or at least complemented by a rights-based (private law) understanding of the citizen.[5] A sphere of private law activity independent of direct state intervention gradually evolved. But the dominance of public law concepts since the Muscovite period left Russia with little in the way of a native private law tradition.[6] The necessity of establishing a national law to regulate the private (personal and proprietary) relationships of those Russians who were entitled to exercise individual rights was a driving force behind attempts to codify the laws during the reign of Nicholas I (1825-55).[7]

Lacking a private law tradition and private law experts of their own, Russian autocrats turned to Europe to recruit professors for the law faculties established in the early nineteenth century.[8] These professors exerted a decidedly western influence on Russian private law development, an influence apparent in the law code (*svod zakonov*) enacted in 1835, in the Judicial Reform of 1864, and in legislation and court decisions later in the nineteenth century. The codification of Russian law brought into Russian private and even public law many of the complex legal concepts worked out in continental Europe through centuries of interaction between received Roman law and native legal custom. Infusion of this borrowed law made codified Russian law inaccessible to the untrained official. The legal expert, trained in the foundations of European law, became an essential employee in the law courts and in those governmental offices and agencies subject to the rules of the law code. There was now a specialized knowledge base accessible only to the trained expert. And legal experts were able to impose a western imprint on Russia's further legal development.

Simultaneously, the government was seeking through law to make the rules by which it operated more specific and formal. The tendency to depersonalize administrative operations through public (administrative) law, to formalize procedures (*deloproizvodstvo*), and to define intragovernmental organizational relationships more precisely created a need for increasing numbers of employees formally trained in law and legal procedure to staff administrative as well as judicial offices.[9] Earlier attempts to improve the educational profile of state officials increased the number of non-noble state officials, a matter of concern to both the nobility and autocracy. To bring more of the nobility into the ranks of educated officialdom meant restricting access to education and creating incentives to attract the nobility. Nicholas I established the School of Jurisprudence (*Uchilishche pravovedeniia*) to accomplish this goal. With admission restricted to the nobility, the School of Jurisprudence provided central governmental institutions with officials trained in the law. The legal training at the school was dominated by a historicist legal philosophy utilizing catechismal learning of statutes and procedures. But the professors, in the interstices of state curricular control, succeeded in imparting to their students respect for the law and a sense of vocation. The School of Jurisprudence provided much the same sense of camaraderie, *esprit de corps*, and purpose among its students as had the Cadet Corps among its members in the late eighteenth century.[10]

Graduates of the School of Jurisprudence advanced quickly in the central institutions of government, particularly in the Ministry of Justice, the departments of the Senate, and the Codification Commission. Graduates of the new university law faculties augmented the ranks of the legal experts in state service. School of Jurisprudence graduates (called *pravovedy*) were imbued with an idealistic and romantic identification of work in the law with personal fulfillment. Together with the university graduates, generally sons of high- and intermediate-rank civil and military officials, they forged an emotional and intellectual attachment to their discipline and an ethos of dedication to the law and service to their nation. They worked in the often frustrating confines of the ministerial bureaucracies, but for a growing number, their allegiance was to the law itself, transcending their particular position.[11]

The influx of trained legal experts into central governmental institutions had little immediate effect on the courts or the activity of "lawyering." The court systems remained disjointed and separated according to the estate (*soslovie*) jurisdictions they served. Although judges and court officials were increasingly appointed from among the trained jurists, most judicial posts, particularly in the lower and provincial courts, were held by untrained officials.[12] Lawyers (known as *striapchie*, meaning "representatives," and less politely as *iabedniki*, meaning "slanderers") were simply lay representatives of parties to a court action. With a few exceptions (peasants of crown lands, minors, clergymen, and ex-convicts), anyone could act in the capacity of a *striapchii*. They were unorganized, unevenly educated, and unregulated. The procedures in the courts were cumbersome and formal, relying on written proceedings, so the *striapchii*'s work was restricted to writing documents and, more often, greasing the gears of the judicial machinery.[13]

The indispensability of formally trained jurists to the governmental institutions of mid-nineteenth-century Russia and their ability to rapidly advance in service because of their hereditary rank, their family ties, and their accelerated acquisition of higher state service grades through education put the *pravovedy* in key positions when the issue of court reform became urgent. Court reform had been on the state's agenda since the codification of Russian law under Nicholas I. The preparation of reform proposals was entrusted to the Second Section of the Tsar's Chancellery under the direction of D.N. Bludov. Its draft proposals came under severe criticism in the late 1850s. Leading the critics were *pravovedy* employed in the Naval Ministry who successfully stalemated deliberations on Bludov's proposals in the State Council, the chief legislative-advisory chamber. In 1861, the emancipation of the Russian serfs forced a thorough reconsideration of the issue of court reform. The estate-based court systems could not accommodate demands resulting from the competition of individual rights possessed by all citizens. With progress on Bludov's proposals stopped, the responsibility for drafting a court reform was shifted to the State Chancellery, a staff office responsible to the State Council. *Pravovedy* comprised the majority of the State Chancellery staff. Under the leadership of S.I. Zarudnyi, himself a trained legal expert, these legal experts led "a fight for a court procedure that would allow the jurist to come into his own—an emancipation of legal expertise."[14]

The new legal officials "did not yet comprise a group of professional jurists."[15] They lacked formal organization, official recognition of their monopoly over the knowledge base, a code of ethics, and a form of self-regulation. But they did possess a strong sense of what many who have studied professions call a "service ideal." They could lay claim to a specialized knowledge base and to training in the techniques of their craft, even if official recognition was not yet forthcoming. Moreover, the *pravovedy*, at least in the capital cities, exhibited a strong desire to form associations, known as circles (*kruzhki*).[16]

The Judicial Reform of 1864 was a benchmark in the legal expert's progress toward professional status, not least because it was the product of the legal experts' work, illustrating the state's dependence on them. The judicial reform also ratified the "emancipation of legal expertise" sought by the *pravovedy*. By creating a legal system based on "lawyers' law," it marked a definite movement in Russia toward greater complexity in law and legal procedure. It led to the import of the "legal technology" of Europe, that is, procedural rules and adjudicative and appellate processes.

By recognizing a scientific element in judicial reasoning and tacitly admitting that not all litigation could be resolved by the mechanical application of literal statutory rules to specific situations, the reform enhanced the claims of the *pravovedy* to a monopoly over this knowledge base or technology. It thus acknowledged that the legal expert was to play a policy-making role in the legal system. [17] To assure that only qualified persons made policy decisions, the reform established educational and experiential requirements for juridical activity and judicial office. [18]

The special status legal experts achieved through the Judicial Reform of 1864 was apparent. The reform eliminated the *striapchii* and replaced him with the lawyer (*prisiazhnyi poverennyi*), who alone had the right to represent individuals in court. The lawyer was given the right to membership in a bar (*sovet prisiazhnykh poverennykh*) which controlled entry into the lawyer's guild, decided disciplinary matters involving lawyers, and autonomously performed a variety of administrative functions relating to attorneys. State prosecutors and judges also achieved greater recognition as a result of the judicial reform. Former military officials no longer qualified for court positions. Prosecutors and judges were to hold law degrees and to have served specified periods in the courts. [19]

Russia frequently borrowed law and legal techniques (legal technology) from continental Europe. This transfer of legal technology was most pronounced in the Judicial Reform of 1864 as legal experts, trained in Europe or by European professors, conducted extensive research on European legal procedures. Comparative legal history is rich in examples of such transfers. It is common for nations to adopt similar legal technology at particular levels of economic development. [20] But legal technology is not necessarily portable. It evolves within and affects specific social, economic, political, and cultural constructs. As a set of mechanisms for stating a society's ideal of behavior, for regulating behavior, and for resolving disputes, legal technology embodies a culture of its own—a legal culture. [21]

The Russian government's intention in borrowing legal technology from Europe was to accommodate the personal and proprietary relationships resulting from changes in the structure of society. It did not seek to diminish its own economic and political control. But the legal technology it borrowed included a legal culture of individual rights superior to the right of the state to interfere in society. [22] Russian legal experts embraced this individualistic legal culture while the autocracy failed to abandon its traditional attitude toward governance. The conflicting legal cultures of the legal experts and the autocracy significantly affected the professionalization of the law occupations.

Legal Occupations and Professionalization

To what extent did the Judicial Reform of 1864 transform Russian legal experts into professionals? Who were the law professionals and how was their professional status defined? Was the reform followed by any movement among legal experts toward the status of a profession?

If developments in the Russian legal world are treated as analogous to developments in European legal history, it might be argued that the lawyers alone became professionals. In most national contexts, a study of the legal profession would focus almost exclusively on the lawyer.[23] Other occupations requiring legal training or associated with legal processes (judges, prosecutors, law school faculty) are considered to be distinctly different occupations or professions to which lawyers have access. The Russian situation may seem analogous. It appears that the lawyers gained for themselves the attributes of a modern profession. The lawyer possessed specialized training, enabling him to claim a monopoly over the technical skills implicit in the knowledge base of the law. Admission to the bar and registration with a court comprised a licensing procedure which carried state recognition of the lawyer's professional status. The bar was an autonomous, self-regulating, occupational association which immediately set to work producing a code of ethics. These traits comprise the consensual attributes of a modern profession.[24]

By this definition, it would appear that Russian lawyers became professionals after 1864. But other legal experts, as esteemed as their status may have become after the judicial reform, were not professionals. They did not possess autonomous occupational associations, did not themselves determine entry into their ranks, and did not pass through any occupationally controlled licensing procedure in their careers. According to this definition, the Russian lawyer was a professional; the Russian state legal official was not.

In Russia, however, formal criteria of professional status may not be the most appropriate way to define a profession. The criteria most commonly used are those derived from studies of "western" professions. Their application to Russian occupations assumes not only that the conditions in which a given occupation attempted to gain professional status were alike in Russia and the West but also that the Russian occupation wanted or required the same things from professional status as did its western counterpart.

In the Russian context, multiple factors mitigate against applying western sociological criteria of professional status to the law occupations. In contrast with legal systems in which the educational patterns of lawyers and state legal officials followed different paths, all legal experts in Russia owed the status they gained in 1864 to their common heritage as descendants of the *pravovedy*. The Russian lawyer and the state legal official underwent the same educational preparation for their careers. They attended the same schools and heard the same lectures. The lawyers after 1864 were not at all related to the prereform *striapchie*. The prosecutors and judges bore little resemblance to the men who filled their positions before the reform.[25]

The lawyer and the state legal official had separate employment settings, the former as an independent professional, the latter as a state employee. Yet the state legal official was also quite separate from the rest of administrative officialdom, and both the lawyer and the state legal official shared a common work environment—the reformed court system—which was itself an autonomous set of institutions within the state structure. Although employment patterns of Russian legal experts were similar to those of European jurists, they contrasted with Anglo-American legal systems, where all legal professionals were lawyers and where judges and prosecutors were chosen from the ranks of the lawyers. Moreover, there was a great deal of one-way career change, as large numbers of state legal officials periodically entered the bar. Even if the state legal official did not have an officially recognized occupational organization, he was not so distant from the lawyer in terms of influencing entry into state legal careers, establishing "professional" ethical norms, and enforcing these norms through disciplinary authority over his peers.[26]

The attitudes of the Russian legal professionals themselves were not uniform, as conflicts within the legal profession after 1864 indicate. Lawyers and state legal officials used a variety of terms to describe themselves. Some simply used their occupational titles, such as *prisiazhnyi* (a short form of the Russian term for lawyer), *sud'ia* for judge, or *prokuror* for state prosecutor. Others preferred terms with more metaphoric value, like *advokat*, a term for a lawyer which connoted political independence and social service. Although the term *advokat* was the preserve of the attorney alone, both lawyers and state legal officials often referred to themselves as *iuristy* (jurists), a term connoting the scientific and intellectual elements of jurisprudence. In the opposite direction, the term *pravoved*, used by the prereform legal experts, appears to have been relegated to academicians who themselves seemed to prefer the term *iurisprudent* (jurisprudent).[27] Many of these terms cut across specific legal occupations, particularly *iurist*, which was used by lawyers, judges, prosecutors, and law school professors.

Outsiders' views are no more clear in distinguishing the members of specific legal occupations as professionals and others as nonprofessionals. Many viewed the lawyers as they had viewed the *striapchie*—with suspicion.[28] Many considered the judges and prosecutors in the reformed courts as no more than state officials.[29] But some regarded the status of the lawyer and his corporate organization quite highly, referring to members of the bar as the *advokatskoe soslovie*, literally a class of lawyers. Conservatives often used the pejorative term *iuridicheskii* or *sudebnyi element*, the "juridical element."[30] This term most specifically referred to the state legal officials who, in the period of "counterreforms," refused to compromise their ideals of due process in order to serve the interests of the state administration. But lawyers were also an essential part of the juridical element.

The judicial reform created three types of law occupations: the lawyer, the state prosecutor, and the judge. Each was radically different from its prereform counterpart.

Lawyers

The technical innovations introduced into private law and court pleading by the judicial reform required formally trained lawyers. After thoroughly examining the forms of legal representation in England and continental Europe, the *pravovedy* adopted a variant of the French and Austro-German legal representative. The Russian lawyer was to enjoy the corporate organizational freedom of the French lawyer, but contrary to the French and British systems, there were to be no gradations of legal representation in Russia.[31] The State Council, responding to conservatives' fear of replicating the radical French *avocat*, decided to name the Russian lawyer the "sworn attorney" (*prisiazhnyi poverennyi*), although lawyers often referred to themselves as "advocates." The Notarial Code, an often overlooked part of the judicial reform, relegated some of the less demanding legal tasks performed by solicitors in England to the Russian notary, who did not require the same education or training as the lawyer. This created a distinct subprofessional, an important factor in preventing intraprofessional divisions according to levels of expertise as occurred in other professions in prerevolutionary Russia.[32]

A significant innovation of the 1864 reform was the establishment of specific educational and experiential requirements for registration with the court as a lawyer and membership in the bar. Only those holding degrees from a university law faculty or a law school were eligible to become lawyers. With this degree, the prospective lawyer embarked on a three-stage process leading to full recognition as a lawyer: admission to the status of lawyer-in-training (*pomoshchnyi prisiazhnyi poverennyi*), completion of a five-year apprenticeship under the supervision of a patron-lawyer, and formal admission to the bar with accompanying registration in a regional court.

According to the judicial reform, the law school graduate only needed acceptance into the practice of a registered lawyer to be entered on the rolls as a lawyer-in-training. However, following the lead of the St. Petersburg bar, most regions adopted further restrictions on candidates.[33] A five-year apprenticeship ensued. In some areas, lawyers-in-training enjoyed their own form of organization under a committee or commission of the Council of the Bar. In other areas, there was no formal supervision save that of their patron. In most areas, the lawyer-in-training was permitted to conduct actual cases (particularly after 1874, when lawyers-in-training could register as "private attorneys"), and everywhere the lawyer-in-training was scrutinized in his behavior and ethical conduct by members of the bar. At the end of the five-year apprenticeship, the Council of the Bar conducted a final screening of the candidate's abilities and character, and the council registered his admission with the superior court of the region. Final admission to the bar was not taken lightly.[34]

The Council of the Bar was itself regionally structured, having no national directorate or administration, although the St. Petersburg and Moscow regional councils were generally recognized as leaders in establishing standards and policies. Each regional organization took the form of a Council of the Bar. Although the judicial reform provided for these Councils of the Bar and defined their functions and responsibilities, the formation of a council in any region depended on the initiative of the lawyers. If twenty or more lawyers were registered in the regional appellate court, they could request formation of a Council of the Bar. If registered lawyers numbered between ten and twenty, they could request formation of a "branch" of a nearby council, attached to the circuit court of the region. A Council of the Bar could only exist in the jurisdiction and locus of an appellate court—a Chamber of Justice (*sudebnaia palata*). This limited the number of councils that could be established, but it also afforded the councils greater professional independence, since the jurisdiction of the Chamber of Justice was not contiguous with provincial or district administrative boundaries. Each Council of the Bar therefore enrolled lawyers from two or more provinces. The result was the relative immunity of members of the bar and the bar itself from local administrative influences.

The Councils of the Bar gave Russian lawyers the capability of controlling entry into the profession and wielding disciplinary authority over colleagues. The councils performed a variety of administrative functions: admitting lawyers to the profession, accepting their resignations, and instituting disbarment proceedings. They enforced those rules of conduct for lawyers which were included in the judicial reform, and they augmented these statutory rules with ethical codes drafted by the lawyers themselves.[35] They instituted and conducted disciplinary proceedings against member lawyers for violations of these rules of conduct, employing sanctions ranging from a reprimand to disbarment. They also appointed legal counsel for indigents and persons requesting such assistance.[36] The Councils of the Bar also made recommendations to the Ministry of Justice for fee scales which would govern disputes between a lawyer and his client over fees.

The Councils of the Bar provided lawyers with greater professional autonomy and self-regulation than was enjoyed by most other prerevolutionary Russian occupations. But the councils were not entirely free from governmental intervention and restriction. The formation of a council was subject to approval by the Ministry of Justice. Between 1865 and 1875, Councils of the Bar were established in St. Petersburg, Moscow, and Khar'kov. But in 1875, the Ministry of Justice, reassessing many of the provisions of the 1864 reform and the government's attitudes toward lawyers in general, clamped a moratorium on the establishment of new councils that lasted thirty years. After 1889, the ministry also prohibited the formation of new "branches" of existing councils. In 1904, the Ministry of Justice permitted the opening of six new councils, but none of these was permitted to establish "branches."[37] Outside of European Russia, councils were established only in Irkutsk and Omsk. Notably absent from the list of cities with councils were the non-Russian cities of Warsaw and Kiev, and cities in the Caucasus and the Baltic provinces.

Where councils or their branches did not exist, the functions usually performed by the Councils of the Bar were assumed by the regional circuit courts. The small number of councils is explained in part by the concentration of the overwhelming majority of Russian lawyers in the major urban centers of European Russia.[38] In many rural areas there was a severe shortage of lawyers.[39] Nevertheless, the government's reluctance to approve the formation of more councils and its ban on the formation of branches were points of contention between the lawyers and the government. The existing councils argued that they exerted far greater disciplinary supervision over lawyers than did the circuit courts in areas where councils did not exist. Judging by the public criticism of rural legal representation, their arguments appear substantiated.[40]

The councils were not entirely free in their exercise of professional self-regulation. In disciplinary actions, the council was only a first instance. The accused or a state prosecutor could appeal a ruling of the council to the court under which that council (or branch) had been established. And the court could overturn council decisions in matters of professional discipline. When a lawyer was charged with common criminal actions, he was subject only to court trial. If a council chose to overlook a lawyer's indiscretion, the superior court or a state prosecutor could demand disciplinary proceedings in the council.[41]

Nor did the councils have total authority in determining admission to the bar. Requirements for admission were listed in the judicial reform, and the councils both enforced these requirements and added to them. But the government could intervene as well. After 1889, for example, an imperial order prevented the registration of Jews as lawyers. Jews were permitted to remain in the status of lawyers-in-training, and as such to carry on cases. This order was relaxed between 1905 and 1912. Many of the most famous lawyers in prerevolutionary Russia were Jewish, some achieving fame while in the status of lawyers-in-training for a number of years.[42]

Perhaps most critically, the councils did not enjoy a monopoly over personnel performing the functions of attorneys. In 1874, the government created the status of "private attorney" (*chastnyi poverennyi*), ostensibly because of a shortage of lawyers in many areas where the judicial reform had been introduced.[43] Virtually anyone could register as a private attorney, with practice restricted to those courts in which he was registered. The private attorney was not required to possess a law degree. Supervision and discipline of private attorneys was exercised by the courts in which they were registered rather than by the Councils of the Bar.

Despite these limitations and the absence of a complete monopoly over the practice of law, the Russian lawyers possessed greater independence as professionals than most other groups. Because they were geographically concentrated in areas where Councils of the Bar existed, most Russian lawyers enjoyed the benefits of corporate organization and were often referred to as an estate because they possessed specific rights derived from their professional status.

State Legal Professionals

Prosecutors and judges might appear to be outside our definition of law professions. They were not members of a "free" profession. They did not possess the corporate, self-regulating organizations of the lawyer. They were state employees. But to eliminate the state legal offices from a definition of the legal profession is to say that some of the legal profession's most eloquent spokesmen were not members of the profession.

The judicial reform established educational and training qualifications for the state legal employee as it did for the lawyer. Except for justices of the peace, who were elected by local *zemstvo* assemblies, all judges and state prosecutors in the reformed court system were appointed by the minister of justice.[44] A law degree was a prerequisite for appointment to offices in the reformed courts. And although state legal officials did not enjoy self-administration through autonomous organizations like the Councils of the Bar, they generally enjoyed tremendous influence over nominees for appointments to vacancies in their courts.[45]

Future state legal officials underwent the same educational training as lawyers, in the same schools, and generally with the same enthusiasm and dedication to professional ideals.[46] The law school graduate opting for a state legal career began his postgraduate training as a "candidate for court office," registering with a court and accepting a series of what were usually temporary appointments until an appropriate vacancy occurred. Unlike the lawyer, whose fortune depended on his ability to attract clients or to gain publicity through trial action, the state legal official followed a rather routine career path, at times serving in the bureaucracy, at times in the judiciary, and at times in special posts which enhanced his ability to gain access to higher level positions. This career path was partially imposed by the judicial reform, which required that appointees to higher courts have specified years of experience in lower court positions or in ministerial legal work. It was also partially a result of informal norms, as certain court positions in certain cities became stepping stones to specific positions in higher courts. After the 1860s, career patterns of those who reached the most prestigious state legal positions in the Courts of

Cassation indicate a regularity that cannot be coincidental.[47] Although there were scattered cases of ministerial appointments to high courts of persons who had gained the majority of their postgraduate experience in administrative offices, the pre-1864 practice of appointing such persons to top judicial posts became the exception. The prereform tendency toward appointment of trained jurists to state judicial and prosecutorial positions became a firm rule after the judicial reform.[48] Thus, to the degree that "professionalization" is defined as the restriction of career access to experts trained in a "limited access" knowledge base, the state legal officials became professionals.

State legal officials also enjoyed a certain degree of independence. The reformed court system represented a remarkably autonomous set of institutions. All disciplinary authority over state legal officials was lodged in this court system, particularly in the Disciplinary Bench of the Court of Cassation. Thus, disciplinary authority over prosecutors and judges was, by statute, in the hands of other prosecutors and judges.[49] Although behavioral codes for judges and prosecutors were included in the judicial reform, much was left to the discretion and interpretation of the courts which, like the Councils of the Bar, augmented legal standards through their own precedent rulings in disciplinary cases.[50] Under the judicial reform, judges were granted irremovability (*nesmeniaemost'*) from office, except for felony violations or through disciplinary decisions of superior court judges.[51] Prosecutors were in a more vulnerable position. Although holding court positions, they were direct subordinates of the Ministry of Justice. They could be promoted, demoted, or transferred, and they were more likely to encounter administrative pressures in their prosecutorial work.[52]

In spite of the absence of a formal occupational organization for state legal officials, evidence suggests that the lawyers and the state legal officials had more in common as professionals than they had differences. The issue of occupational autonomy for lawyers was decided by the 1864 statutes. For the state legal official, autonomy and intra-occupational disciplinary authority was achieved de facto. Accepting these attributes as operational for both groups, the actual career status and the rights enjoyed by all legal occupations in Russia differed only in degree. The lawyer's organization, the bar, was formally recognized by the state, but it was also severely restricted. The state legal officials, while lacking an officially recognized occupational organization, enjoyed certain de facto privileges as professionals. To the extent that the lawyers were professionals, the state legal officials were professionals detached from the main body of their profession.

A Russian Variant of Legal Professionalism

If the application of sociological conventions deduced from the experience of western professions to the Russian legal occupations leads to ambiguous definitions, the history of these occupations between 1864 and the beginning of the twentieth century helps us toward a more useful definition. In the half century after the 1864 reform, there is evidence of continuity and consistency in the professionalization of Russia's legal occupations, but the history of the legal occupations in this period also forces us toward a more behavioral and attitudinal definition of the Russian legal profession.

The transfer of western legal technology to Russia brought with it a distinct legal culture, the most novel aspect of which for Russians was the emphasis on individual rights. The *pravovedy* embraced this culture and strove to subject the state itself to new norms. They exhibited a strong dedication to the ideal of a *Rechtstaat*, a society ruled by law not through law. These attitudes led them to guarantee procedural rights and entitlements to defendants, to establish jury trials, to include most "political" crimes in the jurisdictions of the ordinary courts, and to provide for legal counsel and expertise in all court positions. The judicial reform articulated the "legal culture" of the *pravovedy*.[53]

The government, having welcomed the technical contributions made by the *pravovedy,* could not for long welcome the "cultural" baggage these contributions brought with them. In the legal culture of autocracy, society was subordinated to administrative exigencies. The rights of the state, wielded by officials with broad discretionary authority, were superior to any individual's rights. The individualistic legal culture of the reformed courts' procedures was a small autonomous compartment within the larger legal culture of Russia.[54] As long as it did not impede or hinder the governance of society and the achievement of order, it remained relatively free from governmental interference.[55] But when the individual rights it held supreme challenged the rights of the state, intervention was swift and incisive.

Professional initiatives—which in other societies were directed toward internal cohesion, autonomy, and the exclusion of "outsiders" in order to protect material benefits—were in Russia directed toward removing political restrictions precluding the achievement of a more complete professional status. Neither the lawyer nor the state legal official was secure in his professional status as long as the legal culture of his occupation remained compartmentalized in the civil and criminal law courts and inapplicable in the public law arena. Autonomy could only become a viable professional goal after the removal of the causes of professional insecurity. Unfortunately, the cause of this insecurity was the legal culture of autocracy.

There was, therefore, a great deal of continuity between the origins of the legal profession and the goals of many legal professionals throughout the remainder of the tsarist era. Legal professionals confronted government policies that controlled the work environment and employment, and that were philosophically opposed to much of the legal culture in which they believed. The legal occupations can be categorized during the post-1864 period less along occupational-employment lines than by their responses to the government's continued attempts to limit the "cultural" effects of the transfer of legal technology.

The autocracy, in the wake of the Great Reforms, attempted to maintain court processes and structures deemed essential for the economic and personal security of Russians, yet restricted the use of these processes in political arenas. The government was persistent in remolding the law profession. It never won over most lawyers, and it was ónly partially successful with the legal officials in its own employ. When positive influence failed to achieve an acceptable legal profession, the state turned to retaliation against those who did not conform to its view of the legal professional's ethical code.

The government's attempts to shape the lawyer to its ideal took a variety of forms. It sought to limit access to the profession by restricting establishment of Councils of the Bar, particularly in non-Russian areas of the Empire, and by its ban on non-Orthodox lawyers entering the bar. It sought to remove the monopoly of the bar over law practice by creating what was, in effect, a career alternative—the "private attorney." It tried to limit the autonomy of the bar by interfering in disciplinary matters and by sanctioning attacks against the profession in newspapers and the periodical press.[56] It increasingly retaliated against lawyers and against Councils of the Bar for statements made during trial proceedings or for protests lodged as a result of the persecution of individual lawyers, reminding the lawyers that, even if they were members of a "free" profession, they were not free professionals.[57]

Among its own employees, the state took more direct measures. If the autocracy never seemed to understand the importance of the assumptions behind the court procedures established in 1864, it was especially unable to tolerate prosecutors and judges succumbing to procedural restrictions or providing evenhanded instructions to juries in the prosecution of politically important criminal cases. Attempts by the Ministry of Justice to force state legal officials to act more peremptorily in court through administrative pressures more often led to resignations.[58] Many state legal officials, required by their employer to act unethically, simply quit. Most who left state service became lawyers or academicians.

Under Count Pahlen, minister of justice from 1867 to 1878, the ministry began to utilize its control over entry and advancement in state legal occupations to recruit and promote candidates who were more attuned to the "state's interest." One result was an increasing preselection of career options by law school graduates. Those committed to the legal culture of the *pravovedy* increasingly turned to the bar, while those desiring personal career security and rapid advancement in the state legal bureaucracy chose state service.[59]

However, even regarding its own employees, the state's ability to maneuver was limited by statute. It could not create an alternative judiciary, although the establishment of military courts-martial under the "safeguard" legislation of 1881 and ensuing years in effect created an alternative court system.[60] It could not remove judges, and its ability to promote trustworthy officials was therefore blocked at the upper levels of the judicial hierarchy by irremovable incumbents.[61] Its insertion of trustworthy officials into the state legal ranks in the 1870s did not affect the composition of the appellate and supreme courts until the early twentieth century.[62]

When the government failed to create a legal officialdom satisfactory to its own view of legal culture, it altered the work environment of the existing officials through measures known as the "judicial counterreforms."[63] These were attempts to rig procedures and legal contests to the benefit of the state and to handicap those jurists who dared to uphold the law in defiance of state interests. Whole categories of crimes considered as "political" were removed from jury trial, although the state's interest did not seem to fare much better in the special courts to which these trials were shifted.[64] Administrative actions completely bypassing the courts were put into effect.[65] The jury was periodically shorn of its powers.[66] And when all else failed, the government altered the legal technology itself by changing procedural rules.

The effects of these measures on state legal officials were quite counterproductive from the state's point of view. First, many of the most able and dedicated state legal officials left state service and joined the bar, where they were accepted with open arms. Second, although the ministry succeeded in attracting to state service a more homogenous group of law school graduates, the benefits realized from this recruitment were dubious. The ministry wanted officials who would follow orders and perform their tasks bureaucratically. What they produced was a legal official who uncritically performed his task and who, attracted by the less creative work of state legal service, was less well informed of developments in the law and less able to represent the state's interest in the courtroom against a lawyer dedicated to the practice of law as an end in itself.[67] This resulted in cases dismissed on technical grounds or cases overturned by the Court of Cassation (staffed until 1917 with many of the leading jurists in Russia) on the basis that the procedural rights of a defendant had been violated.[68]

The lack of practical benefits from these personnel policies precluded the government's use of the courts to prosecute political crimes. Almost every such attempt ended in embarrassment. In a small but significant way, the government's inability to create a legal officialdom to its own liking contributed to the perpetuation of administrative, extrajudicial measures for silencing its critics.

The responses government actions provoked from lawyers and state legal officials provide a more interesting, if not a more precise, basis for a description of the Russian legal profession than the criteria extracted from western experience. There were at least three varieties of response that closely resemble the intraprofessional differentiation noted in western professions.[69] One response was "careerist," a second "missionary," and a third the response of those who felt compelled to defend the knowledge base of the law in the context of the legal culture in which it was formed and to reinforce the elements of social service inherent in that knowledge base—a response I call "culturalist." Each represents a set of positions defensible for the professional.

The careerist response best represents tendencies within a profession to protect that which it has already gained, to maintain exclusivity, and to present a facade of internal professional unity and conformity. A cynical casting of the careerist response focuses attention on those (primarily state legal officials) who were attracted to the profile of the legal professional as depicted by the government through its personnel policies, who sought personal security through performance of duty, who joined or remained in state legal service with few, if any, reservations about the political policies they would be called upon to defend.

Most western scholarship on prerevolutionary Russian lawyers has focused on those lawyers who fought (quite bravely) for the rights of individuals.[70] There is, however, a good deal of evidence that professional and career motivation was widespread among lawyers. The number of lawyers who actively participated in the Council of the Bar was small, the leadership of the bar remaining an identifiable elite of practitioner-theoreticians. Events in the early twentieth century also point to a larger proportion of careerists in the bar than casual observation might indicate. Evidence is found in the relationship of the Councils of the Bar to lawyers-in-training and specifically to the issue of the establishment and control of legal aid clinics.

The idea of providing legal aid clinics in which the needy could receive legal assistance free or for a nominal fee was originally promoted by the *zemstvo* in the 1860s but was rejected by provincial and central administrators. The idea was rekindled in the 1890s, however, as Russian lawyers pointed to the German lawyers' establishment of Workers' Secretaries. In 1896, the *Likhvitskii uezd zemstvo* proposed a legal aid office. The governor protested and was upheld by the First Department of the Senate.[71] The lawyers, more specifically lawyers-in-training, had established and maintained modest legal aid services since 1870-71 in Moscow and St. Petersburg. However, by the 1890s, these services were used increasingly by persons able to pay for the retention of a lawyer. The needy remained inadequately served by legal assistance in the capitals and almost completely ignored in the provinces where "underground (*podpolnye*) lawyers," enterprising businessmen who set up storefront legal advice offices and who were not qualified attorneys, flourished.[72]

In the 1890s, legal clinics were revived with the support and participation of lawyers-in-training. Undoubtedly, the lawyers-in-training were motivated by general social pressures on their generation and by a political philosophy that celebrated service to the people. But there were intraprofessional reasons for their interest in legal aid as well. In the 1890s and during the first decade of the twentieth century, the lot of the lawyer-in-training had become increasingly frustrating. Attracted to the law profession because of the opportunities it presented for social activism, many found themselves blocked on the path to professional status and relegated to a subprofessional realm. Some were Jews to whom the state had closed the legal profession. Student disturbances and the increasing influx of state legal officials into the ranks of the lawyers delayed others' careers, since the state officials were often given preferential treatment in their applications for entry into the bar. Most lawyers-in-training were in the capital cities where there was already an overabundance of lawyers. They earned meager salaries, found the work assigned by their patrons demeaning, and often needed to seek employment outside of the legal profession.[73] The most politically radical were frustrated by the hesitancy of the Councils of the Bar to admit to full status those lawyers, like A.F. Kerensky, who had gained their fame in political trials.[74] Legal aid work was an outlet for their political as well as their professional urges.[75]

That this was an issue involving careerist concerns and not one which ruffled the political feathers of the lawyers of the bar is clear from the degree to which the lawyers participated in the political actions of 1905-6. Even if the lawyer was inclined toward a kind of professional introspection within his own professional organization, he had not subordinated defense of income and status to his interest in the legal culture of his profession. Of approximately 3,600 lawyers in Russia in 1905, some 2,500 (69 percent) joined the Union of Lawyers formed by leading members of the Councils of the Bar.[76] This political participation is certainly more indicative of the culturalist response which will be discussed more fully below. And it underscores the uneven development of the Russian legal profession. Members of both legal occupations (lawyers and state legal officials) exhibited both careerist and culturalist responses simultaneously. Professionalization in the sense of internal cohesion and exclusivity was proceeding apace within the occupational branches of the law. But the insecurity of the legal culture that formed the foundation of the entire legal profession elicited a common response from both occupational groups.

The "state careerist"—the state legal official who conformed to the government's view of an ideal law professional—remained outside of this common response to political events. He identified much more closely with the state administrative official and with the "state's interest" throughout the events of the early twentieth century. Examples of such officials abound during this period, a result of the long-term effects of earlier personnel policies. Even the Courts of Cassation, dominated attitudinally if not physically by culturalists until the turn of the century, were more firmly in the hands of state careerists who cooperated fully with the Ministry of Justice in securing interpretations of the law desired by the ministry.[77]

The missionary was the product more of social and political influences than professional developments. Almost always a professional lawyer or lawyer-in-training, the missionary, cloaked in the mantle of professional autonomy and dedication to the law, nevertheless seemed to have an attitude toward law mirroring that of the autocracy. The missionary, like the government, sought to use the law for a purpose, in this case to embarrass and where possible drive cracks into the edifice of the autocracy's legal culture. The missionary, although occasionally criticized by the culturalist, who found the employment of the law in the pursuit of political ends repugnant, became the leading edge of the culturalist response. The law profession could tolerate a handful of "hotheads" whose fame rested on their participation in high-profile political trials. But it could not tolerate the government's attacks on these missionaries for exercising their rights as professionals.[78] Gradually the distinctions between the missionary and the culturalist eroded. A.F. Kerensky, a typical missionary whose entry into the bar had been delayed because of the council's reticence to sanction his actions, became a hero of the culturalists in 1917.[79]

The culturalist response cut across occupational boundaries in the legal profession. It was the culturalists who most clearly carried on the tradition of the *pravovedy*: a vigorous dedication to the western-oriented knowledge base in the belief that it was superior to parochial political ideology. In the political situation of prerevolutionary Russia, the legal culture of the legal profession itself became a political ideology. Unfortunately, the culturalist's strength was also his weakness; his moral righteousness and his dedication to "due process" prevented participation in forceful political action.

The culturalist response to the judicial counterreforms of the 1870s and 1880s was led by men who themselves had worked on drafting the judicial reform early in their careers. And the culturalist response to revolution and reaction in the early twentieth century was led by men who considered themselves colleagues of the *pravovedy*. The direct link between the culturalist and the *pravoved* was provided by the culturalist's formal organization—the law society.

The law societies provided an interesting contrast with the bar. Unlike the bar, they were not formal organizations sanctioned statutorily by the judicial reform. They were not specifically oriented toward either occupational branch of the legal profession; they were open to all. The law societies, given the difficulty of maintaining an occupational definition of the Russian legal profession, more closely resembled the typical western professional organization than did the Russian bar.

The first law society, founded in Moscow in 1863, was a coalescence of informal associations that had evolved among the *pravovedy* of Moscow.[80] The remaining law societies, located in St. Petersburg and in many provincial cities, were formed during the 1870s, a time when the principles of the judicial reform, the lawyers, and the state legal officials were all under increasing criticism. Lawyers were criticized for their manipulation of juries and for defending admittedly guilty persons. Prosecutors were forced to choose between their personal ethical standards and those of their employer, the Ministry of Justice. The government was attempting to cleanse the legal technology borrowed in 1864 of its cultural accoutrements. Moreover, the law societies, formed in a time of attacks on the legal culture of the *pravovedy*, in many instances traced their origins to informal circles of *pravovedy* which had existed since the early 1860s.[81]

The law societies became vehicles for the continuing transmission of the legal professional's culture. They were forums for interaction and means of continuing education of legal professionals. They were also a mechanism of mutual support. Their purpose was to disseminate relevant and innovative ideas about the law to professionals, to formulate responses to legislative proposals, to express views on legal problems facing Russian society and on the social foundations of those problems, to reinforce the moral basis of their profession's activities and the ethical standards which governed them, and to stress the social service role of jurists. Law societies sought to unite the voices of the lawyer, the prosecutor, and the judge into a "harmonious choir."[82]

The societies strove toward these tasks through regular meetings at which members and invited guests delivered papers and commentaries. More important, they published journals which became the basis of the Russian juridical press.[83] Free from prepublication censorship, these journals nevertheless remained moderate in tone, restricting their contents to the world of Russian law and jurisprudence. Within this world, the influence of the journals and the societies was tremendous, but, as noted earlier, the world in which the professional's legal culture was an accepted principle was institutionally separate from the administrative agencies of the government which operated according to a different legal culture.

The law societies, like the Councils of the Bar, suffered from their inability to work on a national level. One Congress of Russian Jurists was held in Moscow in 1875 under the sponsorship of the Moscow Law Society, but attempts to convene a second congress were repeatedly put off by the government.[84] For reasons related to the underdevelopment of provincial law societies, attempts at close cooperation among the societies led to only sporadic exchanges of papers and mutual discounts on publications.[85] But through their journals, the societies reached a national readership of professionals.

The law societies were more successful in presenting the law professional in Russia as a colleague of European law professionals.[86] The St. Petersburg Law Society, for example, formed the Russian Group of the International Union of Criminalists and in 1890 hosted an international conference on prisons. It affiliated with societies of legal professionals in France and Germany, and supported other professional societies in Russia in their public ceremonies and fundraising activities.

The law societies, physical extensions of the "circles" of *pravovedy* which formed in the 1850s and 1860s, also illustrate the continuity within the legal profession from 1864 to 1917. Most of the leaders of the Russian Councils of the Bar were also members of law societies, as were the leaders of the Union of Lawyers in 1905. The founders of the Kadet Party were also leaders of the law societies.[87] Yet the law societies appear to have been dominated by state legal officials and law academicians.[88]

Conclusion

An occupationally based definition of the Russian law profession yields ambiguity. It paints the lawyer as the only legal professional and relegates state legal officials and academicians, both of whom shared the professional "culture" of the lawyer, to a quasi-professional status. However, an attitudinal definition centering on the responses of legal professionals to the restrictions imposed on them by the state yields a picture of continuity in the legal profession which must be considered as including both lawyers and state legal officials. Moreover, the legal profession, defined attitudinally, possessed its own formal professional organization—the law society—which fulfilled the responsibilities associated with western professional organizations more directly than did the Councils of the Bar.

The Russian law profession never fully succeeded in gaining the security that most professions desire, in part because the profession's knowledge base was itself never entirely secure from externally imposed redefinition. This knowledge base encompassed the legal technology and the legal culture transferred from Europe in 1864. It was adopted by the autocracy to meet specific needs occasioned by economic development and the granting of personal and proprietary rights, but Russian rulers never intended that the private law technology apply to the functions of governance or that the rule of law should accompany this technology into Russia.

The rule-of-law legal culture, however, did become the basis of the Russian law profession. The government attempted to separate the legal technology it had borrowed from its cultural dimension, but at best it only restrained the "spinoff" of this legal culture. The carriers of legal culture, the legal professionals, served as a living critique of the inconsistencies of Russian development and governmental policy.

Notes

1. H.M. Vollmer and D.L. Mills, eds. *Professionalization* (Englewood Cliffs, NJ: Prentice-Hall, 1966), 1-45.

2. M. Raeff, *Mikhail Speransky: Statesman of Imperial Russia* (The Hague: Nijhoff, 1957), 320-46.

3. I. Bocharov, "V pravitel'stvuiushchem senate," *Russkaia starina* 44 (1884): 163. Also, S. Kucherov, *Courts, Lawyers, and Trials Under the Last Three Tsars* (New York: Frederick A. Praeger, 1953), 5-7.

4. Richard Wortman, *The Development of a Russian Legal Consciousness* (Chicago, IL: University of Chicago Press, 1976), 1-33.

5. V.O. Kliuchevskii, *Istoriia soslovii v Rossii* (Petrograd, 1918), presents an interpretation of *soslovie* that defines this social stratification as moving from one of obligation categories to one of exclusive personal and proprietary rights.

6. A.I. Kaminka, *Ocherki torgovogo prava*, vyp. 1 (St. Petersburg, 1912), 78-79; and G.F. Shershenevich, *Nauka grazhdanskogo prava v Rossii* (Kazan', 1893), 1-23, make the argument that Russian civil law was constructed almost entirely on European borrowings.

7. M. Raeff, "Codification et droit en Russie imperiale: Quelques remarkes comparative," *Cahiers du Monde Russe et Sovietique* 20, no. 1 (January-March 1979): 5-12; and M. Raeff, *Speransky*, 325.

8. Wortman, *Development*, 35-50.

9. Ibid.

10. Ibid., 198-234.

11. Ibid.

12. Richard Wortman, "Judicial Personnel and the Court Reform of 1864," *Canadian Slavic Studies* (Summer 1969): 226-27.

13. I. Bocharov, "V pravitel'stvuiushchem senate," 163.

14. Wortman, *Development*, 234.

15. Ibid.

16. Ibid., 252-54.

17. A.D. Gradovskii, "O sudebnom tolkovanii zakonov," *Sobranie sochinenii*, vol. 7, (St. Petersburg, 1907), xxxii, discusses the radical change in judicial functions which resulted from the Judicial Reform of 1864.

18. *Svod zakonov*, vol. 16, pt. 1, Uchrezhdenie sudebnykh ustanovlenie, arts. 263-67.

19. Wortman, *Development*, 275, describes some of the friction between administrative officials and the judiciary, often resulting from the administrators' feeling that they were being affronted by upstart officials.

20. Lawrence M. Friedman, *The Legal System: A Social Science Perspective* (New York: Russell Sage Foundation, 1975), 194.

21. Ibid., 194-222.

22. Wortman, *Development*, 255, offers an excellent summary of the legal culture that permeated the law schools and that became the legal culture of the law professional after 1864.

23. Kucherov, *Courts*, 119.

24. Vollmer and Mills, *Professionalization*, 1-45.

25. Kucherov, *Courts*, 120-21.

26. The degree to which state legal officials had access to teaching positions in the law schools indicates that they had a strong influence over the formation of attitudes among prospective law professionals. See, for example, D.I. Shakhovskoi, ed., *S.A. Muromtsev: Sbornik statei* (Moscow, 1911), 14-36. Service records show that a number of state legal officials served as either full-time professors or as lecturers during their careers. Ia.Ia. Chemadurov, for example, taught criminal procedure at the School of Jurisprudence from 1861 to 1866 between the jobs of chief prosecutor of the First Department of the Senate and prosecutor in the St. Petersburg Chamber of Justice. Rossiiskii gosudarstvennyi istoricheski arkhiv (hereafter RGIA), f. 1363 (Criminal Cassation Department), op. 8, d. 821. During his tenure as both chief prosecutor of the Criminal Cassation Court and later as Senator in that court, V.K. Sluchevskii continuously held a professorship at the Aleksandrov Military-Juridical Academy. RGIA, f. 1405 (Ministry of Justice), op. 528, d. 196.

27. The term *zakonoved,* a word meaning a student of the statutes used prior to the judicial reform, appears to have dropped out of use, for it implied that a legal expert was one who learned the statutes, not the science of law.

28. Kucherov, *Courts*, 119-120.

29. On the sense of contemporaries that the state legal officials were becoming more bureaucratic in the performance of the jobs, see G.L. Verblovskii, "Grazhdanskoe sudoproizvodstvo," *Zhurnal Ministerstva Iustitsii*, no. 8 (June 1895): 1-38.

30. A.A. Polovtsov, *Dnevik gosudarstvennogo sekretaria A.A. Polovtsova*, vol. 2 (Moscow, 1966), 336.

31. Kucherov, *Courts*, 119-120.

32. On intraprofessional stratification, see the essays in this volume by Harley D. Balzer, Julie V. Brown, and John F. Hutchinson.

33. Kucherov, *Courts*, 131-41.

34. M.P. Karabchevskii, *Chto glaza moi videli*, vol. 2 (Berlin, 1922), 18-19.

35. Kucherov, *Courts*, 182-96.

36. Russia did not have a corps of public defenders. All lawyers, and sometimes lawyers-in-training, were obligated to accept all cases to which they were appointed as public defenders, being paid for such services out of funds earmarked from the budget of the Ministry of Justice. Ibid.

37. Ibid., 130.

38. M.H. Gernet, ed., *Istoriia russkoi advokatury*, vol. 2 (Moscow, 1916), appendices.

39. "Feldshera iurisprudentsii," *Sanktpeterburgskie vedomosti*, no. 307 (1903).

40. Ibid.

41. Kucherov, *Courts*, 161-63.

42. The ban on Jewish enrollment was to have been followed by a quota for Jews by the Ministry of Justice. Although quotas were never established, the ban remained in effect. Jews who were lawyers-in-training when the prohibitions went into effect remained in that status until the prohibitions were lifted. Ibid., 274-80.

43. Ibid., 155-59.

44. Ibid., 92-93.

45. Ibid., 93.

46. A.F. Koni, *Sobranie sochinenii*, vol. 7 (Moscow, 1966-69), 70-124.

47. Of fifty-two senators appointed to the Criminal Cassation Court between 1891 and 1911, twenty-nine had held previous positions as chairmen or prosecutors in Chambers of Justice, fourteen were promoted from within the prosecutorial staff of the Cassation Courts, and only eight were appointed from other departments of the Senate or from offices in the Ministry of Justice—in other words, from outside of the reformed court system.

48. After the initial appointments to the Courts of Cassation upon their establishment in 1866, I could find no appointees except I.P. Otmarshtein and Ia.G. Esipovich (both appointed in 1877) who had served their careers entirely outside of judicial or prosecutorial service. Both of the above were appointed to the Civil Cassation Court after service in the Ministry of Justice.

49. The judicial disciplinary benches were reluctant to convict their professional colleagues of disciplinary violations. For example, of 572 disciplinary cases brought before the disciplinary bench of the Cassation Courts in 1892, only 32 resulted in actual trials for malfeasance and 20 in lesser disciplinary actions. RGIA, "Otchet kassatsionnykh departamentov za 1892," f. 1364 (Civil Cassation Dept.) op. 15, d. 11.

50. The development of norms of judicial conduct by the disciplinary benches can be followed in such articles as N.N. Bystrov, "Polozheniia izvlechenniia iz opredelenii vysshogo ditsiplinarnogo prisutstviia senata," *Zhurnal Ministerstva Iustitsii*, 3 (1906): 269-76.

51. In 1885, the Ministry of Justice gained additional prerogatives in bringing judges and court officials to disciplinary trial, but the law had little effect on disciplinary actions. *Polnoe sobranie zakonov rossiiskoi imperii*, III, vol. 5, 2959, 20 May 1885; and W. Wagner, "Tsarist Legal Policies at the End of the Nineteenth Century: A Study in Inconsistencies," *Russian Review* 54, no. 3 (July 1976): 376-77.

52. One of the more effective methods for controlling the prosecutors was the extensive use of temporary assignments in the early careers of court officials. I.V. Gessen, *Sudebnaia reforma* (St. Petersburg, 1905), 142-46; and Wortman, *Development*, 277-78.

53. Wortman, *Development*, 255.

54. I have developed the idea of institutional separation of the court system from administrative institutions in "Cassation, Judicial Interpretation and the Development of Civil and Criminal Law in Russia, 1864-1917: The Consequences of the 1864 Court Reform in Russia" (Ph.D. diss., State University of New York at Buffalo, 1984).

55. Governmental interference occurred almost exclusively in criminal matters. The civil courts remained essentially untouched by reaction. Karabchevskii, *Chto glaza moi videli*, vol. 2, 16.

56. P.A. Zaionchkovskii, *Rossiiskoe samoderzhavie v kontse XIX stoletiia* (Moscow, 1970), 234-40.

57. Kucherov, *Courts*, 281-96.

58. A.F. Koni, *Sobranie sochinenii*, vol. 2, 83-84, describes the Ministry of Justice's difficulty getting someone to prosecute Vera Zasulich in 1878.

59. Among the tools available to the Ministry of Justice to influence the composition of the state legal occupations were: use of temporary appointments to sidestep the appointment of qualified but undesirable candidates for a particular position; granting civil service rewards (pensions and "orders") to trustworthy officials in the courts; use of nonjudicial sinecures in which trustworthy legal officials could be kept on the service rolls without direct court contact, but with retention of seniority for possible appointment to higher positions at a later time; and eventually the imposition of general civil service regulations (*chinoproizvodstvo*) for prosecutors and judges. I.V. Gessen, *Sudebnaia reforma*, 185.

60. Wagner, "Tsarist Legal Policies," 378-84.

61. Ibid., 365-76.

62. Until about 1906, the Criminal Cassation Court was firmly staffed with culturalist types like A.F. Koni, I.Ia. Foinitskii, N.S. Tagantsev, et al. After 1905, many appointees had backgrounds in the Ministry of Interior "safeguard" commission, and G.G. Chaplinskii was appointed for outstanding service to the state as prosecutor in the Beilis case.

63. Zaionchkovskii, *Rossiiskoe samoderzhavie*, 234-61. Also, see B.V. Vilenskii, *Sudebnaia reforma i kontrreforma v Rossii* (Saratov, 1969), 220-65.

64. Wagner, "Tsarist Legal Policies," 379-80.

65. F.B. Kaiser, *Die Russische Justizreform* (Leiden, 1972), 469-99.

66. Wagner, "Tsarist Legal Policies," 377-85.

67. A.F. Koni, *Sobranie sochinenii*, vol. 4, 126 et seq.

68. Although lawyers have enjoyed the lion's share of praise for the acquittal of political convicts, their success often depended on actions of state legal officials in the trials. Koni's role in the trial of Vera Zasulich is a perfect example of the influence of the judge on the trial outcome. After this trial, the government paid more attention to the role of the presiding judge and his control over trial proceedings. Kucherov, "The Case of Vera Zasulich," *Russian Review* 11, no. 2 (1952): 86-96; "Postanovka voprosov pri vozbuzhdenii somneniia o vmeniaemosti," *Zhurnal Ministerstva Iustitsii*, kn. 1, khronika (1894): 133-47. Prosecutors of the culturalist mold were also active in ameliorating the effects of government reaction. See, for example, I.P. Belokonskii, *Dan' vremeni*, pt. 2, *V gody bespraviia* (Moscow, 1930), 59-61.

69. H.L. Wilensky, "The Professionalization of Everyone?" *American Journal of Sociology* 70, no. 2 (September 1964): 149-58, suggests a tripartite division of professionals as "careerists," "missionaries," and "client-oriented."

70. Kucherov, *Courts*, 297-316.

71. The decision followed a barrage of criticism from the conservative press which viewed the "*zemstvo* lawyer" as no more than an attempt by liberals to attack the land captains. S. Gurevich, "Iuridicheskaia pomoshch' naseleniiu v stolitsakh," *Pravo*, no. 14 (1910): 857-58.

72. S. Gurevich, *Pravo*, no. 15 (1910): 935.

73. "Stazh v tsifrakh i faktakh," *Pravo*, no. 20 (1910): 1253-62.

74. Karabchevskii, *Chto glaza moi videli*, vol. 2, 27.

75. The Councils of the Bar offered them little encouragement and repeatedly attempted to limit the autonomy of the lawyers-in-training in their legal aid work. Kucherov, *Courts*, 133-41. The Moscow Council even abolished the parent group of the legal aid society "Consultation." But the lawyers-in-training reestablished Consultation under the Moscow Assembly of Justices of the Peace. In 1902, the council chambers were rocked by a public dispute between the lawyers-in-training and the council over the rights of Consultation to exclude from participation a lawyer whom Consultation suspected of desiring to materially benefit from legal aid work. The council sought to limit the autonomy of the lawyers-in-training, but it was primarily concerned about keeping the dispute within the council chambers in order to present a façade of professional unity to the general public.

76. Shmuel Galai, *The Liberation Movement in Russia* (Cambridge: Cambridge University Press, 1973) 247, 253.

77. P.A. Kempe, as chief prosecutor in the Criminal Cassation Department of the Senate, was the most influential member of that court. He was particularly amenable to cater to the desires of the minister of justice by holding cases out of the assignment rotation under a prosecutor known to be particularly influential when a particular bench of senators was scheduled to present a case. RGIA, f. 1363, (Criminal Cassation Department), op. 8, d. 462, l. 14, contains a letter from the Ministry of Justice regarding a case of particular concern. Kempe scribbled "hold for A. Kilshtet" (an assistant prosecutor) in the margin. Subsequent correspondence indicated that the ministry's position was upheld in the court.

78. Kucherov, *Courts*, 294.

79. Karabchevskii, *Chto glaza moi videli*, vol. 2, 18-19, describes the council's hesitancy to approve the candidacy of Kerensky and other *partiinye* candidates to the bar.

80. On the links of the Moscow Law Society to prereform circles, see "Istoricheskaia zapiska o Moskovskom iuridicheskom obshchestve," *Moskovskaia universitetskaia izvestiia*, kn. 5, 1865, 343-52.

81. *Iuridicheskoe obshchestvo pri St. Peterburgskogo universtiteta za 25 let, 1877-1902* (St. Petersburg, 1902), 1-2.

82. Koni, *Sobranie sochinenii*, vol. 4, 314.

83. The Russian legal periodical press was not extensive. A handful of private journals appeared in the early twentieth century, such as *Voprosy prava*, *Vestnik grazhdanskogo prava*, *Iurist*, and others. But the basic journals of the law professions were, aside from the *Zhurnal Ministerstva Iustitsii*, the journals of the law societies: Moscow's *Iuridicheskii vestnik* and St. Petersburg's journal, which went under various names, such as *Zhurnal grazhdanskogo i uglovonogo prava*, *Zhurnal iuridicheskogo obshchestva pri St. Peterburgskom universitete*, and *Vestnik prava*.

84. *Iuridicheskoe obshchestvo pri St. Peterburgskogo universtiteta*, 49-59.

85. Ibid.

86. Studies of professionalization note that one of the functions of the professional organization is to establish links with other professional organizations. Vollmer and Mills, *Professionalization*, 227-43.

87. Examples of such crossovers between the law societies, the leadership of the bar, and the Kadet Party are numerous. V.S. Spasovich, chairman of the St. Petersburg Council of the Bar was one of the charter members of the St. Petersburg Law Society. S. A. Nuromtsev, a charter member of the Kadet Party and chairman of the First State Duma, had been chairman of the Moscow Law Society.

88. Of the charter members of the St. Petersburg Law Society, seventeen were state legal officials, ten were professors, and three were lawyers.

10

The Limits of Professionalization: Russian Governors at the Beginning of the Twentieth Century

Richard G. Robbins, Jr.

At first glance, His Excellency the Governor seems out of place in a book dealing with the professions. So many of the professionals discussed in these pages were specialists operating in clearly defined fields. They were the product of technical or scientific educations, possessors of refined skills, and wielders of power and authority based in large part on knowledge not commanded by the general public. The professionals studied in the other essays in this volume frequently saw themselves as members of groups which, by virtue of education and competence, had not only something to offer society, but also a claim upon it. Many professionals felt that their training had shown them the way to make a better world. The public and the state ought to give them autonomy to pursue professional goals and listen to what they had to say.

Governors were, in contrast, agents of the same government that so often inhibited professional strivings. Moreover, the *nachal'niki gubernii* were, even within the context of state administration, classic generalists. Their office called upon them to handle a variety of problems which could not be lumped into any single field.[1] There were no special schools for training governors, and the backgrounds of these men might differ considerably. The governors possessed no skills or esoteric knowledge comparable to those enjoyed by doctors, lawyers, and engineers. Finally, a governorship was not a profession in itself but a job; traditionally, the governors never saw themselves as a clearly defined group, nor did they create an organization to express any collective striving.[2]

Russian governors do not fit easily into the Weberian model of rational bureaucracy.[3] The duties of the governor were so broad as to make stipulations concerning a defined field of competence almost meaningless. Selection did not proceed entirely on the basis of technical qualifications. In matters of hierarchy and strict discipline, the status of the governors did not coincide with Weber's definitions. The governor's position was, in law at least, *vnevedomstvennyi*, or outside the apparatus of any ministry. For this reason, and because of a perceived need to have the governors enjoy wide-ranging freedom of action, disciplinary control by the central ministries, even the Ministry of Internal Affairs (MVD), was imperfect.

But other contributors to this volume have also noted the difficulty of fitting their professionals into the patterns derived from the West. Instead, they have demonstrated a trend in the direction of professionalization rather than focusing on the finished product. And for all that can be said about the nonprofessional character of the governors, an examination of the development of the gubernatorial corps in the nineteenth and early twentieth centuries shows that these officials were affected by a strong tendency toward professionalization. Over the years, this group of elite officials was shaped by a pattern of recruitment and career socialization that put ever greater emphasis on administrative expertise in general and, specifically, on experience in the area of provincial government.

There has been no systematic investigation of the development of the gubernatorial corps before the last quarter of the nineteenth century. John P. LeDonne has given us an excellent portrait of the governors of Catherine the Great,[4] but subsequent generations have been less thoroughly studied. Still, the works of John Armstrong, I.V. Orzhekhovskii, and P.A. Zaionchkovskii have provided us with many useful data. The research of Orzhekhovskii and Zaionchkovskii points to a secular increase in the educational levels of the governors.[5] Armstrong has stressed the importance of in-service socialization and noted the existence of a fairly clear distinction between high officials whose careers were centered in the capital and those who served primarily in the provinces.[6]

My own earlier analysis of changes within the ranks of the governors of European Russia during the years 1879-1903 confirms and develops the findings of other scholars. I have argued that in the quarter century before the February Revolution, the MVD used its de facto control over selection in order to improve the qualifications of the *nachal'niki gubernii*. Not only did the educational levels of governors rise, but a growing number also possessed legal training. It became more and more difficult to obtain a gubernatorial position without having first held a vice-governorship. And vice-governors were increasingly selected from a pool of officials who had spent the bulk of their careers in the provinces. The kind of service which might lead to vice-governorships and governorships became better defined. Special emphasis was placed on holding offices that gave direct experience in handling peasant affairs.[7]

The early years of the twentieth century were a watershed in the development of the gubernatorial corps. Up until that time, the MVD seems to have evolved its pattern of selection informally and perhaps unconsciously. But in 1903 and 1904 it took steps to give its system legal status. In connection with a new law on the land captains (*zemskie nachal'niki*), the ministry proposed to restrict candidacy for vice-governorships and other key provincial offices exclusively to persons who had served in local administrative posts for at least three years. The post of land captain was singled out as a special rung on the ladder leading to a vice-gubernatorial position.[8]

The State Council rejected the specifics of the MVD's proposal because it would have created too shallow a pool of candidates, but it accepted the basic premise.[9] As a result, the 1904 law on the land captains contained the stipulation that

the office of vice-governor . . . is to be filled primarily by persons [who have] served no less than three years in offices, no lower than VI class, of local peasant institutions, or in one of the following posts: marshal of the nobility, chairman of the provincial executive zemstvo board [*uprava*], chairman of the provincial uprava for affairs of the zemstvo economy, and councilor [*sovetnik*] of the provincial board [*gubernskoe pravlenie*].[10]

This new legislation firmly and formally linked vice-gubernatorial selection with provincial and peasant-related service. Significantly, however, this measure was little referred to in subsequent ministry documents relating to appointments. The practice had already become such an established part of ministry procedure that the MVD felt almost no need to make use of the law as a guide to its internal operations.[11]

The selection patterns legalized in 1904 were continued without major change in the years following the Revolution of 1905. If anything, documents on appointments attest to greater regularity in procedures and a continued concern for practical experience.[12] In 1911 Prime Minister P.A. Stolypin reaffirmed MVD policy on the choice of vice-governors, stating that

from candidates for vice-governor the Ministry of Internal Affairs requires the possession of solid administrative experience which the candidate can only obtain by passing, before selection as vice-governor, through a number of less responsible offices. This requirement, in addition to the personal qualities of the candidate, will guarantee his preparation for the job.[13]

What Stolypin had in mind when he spoke of preparatory steps on the road to a vice-governorship is illustrated by his "long list" of vice-gubernatorial candidates. This document, dated 1910, contains just under 160 names. Of these, 75 percent were engaged in provincial service and a slightly smaller percentage (74.2) had made the provinces the main locus of their careers. Of the men serving in provincial posts (120), 34 percent were marshals and 31 percent were permanent members of the provincial committee on peasant affairs (*gubernskoe prisutstvie*). Beyond this, two-thirds of all candidates listed had held at least one post which gave them direct experience in dealing with peasant problems.[14]

The ministry's shaping of the gubernatorial corps by means of education and training is further demonstrated by a comparison of the governors of 1913 with their counterparts a decade earlier. The educational level of the governors of 1913 had declined somewhat. Only 60.3 percent of these governors had higher education, compared to 67.9 in 1903. But the percentage of governors with legal training had jumped from 22.6 percent in 1903 to 34 percent in 1913. Seventy-eight percent of the governors of 1913 had served as vice-governors, and 72 percent held that office immediately prior to their first governorship. In 1903 the percentages had been 68 and 64 respectively. The use of the provinces as a training ground for future vice-governors and governors became even more marked. Of the governors of 1903 who had previously been vice-governors, 72 percent had served primarily in the provinces. By 1913, the proportion was just under 80 percent. The ministry's growing interest in having as governors men who had worked in institutions which gave them direct contact with the peasantry and its problems is also demonstrated by our comparison. In 1903, 45 percent of the governors had had peasant-related experience. By 1913, the number had risen to 56 percent.[15]

The statistical material on gubernatorial education and career patterns shows the MVD's determination to select governors who possessed real expertise in the area of provincial government. This was clearly a major step in professionalizing the gubernatorial corps—building up a group of officials who had similar kinds of training and experience. But did this approach achieve the goal of bringing to the office of governor a professional civil servant whose knowledge and administrative skill were coupled with devotion to duty, honesty, and consistent behavior? Certainly the process of selection and training would facilitate this effort. And on occasion we uncover documents which permit us to see the process of professionalization in operation on an individual basis. The Russian State Historical Archive contains a useful collection of letters from Aleksandr Nikolaevich Troinitskii to his father, Nikolai Aleksandrovich. The younger Troinitskii became governor in Semipalatinsk and Tula provinces in the period 1908-17; the father had been governor of Viatka from 1876 to 1882 and later served as the head of the MVD's Central Statistical Committee. The letters span the bulk of Aleksandr Nikolaevich's life, beginning in the 1870s and ending with the death of Nikolai Aleksandrovich in 1913. The correspondence is by no means complete, and there are whole periods from which no letters have been preserved. Still, they give us a good idea of how the bureaucratic steel was, or could be, tempered.

As the scion of a family of prominent state officials, Aleksandr Nikolaevich began his formal training at the School of Jurisprudence in St. Petersburg. But his education included other, informal aspects. The elder Troinitskii set an example of career success and bureaucratic orderliness.[16] Summers spent on the family estate gave Aleksandr Nikolaevich contact with agriculture and the experience of dealing with peasants.[17] After graduating from the School of Jurisprudence in 1891, the young Troinitskii embarked on a career which seemed designed to point him in the direction of a governorship. His first job was in provincial administration, as a trouble-shooter (*chinovnik osobykh poruchenii*) for the governors of Olonets and Chernigov. In 1895 he became a councilor on the provincial board (*gubernskoe pravlenie*) of Orel province. Beginning in 1896 Aleksandr Nikolaevich served for a year and a half in the land department (*zemskii otdel*) of the MVD, and in 1898 he was assigned to the post of permanent member of the Stavropol provincial committee on peasant affairs (*gubernskoe prisutstvie*). In 1902 Troinitskii became vice-governor in Tobolsk.

The letters written during his provincial service show the growth of Aleksandr Nikolaevich's consciousness and sense of duty. Initially, mundane social concerns take precedence over service. Troinitskii's letters from Chernigov are filled with descriptions of local society and various petty squabbles as the young bureaucrat seeks to make his way and avoid stepping on anyone's toes.[18] Finding a suitable apartment and a roommate to share the cost, the state of his wardrobe, and the prospects of a promotion occupy his mind to the exclusion of almost everything else.[19] The chance to accompany the governor on a tour of inspection of several of the northern counties (*uezdy*) elicits some excitement,[20] but the work itself seems to have been of little interest. Troinitskii notes the filth and rain the inspection party encountered in Starodub. The only bright spot on the trip was a stay with Graf Kleinmikhel and his charming young wife.[21]

But time and experience slowly change Aleksandr Nikolaevich. When, after service in the land department, he takes up his post as permanent member in Stavropol, Troinitskii's letters show an increasing absorption with his duties. The descriptions of local intrigues and personal problems give way to detailed reports on his work. The climax of the process seems to come in the summer of 1899. In a letter written while on a tour of inspection of county institutions, Aleksandr Nikolaevich shows that he has pushed all other concerns aside and has plunged fully into his administrative responsibilities:

Dear Dad,
    I haven't written for a long while, but everything is going well and I am very busy with work. Our project on various fire prevention measures has been approved by the ministry, and they are releasing 61,000 rubles for funding and so now it is necessary to put the project into effect. The project was my creation, and . . . [I] have to write all the orders for getting [things] into motion. I hope it will be of value to the province. The other day *Birzhevye vedomosti* ran a big editorial about the project strongly praising . . . [it]. It is

interesting that the article was printed before we received official word from the ministry. . . .

I've been sitting three days in the village of Moskovskoe, Stavropol county. I have inspected the parish board and the court. . . . [I] stayed here an extra day or two in order to acquaint myself with several important pieces of business I brought from Stavropol. . . . [A]fter the departure of the entire staff of the provincial committee for vacation, there has been no chance to work on major business since I have to write even the minor papers myself. Last night a fire was put out here. In the past there has been arson. How are things with you and the census? What's new in Petersburg? . . .

The heat [here] is terrible, and for work I have to get up no later than 5 A.M. I go to bed late, only after midnight. . . . On Thursday morning, or maybe even tomorrow night, I'll return to Stavropol. . . .[22]

After this letter, all the surviving correspondence between son and father is in the same vein. It is service oriented, with only the slightest reference to family and personal matters. The dominant themes of the subsequent letters repeat and amplify those found above: concern for the development of the provinces, devotion to duty, and pride in achievement.

It would be misleading to insist that Troinitskii's development was typical of Russian governors during this period, but it was not unique. By the early twentieth century, the majority of governors had pursued careers which closely paralleled Troinitskii's. They came to their governorships with extensive provincial experience and, for the most part, significant contact with the peasantry. Men so trained frequently displayed the same concern for the development of the provinces as did Troinitskii. More important, they often demonstrated a style and attitudes which can be called professional.[23]

One of the characteristics which defined the professionals described in the other essays of this collection was the possession of a "knowledge base." Many of the professionals felt that they commanded scientific knowledge or special skills which gave them both dignity and the right to demand autonomy in the pursuit of professional goals. The same sort of outlook would seem to be a characteristic of those governors whom we might label as professional. To be sure, their knowledge base was not as firm or as clearly defined as that of doctors, lawyers, or engineers, but the training and experience of governors enabled them to know Russia as few administrators could. Armed with these insights, many governors felt that they should be free to act on the basis of local needs even if, in the process, they had to challenge or defy the dictates of the center.

Examples of governors who vigorously asserted their autonomy are not difficult to find. At a number of points in his memoirs, I.F. Koshko scoffed at the ignorance that St. Petersburg officials displayed with regard to the situation in the provinces. He was prepared to disregard ministerial directives that he felt were based on a failure to apprehend properly the situation at the local level.[24] M.M. Osorgin's account of his efforts to satisfy the legitimate needs of the striking workers of the Cherniana Ruda factory reveals that he, too, was willing to pursue an independent course in order to handle a local problem not properly appreciated by the central authorities.[25] S.D. Urusov's treatment of the Jewish question in Bessarabia illustrates a similar tendency. Personal observations of the condition of the Jews in that province and their relation to the local Christian population caused the governor to doubt the justice of government policy and led him to adopt a line which was not welcomed by the MVD.[26] The assertion of gubernatorial autonomy by men like Koshko, Osorgin, and Urusov is easily explained in terms of professional values, for these men left memoirs which give us insight into their individual mentalities. It is much more difficult, however, to talk about professional attitudes within the gubernatorial corps as a whole, because the sources are fragmentary and unclear. On occasion we have instances of collective actions by the governors, but the motive and meaning of their positions are not certain.

In the early twentieth century, for example, the governors were given the opportunity to comment on MVD proposals for restructuring provincial government. Central to reform schemes of 1903 and 1908-9 were the strengthening of the governors' power, the firmer integration of the *nachal'niki gubernii* into the MVD chain of command, and major changes in the organization of the provincial bureaucratic agencies that functioned under the governors' direction.[27] For the most part, the governors were ambivalent about these reforms. Generally, they welcomed expansion of their power, but in 1903 a significant number expressed opposition to any change in their supradepartmental status.[28] In 1908-9, governors called to the capital to discuss Stolypin's reform plans opposed several major alterations in the makeup of provincial committees.[29]

Autonomist strivings have been imputed to these cases of gubernatorial opposition to the Ministry of Internal Affairs.[30] But not every student of the question would agree with this interpretation.[31] More important, it is difficult to decide whether those governors who resisted changes proposed by the central authorities did so on the basis of professional considerations (i.e., a sense of special competence derived from training and experience) or simply because of personal motivations. In explaining his opposition to Stolypin's plan to create a provincial council (*gubernskii sovet*), V.F. Dzhunkovskii asserted that the changes desired by St. Petersburg bureaucrats would not result in any real improvements. The existing committee structure had grown up historically and, confused as it was, corresponded with the interests of various local groups.[32] But did Dzhunkovskii's objections stem from a professional conviction that as an experienced local administrator he understood the workings of *guberniia* institutions better than ministry officials? Or did they simply reflect a desire to maintain a comfortable but inefficient status quo?[33]

The historian's difficulty in distinguishing between professional and traditional attitudes among the governors reflects the transitional nature of the corps itself. The existence of specialized training, a distinct knowledge base, and a striving for autonomy all suggest that, at the very least, the process of professionalization was operating within the ranks of the Russian governors. At the same time, however, this development had definite limits. The selection and training of governors did not function automatically or flawlessly. Individuals who lacked the requisite career experience continued to be appointed governors and vice-governors. Even more significant, by no means all of those who went through the regular system of selection absorbed the values that they were expected to acquire, and the ministry retained and promoted men it knew to be incompetent or corrupt.

Documents in the MVD archives contain a revealing example of the problem. In late 1910, Prime Minister Stolypin ordered the MVD's Department of General Affairs to prepare a series of inspections of provincial institutions.[34] The main aim of these *obozreniia* was to study the working of the provincial boards, the governors' chancelleries, and the police.[35] The conference that was established to develop the program for the review explicitly ruled out an examination of the governors' own actions;[36] however, it proved impossible to exclude their work completely from consideration. Indeed, when one of the inspectors, Nikolai Cheslavovich Zaionchkovskii, reached Riazan, he encountered such a scandal that the original goals of the review were soon pushed aside. Zaionchkovskii found a nest of corruption and wild abuse in which the governor and the vice-governor were directly implicated.

In Zaionchkovskii's opinion, Riazan's governor, Prince Aleksandr Nikolaevich Obolenskii, was simply not up to the task of managing the province because his training was inadequate. A graduate of the Corps of Pages, Obolenskii had served exclusively in the military, rising to the post of company (*rota*) commander. During the stormy year 1906, Obolenskii had been effective in restoring order, and in recognition of this service, he was subsequently attached to the MVD for about eight months and then made vice-governor in Kostroma. He worked two years in the latter post, but Zaionchkovskii felt that the experience had not been "a serious administrative school."[37] Later, Obolenskii had participated in an inspection of the Warsaw area, and in 1910 he had been appointed acting governor of Riazan. Still Zaionchkovskii concluded that the administrative experience Obolenskii had acquired was too thin for the work he faced. The inspector commented acidly, "Undoubtedly, after three . . . years of service in the Ministry [Obolenskii] significantly broadened his company commander's horizon to the horizon of, perhaps, a battalion commander. But he did not manage to acquire real life experience or knowledge of the province and its people."[38]

Zaionchkovskii admitted that Obolenskii was hard-working and quite accessible, yet most of his efforts were little more than fruitless wheel-spinning. The governor read diligently the incoming correspondence, edited outgoing letters, studied the journals of the provincial board, and wrote long resolutions on various reports. But Obolenskii never got much beyond the surface of things. The real power in the province was the vice-governor, Vladimir Arsen'evich Kolobov.[39]

Zaionchkovskii described Kolobov as a marked contrast to Obolenskii. If the weakness of the governor underlined the fact that *nachal'niki gubernii* needed lengthy on-the-job training, the activities of the vice-governor showed that experience and competence could not by themselves guarantee the worthiness of an administrator. Kolobov had served extensively in provincial government. He had worked in the governor's chancellery in Podoliia, been a land captain in Kherson province, and a permanent member of the provincial committee on peasant affairs. Before his transfer to Riazan, Kolobov served as vice-governor for two years in Kursk.[40] Zaionchkovskii did not deny that Kolobov knew his business. He was well prepared, energetic, worked hard, and had the provincial board firmly under his control. The problem was that the vice-governor was twisted morally—a "festering sore," in the words of one provincial resident.[41]

Kolobov's interests were far from purely bureaucratic. For example, the vice-governor had adopted the practice of hiring women to serve as clerical workers in the offices of the provincial board. This was done in other provinces, and undoubtedly increased the efficiency of local institutions since the women were often better educated than most of the male clerks.[42] Zaionchkovskii found that in Riazan, however, Kolobov's hiring policies had produced results of another character. In his report Zaionchkovskii noted that

the seven young women employed to work in the provincial board call attention to themselves. Of these, six work in an extremely unsatisfactory manner, but to make up for it, they are distinguished by remarkable behavior. One . . . [of the women] was brought from Kursk by vice-governor Kolobov, and to this day he provides her with more than fatherly protection. Another was photographed at the apartment of the *kapel'meister* of one of the local regiments with two naked friends, and then they were also photographed separately, in the most debauched poses. (I have seen the pictures.) They say this same girl, coming out of the office of the vice-governor, shouted loudly: "He kissed me, he kissed me, he kissed me! . . ." (Of course, this might be unsubstantiated boasting on her part.) A third, who only shuffles papers, also enjoys great favor with Kolobov; a fourth . . . has a close relationship with one of the clerks; a fifth lives openly with one of the secretaries . . .; concerning the sixth, there circulate the most unambiguous rumors. I present this information because the Riazan provincial board is known in the city as the harem of the vice-governor, [a title] that ill befits the highest institution in the province. In Tula and Voronezh women and girls also work for the provincial boards, but nothing like this is heard of there.[43]

Kolobov's hiring practices and his sexual peccadilloes might have been cited as relatively unimportant idiosyncracies had they not been indicative of a greater moral failing. As the day-to-day supervisor of the provincial board, vice-governor Kolobov was also supposed to keep a close eye on the work of the local police. But instead of guiding and restraining these officials, Kolobov aided and abetted the police in shocking abuses of authority. According to Zaionchkovskii, Kolobov had developed a close working relationship with Vladimir Vladimirovich Gofshtetter, the chief of the Riazan city police, and extended to him extraordinary support and protection. As a result, Gofshtetter, "a person of clearly criminal character, terrorized the entire local population and even a significant portion of the government officials. Neither personal inviolability and freedom nor any person's honor and good name were safe from the chief of the Riazan police."[44] Gofshtetter used his powers in a most blatant way, mistreating citizens almost at will. The population was powerless. Zaionchkovskii stated that, "according to the generally held opinion, Gofshtetter was 'untouchable,' struggle with him was impossible."[45] Indeed, things reached such a point in Riazan that Gofshtetter even dared to blackmail Nadezhda Konstantinovna Popova, the wife of the district procurator. The police chief hoped to force her husband to quash several complaints which had been brought against him. When Kolobov learned of Gofshtetter's misdeeds, he supported his protégé to the hilt. The vice-governor even induced the befuddled Obolenskii to go along with the plan, arguing that the affair would give the provincial administration the opportunity to reduce the effectiveness of procuratorial supervision.[46]

In the end, however, the schemes of the governor, the vice-governor, and the police chief blew up in their faces. M.V. Kirilov, a councilor of the provincial board who had been charged with the task of investigating the Popova affair, refused to go along with his superiors.[47] After being subjected to intense pressure to get into line, Kirilov brought matters to the attention of the local chief of gendarmes.[48] Procurator Popov himself became aware of what was going on and demanded that the governor fire Gofshtetter. Instead, the police chief was removed from office and assigned as an assistant police chief (*ispravnik*) in one of the counties.[49] When Zaionchkovskii arrived on the scene, the town was still ringing with the scandal.[50]

The entire tragicomic episode in Riazan was a clear indication that the ministry's rules for training and selection were inadequate to produce a gubernatorial corps that consistently displayed professional attitudes and behavior. Obolenskii had gained his post with insufficient on-the-job training. Kolobov's experience and administrative competence did not prevent his gross misbehavior. Moreover, the MVD's response to Zaionchkovskii's exposé revealed another problem: the unwillingness of St. Petersburg officials to discipline errant governors and other top provincial officials.

The ministry became aware of Zaionchkovskii's main conclusions by August 1911,[51] and received the final version of the report in November. MVD documents dealing with gubernatorial activities quoted the report in 1912 and 1913.[52] Yet the ministry failed to discipline either Obolenskii or Kolobov and soon gave each of them promotions. In 1913 Kolobov became governor in Ekaterinoslav, and in 1914 Obolenskii assumed the post of town governor (*gradonachal'nik*) of St. Petersburg. Kolobov, at least, was apparently unchastened by his experience, for in 1916 he was charged with the same kind of abuse that had shocked Zaionchkovskii five years before.[53]

The Obolenskii-Kolobov affair was not an isolated incident. MVD records contain numerous examples of gubernatorial and vice-gubernatorial misdeeds that went unpunished.[54] These cases seem particularly remarkable given the ministry's strenuous efforts in the years after 1905 to obtain a clearer picture of the behavior of the *nachal'niki gubernii*. Indeed, in 1911 Stolypin ordered the central departments of the MVD to gather all available material on gubernatorial defects.[55] After some difficulties, the ministry was successful in putting this information together, but in only a very few instances did the MVD remove from office governors who engaged in scandalous activity.

Documents in the MVD's archives do not reveal why it disciplined governors so rarely, but several answers suggest themselves. Favoritism based on connections at court and in the administrative hierarchy must have protected many governors from the wrath of their superiors, including the ministers of internal affairs.[56] Beyond this, there was a certain reluctance on the part of the MVD to restrain too closely governors' freedom of action lest they be unable to meet emergency situations when they arose.[57] Finally, ministers may have worried about the repercussions of sacking a governor; such an act could reflect badly both on the service and on their own judgment.[58] As a consequence, the MVD moved cautiously in exercising its power to punish.

Conclusion

By the beginning of the twentieth century, a complex and contradictory situation had developed with regard to the professionalization of the gubernatorial office. The MVD's selection policies had produced a contingent of governors who displayed many of the features we associate with professional administrators. They possessed demonstrable skills and a knowledge base acquired as the result of training and experience. Moreover, these men combined their abilities with a professional consciousness—a clear understanding of what constituted both technical competence and acceptable behavior in the conduct of their duties.[59] But while the number of "professionalized" governors was growing, they were not able to set the tone for the corps as a whole because the MVD continued to appoint and retain men who had dubious abilities and deficient morals. This inconsistent policy reflects the fact that to the very end of its existence the tsarist government remained unclear as to the kind of governors it really wanted. As in so many other areas, Russia's old regime hesitated at the threshold of modernity, realizing that members of a gubernatorial corps who were selected and disciplined according to professional standards could undercut both ministerial and monarchical power even as they enhanced the efficiency and good order of the state.

The fate of the governors and the governorship was thus analogous to that of other professionals and professions in the tsars' Empire. As had often happened, the government initiated the creation of cadres of educated, trained specialists, but then pulled back from the consequences of its action, unwilling to let the process of professionalization run its course. Consequently, the attitudes and administrative style of men such as Troinitskii, Osorgin, Koshko, Urusov, and others like them could not become the defining ethos for the Russian governorship. The gubernatorial corps never fully jelled, and the professionalization of this important office remained incomplete.

Notes

For a more complete discussion of the Russian governorship, see Richard G. Robbins, Jr., *The Tsar's Viceroys: Russian Provincial Governors in the Last Years of the Empire* (Ithaca, NY: Cornell University Press, 1987).

1. "Obshchee uchrezhdenie gubernskoe," vol. 2, articles 263-428, *Svod zakonov rossiiskoi imperii* (St. Petersburg, 1892).

2. Of course governors recognized that they were all in the same administrative boat, and as Frederick Starr has shown, governors could emerge as an effective lobby during times of national crisis. See S.F. Starr, *Decentralization and Self-Government in Russia, 1830-1870* (Princeton, NJ: Princeton University Press, 1972), 122-37. But Heide Whelan's assertion that the governors constituted a special interest group within the bureaucracy is open to question. See H. Whelan, *Alexander III and the State Council: Bureaucracy and Counter-Reform in Late Imperial Russia* (New Brunswick, NJ: Rutgers University Press, 1982), 132. Throughout the late nineteenth and early twentieth centuries, governors communicated with each other on an individual basis, and the MVD called upon them to present their views collectively on various reform plans. See, for example, *Svod mnenii gg. gubernatorov po predlozheniiam ob ustroistve mestnogo upravleniia,* a volume in *Materialy vysochaishe utverzhdennoi osoboi kommisii dlia sostavleniia proektov mestnogo upravleniia* (St. Petersburg, n.d.) and another summary of gubernatorial responses to ministerial requests for information, "Izvlechenie iz otzyvov gubernatorov po voprosu o preobrazovanii gubernskogo upravleniia," Rossiiskii gosudarstvennyi istoricheskii arkhiv (hereafter RGIA), f. Departament obshchikh del MVD (1284) (hereafter DOD), op. 194, d. 150, ch. 1, "Po gubernskoi reforme," 1-56. There was never anything like a regularly

meeting Russian governors' conference. The focus of the *nachal'niki gubernii* was vertical—on their provinces and the center—not horizontal, in the direction of other governors.

3. Max Weber, *The Theory of Social and Economic Organization*, trans. A.M. Henderson and T. Parsons, ed. T. Parsons (New York: Oxford University Press, 1947), 320-41.

4. John P. LeDonne, "Catherine's Governors and Governors-General, 1763-1796," *Cahiers du Monde Russe et Sovietique* 20, no. 1 (January-March 1979): 15-42.

5. I.V. Orzhekhovskii, *Iz vnutrennei politikoi samoderzhaviia v 60-70-kh godakh XIX veka* (Gor'kii, 1974), 81. P.A. Zaionchkovskii, *Pravitel'stvennyi apparat samoderzhavnoi Rossii v XIX v.* (Moscow, 1978), 214.

6. John A. Armstrong, "Tsarist and Soviet Elite Administrators," *Slavic Review* 31 (March 1972): 26.

7. "Choosing the Russian Governors: The Professionalization of the Gubernatorial Corps," *The Slavonic and East European Review* 58, no. 4 (October 1980): 541-60.

8. RGIA, f. 1160 (Zhurnaly departamentov gosudarstvennogo soveta), op. 1, d. 218, "Zhurnaly departamenta zakonov gosudarstvennogo soveta, 1904, ch. 1," 209.

9. Ibid., 209-10.

10. *Polnoe sobranie zakonov*, 3d ed., no. 24388, 19 April 1904.

11. I found only one reference to this piece of legislation in the MVD files. RGIA, f. DOD, op. 46, 1905, d. 214, "Po khodataistvam o predstavlenii dolzhnosti vitse-gubernatora," 31.

12. RGIA, f. DOD, op. 47, 1906, d. 9, "O kandidatakh na dolzhnosti gubernatorov i po khodataistvam ob opredelenii po eti dolzhnosti," 23, 40-50, 92-94, 260-72. Also, Ibid., 1907, d. 98, "O naznachenii . . . grafa Apraksina. . . . , 4-12.

13. RGIA, f. DOD, op. 47, 1911, d. 53, "Po khodataistvam o predstavlenii dolzhnosti vitse-gubernatorov 1911, 1912 g.," 203. Stolypin is quoted in an internal memorandum (*spravka*) dated 8 October 1912.

14. RGIA, f. DOD, op. 47, 1910, d. 325, "Kandidaty na dolzhnosti vitse-gubernatorov po noiabr' 1910 g."

15. Information on gubernatorial careers is derived from *Spisok vysshikh chinov mestnykh ustanovlenii Ministerstva vnutrennikh del po 1913 g.* (St. Petersburg, 1913) and supplemented by materials in RGIA, f. DOD, op. 46 and 47.

16. The elder Troinitskii's "bureaucratic style" is illustrated by the fact that all letters from his children are stamped with the date they were received and the date they were answered.

17. Letter dated 16 July 1885, RGIA, f. N.A. Trointskogo (1065), op. 1, d. 57, "Pis'ma Troinitskim N.A. i A.E. ot ikh detei, 1878-1913," 116.

18. Ibid., letters of 11 November 1892, 19 March and 27 August 1893, 88, 78-79, 82-83.

19. Ibid., letters of 27 August and 21-23 September 1893, 83, 84-85.

20. Ibid., letter of 21-23 September 1893, 85.

21. Ibid., letter of 11 October 1893, 80-81.

22. Ibid., letter of 13 July 1899, 70-71.

23. Among the governors who can be put in this category are A.P. Engel'gardt, I.F. Koshko, I.M. Strakhovskii, P.P. Stremoukhov, and S.D. Urusov.

24. I. F. Koshko, "Vospominaniia gubernatora, chast' II: Perm," 126-32, 553, Bakhmeteff Archive, Columbia University (hereafter BAR), Koshko family papers.

25. M.M. Osorgin, "Vospominaniia 1890-e gody-1905," Rukopisnyi otdel Rossiiskoi gosudarstvennoi biblioteky, f. M.M. Osorgina (215), papka II, d. 2, 168-75.

26. S.D. Urusov, *Memoirs of a Russian Governor,* trans. H. Rosenthal (London: Harper & Brothers, 1908), 171-81.

27. The best recent accounts of these reforms are Neil B. Weissman, *Reform in Tsarist Russia: State Bureaucracy and Local Government, 1900-1914* (New Brunswick, NJ: Rutgers University Press, 1981), 40-46, 124-47; and Francis W. Weislo, *Reforming Rural Russia: State, Local Society and National Politics, 1855-1914* (Princeton, NJ: Princeton University Press, 1990), 207-304.

28. "Izvlechenie iz otzyvov gubernatorov. . . ," RGIA, f. DOD, op. 194, d. 150, ch. 1, "Po gubernskoi reforme," 2.

29. Weissman, *Reform,* 187-88.

30. D.N. Liubimov, "Russkaia smuta nachala deviatisotykh godov, 1902-1906," 31-33, 35-36, BAR, Liubimov papers; P.P. Stremoukhov, "Administrativnoe ustroistvo imperatorskoi Rossii po vospominaniiam gubernatora, pervaia lektsiia," 3, BAR, Kryzhanovskii papers.

31. Weissman, *Reform,* 53-54, 186-88.

32. V.F. Dzhunkovskii, "Vospominaniia za 1909-1910 gg.," Gosudarstvennyi arkhiv rossiisskoi federatsii (hereafter GARF), f. V. F. Dzhunkovshogo (826), op. 1, d. 49, 63-64.

33. On the basis of reading his memoirs and other materials in his archive, I would impute professional motives to Dzhunkovskii, but the explanation given by Dzhunkovskii could have been used by someone simply determined to resist all change in the existing provincial structure.

34. A.D. Abrutsov to N.P. Zuev, 4 November 1910, no. 28307, RGIA, f. DOD, op. 47, 1910, d. 233, "Po vyrabotke programmy obozreniia deloproizvodstva gubernskikh pravlenii, gubernatoriskikh kantseliarii i politseiskikh upravlenii chlenami soveta ministra vnutrennikh del," 3. Similar letters were sent to other members of the Council of Ministers.

35. Ibid., program of the inspection, 47-64.

36. Ibid., Zhurnal soveshchaniia, 12 January 1911, 53-54.

37. Report of N.Ch. Zaionchkovskii, RGIA, f. DOD, op. 47, 1911, d. 342, ch. 2, "Otchet chlena soveta ministra vnutrennikh del deistvitel'nyi statskii sovetnik Zaionchkovskogo po obozreniiu deloproizvodstva Riazanskikh gubernskogo pravleniia i kantseliarii gubernatora i revizii politseiskikh uchrezdenii v 1911 godu," 88.

38. Ibid., 89.

39. Ibid.

40. Information on Kolobov's career is found in *Spisok vysshikh chinov . . .* and RGIA, f. DOD, op. 47, 1907, d. 145, "O naznachenii . . . Kolobova . . ."

41. Report of Zaionchkovskii, RGIA, f. DOD, op. 47, 1911, d. 342, ch. 2, 3.

42. This is an impression based on information found in RGIA, f. DOD, op. 47, 1914, d. 43 v. "Prilozheniia k otchetu N.Ch. Zaionchkovskogo po komandirovke v g. Vil'nu v fevrale 1914 goda," 1.

43. Report of Zaionchkovskii, RGIA, f. DOD, op. 47, 1911, d. 342, ch. 2, 5. (A careful search of the documents preserved in the archives failed to uncover the pictures Zaionchkovskii mentioned.)

44. Ibid., 87.

45. Ibid.

46. Here is the story. Madame Popova was guilty of an indiscretion. Without her husband's knowledge, she had borrowed money from Gofshtetter. (She wanted to help her son who had become estranged from his father.) Gofshtetter then sought to use Popova's indebtedness in order to force her to intervene on his behalf with her husband. When Popova refused, Gofshtetter set up a "sting" operation which could provide witnesses who would testify that Popova, and presumably her husband, had extorted a bribe from the police chief.

Having successfully sprung his trap, Gofshtetter then called Popova to his home and demanded that she do as he had requested. He threatened that if the investigation of his activities was not stopped, "You and your husband will sit in the prisoners' dock." And, he added, "You can call me a scoundrel and a villain as much as you want, I am afraid of nothing." (Ibid., deposition of Popova, 10 May 1911, ch. 1, "Prilozheniia k otchetu . . . Zaionchkovskogo," 111-12).

Terrified and hysterical, Popova turned to the provincial administration for protection from the police chief. But Kolobov, who was acting governor in Obolenskii's absence, decided to use the incident to his and Gofshtetter's advantage. He proceeded to manipulate the affair so that upon Obolenskii's return, the governor was led to believe that Popova was guilty of taking a bribe. Moreover, it appears that Kolobov convinced Obolenskii that the whole business could be used to get rid of procurator Popov and to acquire a "good trump" against the supervision of the courts. (Ibid., report of M.V. Kirilov to Zaionchkovskii, 21 August 1911, 132.) Obolenskii went along. He ordered M.V. Kirilov, a councilor (sovetnik) of the Provincial Board, to undertake an investigation which "officially and legally" would be concerned with Popova's complaint against Gofshtetter. "But actually," the governor added, "secretly give me . . . material which can be used in a letter to the Minister of Justice so that Popov will be removed. . . ." (Ibid.) Obolenskii stuck to this plan even after Kirilov submitted a report which supported Popova's charges.

47. Ibid., M.V. Kirilov to A.N. Obolenskii, 24 June 1911, 128.

48. Ibid., report of Zaionchkovskii, ch. 2, 4.

49. Ibid., 87-88.

50. Ibid., 88.

51. Memorandum (spravka) on Obolenskii, 4 October 1911, RGIA, f. DOD, op. 47, 1910, d. 278, "So spravkami o gubernatorakh kotorye predstavlialis' g. ministru v 1910, 1911 gg.," 114-15.

52. Memorandum on Obolenskii, no date, RGIA, f. DOD, op. 47, 1912, d. 19, "So spravkami o gubernatorakh kotorye predstavlialis' g. ministru v 1912 godu i v 1913 g.," 57-63.

53. This document, a request (*proshenie*) from citizens of Ekaterinoslav, dated 18 February 1916, is found in Kolobov's personnel file. (Prilozheniia k doveritel'nomu pis'mu chlena soveta ministerstva vnutrennykh del. N.P. Kharlamova ot 16 iiuniia 1916 goda o deiatel'nosti Ekaterinoslavskogo gubernatora . . . V.A. Kolobova, RGIA, f. DOD, op. 47, 1907, d. 145, "O naznachenii . . . Kolobova," 1).

54. Various memoranda on gubernatorial misbehavior are to be found in RGIA, f. DOD, op. 47, 1910, d. 278 and 1912, d. 19. Other materials of this sort are found in the same *fond* and *opis'*, 1909, d. 143, "Prilozheniia k otchetu . . . Zaionchkovskogo po komandirovke v Mogilovskuiu gub. ot 18-25 marta 1909 g." 6, 1913, d. 332; "Otchet . . . Zaionchkovskogo po komandirovke v gor. Vologdu 14-21 ianvaria 1913 g." 10-13, 1915, d. 294; "O pricheslenii k Ministerstvu vnutrennikh del tainogo sovetnik Borzenko," 9-10, 13.

55. Memorandum dated 26 February 1911, RGIA, f. DOD, op. 47, 1911, d. 333. "Po zaprosam gg. nachal'nikov tsentral'nykh uchrezhdenii svedenii, kharakteri-zuiushchikh deiatel'nosti gubernatorov," 1.

56. Stephen Sternheimer, "Administering Development and Developing Adminis-tration: Organizational Conflict in Tsarist Bureaucracy, 1906-1914," *Canadian-American Slavic Studies* 9, no. 3 (Fall 1975): 290.

57. In the 1890s the MVD and the Ministry of Justice tried to come up with a new law dealing with governors who committed crimes in office. During the discussions, the MVD argued that governors ought to have broad freedom to act as they saw fit, even if the law was broken in the process. The views of the MVD were most clearly expressed in a communication with the Ministry of Justice dated 25 April 1893, no. 5272, which stated that "to stand mute before purely legal considerations would not be helpful to an official who might be compelled, by special circumstances, to commit one or another violation of the law; and in the work of a governor, responsible for the good order of his region, such circumstances were bound to be encountered." RGIA, f, DOD, op. 46, 1892, d. 113, "Po otnosheniiu Ministra iustitsii ob izmenenii deistvuiushchikh pravil ob otvetstvennosti gubernatorov, za prestupleniia dolzhnosti," 23.

58. I. Blinov, "Nadzor za deiatel'nosti gubernatorov (istoriko-iuridicheskii ocherk)," *Vestnik prava* 32 (September 1902), 74.

59. The memoirs and papers of Russian governors contain frequent evaluations of provincial officials and other *nachal'niki gubernii*. While there was no absolute consensus as to what constituted a good governor or provincial administrator, there was general agreement that solid knowledge of local government was crucial. Administra-tive skills had to be combined, however, with certain moral and personal qualities. These included a capacity for hard work, seriousness, tact, ability to handle people, firmness, and determination to follow an even course through the storms of party and group conflict. Governors who pursued consistent policies were praised by colleagues who might hold very different political views. See for example, P.G. Kurlov, *Konets russkogo tsarizma: vospominaniia byvshego komandira korpusa zhandarmov* (Petrograd-Moscow, 1923), 76; S.D. Urussov, *Memoirs*, 16, 26; Dzhunkovskii, "Vospominaniia," GARF, f. Dzhunkovskogo, op. 1, d. 47, 114; d. 51, 1912, 28; d. 53, 65-67, 71, 73.

11

Professionalism in the Ministerial Bureaucracy on the Eve of the February Revolution of 1917

Daniel T. Orlovsky

The study of professions has focused for the most part on the development, consolidation, taxonomy, and ideology of certain occupations or functions in conjunction with the emergence of capitalism in the West. Autonomous or free professions, or even heteronomous and semipublic organizations and their expert staffs, are shown to be embedded in a web of social, economic, and political relations whose motor force is the capitalist market.[1] Although the forms of the free professions have roots in the preindustrial guilds of feudal regimes with their aristocratic value structures, the content and ideologies of various modern autonomous professions have been very adaptable to the new challenges and sources of support offered by industrial society. One scholar has even gone so far as to point out that the professional project of the late nineteenth and twentieth centuries has resulted in a merging of the professional with the upper- and upper-middle-class value structures so that these have become virtually indistinguishable.[2] Another, looking at the problems of professionalism in relation to the historically parallel and comparable phenomenon of bureaucratization, has noted that under modern capitalism the free professions have become bureaucratized.[3] This has occurred in terms of actual organization and values, as well as in the fact that the sustaining myth of autonomy has become much more difficult to preserve not only for professional associations, but for those at work in the corporate world, universities, foundations, and in the various sectors of government. At the same time, bureaucracies have become professionalized with the employment in a whole range of institutions of those possessing professional qualifications, skills, status expectations, and so on. From a cursory review of the literature, the problem of professionalism in history is one to be viewed in terms of specific cultures and societies as a necessary first step toward fruitful comparisons and the formulation of theory.

Context is especially important for study of the emerging professions in late tsarist Russia. To give just one analogy, it would make little sense to study the history and fate of Russian liberalism (an ideology not irrelevant to the professions in tsarist Russia) without taking into full account the social and cultural framework within which it had to fight for survival. Russia presents great challenges and opportunities to the student of the professions because in social structure, culture, and institutions it is not "western," and its professional groups cannot be fit easily into the paradigms of sociologists and historians of the western professions. In tsarist Russia, as in its Muscovite predecessor (and we might well argue its Soviet successor), there is no direct counterpart to the capitalist marketplace or to the dynamics of capitalism as the determinant of superstructure. This is not to deny the existence in Russia of a market or even of the tremendous strides toward industrialization and urbanization in the decades prior to the upheavals of 1917. These changes spurred the rise of new social and occupational groups. We should remember that Russia remained an agrarian society, and that in Russia the state mirrored and reinforced a social structure and set of values that make it possible to view the state (or more accurately patterns of social and institutional organization and their supporting values) as a dynamic historical counterpart to the structures of capitalism in the West. At every turn in our study of the professions in Russia, we come upon the state and its bureaucratic apparatus as the parent of occupational groups that in many of their external forms and aspirations corresponded to their western counterparts, but that could never attain comparable autonomy or even express a desire for complete autonomy. In Russia, time and again we see the professionals (and indeed artists, intellectuals, and others) fighting simultaneously for freedom from bureaucratic tutelage and for access to or control of the bureaucracy and state power for their own "projects."[4]

This essay examines professionalism in the central ministerial bureaucracy on the eve of the February Revolution of 1917. Although I am not analyzing a specific group of either autonomous or semipublic professionals (e.g., doctors, lawyers, teachers, engineers, agronomists, etc., all of whom had important connections to the bureaucracy and the larger complex of state service in Russia), I hope to show that the existence of individuals with professional qualifications and aspirations in high posts in the ministerial bureaucracy and the increasing numbers of those with professional qualifications in lower posts is symptomatic of the historical process of professionalization in Russia. In a sense, the ministerial bureaucracy was the power center of the Russian state and the mediator between state and society and thus corresponded to some of the institutions of capitalism in the West. The tension between the ideology of "free professions" and the very real demands, powers, and magnetism of the ministerial bureaucracy was one of the hallmarks of political and social conflict in the last years of the tsarist regime. Even more important, this conflict took place not only between the bureaucracy and those who had begun to break away and form professional associations and markets apart from the state, but it took place in slightly different terms within the ministerial bureaucracy itself, as proponents of rival notions of professionalism and service contended for political power.

The Russian ministerial bureaucracy offers contradictory evidence with respect to the question of professionalism. It is easy enough to make the claim that career tsarist ministerial officials were professional bureaucrats —professional in the sense that their livelihood, status, and power within society derived from full-time officeholding in the state apparatus. But were they professionals in the same sense as members of the so-called free professions (i.e., doctors, lawyers, professors, and teachers) who maintained control over access, a separate education, and a corporate sensibility? Can we use this term to discuss the ministerial official? And most important, does an analysis of these questions shed light on the nature of the professions in Russia generally and the relationship of those professions to the state?

The first tasks then are to define more precisely the ministerial bureaucracy, provide historical background regarding professionalism in the state bureaucracy, and finally to outline in general terms the shape of the autocracy and its service personnel on the eve of the February Revolution.

I use the term "ministerial bureaucracy" to mean the central institutions of domestic administration, which were most often but not always named ministries, along with their provincial hierarchies and the personnel working in both central and provincial offices. As the cornerstone of autocratic government, these institutions existed in mutually dependent and dynamic relationships with the tsar, each other, other high government bodies (the State Council, Senate, Duma, etc.), and committees and commissions in which ministerial officials took part. Individual ministries also faced the problem of developing and controlling their own hierarchies (especially in the provinces) and defining some sort of relationship to outside constituencies in what must be labeled "society."5 The ministerial bureaucracy was the key mediator between state and society during the last decades of the tsarist regime. The bureaucracy, far more than the nascent private sector or free professions, provided the livelihood and means of social mobility for those who were neither peasants nor workers. From a social perspective, the ministries reveal themselves as a microcosm of important changes taking place in the larger society of which they were a part.

My analysis of the ministerial bureaucracy on the eve of the February Revolution is divided into two parts: institutions and personnel. Both of these dimensions of ministerial bureaucracy had their impact on politics and on the course of the revolution.

Institutions

Without describing in detail the formal structure of the ministries or the larger government during World War I,[6] the following generalizations are most important for establishing the political and cultural place of the ministerial bureaucracy in the state system and the relationship of the ministry to the idea of professionalism.

1. *The role of the tsar's personal, as opposed to legal or institutional, power.* This implies the myth versus reality of the tsar's own power and raises the question of rule of law and institutions versus personal power in Russian history. During the late tsarist period, the tension between these two modes of power was particularly strong within the government and the ministerial bureaucracy. The personal and arbitrary grew stronger at the very end of the regime. It was a hallmark of Russian history that personal power was often the focal point of social and bureaucratic opposition to autocratic domestic policy, even as it was a necessity for the implementation of reform. The possibility of the tsar's intervention had many ramifications—from the so-called ministerial checkers and sidestepping of ministerial government during World War I to the duplication of arbitrary relationships at lower levels in what was on paper a highly formal and structured set of hierarchies governed by impersonal rules.[7]

2. *Absence of unity and coordination in government and administration.* This was the case in an operational sense as well as in terms of ideology. In part, the problem derived from the personal power of the tsar and its incompatibility with "regular" or "systematized" ministerial government. In part, it had to do with functional and institutional cleavages, rivalries, competing ideologies, and the like. There had rarely been a stable and effective cabinet or council of ministers, prime minister, or even a shared set of values or administrative ideologies among the highest officials of ministries with very different missions. These problems were acute during the last years of the tsarist regime, particularly during World War I.[8]

3. *The growth of the specialist and technically oriented ministries.* This was the culmination of tendencies dating back to the reform era, and even to the latter part of the reign of Nicholas I.[9] It had to do with the growing primacy of managing the economy in the Empire (including the agrarian question and industrialization) and the entire range of social problems connected with it. The economic and social crises exacerbated by World War I led to a qualitative and quantitative increase in the autonomy and influence of those specialized sectors of the ministerial bureaucracy directly responsible for the economy.[10] This is not to argue that there was "rational" management of the economy or a clear-cut division of labor. Rather, the opposite was the case; there was a welter of competing jurisdictions, overlapping functions,

and confusion. Yet all signs pointed toward an important shift in institutional power as well as to the coming-of-age within the bureaucracy of all sorts of specialists and "professionals."

It is apparent that an organization such as the Ministry of Internal Affairs (MVD), the traditional bastion of autocratic power and symbol of tutelage of state over society (and indeed the home base for a growing number of generalist representatives of the provincial nobility), felt itself on the defensive during World War I, overshadowed and deflated as a result of the growing role of such ministries as Agriculture (MZ), Communications (MPS), Trade and Industry (MTI), and Finance (MF).[11] Yet the victory of the specialized ministries, if we can call it such, was ambiguous at best. True, they became indispensable to the functioning of the economy and to the war effort. They even established something of a monopoly in such matters as food supply and land reform, where they became free to create new relationships with society in the provinces where these things really mattered.[12] But there was no political victory in the struggle for power at the center within the autocracy. The irony was that even as mounting social and economic crises drew the specialists more and more into high-level policy making, the more traditional, generalist sectors of the government (including the MVD) threw their considerable political weight behind their own conception of traditional autocracy and the estate society it supposedly represented. Nicholas himself remained aloof and barely heeded the desire of his ministers to serve him and the dynasty. He dismissed them at will, giving his backing to a military overtly hostile to the civil administration whose functions it was usurping in the war zones. Though power was certainly fragmented during World War I, more of it remained in the hands of autocratic institutions (including the tsar and court) based upon personal power and rooted in traditional estate society.

4. *The emergence of the special councils (Defense, Food Supply, Fuel, and Transportation), the public organizations (Union of Zemstva, Union of Towns, Zemgor, etc.) and various other organs of economic mobilization and supply.* The special councils were chaired by, and in a sense in the domain of, the specialist ministries. Here was another example of how the MVD had been shunted aside when it came to the war effort. It must have been particularly galling to MVD officials, given that the purpose of the special councils was not only to help administer the economy but to define a working relationship with politicians and experts outside the ranks of government. The evolving wartime relationship between the ministerial bureaucracy and the special councils and public organizations produced patterns that would persist under both the Provisional Government and its early Soviet successor.[13]

5. *The assumption by the military of economic functions and the virtual replacement of regular by military administration in enormous areas at or near the fronts.*[14] The role of the military in the demise of autocracy is only now

coming to light. Until recently, the fact that the military assumed such a large role in wartime administration was obscured. The military, through the Special Council on Defense and its own administrative branches such as the Main Artillery Administration, was very much involved in economic decision making. Furthermore, with Nicholas' permission the army set up a dictatorship of military administration in the war zone. The army built its own supply network, entered into independent relations with public organizations, and made decisions that had profound political implications. For example, in western Russia it pursued a modified scorched-earth policy that greatly increased the refugee problem. Military administration was marked by a degree of arbitrariness and unconcern with legality that astounded even MVD administrators. Military leaders had only contempt for ministers and for the Council of Ministers and repeatedly refused to consult with, or even inform, the Empire's regular government. One only has to read the memoirs of General P.G. Kurlov, a notorious tsarist police official who served as a military administrator in the Baltic provinces, to get a sense of the problems and conflicts that surrounded matters of supply, evacuation, pacification of nationalists, and the like.[15] The military role was one more factor working against ministerial bureaucracy in its specialist and generalist sectors, and in its quest for hegemony. As with the tsar and the court, the military could fill vacuums or usurp functions, but it could not really dislodge the ministerial bureaucracy as a social and cultural force. Even establishment of a formal military dictatorship, as had been suggested by General Alekseev, probably would have done little to reverse the structural trends described here.[16]

6. *The problem of provincial administration and the desire of individual ministries to build autonomy through their own provincial hierarchies, apparats, or plenipotentiaries.* For the MVD—as well as for the autocracy, the Provisional Government, and the Bolsheviks—provincial administration was the whole ball game. How to mobilize, administer, and control the population and resources of the provinces (including the non-Russian components of the Empire) was one of the most deeply rooted structural problems faced by the tsarist regime and its successors.[17] On the one hand, the regular civil administration of the MVD was outmoded and lacked reach below the district level of provincial society. By law, the civil governors embodied the notion of personal power, and successive ministers of internal affairs during the last decades of the autocracy attempted to solve the crisis of authority in the provinces by shoring up the power of the governors. They also looked for ways to extend state authority, MVD-style, to the local levels. The specialist ministries, on the other hand, assumed command of growing numbers of local specialists and other officeholders directly subordinate to their respective St. Petersburg ministries rather than to the central MVD or even its governors.[18] In a sense, each specialist ministry had its own microcosmic world of

educational institutions, offices, and other career support systems in the provinces. Provincial and district centers were liberally sprinkled with treasury and state control officials, agrarian, forestry, and fishery experts, railway managers and engineers of all sorts, school and factory inspectors, judges, and prosecutors, to name a few. The ministries controlled their own educational institutions and training programs (i.e., access to the "professions") and provided a kind of cradle-to-grave security for officials who moved up and around provincial offices in well-marked patterns.[19]

Personnel

A social transformation was well under way by early 1917 via the medium of the ministerial bureaucracy. This social transformation worked in a dialectical fashion with institutional and ideological or cultural factors to provide the staying power of the ministerial bureaucracy during the turmoil of 1917 and into the Soviet period. This transformation involved both career patterns and the numerical growth of specialists and quasi professionals. It also involved considerable social mobility, even while reinforcing the long-standing tendency for social mobility to take place within the structures of the state. Once we discard the notion of prerevolutionary society as an estate society neatly divided into legal categories, we can see it more clearly as a variegated and disjointed collection of groups and subgroups along a spectrum that was becoming more and more divorced from estate categories. The essays in this volume provide sound evidence for this point of view in terms of the growing "free" professions, while Alfred J. Rieber has argued it eloquently for the "bourgeoisie."[20] During the last decades of the tsarist regime, the hegemony of ministerial bureaucracy as the arbiter of functional specialization and social mobility was challenged by professions and the private sector. By 1917, these challenges had achieved only partial success, since the professions and the private sector never were able to remove constraints imposed by the state that had nurtured them. One of the results of the revolutions of 1917 was to remove these competitors to ministerial bureaucracy. The professions and private sector were absorbed into that deeply rooted bureaucracy as it reasserted its monopoly over functional specialization and social mobility.

These assertions are based primarily on examination of personnel records (*formuliarnye spiski*) of several hundred of the highest officeholders in the seven ministries of domestic administration (ministers, assistant ministers, department directors and vice-directors and their equivalents, and members of the Council of Ministers); representative samples of middle-level ministerial officeholders such as officials of special missions and section chiefs; and key provincial officeholders such as governors, heads of fiscal chambers, heads of communications districts, and so on.[21] I have also read the personnel records of 137 appointed members of the State Council in 1916, a representative number of Senate files, and random materials pertaining to young officials entering the state service and to the operations of personnel departments in several ministries (Internal Affairs, Agriculture, Finance, and Justice) for 1916 and 1917.[22]

My purpose here is not to repeat the kind of thorough demographic analysis of the late tsarist bureaucracy already offered, for example, by Dominic C.B. Lieven, or the institutional analyses of W.E. Mosse or Don K. Rowney.[23] While evidence on social origins, education, and religion is extremely important, I emphasize something that is played down in other studies—namely, career patterns. I also want to reaffirm the value of evidence such as personnel records in charting social and political developments in late tsarist and revolutionary Russia. The use of such material has been criticized for confirming basic demographic trends but telling us little about the ideology, policies, or historical impact of individuals or the bureaucracy.[24] There is some merit in such criticism, especially if the users of the *spiski* ask only the narrowest questions of the material, take officialdom out of its institutional and political context, and fail to integrate their findings with other forms of evidence. But this does not mean that we should abandon rich materials that can reveal new and unsuspected patterns, or that can substantiate those which we may have suspected or even accepted on the basis of literary evidence. For example, we can verify the assertion made by B.B. Veselovskii (and lucidly developed by Roberta Manning) that the central administration at the beginning of the twentieth century began to co-opt into its ranks men drawn from the provincial nobility who had prior service as marshals of the nobility, *zemstvo* executives, or *zemstvo* delegates.[25] This is an important point, for it lends credence to the idea of a "gentry reaction" and to a close relationship between the powerful MVD and the provincial nobility.

But to fully exploit the possibilities afforded by personnel materials, we must place the MVD's hiring of provincial gentry in the context of the appointment policies of other ministries and the dynamics of career patterns once they shifted from provincial posts to the center. If these provincial gentry appear suddenly as governors who are able to jump immediately to the offices of department director, assistant minister, or even minister (which indeed was often the case from 1900 to 1917 and which would almost never have been the case from 1861 to 1881), does this not suggest new or renewed sources of social influence for MVD policy and the particular role of the MVD as a corporate-interest body within the autocracy? The Khostovs, Shtiurmers, and many others who emerged from the provinces were clients of those more powerful than they and dragged their own clients with them to assume the highest positions in the government, including chairman of the Council of Ministers and membership in the State Council.[26] The personnel records can reveal the patterns of officeholding and the connections between clients and patrons, and also demonstrate that at least one part of the autocratic government had very specific social roots that were reinforced as 1917 drew near.

If the *zemstvo* was a microcosm of the larger Russian society (with its third-element specialists and its estate representatives), it is possible through the *spiski* to establish similar distinctions in the ministerial bureaucracy as a whole. Evidence on social origins and mobility, education, and career patterns reveal the shape of the service state and its supporting society. As Vice-Governor Kondoidi of Samara wrote in regard to the emergence of the third element in the *zemstva*, "Some will be pleased by this news and others will be dismayed, but all will agree with me that in the life of the zemstvo one can now see the participation of a new factor belonging neither to the administration nor to the ranks of representatives of local estates."[27] If by administration here we accept that he meant traditional MVD administration, we can see an analogy between the *zemstvo* experience and the growing impact of specialists on the ministerial bureaucracy.

Let us look first at the specialized ministries. After a brief discussion of each ministry and the demographic profiles and educational levels of their highest officials, representative career patterns will be summarized. Then, we shall discuss some special features of appointments to the minister and vice-minister ranks (referred to as "ministerial checkers" because of the frequent changes in personnel) during World War I.

Ministry of Communications (MPS)

This highly specialized ministry had primary responsibility for the state's railways, waterways, and assorted public works. The importance of transport during the war and revolution needs no recounting here, nor does the role of the railway workers under the jurisdiction of this ministry.[28] As to its own high officials, a sample of ten drawn from 1916 records reveals only three born into the hereditary nobility; the remainder were born into the petty bourgeoisie (*meshchanstvo*) or were the sons of lower officeholders. Virtually all held the rank of civil engineer and had degrees from the Institute of Communications Engineers (named for Alexander I), the Nicholas Engineering School and Academy, or the Mining Institute. Their careers were all highly routinized and predictable, with long periods of early service in the provinces—on the railroads, in the *okrug* administrations of the MPS, in the waterway administration, and so on.

Career Patterns:

Ivan Nikolaevich Borisov—Assistant Minister, 1916. Born 1858. *Meshchanin.* No property. Orthodox. Married the daughter of an honorary citizen. Graduated in 1884 from Alexander I Institute of Communications Engineers with rank of civil engineer. Entered railroad service as a collegiate secretary in the Temporary Directorate of State Railroads. During the 1880s and 1890s he moved up to various positions with different railroads. In 1895 he was appointed assistant chief of service for the Baltic-Riga Railroad. He moved up the managerial ladder in another provincial railroad and in 1906 was named chief of the Vistula Railroad. By 1911, he was an actual state councilor working in the central ministry as director of the operations section. In 1913, he became a member of the Engineering Council; in 1914, chief of the Railroad Director-ate; and in 1916, assistant minister of communications.[29]

I.P. Kalinak—Chief of the Directorate of Internal Waterways and Roads, 1916. Born 1870. Son of a collegiate councilor. No property. Orthodox. Graduated in 1894 from Alexander I Institute of Communications Engineers as civil engineer and collegiate secretary. Immediately entered the Waterway Administration in the provinces. Junior inspector in the Waterway Administration, 1905. Taught at the Alexander Institute, 1909. Chief of the Waterway Section in the Waterway Administration, 1910. Actual state councilor (*Deistvitel'nyi statskii sovetnik*), 1913. Chief of the Waterway Directorate, 1916.[30]

One further point should be made. In many of the records of MPS officials who rose to manage railroads and in some cases to become directors of MPS *okruga* and high central MPS officials, we note various periods of work as managers on privately owned railroads.

Ministry of Agriculture (MZ)

The Ministry of Agriculture had become an important and extremely powerful ministry during the last decade of the tsarist regime.[31] Formed from the old Ministry of State Domains in 1894, the MZ came to fulfill the government's need, so evident since 1861, for a specialist apparatus to take primary responsibility for the agrarian question (particularly land reform), as well as for the Empire's natural resources (forests, fisheries, certain minerals, etc.). MZ specialists dominated the implementation of the Stolypin agrarian reforms in the years immediately prior to World War I. These specialists established a presence in the provinces and an institutional base that extended right through 1917 and on into the 1920s. In so doing, the MZ and the specialists supplanted the MVD with its traditional law-and-order and social-class management concerns. During World War I, the MZ also came to overshadow the MVD in the crucial area of food supply. The MZ was the parent ministry of the Special Council on Food Supply, and its plenipotentiaries (*upolnomochennye*) became state procurement agents in the ongoing attempt to feed the military. By the end of 1916, the MZ was able to launch the well-known Rittikh procurement campaign (Rittikh was the minister of agriculture at the time), which clearly foreshadowed other forms of forcible grain requisition that awaited Russia under the Provisional Government and the Bolsheviks.[32] After February 1917, the MZ became the sponsor of state monopolies of grain, fixed prices, and the land and food supply committees (the latter quickly came under the control of a new Ministry of Food Supply). Its ministers and vice-ministers included the Kadet A.I. Shingarev and many Socialist-Revolutionary leaders and agronomists such as V.M. Chernov, P.A. Vikhliaev, S.L. Maslov, L.A. Kalegaev, A.N. Chelintsev, and A.V. Chaianov, all of whom went on to serve the Soviet state. The MZ, like other specialist ministries, had a very highly specialized departmental structure with a strong presence in the provinces.

In looking over the 1916 personnel records of the department directors, high-ranking officials of special missions, members of the Council of Ministers, and the highest-ranking provincial officeholders, we find a preponderance of men (70 percent) listing their fathers as clergymen, petty bourgeoisie, merchants, low-ranking military officers and officials, honorary citizens, and the like. The few men born into the hereditary nobility were, with one exception, landless (although records are not always accurate in this regard). The high officials attended the following educational institutions: Petrovskii Agricultural and Forestry Academy, Moscow Agricultural Institute, Mining Institute, the natural science faculties of several universities, the Forestry Institute in St. Petersburg, and the Horticultural Academy. Most graduated with professional diplomas, qualifications as agronomists, or with higher degrees in agriculture (*kandidaty sel'skogo khoziaistva*). The careers of these men reveal an unfailing pattern of service in the provincial apparatus of the MZ, beginning with service in a given region's agricultural schools as teachers or as junior forestry officials or their equivalents in other branches of the ministry. Eventually they worked their way up as agricultural or forestry inspectors, agronomists, and in similar positions. Sometimes, they spent short periods employed by *zemstva* or even served as MVD land captains.

The generalist types in the MZ (and there were a few, such as G.V. Glinka, assistant minister of agriculture in 1915-16) usually came from the hereditary nobility and attended the law faculties of the universities. They had served earlier in their careers in the most significant generalist ministry, the MVD, either in its provincial organs, or in the Resettlement Directorate that until 1905 had been part of the MVD, or as marshals of nobility. In social background and career profile, such men were similar to the generalists who dominated the MVD.

Career Patterns:

Nikolai Dmitrievich Sukhodskii—Vice-Director, Forestry Department, 1916. Born 1863. Son of collegiate assessor. No property. Orthodox. Graduate of the St. Petersburg Forestry Institute with title forestry specialist, first class (*lesovod pervogo razriad*). Began career in 1887 as assistant forester in the

Vil'no-Kovno Directorate of State Properties (precursor of the MZ's provincial directorates), Sventsianskoe Forest Administration (*lesnichestvo*). Taught at local forestry school, 1889. Wrote a thesis and was named an academic forester, first *razriad* and then moved up the forestry ladder in various provinces in addition to teaching. Junior forest inspector in Voronezh province and manager of a forestry district, 1896. Section chief, Forestry Department, central MZ, 1902. Vice-director of Corps of Foresters, 1908. Vice-director of Forestry Department, 1916.[33]

A. E. Kas'ianov—Member, Council of MZ and Official of Special Missions. Born 1859. Son of a state peasant of Orel Province. No property. Married the daughter of a hereditary nobleman who owned land in Nizhnii Novgorod and Simbirsk provinces. Orthodox. Graduated from a provincial institute of agriculture and forestry but moved on to study at the Petrovskii Academy in the Agricultural Department. Graduated in 1887 and did brief military service before entering the reserves in 1888. Elected chair of the Makar'ev district *zemstvo uprava* in Nizhnii Novgorod Province, 1893. Maintained this post while climbing up the rank ladder. Permanent member of the Nizhegorod Provincial Governing Board for *Zemstvo* and Town Affairs, 1901. Duma elector, 1907. Member of provincial statistics committee, 1909. MVD chose him as member of conference on introducing *zemstva* to the western provinces, 1911. Permanent member of Kiev Provincial Board, 1911. Official of Special Missions V in MZ and senior specialist in agriculture, Department of Agriculture, 1912. Promoted for excellence to actual state councilor (*deistvitel'nyi statskii sovetnik*), 1915. Assistant to chief MZ plenipotentiary for food requisitioning for the army, 1915. Member of the council of the MZ, 1916. Remained in MZ until co-opted as a senior inspector by the new Ministry of Food Supply, 28 August 1917. Transferred back to the MZ as official of Special Missions IV on 9 September 1917, then vice-director of Department of Agriculture.[34]

As may be seen, even some of the MZ specialists served for periods in the *zemstva*, MVD provincial organs, etc. This was also true of such ministers as Rittikh and Naumov.

Ministry of Justice (MJ)

Ministry of Justice careers are somewhat harder to interpret because of the problem of professionalism and the law. MJ officials were trained in the juridical faculties of the universities or in the elite law schools and developed a "legal consciousness" or sense of professionalism even while working in the apparat.[35] Again, we see the curious type of Russian "free profession" emerging within the state apparat. Yet in the late nineteenth and early twentieth centuries, this branch of the profession grew up alongside attorneys (*advokaty* and *prisazhennye poverennye*) independent of the service hierarchy. MJ officials (particularly prosecutors) and judges were a mixed lot. Many clearly had acquired "legal consciousness," but many also exhibited attitudes reminiscent of generalists and police officials, and indeed many transferred to the MVD during their careers. According to A. Dem'ianov, assistant minister of justice in 1917, the ministry of I.G. Shcheglovitov (1906-15) brought to the fore large numbers of pure careerists who expressed a particularly reactionary spirit in their judicial work, a spirit that included enormous hostility to independent attorneys such as Dem'ianov (who, along with many such attorneys, happened to be a popular socialist).[36]

The MJ was also divided along class lines. It had an aristocratic element, most often comprised of graduates of the Imperial School of Jurisprudence or the Law Faculty of St. Petersburg University, and a lower gentry service class and *raznochintsy* element that formed the backbone of the professional judicial cadres of the ministry.[37] The MJ professional career was also extraordinarily predictable and stable (judges, of course, were protected by tenure). It was so predictable that rather than providing actual career examples, I will offer the general pattern.

Career Pattern:

> After graduation from the law faculty, the young official generally applied for work in one of the circuit courts, then worked in the prosecutor's offices, finally reaching the level of the *sudebnaia palata*, the highest judicial post in the provinces. Usually, these positions entailed moves from province to province. A typical pattern of officeholding might include a first position as an assistant secretary in an *okruzhnyi sud,* then as a judicial investigator for that court, next into a prosecutor's office in another province, followed perhaps by the same post elsewhere. At this point, the official might move into the courts themselves as a member, interspersed with periods of service at higher prosecutorial levels. Finally, he would become chair of an *okruzhnyi sud* followed by membership in a *sudebnaia palata*, or he might be co-opted into one of the departments of the Senate or into the central MJ.

The Dem'ianov memoir is a particularly rich source on changes in the Ministry of Justice after the February Revolution. Dem'ianov served successive ministers of justice: A.F. Kerensky, P.N. Pereverzov, I.N. Efremov, A.S. Zarudnyi, and P.N. Maliantovich. Dem'ianov ran the personnel section of the MJ (among other duties), and he provides a clear picture of just how and why the tsarist regime's MJ officials and judges were retained, and who moved into official positions from outside the ministry. It is very clear that the revolution meant triumph for the *advokaty* and *prisiazhennye poverennye*, who rapidly filled not only the highest posts in the central ministry but representative positions throughout the provinces.[38] Dem'ianov argues that many talented young people had simply stayed away from the MJ under Shcheglovitov. He also points to two important trends relevant for our study of the tsarist regime and the Provisional Government: first, that the ministers themselves were appointed, not for their judicial skills or knowledge, but because of personal qualities, party affiliation, and general visibility (those named above included four socialists and the Progressive Efremov, who served a very short time); and second, that appointment at all levels from assistant minister down to low-ranking provincial posts involved clientelism. The pupils appointed their teachers and their colleagues at the bar who also often happened to be their former law school classmates or party comrades. At no time did the Provisional Government abandon the tsarist regime's commitment to tenure for judges, although had Dem'ianov had his way, the Provisional Government would have abrogated it for a very short time at least to accomplish the necessary purges of "conservative" judicial personnel. Through the spring and summer of 1917, Dem'ianov argued for maintaining the tenure principle, preferring to use moral suasion to convince people that they would not fit into the new order. He managed to cajole many officials into retirement. Sometimes his personnel activities led to ironic outcomes. For example, the only way he could get rid of Reinbot, the chairman of the Petrograd District Court who was famous for his role in the Beilis affair, was to promote him to the Senate and give him a raise.

Ministry of Education (MNP)

This was a small ministry with few central departments. The department directors in 1916 were from peasant, clergy, and petty-bourgeois social backgrounds.[39] High officials were drawn almost exclusively from low-ranking social groups and service personnel. Almost all served as teachers before moving into school administration. The usual path to top ministry posts began with work as a teacher followed by service in the provincial school inspectorates. The top provincial post in the MNP, that of inspector for one of the educational districts, was the usual springboard to a high central ministry post.

In March 1915 an MZ departmental official, P.F. Surin (born a peasant), was named director of the Department of Education. P. Ignat'ev, who was named minister of education at the same time, made the appointment. Surin was obviously an experienced departmental manager, not an educator or educational administrator, and the *spisok* makes clear the connection of the men. Ignat'ev had been director of the MZ Department of Agriculture in 1909 and he evidently wanted this trusted *chinovnik* at his side upon taking up ministerial responsibilities.[40] This was common practice in the ministerial bureaucracy and an important type of clientelism in the history of Russian and Soviet administration.[41]

Ministry of Trade and Industry (MTI) and Ministry of Finance (MF)

The Ministry of Finance archives yielded a disappointing amount of data on personnel matters. There was available, however, rich material on high MF personnel for 1917 and on the question of MF Fiscal Chamber (*kazennaia palata*) appointments in the provinces prior to the February Revolution.[42] A list from June 1917 of some forty top MF administrators reveals almost complete continuity from the tsarist regime.[43] Moreover, almost all of these men had spent their entire careers, dating back to the 1880s and 1890s, in the MF. There appears to be a higher representation of hereditary noblemen among these high officials—men who were graduates of the Alexander Lycée and the major universities—than among some of the other specialist ministries described above.

On-the-job training in the ministry was common, though among young officials in both the MF and MTI there were men from *raznochintsy* groups who were educated in polytechnical and commercial institutes, real gymnasia, and engineering institutes. Also in the MF there seems to have been a rather sharp split between provincial and central service. Fiscal Chamber careers were a kind of specialty, and these provincial *chinovniki* appear not to have advanced into the departmental structures of the central MF. The departmental officials, on the other hand, worked for many years at their specialties at the center. In the Ministry of Trade and Industry a similar situation existed with the provincial tariff and factory inspectors, as opposed to departmental officials, at the center. By 1916, the financial institutions of the Empire represented a very powerful sector of the ministerial bureaucracy with its own service patterns, clientelism, links to private industry and banking, and so on. Yet, ultimately, these institutions could not establish hegemony within the tsarist government. To understand one of the main stumbling blocks to such hegemony we must now turn to the Ministry of Internal Affairs and its personnel.

The Ministry of Internal Affairs (MVD)

Despite the inroads of the specialist ministries (particularly Finance and Agriculture), the MVD was still extremely important in the high politics of the autocracy. In the ministerial bureaucracy, the MVD best expressed the tradition of bureaucratic tutelage and a mode of administration and politics based on personal power that was hostile to the rule of law and institutions. During the nineteenth century, the powerful figures in this ministry had usually been generalists; their concerns largely revolved around the vague and often contradictory goals of public order and "improving the general welfare." The MVD housed the police (both political and executive after 1881) and had general responsibility for provincial administration. It had also been the home base for bureaucratic renovators who desired to move autocracy away from the worst features of personal power toward rule of institutions and law.[44] The MVD was at the center of virtually all attempts to reform or even simply to maintain autocracy during the last decades of the tsarist regime, and ministers such as

Plehve, Sviatopolk-Mirskii, and Stolypin used the ministry as a power base from which to play high autocratic politics.

The MVD was full of contradictions and conflicting value systems among its own professional staff. After 1911, at a time when the autocracy required enormous political sophistication and administrative skill to integrate the Empire and its disparate nationalities and social groups, the MVD was headed by a series of mediocre political appointees drawn in surprisingly large numbers from provincial nobility and officialdom. These men usually had close ties to the court or to high officials who themselves had such ties, and personnel records and other evidence reveal a web of traditional kinship, marital, and clientele relationships. [45] The ministry retained enormous negative power to block initiatives by other ministries and various political and economic interests right up to the February Revolution. By that time, the pressures of the war had made the war effort, administration of the economy, and solution of the agrarian question (which were all concerns of the specialist bureaucracy) the prime tasks of government. During the war, as we have seen, the MVD became more and more isolated from economic functions and administration, especially in the provinces, and also grew weaker because of the structural flaws in tsarist provincial administration and the social and economic crises of the countryside. Its power at the center was weakened by its too close attachment to the person of the tsar, the dynastic principle, and the police ethos and fear of rule of law and institutions shared by so many of its professionals.[46] On the eve of February 1917, the MVD had lost its capacity to promote the wealth and well-being of the Empire or to maintain order.

The influx of provincials into the MVD is a fascinating phenomenon. High MVD officials took some pains to distance themselves in terms of ideology, vision, and level of administrative skill from these newcomers. For example, S.E. Kryzhanovskii, the author of the June 1907 electoral law and a talented and influential bureaucrat (he was almost made minister at the time of the February Revolution), measured his own sense of professionalism in terms not simply of loyalty to the autocrat, or even to the state, but to the primacy of administration and real political skill. In his memoirs, he describes the ministry of D.S. Sipiagin, one of the provincial officeholders who suddenly found himself at the very top of central government institutions.[47] For Kryzhanovskii, Sipiagin exemplified an old-fashioned provincial governor; he was an outmoded and overblown autocrat (*khoziain*) of a province who wished to impose upon the central ministry, and indeed upon the entire Empire, patterns of administration and politics derived from the highly personalized office of the governor.

To some extent, the emergence of provincial types in the MVD central hierarchy was the result of a sense in the ministry that it required men with actual experience in the provinces, men who were close to provincial society (both the nobility and peasantry). As Richard Robbins has shown,[48] the MVD made a real attempt to "professionalize" and regularize its governor and vice-governor appointments. It wanted skilled, experienced provincial administrators in those posts, and its list of candidates in 1916 reveals that the MVD had in fact taken great care to pinpoint experienced officeholders (among marshals, *zemstvo* and government officials, etc.) with real personal leadership qualities.[49] One of the complaints lodged against Prince L'vov for his March 1917 decree removing governors and vice-governors and replacing them with *zemstvo* board chairmen was that in many cases the MVD officials were more competent, and even more liberal, than the *zemstvo* men. All of this represented quite a change from patterns of the reform era in the nineteenth century, when governors were often incompetent, lacked administrative skills, and were drawn from the military. Unfortunately, however, the governors who made it to the top of the central MVD hierarchy, and in many cases into the State Council, were not necessarily this younger breed chosen on the basis of merit. They were older, more socially prominent, and fully locked into client and kinship relations with powerful patrons at the center. Also, it must be pointed out that professionalization among the governors certainly had its limits, since the office itself and the dominating ethos of its parent institution were inimical to the stated aims of the professional project.

Career Patterns:

Top MVD officials most often came from high service or landed gentry backgrounds (or both), and many served for a time as marshals of the nobility, land captains, on the boards of *zemstva*, on the mixed governing boards (*prisutstviia*) of the provinces, and as vice-governors or governors.[50] There was a definite decline in straight central ministry departmental careers as compared to the reform era. High officials were almost exclusively educated in the law faculties of the universities, the Imperial School of Jurisprudence and other law schools, the Alexander Lycée, and so on. There was some crossover with the MJ. For example, when A.A. Khvostov became minister for several months in 1916, he brought some of "his" people into the MVD through patron-client relations in such organs as the Main Prison Directorate and the Resettlement Administration of the MZ. Both of these organs were moved about from one ministry to another, an expression of the very potent fact that ministerial units were a form of political capital.

N.P. Muratov—Council MVD, State Council, 1915. Born 1867. Riazan nobility. Educated at Imperial School of Jurisprudence. Judicial provincial career. Kursk civil governor, 1912. Council MVD, 1915. A.D. Protopopov had him do an inspection of the leather industry, 1916.

A.N. Volzhin—Director of Department of General Affairs MVD, then appointed over-procurator of the Holy Synod as the client of A.N. Khvostov with the help of Rasputin, 1915. Moscow nobility. Married to daughter of

A.I. Dolgorukoi. Service as Moscow district marshal of the nobility. Acting governor of Sedlets, 1904. Kholm Governor, 1913. *Gofmeister*, 1914. Director DOD-MVD, 1914.

S.A. Kukol-Iasnopol'skii—Assistant Minister, 1916. Hereditary nobility. Moscow University law, 1884. Married Princess Chavchavadze. Spent sixteen years climbing hierarchy of MVD *zemskii otdel*. Acting chief of Directorate of Military Obligations MVD, 1900. Confirmed as chief, 1901. Traveled officially to many trouble spots in the following years. Assistant minister, ran the ministry while Protopopov was ill, late 1916.

N.A. Kapustin—Assistant Chief of *zemskii otdel*, 1916. Hereditary nobility. Graduate Moscow University law. Landowner, 461 *desiatina*. Land captain, 1891. Into central MVD *zemskii otdel* and up its ladder, 1900. Worked on grain procurement for army, 1916.

After February 1917, the MVD was purged of its leadership, including many top departmental officials, first by the Provisional Government and then by the Bolsheviks. In the specialist ministries, mainly ministers and vice-ministers were purged. The changing relationship with provincial society and what appeared to be an increase in the intensity of clientelism on the eve of the revolution (patterns that manifested themselves in the 1916 State Council as well) seemed to foreshadow patterns of recruitment and clientelism during the early years of the Soviet regime.

The Council of Ministers and Ministerial Checkers

Frequent changes in ministers and their assistants during World War I were an indication of the instability of cabinet government, not necessarily evidence of weak administration. The game of ministerial checkers was not the whole story with regard to operational problems of the ministerial bureaucracy, nor did it indicate any shift in the institutional, social, or cultural tendencies at work in the ministerial bureaucracy during the last years of the tsarist regime. We know that many World War I appointments had much to do with the growing influence of Empress Alexandra, Rasputin, and others close to the court. On the surface, it seemed that Nicholas's personal authority had run amok. It should be remembered, however, that Nicholas viewed more than a few of his appointments as concessions of a sort, and that indeed they were viewed as such by his opponents in the Duma and public organizations (for example, Trepov as chair of the Council of Ministers, Polivanov as war minister, Pokrovskii as minister of foreign affairs, Ignat'ev as minister of education, Samarin as over-procurator of the Holy Synod, and even Protopopov as minister of internal affairs).

There certainly was an element of irrationality at work, given the rapid turnover in some ministries and the fact that a police official and former minister of the interior, Makarov, could become minister of justice; that a minister of justice, A.A. Khvostov, could suddenly become minister of internal affairs; that the state controller, Pokrovskii, could become minister of foreign affairs; and that someone of Shtiurmer's background could rise up to be minister of internal affairs, chairman of the Council of Ministers, and minister of foreign affairs. Nicholas also tapped benign nonentities with no apparent qualifications, such as N.B. Shcherbatov as minister of internal affairs and N.D. Golitsyn as the last chairman of the Council of Ministers. Some career officials prevailed. P.L. Bark, minister of finance, and I.K. Grigorovich, naval minister, served throughout the war until the February Revolution. Those with programs to save the autocracy were inevitably appointed as ministers of internal affairs with disastrous results: for example, A.N. Khvostov, who had served only as governor of Vologda and Nizhnii Novgorod provinces and whose uncle was A.A. Khvostov, the minister of justice and of internal affairs; and A.D. Protopopov, a Simbirsk landowner who had inherited a cloth factory from his uncle (N.D. Seliverstov, a former chief of gendarmes) and who had links to financial circles and the metallurgy industry. Protopopov was a right Octobrist who had served as one of the Duma's vice-presidents. He had been proposed as minister of trade and industry, and certain bankers wanted him appointed minister of finance. They worked unsuccessfully through Rasputin and Doctor Badmeev toward this end.[51]

The ministers constituted a special service and social elite. They alone could transcend the regular career patterns of the officials in their ministries. They were political appointees, either in the obvious sense of their having been chosen by the tsar to satisfy his own perceptions of the Empire's needs, or their rise was the result of patronage. They needed the continued support of the tsar, and usually their patrons as well, to have real impact. In addition, much depended on the degree to which they could get their respective apparats to respond, and on whether they commanded the prestige and ability to gain support among fellow ministers in the council. This was the framework in which ministers operated. Their situation was neither hopeless, nor especially promising—a situation not really different from the position of ministers in other countries. The main difference, aside from the extreme interference of the tsar, was the very fact that these ministers, their ministries, and ministerial bureaucracies were so central to Russian political, economic, and social life. One might suppose that a revolutionary regime, such as the Provisional Government or the Soviet state, might try to smash that bureaucracy or at least attempt to transform it, not simply by removing officials but by changing the structures themselves. The Provisional Government made some effort in this direction, but ultimately came to depend on the ministerial bureaucracy for just about everything.

Table 11.1

Ministerial Checkers in Russia during World War I

Year	Prime Minister	Minister of the Interior	Minister of Justice	Minister of Agriculture
1914	I.L. Goremykin (30 Jan 1914 - 20 Jan 1916)	N.A. Maklakov (16 Dec 1912 - 5 Jun 1915)	I.G. Shcheglovitov (24 Apr 1906 - 6 Jul 1915)	A.V. Krivoshein (21 May 1908 - 26 Oct 1915)
1915		Prince N.B. Shcherbatov (5 Jun 1915 - 26 Sept 1915) A.N. Khvostov (26 Sept 1915 - 3 Mar 1916)	A.A. Khvostov (6 Jul 1915- 7 Jul 1916)	A.N. Naumov (10 Nov 1915 - 21 Jul 1916)
1916	B.V. Shtiurmer (20 Jan 1916 - 10 Nov 1916)	B.V. Shtiurmer (3 Mar 1916 - 7 Jul 1916) A.A. Khvostov (7 Jul 1916 - 16 Sept 1916)	A.A. Makarov (7 Jul 1916 - 20 Dec 1916)	A.A. Bobrinskii (21 Jul 1916- 14 Nov 1916)
1917	A.F. Trepov (10 Nov 1917 - 27 Dec 1917) N.D. Golitsyn (27 Dec 1916 - 27 Feb 1917)	A.D. Protopopov (16 Sept 1916 - 27 Feb 1917)	N.A. Dobrovol'skii (20 Dec 1916 - 27 Feb 1917)	A.A. Rittikh (29 Nov 1916 - 27 Feb 1917)

Conclusion

If we take the simplest set of criteria for professionalism—highly specialized skills based upon extensive training, competence determined by some form of legitimization, self-regulation of ethical behavior, association, and commitment to public service—Russian high ministerial officials on the eve of the revolution should certainly be considered professional. Many were not only

Table 11.1 *(continued)*

Year	Minister of Communications	Over-Procurator of the Holy Synod	War Minister	Foreign Minister
1914	C.V. Rukhlov (29 Jan 1909 - 27 Oct 1915)	V.K. Sabler (2 May 1911 - 5 Jul 1915)	V.A. Sukhomlinov (11 Mar 1909 - 13 Jun 1915)	S.D. Sazonov (14 Sept 1910 - 7 Jul 1916)
1915	A.F. Trepov (30 Oct 1915 - 26 Dec 1915)	A.D. Samarin (5 Jul 1915 - 26 Sept 1915) A.N. Volzhin (30 Sept 1915 - 7 Aug 1916)	A.A. Polivanov (13 Jun 1915 - 15 Mar 1916)	
1916		N.I. Raev (20 Aug 1916 - 27 Feb 1917)	D.C. Shuvaev (15 Mar 1916 - 3 Jan 1917)	B.V. Shtiurmer (7 Jul 1916 - 10 Nov 1916)
1917	E.B. Kriger-Voinovskii (27 Dec 1916 - 27 Feb 1917)		M.A. Beliaev (3 Jan 1917 - 27 Feb 1917)	N.N. Pokrovskii (30 Nov 1916 - 27 Feb 1917)

Source: N.P. Eroshkin, *Istoriia gosudarstvennykh uchrezhdenii dorevoliutsionnoi Rossii,* 3d ed. (Moscow, 1983), 304-5.

full-time career officials, but highly trained specialists. They were professionals not in the sense of free professionals independent of the state, but definitely in the sense of belonging to organizations of high status within the government that were self-regulating associations with a high level of commitment to public service.

If we project our vision forward to the years of revolution, 1917-21, it seems clear that both the strength of professionalism and the strength of the ministerial bureaucracy within the government were stumbling blocks to any major transformation of the occupational structure of Russia under the Provisional and Soviet governments. Since autonomous professions had barely begun to break away from the ministerial bureaucracy, and since the ministerial bureaucracy itself became more and more saturated with specialist professionals and institutions, there was enormous pressure to use professionals as a form of state capital. This pressure came from above (from the political leadership of both revolutionary regimes), from below (from the professionals themselves serving at all levels of the ministerial bureaucracy), and eventually from those professional associations that had taken important strides in the last decades prior to 1917 to continue and even strengthen the traditional connection between the state apparatus and professional activity. Power placed a premium on specialist skills, and ideology reinforced long-held notions of public service. Many professionals willingly served both the Provisional and Soviet governments, and the state itself proved remarkably adept at co-opting and absorbing the professionals and their aspirations.

When we speak of professionals in the ministerial bureaucracy, then, we are really speaking of several groups across a spectrum. On one end, we have specialists (teachers, statisticians, doctors, etc.) at the lower and middle levels of ministerial hierarchies who come closest to the western type and who identify with the ideals of free professions despite the reality of their existence in government hierarchies. Moving to the center of the spectrum, we have higher ranking specialists in provincial and central ministerial hierarchies (engineers, lawyers, financial specialists, agronomists, or those with legal training, and the like), who maintain much closer degrees of identification with the state bureaucracy and who coexist, sometimes uneasily, with their professional counterparts in the private sector. Finally, at the other end of the spectrum, we have the traditional generalist, who whatever his degree of education or specialization within the bureaucracy regards himself morally also as a professional, but in this case as a nonamateur representative of a set of ethical and political norms tied to the autocracy and the deeply rooted traditions of Russian administration. That many of the patterns visible in the ministerial bureaucracy in 1916 should have reappeared during the revolution is no surprise given the strength and dynamism of bureaucratic patterns of organization in Russian political culture. In this way the study of professionalization in the Russian bureaucracy may help us to better comprehend the causality in the emergence of professions in all nonwestern societies and the role of professions in revolutionary change.

Notes

1. See especially, Magali Sarfati Larson, *The Rise of Professionalism: A Sociological Analysis* (Berkeley: University of California Press, 1977); Eliot Freidson, *Profession of Medicine: A Study of the Sociology of Applied Knowledge* (Chicago: University of Chicago Press, 1970).

2. Dietrich Rueschemeyer quoted in Larson, *Rise of Professionalism*, 200.

3. Larson, *Rise of Professionalism*, 178-207.

4. Daniel T. Orlovsky, "The Provisional Government and Its Cultural Work," in *Bolshevik Culture: Experiment and Order in the Russian Revolution*, eds. Abbott Gleason, Peter Kenez, and Richard Stites (Bloomington: Indiana University Press, 1985), 39-56; Sheila Fitzpatrick, *The Commissariat of Enlightenment: Soviet Organization of Education and the Arts Under Lunacharsky* (Cambridge: Cambridge University Press, 1970).

5. I recognize that the idea of a sharp split between state and society is problematic. Bureaucrats are always drawn from "society," and during the late tsarist period many had strong links to constituencies in society, for example, among industrialist and financial groups, the provincial nobility and its organized interest groups, the *zemstva*, the professions, etc. But often these relations were ambivalent and ambiguous, and more important, participation in an institution as an official had a demonstrable impact on the perceptions and actions of individuals.

6. N.P. Eroshkin, *Ocherki istorii gosudarstvennykh uchrezhdenii dorevoliutsionnoi Rossii* (Moscow, 1960), 326-89.

7. Andrew M. Verner, "Autocratic Theory and Practice Before and After October 1905," paper read at the American Historical Association meeting, Washington DC, December 1982; developed in his monograph *The Crisis of Russian Autocracy: Nicholas II and the 1905 Revolution* (Princeton, NJ: Princeton University Press, 1990). See also, V.S. Diakin, *Russkaia burzhuaziia i tsarizm v gody pervoi mirovoi voiny, 1914-1917* (Leningrad, 1967).

8. See especially, A.L. Sidorov, *Ekonomicheskoe polozhenie Rossii v gody pervoi mirovoi voiny* (Moscow, 1973); Diakin, *Russkaia burzhuaziia*; George Yaney, *The Urge to Mobilize: Agrarian Reform in Russia, 1861-1930* (Urbana: University of Illinois Press, 1982), 400-62; and Alfred J. Reiber, *Merchants and Entrepreneurs in Imperial Russia* (Chapel Hill: University of North Carolina Press, 1982), 372-412.

9. W. Bruce Lincoln, *In the Vanguard of Reform: Russia's Enlightened Bureaucrats 1825-1861* (DeKalb: University of Northern Illinois Press, 1982); Richard Wortman, *The Development of a Russian Legal Consciousness* (Chicago, IL: University of Chicago Press, 1976).

10. See the sources in note 8 and Thomas Fallows, "Politics and the War Effort in Russia: The Union of Zemstvos and the Organization of the Food Supply, 1914-1916," *Slavic Review* 37, no. 1 (March 1978): 70-90.

11. Diakin, *Russkaia burzhuaziia*, 163-81, 226-46; see also the reports of the MVD and chairman of the Council of Ministers B.V. Shtiurmer to Nicholas II in *Monarkhiia pered krusheniem*, ed. V.P. Semennikov (Moscow-Leningrad, 1927), 109-70.

12. Yaney, *Urge to Mobilize*, 400-61.

13. See the journals of the *Osoboe soveshchanie po oborone* which functioned throughout 1917 and into 1918; A.L. Kublanov, *Sovet rabochei i krest'ianskoi oborony (Noiabr' 1918 - mart 1920 g.)* (Leningrad, 1975); and M.P. Iroshnikov, *Predsedatel' Sovnarkoma i soveta oborony N. Ul'ianov (Lenin)* (Leningrad, 1980).'

14. Daniel William Graf, "The Reign of the Generals: Military Government in Western Russia, 1914-1915" (Ph.D. diss., University of Nebraska, 1972). See also A.A. Polivanov, *Iz dnevnikov i vospominanii po dolzhnosti voennogo ministra i ego pomoshchnika 1907-1916 g.*, vol. 1 (Moscow, 1924), 117-238.

15. P.G. Kurlov, *Gibel' Imperatorskoi Rossii* (Berlin, 1923), 179-203.

16. Semennikov, *Monarkhiia pered krusheniem*, 225-66.

17. Neil B. Weissman, *Reform in Tsarist Russia: The State Bureaucracy and Local Government, 1900-1914* (New Brunswick, NJ: Rutgers University Press, 1981); William G. Rosenberg, "The Zemstvo in 1917 and Its Fate Under Bolshevik Rule," in *The Zemstvo in Russia: An Experiment in Local Self-Government*, eds. Terence Emmons and Wayne S. Vucinich (Cambridge: Cambridge University Press, 1982), 383-422; Daniel T. Orlovsky, *The Limits of Reform: The Ministry of Internal Affairs in Imperial Russia, 1802-1881* (Cambridge: Harvard University Press, 1981), 133-57.

18. This problem plagued both the Provisional Government and the Bolsheviks after October 1917. See the *Vestnik NKVD* and its successor *Vlast' sovetov* for 1918-19 and the stenographic reports of the Soviet congresses for the same years.

19. Personnel records and other materials found in Rossiiskii gosudarstvennyi istoricheskii arkhiv (herafter RGIA), f. 23, 229, 381, 560, 740, 1162, 1284, 1405—the *fondy* of the following institutions: MTI, MPS, MA, MNP, State Council, MVD, and MJ.

20. Rieber, *Merchants and Entrepreneurs*, 415-27.

21. See note 19.

22. See for example, f. 560, op. 23, d. 566, MF papers concerning the hiring of recent Alexander Lycée graduates (1916); f. 560, op. 23, d. 1154, MF materials on candidates for the offices of manager and assistant manager of provincial Fiscal Chambers; and f. 381, op. 42, d. 29975, MZ correspondence, Chancery MZ (1917).

23. Dominic C.B. Lieven, "The Russian Civil Service Under Nicholas II: Some Variations on the Bureaucratic Theme," *Jahrbucher für Geschichte Osteuropas*, Band 29, Heft 3 (1981): 366-403 and his *Russia's Rulers Under the Old Regime* (New Haven, CT: Yale University Press, 1989); Werner E. Mosse, "Russian Bureaucracy at the End of the Ancient Regime: The Imperial State Council 1855-1915," *Slavonic and East European Review* 57, no. 2 (April 1979): 240-54; Don Karl Rowney, "Higher Civil Servants in the Ministry of Internal Affairs: Some Demographic and Career Characteristics, 1905-1916," *Slavic Review* 31, no. 1 (March 1972): 101-10. See also the essays of Walter Pintner in *Russian Officialdom: The Bureaucratization of Russian Society from the Seventeenth to the Twentieth Centuries*, eds. Walter M. Pintner and Don Karl Rowney (Chapel Hill: University of North Carolina Press, 1980); A.P. Korelin, *Dvorianstvo v poreformennoi Rossii 1861-1904 gg.* (Moscow, 1979); G.M. Hamburg, "Portrait of an Elite: Russian Marshals of the Nobility,

1861-1917," *Slavic Review* 40, no. 4 (Winter 1981): 585-602; P.A. Zaionchkovskii, *Pravitel'stvennyi apparat samoderzhavnoi Rossii v XIX v.* (Moscow, 1978).

24. Daniel Field, "Three New Books on the Imperial Bureaucracy," *Kritika* 15, no. 2 (Spring 1979): 119-47.

25. Roberta Thompson Manning, "The Zemstvo and Politics, 1864-1914," in *The Zemstvo in Russia*, eds. Emmons and Vucinich, 133-75; Roberta Thompson Manning, "Zemstvo and Revolution: The Onset of the Gentry Reaction, 1905-1907," 30-66, and Geoffrey A. Hosking and Roberta Thompson Manning, "What Was the United Nobility," 142-83, in *The Politics of Rural Russia 1905-1914*, ed. Leopold H. Haimson (Bloomington: Indiana University Press, 1979).

26. *Formuliarnye spiski* of 1916 ministers and members of the State Council drawn from the *fondy* in note 19.

27. Quoted in Thomas Fallows, "The Zemstvo and the Bureaucracy, 1890-1914," in *Zemstvo in Russia*, eds. Emmons and Vucinich, 219.

28. William G. Rosenburg, "The Democratization of Russia's Railroads in 1917," *American Historical Review* 86, no. 5 (December 1981): 983-1008. On technical education, the rise of the engineering profession, and the role of the Ministry of Finance, see Harley D. Balzer, "Educating Engineers: Economic Politics and Technical Training in Tsarist Russia" (Ph.D. diss., University of Pennsylvania, 1980).

29. RGIA, f. 229, op. 18, d. 792, ll. 145 ff.

30. RGIA, f. 229, op. 18, d. 3631.

31. Yaney, *Urge to Mobilize*, especially 256-462. On the wartime MZ, see the firsthand account in A.N. Naumov, *Iz utselevshikh vospominanii 1868-1917*, vol. 2 (New York, 1955), 258-583.

32. Yaney, *Urge to Mobilize*, 463-561; Graeme J. Gill, *Peasants and Government in the Russian Revolution* (New York: Barnes & Noble, 1979); J.L.H. Keep, *The Russian Revolution: A Study in Mass Mobilization* (London: Weidenfeld & Nicolson, 1976); and V.I. Kostrikin, *Zemel'nye komitety v 1917 godu* (Moscow, 1975).

33. RGIA, f. 381, op. 41, d. 29802.

34. RGIA, f. 381, op. 41, d. 28815.

35. Wortman, *Development of a Russian Legal Consciousness*; and Brian L. Levin-Stankevich's essay in this volume.

36. A. Dem'ianov, "Moia sluzhba pri vremennom pravitel'stve," *Arkhiv Russkoi revoliutsii*, vol. 4 (1922): 55-129.

37. Personnel records in RGIA, f. 1405.

38. Dem'ianov, "Moia sluzhba," 55-80.

39. Personnel records in RGIA, f. 740, op. 10 (MNP). On the tendency of the Ministry of Education to take over or co-opt education and its administration in the provinces prior to 1917, see Jeffrey Brooks, "The Zemstvo and the Education of the People," in *Zemstvo in Russia*, eds. Emmons and Vucinich, 243-78.

40. RGIA, f. 740, op. 10, d. 25.

41. Daniel T. Orlovsky, "Political Clientelism in Russia: The Historical Perspective," in *Leadership Selection and Patron-Client Relations in the USSR and Yugoslavia*, eds. Bohdan Harasymiw and T.H. Rigby (London: George Allen & Unwin, 1983), 174-99.

42. RGIA, f. 560, op. 23, d. 1142, 1154.

43. RGIA, f. 560, op. 23, d. 1160.

44. Orlovsky, *Limits of Reform.*

45. Personnel records in RGIA, f. 1284, Department of General Affairs, MVD and f. 1162, State Council.

46. See for example, the Maklakov and Shtiurmer reports to the tsar in Semennikov, *Monarkhiia pered krusheniem,* and the introduction by Kurlov to his memoirs, *Gibel' Imperatorskoi Rossii.*

47. S.E. Kryzhanovskii, *Vospominaniia* (Berlin, 1938).

48. Richard G. Robbins, "Choosing the Russian Governors: The Professionalization of the Gubernatorial Corps," *The Slavonic and East European Review* 58, no. 4 (October 1980): 541-60 and the same author's contribution to this volume.

49. RGIA, f. 1284, op. 47, d. 333, ll. 2-31.

50. Summaries drawn from *spiski* in RGIA, f. 1284, op. 47, d. 80, 115, 158, 275, 298, 308, 336, 342, 360, 361; and from State Council records in f. 1162, op. 6.

51. Diakin, *Russkaia burzhuaziia*, 228-29; *Padenie tsarskogo rezhima,* vol. 4, 469; Aleksandr Blok, "Posledniia dni starogo rezhima," *Arkhiv russkoi revoliutsii,* vol. 4, 5-54.

12

Conclusion: The Missing Middle Class

HARLEY D. BALZER

Those who write about Russia, including many Russians themselves, are fond of describing it as a country of extremes. But is this enough to explain the stunted development of the middle class? Ever since Alexander Herzen damned the bourgeoisie for disappointing him in 1848, Russian radicals have tended to ignore or revile middle-class groups, putting their emphasis first on peasants and then on workers. When a few historians did turn to the development of Russia's middle class, they looked to the commercial and industrial bourgeoisie.[1] Many historians devoted attention to the intelligentsia, but most Soviet and many western scholars focused on the "revolutionary" intelligentsia.[2] An alternative line of investigation by western scholars, following the political commentaries of the losers in Russia's revolutions, sought the reasons for the "failure" of Russian liberalism.[3]

Missing from most of these accounts, and playing only a minor role in a few studies, was the professional middle class. The lacuna is surprising, given that recent scholarship on America and Europe emphasizes the professional middle class as an important component of democratic societies.[4] Harold Perkin in his studies of Britain sees professionalism as superseding class.[5] Scholarship on Germany in the past decade has provided a comprehensive portrait of the middle class—commercial, industrial, and professional—in the context of cultural studies and a reevaluation of the fate of German liberalism.[6] In a closely related line of research, scholars of Central Europe have also focused on the correspondence between the civil service and the professions.[7]

Professional specialists were the largest component of Russia's nascent middle class by 1900, and professionals played a more important role in political activity than did the commercial or industrial bourgeoisie, particularly during the Revolution of 1905.[8] As the work of Alfred Rieber, Ruth Roosa, James West, and others has demonstrated, commercial and industrial groups were hardly apolitical, but their activities focused primarily on economic interests, especially tariff policy, rather than high politics. Perhaps most important, they were never united and did not establish effective political institutions. Divisions along lines of geography, economic sector, and market orientation largely precluded making common cause.[9] Many of the professionals, by contrast, did come together at a key juncture in 1905, and by joining their strength to that of other groups managed to alter, if not to change fundamentally, the course of Russia's history. As Kendall Bailes notes in his essay in this volume, the political brew in the spring and summer of 1905 was probably the most potent it ever became in Russia. But beginning with doubts among members of the Academic Union following publication of Bulygin's rescript in August, and in greater measure following the October Manifesto and subsequent general strike, the common ground diminished. It was never again broad enough to provide the basis for a democratic polity.

Following the Bolshevik seizure of power, the regime embarked on a program of deprofessionalization. Contrary to popular images of a monolithic Bolshevik totalitarianism, the policy was confused and not always unidirectional. While nothing comparable to the prerevolutionary professions was permitted, remnants of professional organizations persisted much longer than might have been expected. Perhaps more important, consciousness of professional identity and attempts to assert a role for specialists that included some control over their professional life never vanished.

Deprofessionalization and Social Structure in the Soviet Union

A brief summary of professionals' experience in the Soviet era is valuable for our understanding of Russian society both under communism and since 1991. Professional programs persisted throughout the Soviet period. The tenacity of these professional aspirations suggests that difficulties in reestablishing professional communities since 1991 are less the result of an absence of models, initiatives, or consciousness than symptoms of the stunted development of civic society and an economy that is undermining the social and economic status of professional specialists.

We have seen that some prerevolutionary Russian professionals strove to achieve autonomous corporate identities resembling those of their western and especially their continental European counterparts. In this they were only partially successful. World War I both whetted appetites and limited possibilities; those who participated in the work of the War Industries Committees, the Committee for the Study of Productive Forces (KEPS), Zemgor, and other organizations believed they had proven the value of independent collective action.[10] Most professionals saw in the fall of tsarism an opportunity to implement their professional programs, and between February and October 1917 a plethora of independent professional associations managed to organize.[11] The Bolshevik seizure of power changed these plans.

The Bolshevik government may have appreciated education, but it had little use for independent professional organizations. Bolshevik policies pressured professionals to join large unions in which their numbers and interests were submerged in a sea of blue-collar workers. Maintaining special "sections" for the specialists within large production unions created as many difficulties as benefits.[12] In contrast to the "creeping deprofessionalization" that took place in Germany in the 1920s and 1930s, the process in the Soviet Union was rapid and more thorough.[13] But it was not total. The most misleading aspect of the totalitarianism model in western Sovietology was that it imputed totality to processes and phenomena that were never complete—due to both the limitations on the Soviet state's capabilities and the vagaries of human behavior.

Despite a flurry of edicts in the first months of the new regime, the diminution in professional activity during the Civil War was due as much to general disruption and dislocation as to conscious government policy. In the 1920s, many of the prerevolutionary professional groups were able to reconstitute themselves and play a role in the social life of the new nation. Classroom teachers continued to conduct lessons in the 1920s very much as they had before the revolution; criminal lawyers continued their for-fee activity well into the 1930s; and health-care professionals sought to perpetuate a tradition of public health based on *zemstvo* medicine.[14] Sufficient attention has not been devoted to the capacity of Soviet professionals to maintain their organizations and voice their concerns. While hardly requiring a reevaluation of the status of professionals in the Stalin period, evidence for continuation of prerevolutionary "professional programs" well into the Soviet period helps put the reemergence of these programs in the 1980s in perspective.

If professionals made the transition to the Soviet regime *relatively* more easily than the entrepreneurial middle class, this does not mean the process was devoid of conflict and pain. No one should understate the suffering and physical destruction wrought by Bolshevik policies. Yet even at times of regimentation and repression, the professional programs articulated in the tsarist era proved remarkably persistent. Professional groups continued their search for corporate legitimacy well into the Stalin era and sought to put forward their claims to control aspects of professional life with increasing vigor beginning almost immediately after Stalin's death.

Among professional specialists, *zemstvo* physicians experienced perhaps the easiest transition to Soviet power.[15] After an initial period of conflict, Pirogov Society physicians and Bolsheviks found common ground in perpetuating Russia's public health traditions and combatting epidemics.[16] Lawyers, too, were able to maintain some of their organizations well into the Soviet period. Despite the "tide of legal nihilism" during the Civil War, professional organizations reconstituted during NEP lasted until World War II. The professional legal community was not single-minded, and intense debates existed even in the purge years. In a process very similar to what was seen after the Great Reforms, legal norms for most civil and criminal cases coexisted with massive breaches of those norms in public law.[17] The list of functioning professional communities will undoubtedly be expanded with additional research.[18]

After 1929-30, the issue becomes murkier. Yet if we accept Kendall Bailes's assessment that following the Industrial Party affair political differences of opinion did not go away but rather went "inside," we are led to at least circumstantial evidence that professionals sought to advance elements of their programs even during "high Stalinism."[19] Following Stalin's death, expressions of a desire for increased professional autonomy and international communication reappeared very quickly, and have surfaced repeatedly since.

The Example of Soviet Engineers

This is hardly the place to attempt a full-scale history of Soviet professional specialists. But a brief outline of the fate of the engineering profession may help to provide perspective on a period that has not yet been studied adequately. Archival materials chronicling the activity of the Russian Technical Society and the All-Russian Association of Engineers demonstrate the determination of one group, the technical professionals, and the staying power of their traditional forms of activity in a period of vacillating state policy. Following the February Revolution, engineers returned to the professional agenda they had established before the war. They convened an All-Russian Congress, established an All-Russian Association of Engineers, and articulated demands for salary scales, ethical and contractual standards, job safety, and other professional concerns. Engineers devoted particular attention to establishing an identity distinct from both workers and management.[20]

An emphasis on proletarian leadership largely determined the initial Bolshevik policy toward engineers' professional organizations. However, despite official preference for unions based on specialties that would unite engineers, technicians, and workers, engineers' professional organizations continued to function with remarkable continuity during the Civil War.[21] Recognizing the need for engineering organizations to promote technical knowledge and communication, the Bolshevik government sanctioned continuation of some groups. Conflict over these policies persisted among the leadership, but through the 1920s the combination of sheer necessity and Lenin's injunctions about how the specialists were to be brought to communism were decisive.[22]

Throughout the 1920s, the All-Russian Association of Engineers (VAI) was permitted to continue its activities directed at economic reconstruction and technological development.[23] The Russian Technical Society (RTO) also maintained a precarious existence.[24] While the VAI carried out much of its activity in Moscow, engineers in Petrograd continued to look to the older

Technical Society for organizational leadership. During some of the darkest moments of the Civil War, the government provided financial assistance for these organizations, and they evidently retained some patrons.[25] In 1919 the RTO received a state subsidy amounting to the lion's share of its budget.[26] Influential members of the Bolshevik leadership, including Lenin himself, intervened repeatedly to assist engineers and scientists experiencing political troubles and difficulties with living conditions.[27]

In 1921 the RTO still had over 450 members, most of whom were engineers. While 240 of them had been members before the revolution, 166 (more than one-third) had joined within the past year, indicating that the organization was far from moribund, and that engineers did not perceive the Engineering-Technical Sections (ITS) established under official trade unions as their sole option.[28]

Recognizing the necessity of employing available skilled cadres, during NEP the regime sought to improve engineers' status, material life, and working conditions, and allowed some additional professional activity. This was a period when the government still spoke with more than one voice, and internal debates over policy caused fluctuations and even reversals. At the same time that the fate of the VAI and RTO was being decided, the Union of Scientific Workers was sanctioned, abolished, restored, and again disbanded.[29] The Pirogov Society, too, experienced fluctuations in activity and legitimacy.[30]

In a development reminiscent of tsarist-era practice, the VAI provided an umbrella for other engineering societies that were permitted to join as "collective members."[31] In this way, the Russian Technical Society was able to continue its corporate existence and play a role in economic and technical policy. The sense of engineers having a social role—indeed an obligation to society—carried over from the tsarist era. In 1921 the Technical Society sought to organize committees to assist with famine relief and the reconstruction of Petrograd. The government rejected these initiatives, much to the disappointment of the engineers.[32] The famine assistance in particular harked back to activities organized by the RTO in 1911-12,[33] and it was not the last such initiative. In 1934 engineering societies again put forth proposals to assist with famine relief.[34]

There is also evidence that the influence of internationalist and technocratic ideas continued to resonate. It took little encouragement for some leaders of the RTO and VAI to see in the policies of NEP a major opportunity. In the excitement of the moment, P.I. Pal'chinskii carried the concept further than most of his colleagues.[35] Pal'chinskii considered the engineers (*inzhenerstvo*) to be the only "reliable" group in Soviet society, and the sole entity capable of negotiating successfully with foreign governments or corporations.[36] In 1922 he was at the center of an initiative to create an engineers' joint-venture company to bring foreign capital to Russia. Pal'chinskii asserted that

> Many representatives of the authorities openly acknowledge the *inzhenerstvo* as a social substratum [*presloika*] without the assistance of which any productive activity, even any Soviet economy, is impossible. All this gives us the opportunity to take new steps in the same direction and first of all to create our own organization.

According to Pal'chinskii, foreign concerns were willing to provide credits of one million gold rubles with no collateral "except the good word of the Russian *inzhenerstvo*," provided the engineers were allowed to organize their activity without government involvement. Pal'chinskii and several colleagues actively pursued this initiative in the summer of 1922, but it was a variety of blackmail exceeding what the Soviet government could tolerate.[37]

One of the important continuities in Soviet engineering organizations was their emphasis on maintaining contact with the international professional community. In the late 1920s, the members of VAI discussed participation in an international organization of consulting engineers, and as late as 1927 some engineers still perceived themselves as independent technical consultants.[38] Such behavior might have been expected from the RTO and VAI, which had strong traditions of international activity. But well into the 1930s the ITS and other organizations persisted in asserting the necessity of receiving foreign literature and regularizing foreign travel to insure beneficial results for science.[39]

Engineers like Pal'chinskii with their technocratic musings hardly represented a significant threat to the Soviet government. Yet their activities were more extensive than previously believed, and it is obvious what could be made of such aspirations in a supercharged political environment. Shortly before the VAI/RTO was closed, Pal'chinskii was traveling between Leningrad and Moscow in an effort to revive the Moscow branch of the Technical Society.[40] But, as the government subsequently argued, the organization could not maintain itself financially without private contributions from a few members, a situation that made it even more suspect.[41] At the same time, our image of the mechanisms of repression must be adjusted to take account of the way the VAI/RTO ceased to exist. Rather than being ruthlessly repressed, it was allowed to fall through the cracks in the bureaucracy, a victim of "departmentalism."[42]

The character of professional life in the Stalin era is demonstrated by the fate of the All-Union Council of Scientific-Technical Societies. Established in 1933, this organization was able to convene its first congress only in 1959. The top-down "transmission belt" image of organizational activity came closest to being realized in the Stalin period. Yet even in this environment, engineers persisted in putting forward more ambitious proposals for professional organization. The All-Union Association of Workers of Science and Technology for the Assistance of Socialist Construction (VARNITSO) functioned as something of a lobby for the scientific-technical intelligentsia. Despite its role in the assault on the Academy of Sciences, VARNITSO helped attract some specialists to the Party and provided a mechanism to represent their views. About half of its members were engineers and physicians.[43]

The Engineering-Technical Sections also revived their activities on behalf of specialists in the mid 1930s. In 1934 their Engineer's Bureau drafted a new protocol "On conditions of work for engineering-technical workers," enumerating both rights and responsibilities. In addition to salary norms, special cafeterias, and housing, technical specialists were promised one day in each decennial for scientific work.[44]

World War II and the era of postwar reconstruction was hardly a time for new initiatives in professional organizations. However, as Vera Dunham has demonstrated, it was a period when the professional ethos and reliance on scientific professionalism that had emerged before and during the war became part of the Soviet social contract. Professor Dunham has described this as the "Big Deal" between the regime and the new, largely professional, middle class.[45] Its wartime origins are seen clearly in Korneichuk's *The Front*. Following the war a plethora of popular novels conveyed a similar message of specialist respectability. The emphasis was on lifestyle and ethos, rather than on engineering, but even the "production novels" of the period feature an acceptance of the engineering professional.[46] Eric Duskin has made a case for postwar technical professionalism based on the expansion of the education system in these years.[47] Examples of persisting professional programs are visible in the economic debates, and efforts to assert a professional role can also be seen in the activity of individual scientists and engineers.[48] Following Stalin's death, professional programs were articulated with varying but generally increasing degrees of intensity by diverse groups ranging from physicians and lawyers to military specialists.[49] Calls to establish a Union of Engineers and Scientists represented a striking proposal in a state that executed "technocrats." Most public statements before 1991 were more cautious, using historical materials to make their point rather than risking direct proposals.[50]

During perestroika the list of Soviet professional groups seeking to "normalize" their contact with international professional communities expanded rapidly. They put forth programs of professional activity that drew on their tsarist and early Soviet heritage. While similar in many ways to the professional programs of their colleagues in other nations, most Soviet professionals accepted a degree of "responsible behavior" and self-censorship that set them apart. Western professionals should not be surprised to find that their Soviet colleagues were able to work out an accommodation with a regime that insisted on norms short of what the westerners would regard as "complete" democracy or professional autonomy. The opposition between state and society was not as complete as often suggested, nor was the victory of the state ever as total as is sometimes implied. At some level, the "state" always encompasses and ultimately depends upon elements of society, and individuals frequently perform dual and even conflicting roles.[51]

What is striking about the technical intelligentsia, and indeed the professional intelligentsia as a whole, is the persistence of efforts to assert professional programs. Despite resistance from governments, both tsarist and Soviet, the programs resurfaced repeatedly. And in virtually every case they were specifically Russian/Soviet programs, stressing differences from western models even as they encouraged participation in international professional communities.[52]

Civil or Civic Society?

Modern democracy is overwhelmingly a middle-class phenomenon. Yet for a combination of reasons, historians of Russia and the Soviet Union have tended to ignore the middle class. When they have devoted attention to the bourgeoisie, scholars have focused on the commercial and industrial groups that constituted the counterparts to the working class.[53] But as a drastically changed Russia enters the twenty-first century, it is time to reassess these approaches. The failure of democracy in 1917 was due in no small measure to the inability of Russia's nascent middle class to provide unified and unifying leadership in the face of daunting economic, social, and political tensions. Unable to squelch impulses for empire and territorial gain, Russia's liberals failed to find ways to reconcile competing demands and were overwhelmed by forces advocating far more extreme programs.

During seventy years of Soviet rule the number of educated specialists —the professional middle class—grew tremendously. By the time Mikhail Gorbachev introduced his agenda for reform, there were some forty million professionals in the Soviet Union.[54] If numbers alone were sufficient, Russia would already be a civil, if not a civic, society. But more is required. The discussion of civil society properly begins with Locke and Hobbes, and the distinction between civil and political society was noted by de Tocqueville. But of more central concern to the issues raised here is the use of the term in discussions of the "return of civil society" in postcommunist contexts. While it is fully understandable that participants and scholars emphasized the groups operating in opposition to the state, the stress on liberation frequently diverted attention from issues of political integration.[55]

Many scholars have seized on Jurgen Habermas's writings about the public sphere as a way to frame discussions of civil society understood in a cultural as well as political context. Habermas provides a complex and sophisticated analysis of the interrelationship between state and society in his discussion of the public sphere, but he opposes public and private in a dualistic manner frequently enough that his work can be presented as suggesting they are opposites.[56] In the Soviet and immediate post-Soviet environment, where any dissident who sought autonomy from the totalitarian state was embraced as a harbinger of civil society, many analysts portrayed the issue in these simple terms. In the aftermath of communism, it is civil society, implying independence from the state, rather than civic society, implying an interrelationship, that is in vogue.

The root of the conceptual problem can be seen in the inclusion of Vaclav Havel's "Anti-Political Politics" in a volume on civil society. Havel's courageous, literate, and immensely sane critique of totalitarianism and its technological and rationalistic hubris is a moving tribute to the human spirit. But it is a call to resist the devil, not a prescription for a functioning civic community. Lone opponents of the forces of bloated and anonymous bureaucratic power are brave, and they may form a transnational community of conscience that helps to defeat dictatorships. This, however, is very different from developing a balanced relationship between social forces and the structures of government; it is purely civil, and only tangentially civic.[57]

A simple public-private distinction, like most dualities, obscures as much as it reveals. Examining professions and markets helps us to perceive that the relationship is more usefully formulated as public-private-civic. The civic sphere is not the same as the private sphere—it is a realm in which the public and private interact. Professionals do not seek merely to be independent of the state; rather they seek to achieve autonomy while utilizing the state's power, including its coercive power.[58] Professionals cannot by themselves enforce codes of ethics or limitations on who may practice; for this they require the governmental administrative apparatus. Their preference, of course, is for the state to rely upon the recommendations and decisions of professionals in formulating standards for training, practice, and normative behavior. This becomes complex when some of the professionals are employed by the state, others work in large institutions, and still others engage in "private" practice. But it is nearly impossible to visualize the modern professional matrix separate from its relationship with the state.

The state is intrinsic to most types of middle-class activity. As Russians and others transiting from communism are discovering, markets depend on a developed legal system and myriad other structures that cannot exist independently of the state.[59] The true key to civic society is a relationship with the state in which public and private spheres are demarcated, where conflicts over these boundaries are kept within limits that do not threaten the system, and where the state performs crucial intermediating roles.

In the Russian context, the pervasive and unregulated role of the state made the contradictions particularly acute. In their introduction to the volume *Between Tsar and People,* Edith Clowes, Samuel Kassow, and James West focused on Russian *obshchestvennost'.* Most of the contributors emphasized the cleavages within Russian society, particularly within the middle class, and stressed educated groups' opposition to the state. My own chapter in that volume reflected the ambiguity in professional relationships with the state that Nancy Frieden referred to as "Janus-faced." Like all advocates of social activism and political change, Russian professionals saw the state as a major obstacle. Yet the state was also the provider of education, protector of "civilization," and the most promising agent for programs of social transformation. These tensions can be destructive or creative depending on the mix and context, and the relationship is always in flux. The focus on opposition prevalent in East European discussions of civil society directs attention away from one of the crucial elements of democratic society: the relationship *between* society and the state.

Much of the "civil society" literature generated during perestroika focused on "independent" civic and social activities. This was perhaps inevitable as a reaction to the prevailing model of "totalitarian" systems. Even many of those who rejected totalitarianism wrote about the state "swallowing" society.[60] In this context, scholars who understood that the totalitarianism model, with its lack of any mechanism for explaining change, was a highly imperfect description of post-Stalinist reality pounced on every manifestation of private activity to demonstrate that things were different.

Neither an emphasis on opposition voices crying in the wilderness nor the alternative agenda of "bringing the state back in" offers a satisfactory approach. More promising lines of inquiry have been suggested by scholars examining the state-society interaction in a context of mutual dependencies and the potential for mutual empowerment.[61] The professions with their professional programs dependent on state cooperation illustrate this point particularly vividly. Professionals aspire to a partnership with the state in which the professions formulate standards of training, conduct, and competence, and can rely on the state as the final enforcer of these codes. If the state is not strong enough to police the professional labor market, deal with incompetents, and punish violators, no professional standards will be effective. Thus it is *partnership with the state,* rather than independence from the state, that is the hallmark of civic society. A state too weak too be a partner cannot support civic society. A plethora of "independent" social or economic organizations existing in a chaotic political environment do not produce democratic civic society—they produce corruption, corporatism, and disillusionment.

Neither the tsarist nor the Soviet state ever accepted the civic relationship as legitimate, thus provoking civic-oriented social groups to take radical positions. The rules, boundaries, and character of the relationship are an arena of ongoing conflict in any civic society, but the basic legitimacy of the relationship itself is not on the table for renegotiation.[62] This is the crucial distinction between civic society and various forms of authoritarianism. Corporatist regimes may come closer to the civic model, but by limiting the players to those approved by the regime rather than accepting those who themselves express a desire to play, they are at best quasi-democratic.[63]

Thwarted Societies and Clumsy States

The cold war helped encourage the totalitarianism model of Soviet politics and a historiography emphasizing the "swollen state" in Russia. With this heritage, it is difficult to perceive Russia in the category of "weak" or "soft" states.[64] And it is equally difficult to imagine "strong societies" in the nations of the former Soviet bloc. What we see in the post-Soviet space more often are states that are clumsy. They cannot fine-tune, finding it easier and more congenial to push or squash.[65]

The societies in postcommunist nations are hardly identical, but they do share the traumatic effects of authoritarian rule. In most of them, large educated populations aspire to the social and political roles they perceive among their peers in Western Europe. (The aspirations may be based on an imperfect image of a changing situation, but the model is no less powerful for that.[66]) Many of them managed to organize impressive public and even political movements in opposition to communism, but they have been thwarted in developing genuine civic institutions.

This is not to suggest a single developmental model or stage theory, or a Weberian ideal type. Each society works out its own set of relationships, and existing models are often sources of negative as well as positive examples. Most of the postcommunist societies are seeking to imitate western models while simultaneously adapting them to their own conditions.

In the Russian case, society has been thwarted by administrative opposition and an inability to formulate a coherent set of rules of the game acceptable to all players. Rather than adumbrate rules, leaders have sought to set policy agendas in a fluctuating system. Russia has a clumsy state. Despite all the verbiage about an "iron hand," Russia's government is one of the least efficacious in Eurasia. It cannot collect revenues, it cannot enforce its decrees, it cannot overcome traditional Russian bureaucratic departmentalism, and it is increasingly corrupt. It is crucial to understand the often hazy distinctions among crime, organized crime, and official corruption. It is official corruption, with deep roots in the Soviet era and growing ties to organized crime, that poses the most serious threat to civic society.[67] Corruption makes it less and less possible for the state to be a partner with social organizations. And without the opportunity for a reciprocal relationship with an effective state, social and professional groups remain fragmented and isolated. The belief that no amount of civic organization will produce positive changes in public administration leads to cynicism and anomie among the supporters of democracy, and to calls for a "strong hand" by people desperate for security and certainty in a chaotic milieu.

Reprofessionalization and the New Russian Middle Class

The coup in August 1991 was one of those defining moments in Russia's history like Bloody Sunday in 1905 or the spring of 1917; people who regarded the government as their parent discovered that they were orphans. The events were also similar in that long-simmering frustrations created a united front in opposition to an authoritarian regime. But the unity in each case was short-lived. The longer-term result may be disruptive to both political and professional leadership, since by drawing more participants into political activity, the leading role of the self-appointed radical activists is undermined.[68]

In 1905, and especially in 1917, political parties sought to use labor and professional unions for their particular political and revolutionary purposes. Some unions were essentially branches of political parties. The Bolsheviks were particularly active in this realm, and Socialist Revolutionaries, Kadets, and others all adopted the tactic. In the Soviet era, of course, all professional organizations were Party-dominated. Under the communist regime, professional organizations were diluted and politicized—diluted by being forced to represent all the workers in a field and politicized by being made agents of the Communist Party.

Party domination did not mean unanimity or absence of reformist programs. In more than a few instances, individuals and even groups of individuals joined the Communist Party with the intention of fostering change or even converting it to a Social-Democratic party.[69] But the heritage of Party control has strongly influenced the post-Soviet situation. Rather than creating independent professional organizations to represent the goals of professional groups, there exists a plethora of fragmented but politicized groups purporting to represent the interests of individual professions. Political parties endeavor to create "their" professional unions.[70]

Rather than a single union or a number of subspecialty associations to articulate the interests of jurists, lawyers, engineers, or teachers, Russia has a proliferation of groups connected to specific political parties. The holdover communist unions are an obvious example, and Vladimir Zhirinovsky's *Through-the-Looking-Glass*-named Liberal Democratic Party (LDP) has also been quite active in fostering "professional" unions to support its agenda.

These groups have their own journals and tend to regard professional interests as subservient to their broader political goals.[71]

An important comparative perspective can be derived from recent work on the "voluntary sector" in other nations. Russia's postcoup evolution in many ways resembles the situation in Italy:

> . . . the state's lack of organizational or legislative coherence undermines the possibility of the growth of a regulated *volontariato*. In all contexts, formal affiliation with the state could cost voluntary organizations their autonomy. In Italy, the state's weakness and tendency to be overly politicized present additional difficulties. The failure to develop a national policy regulating the voluntary sector, and the maze of regional laws this failure has left in its wake, bespeak the state's legislative incapacities. The jumble of laws that shape the relations between the government and private organizations, and the patronage-oriented growth of the welfare state itself, evidence an unfortunate politicization.[72]

To the extent that Russian professionals do succeed in reestablishing or reinventing their communities, they will face a set of challenges different from the nineteenth-century context. Many will be employed in large organizations, and this will influence their political as well as economic and status concerns. Steven Brint suggests that the purported "liberalism" of professionals in America is often tied more to their employment in government and the nonprofit sector than to their association with intellectual activity.[73] Their liberalism is frequently conditional, determined by the nature of the specific issues involved; professionals tend to be liberal on civil rights and moral protest, but conservative on economic issues.[74] Brint may understate the importance of changes in economic circumstances over time, but his analysis of the distinction between social trustee professionalism and a market value model is highly relevant to Russian conditions. Brint states that applied science and engineering emphasized specialized skills and discounted social responsibility: "expert professionalism needed no sharp distinction from business enterprise, and it required less separation from the idea of pursuing trade for a profit."[75] Expert professionalism is already becoming a major trend in the post-Soviet world.

A break with the intelligentsia's emphasis on community stewardship and cultural authority, which seems to be an inevitable aspect of Russia's transition, is likely to cause great pain and vocal protest.[76] There are already indications that the Russian intelligentsia's traditional self-absorption is leading to a focus on particularistic concerns rather than broader social issues.[77] The factors that are likely to condition the angst are hardly positive; professional specialists, elevated to a position of unprecedented influence during perestroika, are now experiencing downward social mobility. Teachers, scientists, engineers, and other highly educated specialists are finding that the transition to a market economy undermines not only their prestige, but their very existence. In the case of most professions, only a small elite stratum is doing well financially. Many Soviet professionals are learning that their skills do not transfer easily to the market system. Others are discovering that Russia's transitional economy offers no market for their specialized expertise. And those who depend on the public sector are finding that a government that cannot even pay pensions on time is hardly likely to support education, culture, and science at the levels seen in the Soviet era.[78]

Perhaps the one major exception is the state administrative apparatus, which is still striving to exert control and shows no sign of shrinking. By mid 1995, there were as many bureaucrats in Russia's central administration as there had been in the Soviet Union—for a smaller territory and one half the population. Its growth is reminiscent of the Civil War period, when there was rapid inflation of ration categories.[79] Exceptions can be found among lawyers, physicians, and other groups, but they are generally an elite trained in very different skills than those that were dominant in the Soviet period.

One example of the interaction between old and new structures is visible in the education system. In Russia there are now more than 180 new institutions of higher education but, as was the case before 1917, none has been certified to award state-equivalent diplomas that confer employment rights. Numerous discussions are taking place about mechanisms of certification, frequently involving professional associations, and the fate of these efforts will be an important indicator of the new regime's ability to escape old patterns. Thus far many of the discussions, the sense of being on the edge of achieving an important breakthrough, and concerns about the capacity of bureaucrats to inhibit the consummation of real changes all have a disturbingly familiar ring.

The downward mobility being experienced by Russian and other East European professionals raises a serious danger of their not merely becoming less liberal, but of their turning to authoritarian alternatives. Scenarios outlining a "Weimar Russia" future have become quite popular.[80] Most of these focus on workers and pensioners as the "fodder" for fascist movements. Recent research on Germany, however, suggests that elements of the middle class and professional groups played an important role in the Nazi party.[81] The combination of economic distress and downward social mobility led many professionals not only to abandon liberalism and accept discriminatory policies, but to embrace extremes. A similar analysis has been suggested for Hungary.[82] In these cases, it was the combination of an oversupply of professionals and economic dislocation that led many specialists to support extreme solutions. The Soviet Union unquestionably produced an untenable quantity of scientists and engineers, and it fostered among social scientists, writers, and other cultural workers expectations about working conditions and job security that are completely unrealistic in any market system.[83] The Soviet system also provided secure employment, albeit at a low level of remuneration, for hordes of specialists with marginal skills in education, medicine, law, and other fields.

Even if the threat of fascism might be discounted, a strong nondemocratic current exists within many Russian professional groups. The Council of the Professional Union of Workers in the Academy of Sciences has issued electoral statements evincing a desire for greater old-style government support, rather than expressing an interest in democracy. Many other professional and labor unions have adopted similar "survival" programs, hankering after the security provided by the old system. As the transitional economy continues to produce a larger number of losers than winners, it is likely that the political weight of the professionals will be significantly on the side of nonmarket and redistributional economic programs, with their accompanying bias against reforms and in favor of a more nationalistic policy.[84]

The transition is also undoing one of the modest and imperfect achievements of the Soviet era. For all its inadequacies, the Russian / Soviet experience looks somewhat better than the German when it comes to treatment of women in the professions. Nazi ideology was much more "male," and the roles ordained for women were not occupational. Even when pressed by the exigencies of World War II, German professions did not easily accord women permanent places in the professional occupational structure. In the Soviet Union the prevailing ideology preached equality, but the difference is only relative. Reality differed, often markedly, but the need for at least some formal-rational correspondence between rhetoric and policy provided opportunities for Russian women willing to buck the system.

Debasement of the meaning of "professional" has carried over from the Soviet period. In current (post-Soviet) usage, the term is most often a synonym for competent. Political figures stress the need to have real "professionals" directing the economy, by which they generally mean experienced Soviet *apparatchiki.*

More and more, Russian specialists are coming to recognize that self-interest requires self-policing. The pyramid scams perpetrated by MMM and other organizations led to calls for self-regulation by securities dealers. Responsible bankers (if they can avoid assassination) are striving to impose some order in their industry. But these efforts inevitably merge with other agendas, and they are likely to be chaotic for some time. Lacking well-established civic structures, the voluntary initiatives rarely become dominant and can generate additional conflicts. A sense of just how wild and wooly the ride will be may be derived from a western newspaper account of the appointment of Sergei Lisovsky, a Moscow nightclub owner and entertainment promoter, to be director of advertising for a Russian television station in July 1995:

> Last year he attended a meeting of top advertising executives who gathered to discuss ways to self-regulate their no-holds-barred industry. When the participants agreed to establish a professional association, the moderator, Natalya E. Fonaryova, chairwoman of the state anti-monopoly committee that is supposed to regulate advertising, asked the group how much it was prepared to contribute to set it up.
> No one spoke. Mr. Lisovsky shifted in his chair, and a pistol tucked into his waistband clattered noisily to the floor. Silence again reigned. Mrs. Fonaryova said she dryly commented: "Well, at least we can see what Mr. Lisovsky plans to contribute."[85]

The Lisovskys are not the entire Russian middle class. Western journalists are far more likely to pay attention to a casino where a dwarf presides over rats racing along a neon track than to a private Moscow restaurant offering quiet jazz or a Novosibirsk bankers' club featuring classical music. The entire range exists in Russia. But once again Russia's middle class is failing to overcome its internal conflicts or achieve an institutional setting conducive to democratic political activity. How their diversity will be institutionalized remains a crucial question for the Russian people as they redefine their state.

Notes

1. The characteristic approach was stated by Valentine Bill: "In Russia the merchants and industrialists formed a group distinct and separate from the intelligentsia, and the two groups went their separate ways. For this reason the Russian equivalent for 'middle class,' *sredny klass*, has never become a fully accepted and widely used term of the Russian language." Valentine T. Bill, *The Forgotten Class: The Russian Bourgeoisie from the Earliest Beginnings to 1900* (New York: Frederick A. Praeger, 1959).

For other studies focusing on the commercial and industrial bourgeoisie, see I.F. Gindin, *Gosudarstvennyi bank i ekonomicheskaia politika tsarskogo pravitel'stva (1861-1892 gody)* (Moscow, 1960); L.E. Shepelev, *Tsarizm i burzhuaziia vo vtoroi polovine XIX veka: Problemy torgovo-promyshlennoi politiki* (Leningrad: Nauka, 1981), and *Tsarizm i burzhuaziia v 1904-1914 gg.: Problemy torgovo-promyshlennoi politiki* (Leningrad: Nauka, 1987); Alfred J. Rieber, *Merchants and Entrepreneurs in Imperial Russia* (Chapel Hill: University of North Carolina Press, 1982); JoAnn S. Ruckman, *The Moscow Business Elite: A Social and Cultural Portrait of Two Generations, 1840-1905* (DeKalb: Northern Illinois University Press, 1984); Muriel Joffe, "The Cotton Manufacturers in the Central Industrial Region, 1880s to 1914" (Ph.D. diss., University of Pennsylvania, 1981); Thomas C. Owen, *Capitalism and Politics in Russia: A Social History of the Moscow Merchants, 1855-1905* (Cambridge: Cambridge University Press, 1981), and *The Corporation under Russian Law, 1800-1917: A Study in Tsarist Economic Policy* (Cambridge: Cambridge University Press, 1991);

P.A. Buryshkin, *Moskva kupecheskaia* (New York: Izdatel'stvo imeni Chekhova, 1954; reprint edition Moscow: Izdatel'stvo stolitsa, 1990); and A.N. Bokhanov, *Krupnaia burzhuaziia Rossii konets XIX v. - 1914 g.* (Moscow: Nauka, 1992).

A promising line of analysis integrating study of the working class, industrialists, and technical-managerial groups is presented in Heather Hogan, *Forging Revolution: Metalworkers, Managers, and the State in St. Petersburg, 1890-1914* (Bloomington: Indiana University Press, 1993).

2. For example, Philip Pomper, *The Russian Revolutionary Intelligentsia* (New York: Crowell, 1970). The promising lines of investigation suggested in Mark Raeff, *Origins of the Russian Intelligentsia: The 18th Century Nobility* (New York: Harcourt, Brace and World, 1966) have not been carried through the nineteenth and twentieth centuries.

3. Richard Pipes, *Struve, Liberal on the Left, 1870-1905* (Cambridge: Harvard University Press, 1970), and his *Struve, Liberal on the Right, 1905-1944* (Cambridge: Harvard University Press, 1980); and George Fisher, *Russian Liberalism* (Cambridge: Harvard University Press, 1958, 1969).

4. Burton Bledstein, *The Culture of Professionalism: The Middle Class and the Development of Higher Education in America* (New York: Norton, 1976); Eliot Freidson, *Profession of Medicine: A Study in the Sociology of Applied Knowledge* (Chicago, IL: University of Chicago Press, 1970); and Randall Collins, *The Credential Society: An Historical Sociology of Education and Stratification* (New York: Academic Press, 1979).

5. Harold Perkin, *The Rise of Professional Society: England Since 1880* (London and New York: Routledge, 1989), 25.

6. This literature is vast and somewhat daunting to those of us who are not specialists on Germany. Works I have found particularly useful for comparative purposes include Jurgen Kocka and Allan Mitchell, eds., *Bourgeois Society in Nineteenth-Century Europe* (Oxford and Providence, RI: Berg Publishers Ltd., 1993); David Blackbourn and Geoff Eley, *The Peculiarities of German History: Bourgeois Society and Politics in Nineteenth-Century Germany* (Oxford and New York: Oxford University Press, 1984); Konrad H. Jarausch and Larry Eugene Jones, eds., *In Search of a Liberal Germany: Studies in the History of German Liberalism from 1789 to the Present* (New York and Oxford: Berg, 1990); David Blackbourn and Richard J. Evans, eds., *The German Bourgeoisie: Essays on the Social History of the German Middle Class from the Late Eighteenth to the Early Twentieth Century* (London and New York: Routledge, 1991, 1993); Jonathan Sperber, "State and Civil Society in Prussia: Thoughts on a New Edition of Reinhart Kosellecks's *Preussen zwischen Reform und Revolution,*" *Journal of Modern History* 57 (1985): 278-96.

For a first attempt to carry out a similar research agenda covering Russia, see Edith W. Clowes, Samuel D. Kassow, and James L. West, eds., *Between Tsar and People: Educated Society and the Quest for Public Identity in Late Imperial Russia* (Princeton, NJ: Princeton University Press, 1991).

The German language permits distinction between *Wirtschaftsburgertum* (entrepreneurs and managers in industry, commerce, banking, and business) and *Bildungsburgertum* (lawyers, judges, doctors, professors, Protestant clergy, engineers, scientists, and the academically trained civil servants). Russian historiography, like that of continental Europe, has devoted far more attention to the former than the latter. Kocka and Mitchell, eds., *Bourgeois Society in Nineteenth-Century Europe*, x.

7. Charles E. McClelland, *The German Experience of Professionalization: Modern Learned Professions and Their Organizations from the Early Nineteenth Century to the Hitler Era* (Cambridge: Cambridge University Press, 1991); Geoffrey Cocks and Konrad H. Jarausch, eds., *German Professions, 1800-1950* (New York: Oxford University Press, 1990); and Mária M. Kovács, *Liberal Professions and Illiberal Politics: Hungary from the Habsburgs to the Holocaust* (New York: Oxford University Press, 1994).

8. Russian census data make it difficult to derive precise numbers for professionals and other groups that were not part of the traditional estate structure. Some local surveys suggest that if the liberal professions and salaried employees are grouped together, the professional middle class outnumbered the commercial and industrial bourgeoisie. Donald Raleigh provides statistics on the population in Saratov in 1916 (admittedly a time of upheaval and sizable movement of population) that were collected in a local census using categories much closer to those common in western social analysis. The data showed 36,019 individuals (15.5 percent of the population) belonging to the "professional middle class" and 22,879 (9.8 percent) in the "commercial middle class." Together the two groups constituted 25 percent of the urban population in Saratov. Donald J. Raleigh, "The Impact of World War I on Saratov and Its Revolutionary Movement," in *Politics and Society in Provincial Russia: Saratov, 1590-1917*, eds. Rex A. Wade and Scott J. Seregny (Columbus: Ohio State University Press, 1989), 258-59. There is also statistical as well as anecdotal evidence that the professionals were more politically active than other elements of the middle class. In Moscow, specialists were more likely to be members of the city Duma. Robert W. Thurston, *Liberal City, Conservative State: Moscow and Russia's Urban Crisis, 1906-1914* (New York: Oxford University Press, 1987), 66-68, 73-74.

9. Rieber, *Merchants and Entrepreneurs*; Ruth Amende Roosa, "The Association of Industry and Trade, 1906-1914" (Ph.D. diss., Columbia University, 1967); James L. West, "The Moscow Progressists: Russian Industrialists in Liberal Politics, 1904-1914" (Ph.D. diss., Princeton University, 1974); and Edvard Vishnevskii, *Liberal'naia oppozitsiia v Rossii nakanune pervoi mirovoi voiny* (Moscow: Izdatel'skii tsentr "Rossiia molodaia," 1993).

10. Lewis H. Seigelbaum, *The Politics of Industrial Mobilization in Russia, 1914-1917: A Study of the War-Industries Committees* (New York: St. Martin's Press, 1983); and Kendall E. Bailes, *Science and Russian Culture in an Age of Revolutions: V.I. Vernadsky and His Scientific School, 1863-1945* (Bloomington: Indiana University Press, 1990).

11. Peter Krug, "Russian Public Physicians and Revolution: The Pirogov Society, 1917-1920" (Ph.D. diss., University of Wisconsin, 1979), chapter 4; Kendall E. Bailes, *Technology and Society Under Lenin and Stalin* (Princeton, NJ: Princeton University Press, 1978), 41-43; Eugene Huskey, *Russian Lawyers and the Soviet State* (Princeton, NJ: Princeton University Press, 1986), 30-33; and Samuel Ramer's contribution to this volume.

12. L.V. Ivanova, *Formirovanie Sovetskoi nauchnoi intelligentsii, 1917-1927* (Moscow: Nauka, 1980), 207 ff.

13. In both cases deprofessionalization resulted from a combination of economic reversals, oversupply relative to the existing labor market, and political pressures. On Germany, see Konrad H. Jarausch, *The Unfree Professions: German Lawyers, Teachers, and Engineers, 1900-1950* (New York: Oxford University Press, 1990) and "The Decline of Liberal Professionalism: Reflections on the Social Erosion of German Liberalism, 1867-1933," in *In Search of a Liberal Germany,* eds. Jarausch and Jones, 261-86; and McClelland, *The German Experience of Professionalization.* Also see Kovács, *Liberal Professions and Illiberal Politics.*

14. Larry E. Holmes, *The Kremlin and the Schoolhouse: Reforming Education in Soviet Russia, 1917-1931* (Bloomington: Indiana University Press, 1991); Huskey, *Russian Lawyers;* Krug, "Russian Public Physicians"; and Susan Gross Solomon and John F. Hutchinson, eds., *Health and Society in Revolutionary Russia* (Bloomington: Indiana University Press, 1990).

15. Krug, "Russian Public Physicians," 176 ff., 291-92; and Samuel C. Ramer, "Feldshers and Rural Health Care in the Early Soviet Period," in *Health and Society in Revolutionary Russia,* eds. Solomon and Hutchinson, 121-45.

16. Krug, "Russian Public Physicians," 203-9, 283-84. Julie Brown notes the implications of the majority of physicians being public employees. Julie V. Brown, "The Deprofessionalization of Soviet Physicians: A Reconsideration," *International Journal of Health Services* 17, no. 1 (1987): 65-76.

17. Huskey, *Russian Lawyers.* Huskey attributes the longevity of Councils of the Bar to their unimportance. However, by relying on Mark Field's questionable assertions about private physicians in the tsarist period without using the more nuanced work of Hutchinson, Krug, and Frieden, he misses important similarities between lawyers and physicians in the 1920s. Also see Peter H. Solomon, "Soviet Criminal Justice and the Great Terror," *Slavic Review* 46, no. 3/4 (Fall/Winter 1987): 391-413; and Huskey, "Local Political Power and Soviet Criminal Justice, 1922-1941," *Soviet Studies* 37 (July 1985): 305-29.

18. For examples, see A.G. Kavtaradze, *Voennye spetsialisty na sluzhbe Respubliki Sovetov, 1917-1920 gg.* (Moscow: Nauka, 1988); Mark Adams, "The Founding of Population Genetics: Contributions of the Chetverikov School, 1924-1934," *Journal of the History of Biology* 1, no. 1 (1968): 23-39 and his "Science, Ideology and Structure: The Kol'tsov Institute, 1900-1970," in *The Social Context of Soviet Science,* eds. Linda L. Lubrano and Susan Gross Solomon (Boulder, CO: Westview Press, 1980), 173-204; Bailes, *Science and Russian Culture in an Age of Revolutions;* Paul R. Josephson, *Physics and Politics in Revolutionary Russia* (Berkeley: University of California Press, 1991); Mary Schaeffer Conroy, *In Health and in Sickness: Pharmacy, Pharmacists and the Pharmaceutical Industry in Late Imperial, Early Soviet Russia* (Boulder, CO: East European Monographs, distributed by Columbia University Press, 1994); Hugh D. Hudson, Jr., *Blueprints and Blood: The Stalinization of Soviet Architecture, 1917-1937* (Princeton, NJ: Princeton University Press, 1994). For additional material on architects, see Iu.S. Iaralov, ed., *100 let obshchestvennykh arkhitekturnykh organizatsii v SSSR, 1867-1967* (Moscow: Soiuz arkhitektorov SSSR, 1967); S. Frederick Starr, *Melnikov: Solo Architect in a Mass Society* (Princeton, NJ: Princeton University Press, 1978); Starr, "Visionary Town Planning During the Cultural Revolution," in *Cultural Revolution in Russia,*

1928-1931, ed. Sheila Fitzpatrick (Bloomington: Indiana University Press, 1978), 207-40.

The work of a number of younger scholars is extending analysis of more professional groups into the Soviet period. These include Julie Kay Mueller, "A New Kind of Newspaper: The Origins and Development of a Soviet Institution, 1921-1928" (Ph.D. diss., University of California at Berkeley, 1992), and her "Soviet Journalists: Cadres or Professionals?" paper presented at the 27th National Convention of the American Association for the Advancement of Slavic Studies (AAASS), October 1995; Mark S. Johnson, "Russian Educators, the Stalinist Party-State and the Politics of Soviet Education, 1929-1939" (Ph.D. diss., Columbia University, 1995), and his "The Politics of Professionalism in Interwar Soviet Education," paper presented at the 27th National Convention of AAASS, October 1995.

19. Bailes, *Technology and Society*, 140. Evidence supporting Bailes's view regarding conflicts in the leadership during the 1930s has recently been provided in O.V. Khlevniuk, *Stalin i Ordzhonikidze: Konflikty v Politbiuro v 30-e gody* (Moscow: Izdatel'skii tsentr "Rossiia molodaia," 1993).

20. Bailes, *Technology and Society*, 42-43; Balzer "Engineers in Russian and Soviet Society: Rise and Decline of A Social Myth," in *Science and the Soviet Social Order*, ed. Loren Graham (Cambridge: Harvard University Press, 1990), 141-67, note 146-47.

21. The slightly altered professional program of Russian engineers can be seen in the agenda put forth by the Union of Transport Engineers in 1918. They sought to regularize the position of their union and establish the rights and responsibilities of engineers in the workplace. Their concerns included rules for hiring and terminating employees, requirements for settling accounts, payment for overtime work and travel, vacations, sick leave, and norms for salaries which included provisions for inflation. It is striking that these engineers sought to negotiate, not with the government, but with the Petrograd Society of Factory Owners. Rossiiskii gosudarstvennyi istoricheskii arkhiv (hereafter RGIA), f. 150, op. 2, d. 92. Petrogradskoe obshchestvo zavodchikov i fabrikantov. Otdel truda. "Materiali Komissii po voprosu o tarife inzhenerov (Zhurnaly zasedanii soglasitel'noi komissii ob inzhenerakh za ianvar i iiul' 1918; soglashenie mezhdu Petro. otdelenii vserossiiskogo soiuza inzhenerov i obshchestvom zavodchikov i fabrikantov o prieme, uvol'nenii inzhenerov, normakh rascheta, ob otpuskakh i po drugim voprosam; obshchee polozhenie ob usloviiakh raboty i oplate truda chlenov soiuza inzhenerov putei soobshcheniia.)," 1918.

22. Bailes, *Technology and Society*; Ivanova, *Formirovanie*; and S.A. Fediukin, *Velikii Oktiabr' i intelligentsiia* (Moscow: Nauka, 1972).

23. Gosudarstvennyi arkhiv rossiiskoi federatsii (hereafter GARF), f. 5548, op. 1, d. 1; and G.G. Khaliulin "Sibirskoe otdelenie vserossiiskoi assotsiatsii inzhenerov," in *Iz istorii sovetskoi intelligentsii (Materialy II simpoziuma po istorii rabochego klassa, krest'ianstva i intelligentsii Sibiri)* (Novosibirsk: Nauka Sibirskoe otdelenie, 1974), 99-107. Khaliulin calls for recognition by Soviet scholars that the role of the VAI in the 1920s was "more complex" than one-sided Soviet interpretations have suggested.

24. RGIA, f. 90, op. 1, d. 864.

25. A.I. Kardash, "Organizatsiia nauchno-tekhnicheskikh obshchestv v SSSR (1921-1929)" (Kandidat diss., Moscow, Lamumba University, 1968); and Ivanova, *Formirovanie*.

26. RGIA, f. 90, op. 1, d. 21, l. 30 ob.

27. Ivanova, *Formirovanie*, 22-26; and Bailes, *Technology and Society*, 47-53.

28. RGIA, f. 90, op. 1, d. 12, l. 1. Compare the statistics on Pirogov Society membership in the 1920s in Krug, "Russian Public Physicians," 269-70.

29. Ivanova, *Formirovanie*, 213-15, 218-19.

30. Krug, "Russian Public Physicians," 269-72; and Ramer, "Feldshers," 270-76.

31. Khaliulin, "Sibirskoe otdelenie," 100. The RTO and VAI thus became intricately intertwined. At the same time, in this period the RTO became more of a professional society than it had been in the tsarist period.

32. RGIA, f. 90, op. 1, d. 12, l. 2-3.

33. RGIA, f. 90, op. 1, d. 97.

34. GARF, f. 5587, op. 1, d. 10, l. 184.

35. On Pal'chinskii's career, see Loren Graham, *The Ghost of the Executed Engineer: Technology and the Fall of the Soviet Union* (Cambridge: Harvard University Press, 1993).

36. RGIA, f. 90, op. 1, d. 21, l. 60-60ob.

37. RGIA, f. 90, op. 1, d. 21, l. 59-61 and f. 90, op. 1, d. 145, l. 47-49 ob.

38. Rossiiskii gosudarstvennyi arkhiv ekonomiki (hereafter RGAE), f. 3429, op. 7, d. 2336, l. 11, VSNKh Scientific-technical Department. Policies throughout the period 1921-28 were ambiguous, confused, and confusing. We should not read back, even from the vantage point of 1930, how the situation appeared in 1928. Along with the large number of private traders and craftsmen who operated during NEP, there existed a significant community of specialists in the free professions. Alan Ball cites physicians, dentists, and architects along with engineers. There was even a private airline based in Ukraine that was not expropriated until 1929. Alan Ball, *Russia's Last Capitalists: The Nepmen* (Berkeley: University of California Press, 1988), 146.

39. RGIA, f. 90, op. 1, d. 29, l. 30. Protocol of session of Gosplan Bureau of Congresses, "O zadachakh i nuzhdakh nauchno-tekhnicheskogo obshchestvennosti," January-April 1929. Also see RGIA, f. 90, op. 1, d. 102; and L.I. Pystina "Organizatsiia i pervyi etap deiatel'nosti inzhenerno-tekhnicheskikh sektsii profsoiuzov Sibiri," in *Iz istorii sovetskoi intelligentsii*, 90-99.

40. RGIA, f. 90, op. 1, d. 146.

41. RGIA, f. 90, op. 1, d. 29, l. 25ob-26 and 37ob-38. By this time there was no question of state subsidies.

42. The account of the bureaucratic dithering is in RGAE, f. 3429, op. 7, d. 2363, and Kardash, "Organizatsiia nauchno-tekhnicheskikh obshchestv v SSSR." See also, J. Arch Getty's descriptions of chaotic administrative practices in *Origins of the Great Purges: The Soviet Communist Party Reconsidered, 1933-1938* (Cambridge: Cambridge University Press, 1985).

43. Loren Graham, *The Soviet Academy of Sciences and the Communist Party, 1927-1932* (Princeton, NJ: Princeton University Press, 1967); Bailes, *Technology and Society*; and L.M. Zak, "Sozdanie i deiatelnost' VARNITSO v 1927-1932

godakh," *Istoriia SSSR*, no. 6 (1959): 94-107, and his "Varnitso v gody vtoroi piatiletki," *Trudy Moskovskogo gosudarstvennogo istoriko-arkhivnogo instituta*, t. 14 (1960): 273-98.

44. GARF, f. 5587, op. 1, d. 10, l. 62-63ob.

45. Vera Dunham, *In Stalin's Time: Middleclass Values in Soviet Fiction* (Cambridge: Cambridge University Press, 1976).

46. Ibid.; Katerina Clark, "The Changing Image of Science and Technology in Soviet Literature," in *Science and the Soviet Social Order,* ed. Graham, 259-98; and Balzer, "Engineers: The Rise and Decline of a Social Myth."

47. James Eric Duskin, "Recreating the Technical Intelligentsia: The Politics of Recruiting and Training Soviet Industrial Specialists, 1945-1950" (Ph.D. diss., University of Michigan, 1993).

48. Werner G. Hahn, *Postwar Soviet Politics: The Fall of Zhdanov and the Defeat of Moderation, 1946-1953* (Ithaca, NY: Cornell University Press, 1982); and Moshe Lewin, *Political Undercurrents in Soviet Economic Debates: Bukharin to the Modern Reformers* (Princeton, NJ: Princeton University Press, 1974).

49. I first made this point in a review article, "The Soviet Scientific-Technical Intelligentsia," *Problems of Communism* 31 (May-June 1982): 66-72. For a good compendium of preperestroika professional activity, see *Sovetskaia intelligentsiia. Slovar'-spravochnik* (Moscow: Politicheskaia literatura, 1987). See also two volumes published by the Academy of Sciences of the USSR, *Sotsial'noe razvitie sovetskoi intelligentsii* (Moscow: Nauka, 1986); *Sovetskaia intelligentsiia i ee rol' v stroitel'stvo kommunizma* (Moscow: Nauka, 1983); Robert Rand, *Comrade Lawyer: Inside Soviet Justice in an Era of Reform* (Boulder, CO: Westview Press, 1991); and Louise I. Shelley, *Lawyers in Soviet Work Life* (New Brunswick, NJ: Rutgers University Press, 1984). For a good overview, see Blair Ruble, "Stepping Off the Treadmill of Failed Reforms?" in *Five Years That Shook the World: Gorbachev's Unfinished Revolution*, ed. Harley D. Balzer (Boulder, CO: Westview Press, 1991), 15-18; and Moshe Lewin, *The Gorbachev Phenomenon* (Berkeley: University of California Press, 1987), 46-52. Also see Anthony Jones, ed., *Professions and the State: Expertise and Autonomy in the Soviet Union and Eastern Europe* (Philadelphia, PA: Temple University Press, 1991).

50. See for example the republication of P.K. Engel'meier's "Sovremennye zadachi inzhenerstva," in *Vestnik vysshei shkoly* (February 1989): 74-79 (the original appeared in *Inzhenernyi trud*, no. 7 (1925): 6-10). More recently the journal *Inzhener* has been resuscitated, with a masthead specifically referring to the prerevolutionary publication.

51. The literature on "civil society" in Russia has grown rapidly. The strongest case was made by S. Frederick Starr, "A Civil Society," *Foreign Policy* 70 (Spring 1988): 26-41. The argument is amplified by Starr in his "New Communications Technologies and Civil Society," in *Science and the Soviet Social Order*, ed. Graham, 19-50. Sociological data are provided in Blair Ruble, "The Social Dimensions of Perestroika," *Soviet Economy* 3 (April-June, 1987): 171-83; and Ruble, "Stepping Off the Treadmill of Failed Reforms?" 13-30. The most comprehensive presentations are Lewin, *The Gorbachev Phenomenon*; Martin Walker, *The Waking Giant: Gorbachev's Russia* (New York: Pantheon Books, 1988, 1986); and Basile Kerblay,

Gorbachev's Russia, trans. Rupert Sawyer (New York: Pantheon Books, 1989). Many of the trends noted in Kerblay's book are visible in his earlier *La Société soviétique contemporaine* (Paris: Librarie Armand Colin, 1977). Other works that presaged the civil society analysis include Moshe Lewin, *Political Undercurrents in Soviet Economic Debates*; Erik P. Hoffmann and Robbin F. Laird, *The Politics of Economic Modernization in the Soviet Union* (Ithaca, NY: Cornell University Press, 1982); and their *Technocratic Socialism: The Soviet Union in the Advanced Industrial Era* (Durham, NC: Duke University Press, 1985); and Jerry Hough, *The Soviet Union and Social Science Theory* (Cambridge: Harvard University Press, 1977), particularly chapters 2 and 4.

52. For a discussion of the continuities, see Boris Kagarlitsky, *The Thinking Reed: Intellectuals and the Soviet State from 1917 to the Present,* trans. Brian Pearce (London and New York: Verso, 1988).

53. In a similar juxtaposition, historians of the peasantry focus on the gentry opposition to peasant demands for land and self-rule. A comparable phenomenon is visible in historiography of modern Germany. See Blackbourn and Evans, eds., *The German Bourgeoisie.*

54. One measure of the development of the Soviet professional middle class was the proliferation of sociological studies analyzing the intelligentsia. For example, Akademiia nauk litovskoi SSR. Institut filosofii, sotsiologii i prava; and Pribaltiiskoe otdelenie sovetskoi sotsiologicheskoi assotsiatsii, *Sotsial'naia kharakteristika novykh otriadov intelligentsii* (Vilnius, 1979); M.N. Rutkevich et al., *Vysshaia shkola kak faktor izmeneniia sotsial'noi struktury razvitogo sotsialisticheskogo obshchestva* (Moscow, 1978).

55. This is not just a post-Soviet problem. See Alfred Stepan, "State Power and the Strength of Civil Society in the Southern Cone of Latin America," in *Bringing the State Back In,* eds. Peter B. Evans, Dietrich Rueschemeyer, and Theda Skocpol (Cambridge: Cambridge University Press, 1985), 317-46, particularly 318; and Augustus Richard Norton, ed., *Civil Society in the Middle East* (Leiden: E.J. Brill, 1995). The first analysis I read that discussed the problem of confusing spontaneous activity "from below" with civil society in the Soviet Union was by Thane Gustafson, "A Civil Society in the Soviet Union?" *Sovset' News* (The on-line newsletter of the CSIS Soviet Studies Program) 5, no. 4 (2 October 1989).

56. Habermas maintains a focus on discourse and "public opinion." In seeking to untangle, or more accurately to elucidate, the relationship between the public of property owners and the public of private individuals he talks about "the political emancipation of civil society from mercantilist rule and from absolutistic regimentation in general." Jurgen Habermas, *The Structural Transformation of the Public Sphere: An Inquiry into a Category of Bourgeois Society* (Cambridge, MA: MIT Press, 1989), 56.

57. Vaclav Havel, "Anti-Political Politics," in *Civil Society and the State,* ed. John Keane (London: Verso, 1988), 381-98. Also see the contributions to the same volume by Mihaly Vajda, "East-Central European Perspectives," 333-60; and Z.A. Pelczynski, "Solidarity and 'The Rebirth of Civil Society,'" 361-80. A similar enthusiasm for the oppositional as distinct from the integrational aspects of civil society can be seen in Vladimir Tismaneanu, *Reinventing Politics: Eastern Europe from Stalin to Havel* (New

York: The Free Press, 1993, 1992), particularly 153 ff.; and Vladimir Tismaneanu and Michael Turner, "Understanding Post-Sovietism: Between Residual Leninism and Uncertain Pluralism," in *Political Culture and Civil Society in Russia and the New States of Eurasia*, ed. Vladimir Tismaneanu (Armonk, NY: M.E. Sharpe, 1995), 4-5. Also see Norton, ed., *Civil Society in the Middle East.*

Ernest Gellner makes a similar distinction between civil society and democracy. In Gellner's formulation, civil society points to the preconditions and social context for democracy, and he sees it as a more realizable goal. What he means by democracy is essentially what I have in mind when I use the term civic society. *Conditions of Liberty: Civil Society and its Rivals* (New York: Allen Lane, The Penguin Press, 1994), 184-89, 211.

Recent scholarship has offered a valuable corrective to the emphasis on opposition between civil society and the state. See M. Steven Fish, *Democracy from Scratch: Opposition and Regime in the New Russian Revolution* (Princeton, NJ: Princeton University Press, 1995), chapter 3; and Victor M. Perez-Diaz, *The Return of Civil Society: The Emergence of Democratic Spain* (Cambridge, MA: Harvard University Press, 1993), chapter 2.

58. Harold Perkin states this quite concisely in *The Rise of Professional Society*, 13.

59. Again, Perkin's formulation is apt: "The free market itself could not exist but for the state. Without regulation to set the terms of the market, hold the ring between buyer and seller, determine the meaning and transfer of ownership, and uphold the law of contract, the market would collapse into chaos." Ibid., 13.

60. Robert C. Tucker, "Swollen State, Spent Society: Stalin's Legacy to Brezhnev's Russia," in *Political Culture and Leadership in Soviet Russia* (New York: W.W. Norton, 1987), 108-39. (The original appeared in *Foreign Affairs* [Winter 1981-82]: 414-35.) A similar assessment from the totalitarianism perspective is found in Zbigniew Brzezinski, "Soviet Politics: From the Future to the Past?" in *The Dynamics of Soviet Politics*, eds. Paul Cocks, Robert V. Daniels, and Nancy Whittier Heer (Cambridge: Harvard University Press, 1976), 337-54, especially 344-45.

61. Evans, Rueschmeyer, and Skocpol, eds., *Bringing the State Back In.* The "contingent" approach is presented in Joel S. Migdal, Atul Kohli, and Vivienne Shue, eds., *State Power and Social Forces: Domination and Transformation in the Third World* (Cambridge: Cambridge University Press, 1994). For a thoughtful analysis of the Soviet experience in the 1920s from the perspective of an interactive state-society relationship, see Lewis H. Siegelbaum, *Soviet State and Society Between Revolutions, 1918-1929* (Cambridge: Cambridge University Press, 1992), particularly the theoretical discussion on pages 2-4.

62. See Guillermo O'Donnell and Philippe C. Schmitter, *Transitions from Authoritarian Rule: Tentative Conclusions about Uncertain Democracies* (Baltimore, MD: Johns Hopkins University Press, 1986), 66-69.

63. Charles S. Maier, *Recasting Bourgeois Europe: Stabilization in France, Germany and Italy in the Decade after World War I* (Princeton, NJ: Princeton University Press, 1975); and Guillermo A. O'Donnell, "Corporatism and the Question of the State," in *Authoritarianism and Corporatism in Latin America*, ed. James M. Malloy (Pittsburgh, PA: University of Pittsburgh Press, 1977), 47-87.

64. The terms are taken from Joel S. Migdal, *Strong Societies and Weak States: State-Society Relations and State Capabilities in the Third World* (Princeton, NJ: Princeton University Press, 1988). At least some of the post-Soviet nations fit the definition of "quasi-states" offered by Robert Jackson: "deficient in the political will, institutional authority, and organized power to protect human rights or provide socio-economic welfare." Robert H. Jackson, *Quasi-states: Sovereignty, International Relations and the Third World* (New York: Cambridge University Press, 1990), 21. The Russian scholar Andrei Kortunov has suggested that there is now a category of "virtual state" that exists only in the minds of western diplomats—he would put Belarus and Tadzhikistan in this category.

65. See Charles E. Lindblom, *Politics and Markets: The World's Political Economic Systems* (New York: Basic Books, 1977), 65-75 on the "thumb." Timothy Colton has picked up Lindblom's thumb theme in his portrait of Boris Yeltsin: Timothy J. Colton, "Boris Yeltsin, Russia's All-Thumbs Democrat," in *Patterns in Post-Soviet Leadership,* eds. Timothy J. Colton and Robert C. Tucker (Boulder, CO: Westview Press, 1995), 49-74. The specific reference to Lindblom is on page 50. For a good discussion of the phenomena of parallels and convergence, see A.L. Kroeber, *Anthropology* (New York: Harcourt, Brace and Co., 1923, 1948), 464, 540 and passim.

66. On this point, see Theodore H. Von Laue, *The World Revolution of Westernization: The Twentieth Century in Global Perspective* (New York: Oxford University Press, 1987).

67. On official crime in the Soviet period, see Konstantin Simes, *USSR: The Corrupt Society: The Secret World of Soviet Capitalism* (New York: Simon and Schuster, 1982); Arkady Vaksburg, *The Soviet Mafia: A Shocking Exposé of Organized Crime in the USSR* (New York: St. Martins Press, 1991); and William A. Clark, *Crime and Punishment in Soviet Officialdom: Combating Corruption in the Political Elite, 1965-1990* (Armonk, NY: M.E. Sharpe, 1993). In *Comrade Criminal: Russia's New Mafiya* (New Haven, CT: Yale University Press, 1995), Stephen Handelman has provided a good treatment of the post-1991 period, though he unaccountably ignores the work of Simes, which would have strengthened his analysis of the Soviet-era roots of the phenomenon. Also see Annelise Anderson, "The Red Mafia: A Legacy of Communism," in *Economic Transition in Eastern Europe and Russia: Realities of Reform,* ed. Edward P. Lazear (Stanford, CA: Hoover Institution Press, 1995), 340-66. For an important comparative perspective, see Richard Lotspeich, "Crime in the Transition Economies," *Europe-Asia Studies* 47, no. 4 (June 1995): 555-90.

68. Jonathan Sanders, "The Union of Unions: Economic, Political, Civic and Human Rights Organizations in the Russian Revolution of 1905" (Ph.D. diss., Columbia University, 1985); and Ziva Galali y Garcia, *The Menshevik Leaders in the Russian Revolution: Social Realities and Political Strategies* (Princeton, NJ: Princeton University Press, 1989). The issues of elite-driven (top-down) versus "proletarian" (bottom-up) democratic transition have recently been discussed by Charles Tilly, "Democracy is a Lake," in *The Social Construction of Democracy, 1870-1990,* George Reid Andrews and Herrick Chapman, eds. (New York: New York University Press, 1995), 365-87, here 366-68, 382.

69. Personal communications.

70. This may be a phenomenon related to historical circumstances in the evolution of professions. See Steven Brint, *In an Age of Experts: The Changing Role of Professionals in Politics and Public Life* (Princeton, NJ: Princeton University Press, 1994), 4.

71. One clue to the Communist Party or LDP leanings of a group is the appellation "independent" in its name; in the wake of the Soviet Union's demise, groups calling themselves "*nezavisimii*" (independent) have frequently been those that are in fact the "*samii zavisimii*" (most dependent), that is, most closely tied to old structures.

72. Ted Perlmutter, "Italy: Why No Voluntary Sector?" in *Between States and Markets: The Voluntary Sector in Comparative Perspective,* ed. Robert Wuthnow (Princeton, NJ: Princeton University Press, 1991), 157-88. Comparisons between Russia and Italy have long been a favorite topic for demographers and economists, due to the similarity in GNP (and, one suspects, opportunities to visit Bellagio). A recently translated volume on Italian professions suggests a number of important parallels that should be taken up in future work on Russian professions. Maria Malatesta, ed., *Society and the Professions in Italy, 1860-1914,* trans. Adrian Belton (Cambridge: Cambridge University Press, 1995).

73. Brint, *In an Age of Experts*, 14. It is important to compare the situation with Russia, where the intelligentsia was almost synonymous with liberalism and radicalism for a long time.

74. This is not quite Phil Ochs's assessment of "ten degrees to the left of center in good times, ten degrees to the right of center when it concerns them personally," but there is a strong resemblance. Phil Ochs, "Love Me I'm A Liberal," Barricade Music, ASCAP.

75. Brint, *In An Age of Experts,* 7-8.

76. Ibid., 15. The phenomenon was noted more than a decade ago in a different context by Kagarlitsky, *The Thinking Reed,* 97-102.

77. For example, see the three volumes edited by S.A. Kugel', *Intellektual'naia elita Sankt-Peterburga* (St. Petersburg: Izdatel'stvo Sankt-Peterburgskogo Universiteta. Chast' I, 1993; Chast' II, Kniga 1, 1994; and Chast' II, Kniga 2, 1994).

78. Contemporary Russian scholarship reflects both the development of historical treatments of the middle class and the interest in new social phenomena. Social scientists are devoting their attention to new elites, the "new middle class," the businessmen and entrepreneurs, and to the new poor. Thus far, there has been little attention to the professional middle class. For a concise summary of work on the entrepreneurs and a good bibliography, see T.I. Zaslavskaia, "Biznes-sloi rossiiskogo obshchestva: sushchnost', struktura, status," *Sotsiologicheskie issledovaniia,* no. 3 (1995): 3-12. Also see I.A. Gol'denberg, "Khoziaistvenno-sotsial'naia ierarkhiia v Rossii do i posle perestroiki," *Sotsiologicheskie issledovaniia,* no. 4 (1995): 14-27; O.V. Perepelkin, "Rossiiskii predprinimatel': shtrikhi k sotsial'nomu portretu," *Sotsiologicheskie issledovaniia,* no. 2 (1995): 35-40; M. Kivinen, "Perspektivy razvitiia srednego klassa v Rossii," *Sotsiologicheskii zhurnal,* no 2 (1994): 134-42; and M.F. Chernysh, "Sotsial'naia mobil'nost'' v 1986-1993 godakh," *Sotsiologicheskii zhurnal,* no. 2 (1994), 130-33. Marc Garcelon's doctoral dissertation is the first systematic treatment of the subject. Marc Garcelon, "Democrats and Apparatchiks:

The Democratic Russia Movement and the Specialist Rebellion in Moscow, 1989-1991" (Ph.D. diss., University of California at Berkeley, 1995).

79. Daniel R. Brower, "'The City in Danger': The Civil War and the Russian Population," in *Party State, and Society in the Russian Civil War*, eds. Diane P. Koenker, William G. Rosenberg, and Ronald Grigor Suny (Bloomington: Indiana University Press, 1989), 58-80. Data on the growth of the Russian apparat were presented by Eugene Huskey in a lecture at the Kennan Institute on 12 June 1995 and reported in a Kennan "Meeting Report," vol 12, no. 18.

80. For example, see Galina Starovoitova, "Weimar Russia" *Journal of Democracy* 4, no. 3 (July 1993): 106-9.

81. Jarausch, "The Decline of Liberal Professionalism," 273-80, and *The Unfree Professions*, 80 ff.; Blackbourn, "The German Bourgeoisie," in *German Bourgeoisie,* eds. Blackbourn and Evans, 29-30; and Michael H. Kater, *The Nazi Party: A Social Profile of Members and Leaders 1919-1945* (Cambridge: Harvard University Press, 1985).

82. The second chapter of Kovács's *Liberal Professions and Illiberal Politics* on the rise of neoconservatism is particularly important for post-1991 Russia.

83. I vividly remember a conversation in 1986 with an actor friend who was complaining about his low salary and dormitory accommodations. I pointed out that many young thespians in the U.S. park cars and wait on tables to make ends meet. His response was to state that "I have a higher education in theater," with the clear implication that such menial work was not acceptable. I should add that this particular individual has found a profitable niche in the new system, but he is not typical. (Then again, one of the important characteristics of the Russian transition is that everyone is atypical.)

84. "Profsoiuz-za soiuz," *Poisk* 332, no 38 (16-22 September 1995), 1. On the broader issue of increasing difficulty in implementing the transition over time, see Adam Przeworski, *Democracy and the Market: Political and Economic Reforms in Eastern Europe and Latin America* (Cambridge: Cambridge University Press, 1991), and his *Sustainable Democracy* (Cambridge: Cambridge University Press, 1995), 67-85.

85. Alessandra Stanley, "Russian State TV Channel Says Let's Make a Deal," *The New York Times*, 26 July 1995, A3.

Index

For Product Safety Concerns and Information please contact our EU
representative GPSR@taylorandfrancis.com
Taylor & Francis Verlag GmbH, Kaufingerstraße 24, 80331 München, Germany

9 781563 247484